THROWN AMONG
STRANGERS

THROWN AMONG STRANGERS

STRANGERS

The Making of Mexican Culture in Frontier California

DOUGLAS MONROY

UNIVERSITY OF CALIFORNIA PRESS
BERKELEY   LOS ANGELES   OXFORD

University of California Press
Berkeley and Los Angeles, California

University of California Press, Ltd.
Oxford, England

© 1990 by
The Regents of the University of California

Library of Congress Cataloging-in-Publication Data

Monroy, Douglas.
    Thrown among strangers : the making of Mexican culture
in frontier California / Douglas Monroy.
      p.   cm.
    Includes bibliographical references.
    ISBN 0-520-06914-5 (alk. paper).—ISBN 0-520-07041-0 (pbk. :
alk. paper)
     1. California, Southern—Race relations. 2. Indians of North
America—California, Southern—History. 3. Mexican Americans—
California, Southern—History. 4. Acculturation—California,
Southern—History. I. Title.
F867.M69 1990
305.8′009794—dc20

                                          89-49035
                                          CIP

Printed in the United States of America

1 2 3 4 5 6 7 8 9

To my parents,
Jaime González Monroy and Theada Erikson Monroy
with love, esteem, and thanks

Contents

vii

Illustrations

The only way to continue is to tell a story and there is no other way. Your children will not survive unless you tell something about them—how they were born, how they came to this certain place, how they continued.

Simon Ortiz, *A Good Journey*

The story invites comment. Indeed it creates it, for even total silence is taken as a comment. The comments may be spiteful or bigoted, but, if so, they themselves will become a story and thus, in turn, become subject to comment. How is it that F . . . never lets a single chance go by of damning her brother? More usually the comments, which add to the story, are intended and taken as the commentator's personal response—in the light of that story—to the riddle of existence. Each story allows everyone to define himself.

John Berger, *Pig Earth*

Introduction

Every California schoolchild's first interaction with history begins with the missions and Indians. It is the pastoralist image, of course, and it is a lasting one. Children in elementary school hear how Father Serra and the priests brought civilization to the groveling, lizard- and acorn-eating Indians of such communities as Yang-na, now Los Angeles. So edified by history, many of those children drag their parents to as many missions as they can.

Then there is the other side of the missions, one that a mural decorating a savings and loan office in the San Fernando Valley first showed to me as a child. On it a kindly priest holds a large cross over a kneeling Indian. For some reason, though, the padre apparently aims not to bless the Indian but rather to bludgeon him with the emblem of Christianity. This portrait, too, clings to the memory, capturing the critical view of the missionization of California's indigenous inhabitants. I carried the two childhood images with me both when I went to libraries as I researched the missions and when I revisited several missions thirty years after those family trips. In this work I proceed neither to debunk nor to reconcile these contrary notions of the missions and Indians but to present a new and, I hope, deeper understanding of the complex interaction of the two antithetical cultures.

Until recently the missions were the only piece of Spanish or Mexican California history children heard about in the public schools, in spite of the centrality of subsequent events concerning Mexicans to the history of the state. Only Carey McWilliams wrote and kept alive what later came to be known as Chicano history. Most people of Mexican descent knew, at least vaguely, that their families were part of a history. But this history received no validation or acknowledgment because it received no attention either in schools or in the dominant culture. Then came that resultful era, the sixties, when the struggle of the United Farm Workers, under the leadership of Cesar Chavez, and the youthful explosion of *chicanismo*, including the Brown Power movement, catalyzed Mexican American consciousness of both the present and the past.

In the seventies Mexican Americans began to affirm the existence of a Chicano history in writings that reflected the different self-conceptions, self-definitions, and strategies of Chicanismo. Were these newly defined Chicanos an internal colony, or a superexploited sector of the working class, or erstwhile Mexicans isolated from the home country, or only the latest immigrant group waiting for acceptance into American society? The new Chicano historians wrote history refracted through the prism of these political and cultural exigencies. They seemed to agree that Mexicans in the United States were an oppressed group (though the nature of that condition was imprecisely defined and hotly debated) who resisted their disparaged condition to various degrees.

These political and cultural considerations are still of importance, of course. My answer, however, to the question of definition is simply that Mexican Americans/Chicanos/Hispanic Californians are a product of history, a history as yet written incompletely. Many books, scholarly and popular articles, and even some fiction about old California tell of the missions, or the Indians, or the ranchos, or the Mexican War, or the Gold Rush, or the Anglo settlement of nineteenth-century California. I set out to understand the history of the Mexican people—"how they were born, how they came to this certain place"—and to add this neglected aspect to the history of southern California. The point here, as regards Chicano history, is that the situation of Mexicans in California derives from the outcome of the interaction of Indians in California with those Europeans and Americans who, along with their productive institutions and notions of other, sought to hold sway over them. On the journey to this understanding I found that history proved more complex and more interesting. One cannot understand discretely either the history of any one people or any one of their many categories of existence. This book is still a history of Spanish and Mexican California, but only because these peoples dominated the landscape during the years under study. It is as much a history of the Indians because, first, they are worthy of historical analysis and, second, the history of Spanish, Mexican, and Anglo California cannot be understood apart from the relationships these people entered into with the native inhabitants. My sometimes-difficult, sometimes-tedious, but usually inspiring expedition through the documents of early California history has shown me that understanding can only come from a sympathetic hearing and critical analysis of the stories of all these people. The Spanish and the Anglos have had their stories told for a long time, and in the last two decades so too have the Indians and the Mexicans. Now it is time for the whole history, and that is what I have tried to write in this book.

An array of these sorts of relationships of Spanish and Mexican California are here dissected and analyzed. I hope that my readers will bear with all of these differing accounts in the various sections of the book. The same things did not happen to everyone in Spanish and Mexican southern California, and when they did, different people had profoundly different perceptions of the events. Not everyone, therefore, had the same story. To approach the truth, we must know as many of these stories as can reasonably fit into this narrative. Epistemological questions arise from this methodology. The existence of differing accounts of the same event means that someone is not telling the truth. How do we know who is accurate? Does the fact that one person's telling includes obvious fabrications delegitimate his or her entire reckoning? Can we conclude anything definitively or are our views of society and culture at best a series of subjectivities to which different people adhere? It is the historian's job to analyze critically these multifarious chronicles—to deconstruct them, if you will—and discern where there is truth. I have done so using the insights of political economy, psychology, anthropology, social theory, feminism, and, of course, historical analysis. Through this process I have constructed with integrity and empathy—an impossible task, had I adhered to only one category of historical investigation—my own view of this history, which I think is a more complete one than has been written heretofore. Such a frankly interpretive effort is a risky undertaking, and I hope that differences with my point of view will be creative ones that produce yet-fuller understandings of these historical characters, cultures, and epochs.

The consistent theme of this book—the experience of people being thrown among strangers, usually because of the demands of labor, in southern California—seeks to illuminate how cultural and historical change happens. I take the view that such change happens when there is interaction, which may be conflictual, adaptive, and even lethal, with "others" and when the weight of historical development encounters the perceived exigencies of a later historical moment. From the aboriginal inhabitants to the Californio dons to the Mexican immigrants of the late nineteenth century, cultural change occurred when the actions of various people and the events of history broke down or delegitimated the old ways. When people then adapted, rebelled, retrenched, or suffered physical and cultural decay, they made history, be it tragic, foolish, heroic, comic, pathetic, boring, or confounding. The evidence accumulated and digested in this book suggests that work on this frontier, as regards first Spain and Mexico and then the United States, has been central to understanding how and why different cultures interacted with one another. Thus, the narrative revolves around the nature of work, ideas about who should do it and under what conditions, and peoples' cultural handling of changes in life and labor.

In part 1 I examine the interaction of the native and Iberian cultures through the institution of the mission in California as a whole. For the Indians, time had been essentially circular. At this historical moment, the late eighteenth century, "el Camino Real" reached them and the Indians were thrust onto the highway of European history, an event of monumental consequences for them. The padres' civilizing efforts, the Indian responses based on their own cultural presuppositions, and the role of the civil authorities, especially the soldiers, provide the substance of this initial era of Mexican and Spanish California history. In part 2 I proceed to analyze, by examining rancho southern California, what the mission period bequeathed to the history of Mexicans before and after the Mexican War of 1846–48. The relationship between the rancheros and the Indians who labored on their lands is central to this era. Part 2 pursues an analysis of how that legacy continued through the Anglo period in southern California, where most Mexicans lived after the 1850s. The demise of the Indians, a process traced from their first interactions with the Iberian soldiers to their end in the City of the Angels, and their replacement with Mexicans from south of the border, completes this historical venture.

The activities and relationships of common people, as well as of elites, come into this analysis. These active associations, which people assume with varying degrees of choice, are a cause of historical change in the arenas of popular culture, ideology, and relations of political and economic power. When those who work enter into production, they do not simply engage the land, tools, and machines; they commence an interconnection with those who control such means as well. Elites, whether in Madrid, Mexico City, Washington, or Los Angeles, influenced such matters as the body discipline of mission Indians in the eighteenth century and the alienation of Mexican lands in the nineteenth century. Structural changes in the regional economy contributed to the final destruction of the Indians in the mid-nineteenth century and the new trappings of work for Mexican immigrants in the late nineteenth century. The most salient features of racial conflict were rooted in each culture's antithetical lifeways in the 130 years covered here. Furthermore, political, economic, racial, and sexual domination is of crucial importance in the forging of social and cultural history.

Many Spanish words are used to tell this story—not only such permanent immigrants into the English language as *patio, taco, cañon, rodeo*, and even the word *California* itself but also *gente, americano, raza, chicano, mexicano, bandido, rancho,* and others that enrich and make more precise this historical venture. Indeed, I have sometimes opted to use the very words by which the people in this book described certain others. Thus, since Spaniards or Californios referred to the native inhabitants of California as *indios,* I often use that word to convey their viewpoint. Similarly, when Mexicans or Californios encountered Anglo-Americans, they called them *americanos,* and that is the word I use when I am describing the Spanish-speaking peoples' perceptions of the newcomers from the east.

It has been a good journey for me. From the stories I heard on it, I learned much about not only Indians, Iberians, Mexicans, and Anglos but also the riddle of existence. I want to share this knowledge with my readers in the most accessible way. The tone, and often the form, adopted here is more literary than is customary in the social sciences. It should become clear that the style borrows from the tradition of the greatest of California, Western, and Southwestern historians, Hubert Howe Bancroft, and from notions of Indian storytelling. As Leslie Marmon Silko says in her novel, *Ceremony,* "You don't have anything / if you don't have the stories." In a good story there is much to be learned and much insight to be gained: "I will tell you something about stories, / They aren't just entertainment. / Don't be fooled."

I am grateful to the librarians at The Colorado College Library, the Huntington Library, the Newberry Library, the Bancroft Library at the University of California, Berkeley, and the Special Collections Library and the Chicano Studies Library at the University of California, Los Angeles. The Colorado College facilitated this work by granting me leave and by supplying generous financial support. David Gutierrez and Vicki Ruiz read and thoroughly critiqued the manuscript. I thank them for improving this book significantly. At the University of California Press, Stephen Rice kindly and resolutely guided this work from bulky manuscript to finished book, and Richard Miller significantly improved the language. Mary Friedrichs assiduously edited the first draft and supported me dearly through much of this project.

Part One

Burials

Let processions be ordered, let solemn festivals be celebrated, let the temples be filled with boughs and flowers. Let Christ rejoice upon earth as he does in heaven, to witness the coming salvation of so many people heretofore given over to perdition.

Christopher Columbus, 1493

Such, then, is the issue: if its [California's] inhabitants are addicted to independence.

un particular in the
Archivo General de México

The denial of the daimonic means only that the earth spirits will come back to haunt us in a new guise.

Rollo May

The dream of reason produces monsters.

Francisco Goya

Chapter One

If Its Inhabitants Are Addicted to Independence

Spain and the Indians of Alta California

The women of Isanthcag-na ran to the brush, and the men hastened to put out their fires in their round huts, when the people first sighted the strangers. These must be gods, for they created fire when they struck wood against small pieces of flint. Yet when one of them fired a musket at a bird and killed it, they knew, terrified as the sound and flash made them, that these strangers were men, like their own, who took life. No Y-yo-ha-rivg-nain, or Giver of Life, would act this way. When the peoples of Isanthcag-na, the more populous Yang-na located to the east, or of the other villages accepted the gifts of corn and beans from the hairy Iberians, they quickly buried them in a safe place away from the village. Their one god, Qua-o-ar, had already given them their food—the staple acorn along with deer, coyote, snake (not rattler, though), raccoon, skunk, crow, blackbird, plus all kinds of berry, wild sage, and the esteemed roasted grasshopper. It was not that the strangers' food was necessarily poisonous, only that each people's world had its own food, and the corn and beans were not of theirs. Soon, however, their suspicions heightened about this food when two of the men found that huge stalks and plants protruded through the earth where they had buried the alien victuals. The wizards "pronounced it white witchcraft," according to two of the people, whom the Spanish renamed Gabrieleños after the mission that would bring them the European god—who took as well as gave life—and everlasting salvation.[1]

The Iberians' accounts of these events were very different from the villagers'. When the padres arrived in 1771, "a great multitude of savages . . . appeared and with frightful yells attempted to prevent the founding of the Mission. . . . One of the Fathers produced a canvas picture of Our Lady of Sorrows." Fray Pedro Cambón recorded that "at the sight of it they became as if transfixed in wonderment, and all of them threw their bows and arrows on the ground, as 'Tomeares' or Chiefs took from around their necks the necklaces they value so highly . . . and placed them at the feet of the Sovereign Queen of the Angels." Father Junípero Serra, as close to a patron saint of California as there is, related to the viceroy of New Spain that "the start of this mission gave promise of great things both on the spiritual and temporal side." Again the mother of the son of their god worked her wonders:

As for the Indian women, when the Fathers showed them a beautiful painting of the Most Blessed Mary, artistically executed, . . . they were so taken with it that they could not tear themselves away from it. They went to their homes and came back loaded down with seeds and provisions, which they offered to the holy image. . . . It is easy enough to say their actions were prompted by the foolish idea that the Most Holy Virgin was to eat them. But the very sight of how intent they were, and how much in earnest, touched one to the heart, and made one feel sure that they would pay even greater homage to the Great Queen when in the light of the faith they would come to know how exalted she was.

These passages reveal a clear dissonance between the views of the Iberians and the native inhabitants about their first meetings at the place that would become Los Angeles.[2]

This inconsistency is not simply ironic. Patterns of life and labor in California and the Southwest of the United States, which prevail to the present day, arose in part from the Europeans' peculiar notions about these people they called Indios.[3] Indeed, their various interactions with the California

Indians originated the area's labor system and begot the social relations between Spaniards and natives. But more than issues of who should actually work and who should control labor and its products comprise production relations. History shows that production happened not simply when people, land, capital, and markets were brought together. Those invisible bonds we call culture, peoples' customary habits and preferences for how life should be carried on, bore heavily on the emergence of production in California. The Indians' techniques for engaging the land to produce their subsistence would need to undergo profound alteration when the Europeans brought a new labor system to replace their customary ways. However, the production system that actually emerged upon the landscape derived from the forced union of European and native cultures, resembling neither genuinely but representing instead the Indian adaptation to the demands of Iberian imperialism. Thus in this chapter I will first describe and analyze the Indian lifeways of southern California both because they are important to understand for their own sake and because we must know how Indians lived if we are to understand the difficulty they had emulating how the Spanish wanted them to live. Next comes an analysis of the Europeans' vision for the Indians and their strategies for realizing their objectives. We will see how Spanish geopolitical ambitions and fears, coupled with a usually sincere desire to make the "heathens" into *gente de razón,* or "people of reason," laid the foundation for California's rural and urban industrial system. Feudal Castilian assumptions about race, civilization, religion, and the relations between fathers—familial and priestly—and their women and various "children," all came to bear on the social relations that prevailed. Later, in 1848, the Anglo-American military would formally capture this land, replete with those social relations, for capitalist labor and exchange markets.

Indios

Of course, these were not the first native peoples the Spanish had encountered in their quest for converts, gold, and empire in what they perceived as the New World. Not only weapons but particularly disease and interimperial rivalries had already thoroughly subdued the peoples that occupied the viceroyalty of New Spain. Establishing their empire where the warrior Aztecs were only the most recent of *tollanes,* or imperial city-states, the Iberians pushed northward as early as the famous and ill-fated Coronado expedition of 1540. There, at their far frontier, they encountered Pueblo Indians of the Rio Grande Valley, who engaged in irrigated agriculture more sophisticated than the Europeans' and for the most part lived peacefully with one another. Nearly two hundred years before their efforts in California, the Spanish attempted to assimilate these Indians into their civilization and empire. These people, whose religion had enabled them to live successfully on the land for generations, revolted at the Spanish efforts to remake them, and they cast out the intruders in 1680. But the Spanish once again tried to "civilize" the native inhabitants of the northern frontier in 1769, this time in California.

Unbeknownst to most Europeans, the natives they encountered varied more widely than did the different European peoples themselves. To the Spanish they were all *gentiles* (heathens), though the adjectives preceding this word ranged from *miserios* (miserable) to *desgraciados* (wretched) to *pobres* (poor). In the medieval European world, where God and the Devil competed incessantly for the souls of humans, it made sense to lump all these gentiles together as Satan's children. The California ones, said Juan Bautista de Anza, captain of the Presidio of Tubac (whom Viceroy Bucareli charged with forging an overland route from Sonora to Monterey, California, in 1774), were "fit subjects of the enemy of the human race, who has them in his power." This mind-set and the experience of the Franciscan padres with the Indians of the interior of Mexico, especially in the Sierra Gorda region where many of the Alta California padres had labored previously, precluded an empathic or nuanced understanding of the "heathens."[4]

Although the Indians of the Western Hemisphere shared many religious beliefs, they differed in how they organized their families, production, and cosmos (their material and spiritual universe). Difficult as it is for non-Indians to understand genuinely the Indian worldview, we must do so if we are to fully comprehend the nature of the California natives' interaction with the Iberians. We must know how they existed in their relations with the land, animals, people, language, and cosmos to understand how the mixing with Iberian ways drastically altered their culture. What follows is yet another European-minded writer's attempt to explicate these Indian relationships. The very means employed here, the written word, is problematic. The tradition of all Indians has always been an oral one; writing cannot provide knowledge of traditional ways. Indians have always learned those ways through a spoken relationship with one's elders. As Russell Means has pointed out with respect to Lakota (Sioux) culture, an Indian mind-set "can only come from the traditional ways, the traditional values that our elders retain," and moreover it "must come from the hoop, the four directions, the relations; it cannot come from the pages of a book or a thousand books." Nevertheless, I shall proceed to abstract the Indian world in these "dry leaves of a book" using an approach that emphasizes these relations and contrasts what is known of California Indian ways and those of other native peoples, especially the Pueblos.[5]

The people the Spanish called Gabrieleños and Fernandeños, after the names of missions, occupied most of what is now Los Angeles County as far north as Topanga (from *to-pang-na*, meaning "place where the mountains run out into the sea"), south into present-day Orange County, and Santa Catalina and San Clemente islands. The people of the village of Yang-na, now the cite of downtown Los Angeles, lived in round thatched houses, gathered acorns, berries, and grasshoppers, and hunted small game, and were seminomadic, moving from the valleys to the hills as the weather suggested. They, like their neighbors to the south, the Luiseños, Juaneños, and Diegueños, spoke a Shoshonean dialect, in the Uto-Aztecan family of native languages. Their neighbors to the north beyond *topang-na*, which marked the edge of their world, were Chumash-speaking. Typically, they had no names for themselves; they were simply "people," the inhabitants of their small worlds, attached primarily to a particular spot and then to blood kindred of that place. To the people of Yang-na however, the Chumash were *pavajmkar,* or "in the water"; the Luiseños termed the Gabrieleños *tumangamal-um,* or "northerners"; the Paiutes were *mamajtan,* or "two days out on the desert," to the Gabrieleños. Sometimes the peoples referred to one another by diet—as "fish eaters," for example. The "northerners" believed that Qua-o-ar, or Chingichnich, as the Luiseños and Juaneños called their creator, had led them to their places. There were about eighteen thousand such Shoshoneans, with about ten thousand within the territories of the southern missions living in clan-based groups of from thirty to one hundred persons.[6]

As in most cultures, Shoshonean social organization proceeded from its most basic unit, the family. Unlike among the several Puebloan groups to the east, these families were patrilineal. The Pueblos, who also called themselves "people," though usually of a particular place, live today, as they did then, in adobe towns of up to a thousand inhabitants, raise corn, squash, and beans, remain permanently near their places of emergence, and are matrilineal. Much can be learned about Pueblo society because many of their villages are still occupied and flourishing along the Rio Grande. Unfortunately, all too little can be found out about the Gabrieleños, Luiseños, or other Indians of southern California simply because they have nearly all disappeared. Ultimately, their dispersal is the most significant result of the interaction of these people, who had lived with the land for at least three thousand years, and the Europeans who would bring them "civilization." Nevertheless, the fragmentary evidence can tell us something about their society and its tensions.

For the agricultural Pueblos, the idea of mother is all-important; seeds planted in her womb, the earth, become the corn on which the people depended, a notion that corresponds to their matrilineal patterns of descent and inheritance. The male sun, the archetypical fertilizing agent, and mother earth, associated with the Corn Maiden in Pueblo culture, are on much more balanced footing in agriculturally oriented societies. So too has the household in these patriarchal societies sought such balance, though not equality, in its male-female relations. By contrast, the hunting-and-gathering Shoshonean societies revolved around the idea of father. In California a man presented his bride's family with payment in exchange for her. Although essentially a ceremonial purchase, the larger the payment, the more enhanced the status of the bride and groom, and she was now his. In Shoshonean culture a man could kill his adulterous wife (though he usually exchanged her for her lover's spouse). He worked her harder than himself; she was responsible for cooking and maintaining the household. A chief could have several wives if he could afford to marry and support them. Among the Chumash and Shoshonean peoples of southern California one descended from one's father. Their little bits of property were passed from fathers to sons.[7] How patrilineality translated into day-to-day life for Indian women remains difficult to gauge, though generally speaking, women have fared significantly better in the home when it has been theirs not only to keep up but to control and pass on as well, and when mother earth and father sun have been more equal in the temple.

Fermín Lasuén, father president of the California missions from 1785 to 1803, all too invested in blaspheming Indian lifeways, asserted in 1801 that women "in their native state . . . are slaves to the men, obliged to maintain them with the sweat of their brow. They are ill-treated, trampled on by them even to the point of death if . . . the women have made no provision of food for them." This statement was typical of Europeans who sought to have leisured wives as a sign of their civilization. But an actual Gabrieleña related through her Scottish husband that "in case her 'Lord' ill used her, and continued to beat her in a cruel manner, she gave advice of it to her kin, who in consequence collected together all the money which had been paid in at the marriage, and taking it in deputation to the husband's hut, left it with him, leading off the wife. They immediately married her to another." This testimony tells us three things. First, Gabrieleñas were at least sometimes physically abused. Second, their families of origin afforded them some protection against such abuse. Third, Gabrieleñas were their men's to pass from father to husband. Again, most aspects of Gabrieleño and other southern Cali-

fornia Indian household relationships are still unknown. Yet
such power relations between these Indian women and men
had crucial repercussions for their societies when the missionaries arrived on the scene.[8]

The relationship of Native Americans to nature—important
both for understanding their troubled interaction with the
Europeans and in its own right—remains enigmatic for non-
Indians, even those sympathetic to Indian culture and to the
plight of the earth. The accumulationist, industrialized cultures of the North Atlantic saw a justification for the removal
of Indians from their lands in what appeared to them to be
the Indians' gross passivity toward developing those lands.
Today some people from these enterprising cultures have found
Indian attitudes toward nature attractive as models for the appropriate and virtuous way to treat that which is indeed the
mother of us all, the earth. What even they often fail to realize, though, is that there is more to their concepts than
harmony with nature. Without being any more or less noble
than other peoples, all Indians in their ideal culture have
understood themselves and their worlds to be relentlessly interconnected in a fashion not necessarily based on morality.
In such a continuously woven fabric not even one thread can
be snarled or mussed lest the whole fabric be jumbled. Indians have understood that they have been tapping into the
ecosystem and expropriating plants and animals for their survival. The earth in turn has demanded reciprocation. The
people, anxious about continuing, then have had to apologize
and give back, in the form of rituals, offerings, or mere thanks,
in order for life to continue as they have known it. Indians
have known that when they took from nature, they created
disharmony. Through rituals they have sought to restore harmony, though because humans have always had to take from
nature for survival, they have always been alienated from it
to some degree. The form these ceremonies have taken has
varied greatly from tribe to tribe. (For example, the Plains
tribes held the buffalo sacred, whereas the Pueblos revere
corn.) For all Indians, however, nature and its beings have
had power. Nothing has been an object; everything has had
an existence. This power has been used for good and for evil,

and only the correct rituals and intercessions of shamans can ensure that the power is used for good. In Indian cultures each person has not been free to choose a relationship to nature; instead, he or she has always had to engage in the proper rituals and practices that have brought success to the people since time began. The individual has had no freedom to act in ways different from those of the ancestors; indeed, the individual has had little place in such archaic, theocratic cultures. Such pursuits allegedly pulled a thread from the fabric, disrupted the inexorable linkages, used nature's power for ill, and explained chaos when it came to the people. Each Indian world has had its own interconnections appropriate only to that particular world. That is why Indian peoples have differed so much at the same time as their notions about the relations of human beings to nature have had so much in common. These ways can never be adopted in other worlds; each culture has had to weave its own fabric and then ensure that no threads are pulled. Southern California Indian culture was no exception to this pattern.[9]

Though noticeably unfree to the industrialist and commodity-oriented personality, Indian ways largely stood the test of time; they had lived successfully with the land. One example of this success is revealed in the exasperated complaints of many Europeans about the fleas. Said Father Serra, "We were covered with them." An Anglo narrator moaned, "Still, notwithstanding the washings and the airing, this bed is but a whited sepulchre, concealing in the interior a pestilential wool-mattress, the impregnable stronghold of millions of *las pulgas.*" Yet Indian people seem to have had the problem solved. The French explorer la Pérouse noted about the California natives, "The Indians say, that they love the open air, that it is convenient to set fire to their house when the fleas become troublesome, and that they can build another in less than two hours." In California the Indians torched their huts and moved from the valleys to the hills to escape the heat, leaving the fleas crackling in their blazing houses.[10]

Did the shape of these houses give California Indians some of this otherworldly power? Again, sadly, evidence is lacking, but we can glimpse here something in the Indians' spirit world

that is clearly different from European conceptions of religion. We know that for the Lakota, the circular shape of their
homes helped link the people with the cosmos. The circle
gave many Native Americans a power similar to that which
the pyramid shape gave the ancient Egyptians. It is clear that
southern California Indians built round houses; whether they
understood this practice as empowering is uncertain. La
Pérouse noted that their houses were "the most wretched that
are anywhere to be met with . . . [but] round." Miguel Cos-
tanó, an early diarist of California, observed with respect to
Chumash houses near present-day Ventura, "We . . . came
in sight of a real town—the most populous and best arranged
of all we had seen. . . . We counted as many as thirty large
and capacious houses spherical in form." He continued, with
respect to some people slightly to the north, "They live in
towns, the houses of which are spherical in form, like the half
of an orange." Though these chroniclers differed on the quality of life within reed houses, there can be no doubt but that
they were round in southern California. There is further evidence that the circle figured importantly in Native American—Shoshonean and Chumash—cosmology. For example, in
one of the southern California Shoshoneans' origin myths, the
father of a wronged young woman after her death "threw his
gaming hoop in four directions." For the Gabrieleños, Bernice Johnson notes, "always in the center of a circular painting was a hole which typified death and the hereafter, and
the circle itself represented the 'whole world.' "[11] It appears,
then, that the circle had some significance for these people.
It is another example of how they understood themselves to
be part of their world, relentlessly associated with all aspects
of that world, spiritual and material. Their mission houses
would be infinitely different.

Clusters of these houses formed the geographic underpin-
ning of native Californian social organization. Surely the different peoples had no nations, though they did have headmen. Each largely patrilineally hereditary chief bore the name
of his village followed by *-pik* (yang-na-pik, for example).
Whereas non-Indians are accustomed to watching their political leaders accumulate goods, or to persons having become

leaders because of their previous accumulations, an Indian bigman traditionally often gave away his own, or apportioned all of the people's, largesse. Societies based on such redistributive principles are difficult for non-Indians to penetrate and genuinely understand. Among the Juaneños a chief directed the peoples' hunts or food gatherings and commanded the largest part of this sustenance. But he gave it away to the neediest, entertained visitors with it, and generally dealt out subsistence. This giving was not out of pure generosity, however. For his bestowals the chief received utmost deference and the privilege of multiple wives, who were important to the preparation of the bigman's dispensations. A chief's liberality elevated his status more than his effectiveness at personal accumulation. (A Juaneño chief had to hunt his own subsistence.) Thus his exalted position in the hierarchy served to allot the people's provisions in a communal and roughly egalitarian (for the men) fashion. Moreover, these gifts of food helped to ensure the social solidarity of the group. The return on the gift was the legitimation of the headman's absolute authority as well as the reciprocity and sense of communion the people would then feel for their leader.[12]

It is important to remember, though, that such goods demanded such social treatment only within the Indians' small universe. Again, rules regarding such matters were more practical than ethical because they kept the world in proper balance. Different rules governed everything beyond *topangna*, the literal end of their world. Other people's victuals and accouterments, indeed the other people themselves, often fell outside the tribal code. Not "for conquest, but for revenge" of a "theft, a slight to a chief, the seizure of a woman, [or] perhaps also the conviction that witchcraft had been practiced" did Indian "wars" happen, according to Kroeber. With little to bind the different peoples who lived in proximity to one another, they often resorted to violence for retribution. Although each group usually presented an unassuming presence on the landscape, Californian inter-Indian relations were hardly harmonious. There emerged no broad political or spiritual authority beyond their small bands to bind them to any sort of agreement on the need to end what we would likely see as the destructive imprudence, indeed folly, of these wars. Thus, the California Indians never could forge a unified response to any of the invaders of their land as long as this tribal structure and rivalry prevailed. These hostilities might appear more quaint than imperial, but the participants took them seriously and waged them mercilessly. The opposing warriors were killed on the spot, with women and children receiving the same treatment or being captured and incorporated into the tribe. This warring produced grief for the Indians, who, according to la Pérouse, "are so strongly attached to their friends." The Frenchman added that "when they are called to their remembrance they shed tears, though they may have lost them for a considerable period." Relatives made strenuous efforts to recover the remains of their dead, even paying their enemies for them.[13]

In some ways warring is simply and purely something that males do; in other ways it is integral to the entire culture. Among the Juaneños the women prepared food, which the chief supplied them, and then accompanied the men on the campaigns as carriers of provisions and retrievers of spent arrows. But in warrior cultures males generally have greater value. Moreover, wars historically have killed more men than women, and thus more men, particularly fierce ones, have been needed and valued. According to anthropological literature, the fiercer the men become in warrior cultures, the more sexually aggressive they are and the more patriarchal culture devalues and exploits its women. In this way destructive maleness was reamplified among the Shoshoneans when they had to seize women to raise more fierce men, which caused wars and the need for yet more fierce men. The women, moreover, had little choice but to submit to the men, on whom they and their children depended for protection against merciless enemies. The example of the Pueblo cultures verifies this analysis. They did not war much, and Pueblo women and men have stood on nearly equal footing in the abodes of both the blessed and the mortals. The more a society has warred, the more its men have dominated. This way of being proved a central aspect of the lifeways of the Indians the Spanish encountered on the California coast.[14]

Men did have an escape from warring, however. Much like the Lakota and some other tribes, a Juaneño could be *kwit.* If for whatever reasons a male youth rejected what his culture considered masculine and opted for socially defined female proclivities, society did not reject him or his tendencies. Kroeber says that femininity and transvestism "were readily recognized and encouraged to manifest themselves as natural. Such 'women' were prized as robust workers, and often publicly married."[15]

It cannot be said that southern California Indians never transcended the pragmatic mind-set of making the world function through ritual and anxious repetition of the tried and true ways of their ancestors. The jimson weed, when powdered and drunk, transported the imbiber to the supernatural. Its consumption was intimately related to the worship of Chinigchinich, or Qua-o-ar to the Gabrieleños, but was also of crucial importance for the initiation of boys into male society, curing of diseases, protection from arrows and snake bites, and fortune in hunting.[16]

Generally shamans were trusted to cure diseases because they were the only ones considered capable of removing the object that was causing the sickness. Again, as Kroeber notes, "information on these matters is tantalizingly scant and vague." We do know, however, that shamans could manipulate the "power" for good or for evil. Indeed, malevolent or incompetent shamans were held responsible for most diseases. It was the job of another, good shaman to remove whatever thing was causing the trouble, usually by sucking it out together with blood. Smoking and singing often accompanied these rites as ways of calling on supernatural help or recalling the practices that had brought success in the past. The common folk used a number of vegetal remedies to cure ailments and wounds.[17] Most diseases originated within a tribal people's own world and could, therefore, only be cured through remedies appropriate to that world. Diseases from other worlds, such as Europe, would prove far more problematic for a shaman and consequential for the California Indians.

Clearly, life was a thoroughly spiritual undertaking for the Indians of California, as it has been for all Native Americans.

Perhaps it is better to say that their world was a wholly integrated one in which the *totality* of existence could not be disintegrated and compartmentalized into the spiritual and material realms. Spirits were immanent in everything in the world. This concept had crucial meaning for Indian ways of producing their subsistence as well. Animals were not simply meat for the taking, nor were plants considered to be insensitive. For all Native Americans all creatures, whether two-legged, four-legged, or winged, have had a psychological makeup or spirit. The different tribes' traditional stories about the animals, which tell about the peoples' proper relationship to them, have varied tremendously. In many of these stories, though, humans and animals originated or emerged at once, could speak to one another in previous epochs, and had crucial functions in the world. This worldview made for a relationship between humans and other animals that European-minded people cannot conceptualize; one sort of creature was no more or no less important than another. Among the Gabrieleños, for example, porpoises watched the world, always circling around it to ensure order. In this context it is easy to see how a Gabrieleño did not want to do anything that would upset the porpoises or their function. Following this logic, to secure an animal for meat, the proper arrangements, both material and spiritual, needed to be made with the companion creature for humans to appropriate it. Proper ritual was in this way as important to the holy undertaking of the hunt as the bow and arrow or snare. Because the animal was a sensible and spiritual creature of the same interconnected cosmos, a hunter likely felt guilt about killing the animal, however necessary for human survival. As Christopher Vecsey explains, "Indians apologized to the animals they killed. . . . At the same time, Indians manipulated animals; they thanked them in order that they might kill them in the future." Proper respect had to be paid to the animal's soul before and after the kill if its soul was to allow its material self to become food for the people when it was reborn. Each, the hunter and the hunted, understood its role in the grand scheme of things. Many Indians believed that the hunted submitted to its destiny willingly if they made the proper observances. There was much to do and much to pay attention to when Indians interacted with nature to produce their livelihoods.[18]

Yet despite all this activity, Europeans and Anglo-Americans consistently perceived Indians as lazy. Juan Bautista de Anza, in a typical Spanish characterization of the people he encountered in California, referred to a "free tribe that is indolent by nature." These people were obviously neither indolent nor free. But their work rhythms gave this impression to all who observed them from an accumulationist perspective. Indians worked intermittently rather than steadily, as survival and nature, rather than a daily schedule or clock, demanded. Most of their food was seasonal; acorns ripened and grasshoppers were abundant in a wingless stage only at particular times. Moreover, ritual may have required that certain animals be killed only at the time deities prescribed, as was true with other tribes. At these junctures people exerted themselves steadily and intensely in a disciplined fashion to procure their livelihoods. The men hunted, and the women gathered and stored food for lean times. Then they rested and loafed. In addition, their ecosystem could not tolerate intensive, accumulationist exploitation—there were only so many animals and oak trees. For this "affluence without abundance" they worked less than people with a plethora of labor-saving devices, maybe ten to fifteen hours a week excluding rituals, and produced only as much as the need for food and shelter demanded, with a work rhythm the environment dictated.[19]

The native people of California followed the ways of their ancestors and, in return, they survived. For them, acting in history meant the repetition of these ancient ways. Repeating their ceremonial dances connected their bodies to these historical cycles and to their ancestors, and interwove their flesh and their spirits with the cosmos. Time existed as a line on a cylinder in which they emphasized that which could and should be repeated for the cosmos to continue. Their myths, their sacred history, told them how to be. They had to exist in the ways they always had, or, in Mircea Eliade's words, practice "the cyclical recurrence of what has been before, in a word, eternal return." Little did they know, or could they know, that a tribe of strangers from a place called Iberia, who had already visited them but gone away, were growing increasingly worried about incursions by a people from Russia. Decisions made as a result of these fears would quickly shred the delicate fabric their ancestors had so carefully woven over thousands of years. They would be thrown into a European conception of linear history, complete with its notion of progress. Now the passage of time would take these native people to new places in their relationship to the cosmos.[20]

Iberians

The ambiguous terminology thus far used to describe the Europeans who would dominate these Indians—Iberians, Spaniards, Castilians—reflects the ambiguity about precisely who they were. I have chosen to refer to all these various peoples of present-day Spain—Andalusians, Catalans, Basques, Galicians, and Castilians—as Iberians because they were not Spaniards. Although "Iberian" often denotes the pre-Roman inhabitants, it nevertheless seems a better term to me than "Castilian," as a minority of the priests or soldiers in California was from Castile, or "Spanish," as a nation of Spain did not come to be until the late eighteenth century. The crown of Castile actually ruled much of the Iberian peninsula essentially as its private estate. Catholicism and a desire to get rid of Moors and Jews unified the peoples of these various regions. Isabel and Ferdinand, already having united the crowns of Castile and Aragon by marrying one another, achieved Castilian dominance when they cast out the last of the Moors from the peninsula in 1492, the same year they sent the Genoan on his famous voyage. The so-called Reconquest, that long and bloody series of campaigns against the Moors, contributed roundly to the vanquishing personality of the conquistadores. The influences on that personality, though, go back two thousand years. First, the Romans conquered the region; then, in turn, the Goths decimated it and the Moors secured it for Islam. Finally, the various Iberians themselves moved to conquer, in the process collecting much booty as a consequence of defeating infidels. In the name of the Sacred Faith it had restored, the military disposition reigned supreme in Iberia. Military heroes even replaced some of the old feudal nobility; thus militarism and conquest earned a person prestige. Unlike the diffuse expressions of violence among California Indians, the crown unified and focused the malevolence of the Iberians.

By no means did Basques or Catalonians all feel themselves to be Spaniards, however. Indeed, they still do not. Nevertheless, the Castilian crown directed people from all over the peninsula to what they perceived as the New World. Like most European elites of the time, the different groups of Iberia went in search of new lands, new trade, and new heathens to loot. Heady from their victory over the Moors, the Iberians sought to break the Arab and Italian monopolies on trade with Asia. Fortune seekers, priests, the unemployed, and the sundry ambitious of the Iberian peninsula all came to the Americas and empowered the Castilian crown with the wealth and prestige they brought back. Castile was vibrant. It gathered together enough people and energy to control nearly the whole of the inhabitants of what is now Latin America. Of course, the English defeat of their armada in 1588 marked the beginning of the decline of Castile, and by the mid-eighteenth century it was a tired empire, indeed. Visions of fantastic wealth had been played out, the mines had already yielded up most of their easy and superficial wealth, European diseases had decimated an astounding 90 percent of the natives on whom the Iberians depended for labor, and factionalism had rent the missionizing effort.[21]

Yet Spain held together its empire. The mid-eighteenth century even saw an economic renewal, and more Spaniards immigrated to New Spain, the viceroyalty that would become Mexico. The reforms associated with the reign of Charles III (1759–88), particularly freer trade and new discoveries of silver, stimulated production in the mines and on the haciendas of New Spain in the two decades before 1800. Moreover, the Indian population revived, swelling the ranks of the labor force. These events primarily influenced the great centers of the viceroyalties of the Spanish empire in the Western Hemisphere: Mexico City, capital of New Spain; Lima, capital of Peru; Bogotá, capital of New Granada; and Buenos Aires, cap-

ital of La Plata. They had little effect on New Spain's far
northwestern frontier, California, where Spain had penetrated
only with a few coastal explorations beginning with Juan
Cabrillo's voyage of 1542. Spain considered it as a way station
for its scurvy-ridden galleons making the voyages from the
Philippines to Acapulco. Interest in California languished for
a century and a half as the threat of largely British pirates
abated on the route to Acapulco and the scurvy was allowed
to take its course. This distant holding finally attracted the
attention of Madrid because of what was to it the ominous
presence of the expansionist Russian empire. In 1767 Madrid
decided that it must secure California from the encroachments of the Russians and the ever-threatening English.[22]

There can be little doubt that it was this Russian threat
that propelled Spain to act in Alta California. Documents in
the Archivo General de las Indias spell out this fear clearly.
Warning of the danger, the viceroy of New Spain, Carlos
Francisco de Croix, wrote to Spain in 1768 "that the Russians
are making efforts to discover new lands, and extend their
commerce." The official response later in the year informed
him of Madrid's plans to counter the menace: "There shall be
an expedition to Monterrey to found a presidio in order to
prevent the Russian effort." Indeed, after 1764 both the Russians and the English (who had recently taken Canada from
the French) looked to the California coast as a profitable place
into which to expand their fur trading. On December 1, 1767,
the Spanish ambassador in Saint Petersburg relayed reports
that the California Indians had killed three hundred Russian
troops who had landed. Though more than likely fanciful, such
reports stirred Madrid to worry about the Russians. Expeditions to California in 1774 reported finding blond Indians, more
evidence of Russian penetrations. The royal court knew it had
to secure the strategic and probably valuable coast by pop-
ulating it with loyal subjects of his Catholic majesty of Castile.[23] The problem was that the remoteness of this frontier
precluded attracting enough Iberians, or even Mexicans, to
hold it effectively against the enemies of the crown. Madrid
resolved this dilemma by fashioning a strategy to transform
those already there into loyal subjects.

To this end in 1769 Spain ordered the founding of presidios, or garrisons, at San Diego and Monterey to accompany what the *Gazeta de Madrid* in 1776 called the "pious Catholic zeal" of the king to convert the "wretched Indians" of California. The double thrust of the military and the priests has confused many historians into debating which was more significant to the crown—religion or military conquest in California. But this analysis should make clear that the military and religion were two sides of the same coin, the effort to create Spaniards out of Indians.[24]

As José de Gálvez wrote to then captain of Baja California, Fernando de Rivera y Moncada, in 1768, the object of the effort in Alta California was "the prompt conversion of many gentiles, the extension of the King's Domains." The energetic Gálvez had come to New Spain in 1765 with the powers of *visitador*, the king's official inspector, and began immediately to deal with a variety of problems all along the northern frontier. His view of the task in Alta California, once he got his orders in 1767, illuminates Spain's intentions. "Make the spiritual conquest," Gálvez instructed Portolá, and "introduce the rule of the King." Fray Juan Díaz chanted a mass for Anza's journey of 1774 to Mission San Gabriel "as an act of thanksgiving to the Infinite Majesty, who deigns to reward with full hands the Catholic zeal, constant piety, and religion of our invincible and most amiable monarch, enlarging his dominions so easily, exalting his arms, and trusting to his fervent charity the task of converting so vast a heathendom to the fold of our sacred religion." Viceroy Bucareli echoed the same holistic sentiment when he entertained "strong hopes . . . of extending, among the many heathen tribes . . . , the dominion of the king and the knowledge of our true religion (which is the principal purpose of his Majesty . . .) by means of the missions." These primary actors in this first of many California pageants accurately reflected the Catholic king's wishes. Charles III said of the coastal lands of California, "They have many fine natural bays and ports, and safe harbors for all manner of boats, and it is known from ruinous experience that enemies of my crown would be seen sheltered in them; in addition this damage could be avoided, and at the appro-

priate time [the natives] could be taught Christianity, and reduced to obedience to my Royal officials." Although the king
did seem concerned mainly with ports and military considerations, and shortly the priests and the army would be feuding with one another anyway, it is clear nevertheless that the
Spanish empire did not separate its California venture into
civil and military halves. Indeed, Gálvez on other occasions
stressed the religious side of the California quest, stating to
Croix, "The primary objective . . . is the bringing of the Faith,
and establishing it in the middle of those Unfortunate Heathens." It must be understood that the feudal-minded Iberians simply proceeded from a worldview that integrated political, productive, and religious activities, though not as
thoroughly as that of Indians. Even Governor Felipe de Neve,
Padre Serra's archenemy because of Neve's later opposition
to missionization, planned that "the natives of these parts will,
in the course of time, develop into useful vassals for our religion and for our state." Most of the relevant documents use
the phrase *conquista espiritual.* As Hernando de Cortez's
chronicler Bernal Díaz opined with respect to the first Castilian conquest, "We came here to serve God, and also to get
rich."[25]

The Spanish would make the Indians into *gente de razón,*
or people of reason. The phrase encapsulates the wholeness
of the Spanish vision for the Indians of California. Of course,
to a Spaniard to be *de razón* meant to be Catholic, Castilian-
speaking, settled into tax-paying towns, working in agriculture, and loyal to his majesty, the king of Spain. But even
more fundamentally, to be *de razón* meant that one's reason,
with some help from the fear of God, would produce an individual who internalized the need to manage, or even renounce, instinct for the good of the social organization. Human reason, moreover, provided the basis for humans technologically to work their will *over* nature. By contrast, for
Indians, human reason studied nature—which included magic.
Such reflection then prepared people to act so as to function
with nature. Nature constantly engaged in biological repro-
duction and encouraged humans to do likewise. The Indians,
apparently, engaged in plenty of such "natural" procreative

activity, to the great trepidation of the Christian padres. The Indians' actions did not seem at all rational to the other culture. Evidently undisciplined Indian instinct, the playground of the devil, seemed to rule the Indians, rather than reason. An anonymous pundit discerned the issue in Alta California nicely, remarking, "Such, then, is the issue: if its inhabitants are addicted to independence."[26]

It was the lot of the Franciscan priests to break the Indians of their addiction to what the Spanish perceived as the Satanic offshoot of liberty and independence—libertinage. The Jesuits, who had labored among the souls of Baja California for seventy years, were cast out from the New World suddenly in 1767. The expulsion was part of a general Bourbon assault on the order. The king sought to reassert royal prerogatives against the always-ambitious Black Robes and against the Catholic church in general. The crown indeed needed bolstering after its humiliating defeat at the hands of the English in the Seven Years War, which Spain entered shortly after Charles III's accession to the throne in 1759. Yet the Jesuit success in Baja California encouraged Gálvez about the chances of missionization producing the settlement of Alta California. The military's management of the Baja California missions, originally intended as a reform measure to give the civil authorities more administrative control, proved disastrous, and in July 1768 Gálvez notified the father president of those missions, Fray Junípero Serra, that priests would reassume control. In spite of Charles III's attempts to upset the old equilibrium between the crown and the clergy, we see repeated here the Spanish mind-set in which the military and the church each furnished part of a single economic and geopolitical pursuit. The Franciscans, headquartered at the College of San Fernando in the interior of New Spain, began the *conquista espiritual* of Alta California under the leadership of Father President Serra with the founding of the first mission, San Diego Alcalá, in 1769.[27]

These were a diverse bunch of spiritual conquistadores who came to Alta California. Many, if not most, genuinely sought to serve God and bring the heathens everlasting salvation. Saint Francis's presentation of self-sacrifice would provide the

model for the undertaking. Serra made his journey north because of "the call of so many thousands of pagans who are
waiting in California on the threshold of holy Baptism." In
his diary he recorded how he traveled on "a road, whose
principal end was the greatest honor and glory of God." The
padres journeyed to the heathens, often barefoot, sometimes
on their knees, to show their compassion for the unfortunates.
(*Passion*, in Spanish *pasión*, derives from the Latin *pāti*, "to
endure," as Christ did on the cross. *Compassion* thus means
"to endure with," which is how the priests often saw their
task. The fathers "endured with" the Indians in their suffering
the lack of knowledge of the Word of God.) But the priests,
we often forget, were men with human passions. In Mexico,
for example, they brawled. On two occasions in the 1780s the
viceroy had to call out the troops to separate Creole and Iberian friars who were clubbing one another in a dispute over
succession to higher office in the church. In a political system
largely closed to nonhidalgos (the word *hidalgo* derives from
hijo de alguién, "child of someone"), the church provided one
of the few routes to power open to ambitious young men—
and some had become priests for this reason in the Hispanic
world.[28]

Father José María Zalvidea was so earnest a fisher of men
at San Gabriel that he learned the Gabrieleño language and
crossed mountains to visit their villages. In a brief diary of
1806 he related one such trip to "the village of Talihuilimit
where I baptized 3 old women, the 1st of 60 years, who had
lost the use of one of her legs." Father Zalvidea had compassion for her and believed in the equality of souls: "To her
I gave the name María Magdalena." The complexity of this
priest emerges in the recollection of an Indian, Julio César,
who "served him as a chorister." He told how Father Zalvidea "was a very good man, but was . . . very ill. . . . He
struggled constantly with the devil, whom he accused of
threatening him. In order to overcome the devil he constantly
flogged himself, wore haircloth, drove nails into his feet, and,
in short, tormented himself in the cruelest manner." Such
physical penance, understood in part as sharing the Savior's

pain on the cross, was not uncommon among the devout. Serra
chastized himself with a whip, too.[29]

Hubert Howe Bancroft wrote, "A curious disease was that
which afflicted many of the early missionaries. It was characterized by melancholy, nervous prostration, and finally per-
turbation of the intellect. . . . Absence from the country invariably worked a cure." Indeed, in the late eighteenth century
California was no land of milk and honey but a harsh and
dangerous frontier where mental equilibrium and discipline
could and did break down. Lorenzo Asisara, a mission Indian
from the north, recalled that a few priests had sexual relations
with Indian women and sometimes drank to intoxication. Fray
Gerónimo Boscana of San Luis Capistrano suffered bouts of
lunacy, and the disparaging reports of his superior hint at carnal relations with his neophytes. An old Californio, José Eusebio Galindo, remembered, "The friar missionaries, who ate
good portions, ordered their fancies, and in general, carried
on a leisurely and comfortable life." Fray Vicente Francisco
de Sarría reported to Madrid on the padres of California in
1817. At San Gabriel one of the two friars' "merit is above
the ordinary," and the other's he considered "distinguished."
But at San Buenaventura the friar's "aptitude was mediocre,"
and at San Luis Obispo Sarría could not "characterize this
padre as having any special fitness or qualifications which I
regard as proper to a missionary."[30] After all, the mission
padres, so thoroughly chronicled and mythologized, were, well,
men.

The crown charged the missionaries with the worldly task
of the *reducción* of the Indians to Christianity. Civil and religious authorities alike agreed on, in Governor Neve's words,
"the prompt reduction of that numerous Heathendom, whose
spiritual conquest will Result in that of yet other Rancherias."
First, the Indians must no longer live "vagrant in the mountains," as Gálvez decreed. To be *de razón* they must be "reduced socially into arranged Pueblos" because concentrated
thus, "the Christian Religion will establish itself in their
Hearts." Reduction of their dominion was the first step in
making the Indians reasonable. (*Reducir* in this context echoes

the Latin *reducere,* which means "to lead back"—in this case to the true faith.) Next, efforts would have to be made "to incline them to go about clothed, beginning to awaken in them the natural Shame of being Seen naked." Father Serra brought not only the word of God but also "clothing of the poor . . . for decency, and modesty, principally for the frail sex." Father Font, noted that "the Christians are distinguished from the heathen in that an effort is made to have them go somewhat clothed or covered, so far as the poverty of these lands will permit." Language also was an important way station on the road to reason, though a stop there was not mandatory, as it was with other manifestations of European civilization. Despite the fact that the government bound them to introduce the Spanish language and further fit the natives for naturalization into the empire, the friars remained rather indifferent to language. They usually repeated church doctrine to the Indians in Spanish, but the padres generally instructed in the native language when they had learned it. Everyday communication proceeded in the Indian vernacular, but only to the extent the padres could speak it.[31]

Once reduced, clothed, and exposed to Spanish, a fuller conversion to Christianity and reason could proceed. It was against the Laws of the Indies to force an Indian to convert: "No government, lieutenant, or alcalde ordinario can or may send armed parties against the Indians with a view towards reducing them into missions . . . [unless] the Indians should cause harm to the Spaniards." This last phrase proved very useful to the army when it came to gathering recruits for Christ; nonetheless, the Indians did have protections, at least in the law. Moreover, they were potentially the spiritual equals of the Europeans. The Indians "are not only capable of understanding the Catholic faith," pronounced Pope Paul III in 1537, "but, according to our information, they desire exceedingly to receive it." Although the last part is questionable given the proven success in the world that the Indians' religion had brought them, it is at least clear that the road to European civilization was an open one.

Missionization was hardly the be-all and end-all of the Spanish endeavor. The loyal subjects of his Catholic majesty

needed to be independent enough to live without their shepherds, the priests. The Laws of the Indies maintained that
"the Spaniards, to whom the Indians are entrusted, should
seek with great care that these Indians should be settled into
towns, and that, within these, churches be built so that the
Indians can be instructed into Christian doctrine and live in
good order." The Indians technically owned the mission lands
and, once civilized, would realize their patrimony as the missions were transformed into pueblos, or towns, and the friars
moved on to new spiritual conquests. Ten years was the prescribed apprenticeship in the mission.[32]

Gálvez decreed that "there are very special circumstances
that promise to locate in California some well-formed, civilized, and fortunate pueblos." As early as 1503 the Castilian
crown had decreed the settling of Indians into towns with a
church and a priest. Juan de Zumárraga, archbishop of New
Spain (1528–48), maintained that New World towns would be
planned "according to and like those of the people who live
in our realms." These towns, according to the Laws of the
Indies, would have the traditional plaza for fiestas and a com-
mons "large enough that although the population may experience a rapid expansion, there will always be sufficient space
where the people may go for recreation and take their cattle
for pasture without them making any damage." The people
were guaranteed common access to water, which the pueblo
officials administered as a public trust. Of course, to become
such *pobladores*, learning and internalizing European ways of
production, it was of utmost importance for schedules and
clocks to guide their labors. As Viceroy Croix instructed Lieutenant Fages, the "missionaries can teach the Indians those
practical trades they are able to learn and for which they are
destined to become useful to themselves and to the state."
Their territory reduced, lands the "vagrants" had previously
used would be available for more Hispanic settlers. It was a
very neat system in its ideal form: European feudal civilization and its social relations would arise among the transformed "heathens" of Alta California. Indeed, since the natives
had no culture the Europeans could discern, this ideal could
be planted in virgin soil and bring forth a showpiece of Ibe-

rian civilization. The new Christians would owe loyalty to the king, thus securing his territory, and would pay taxes. The crown would be reciprocally obligated to sustain the Indians' new-found faith and protect the lands they were entitled to use as lieges.[33]

Such was the vision that the padres carried to Alta California when they founded Mission San Diego in 1769 and Mission San Gabriel Archangel in 1771. Fray Font noted that "God was guiding us and the Virgin Mary was our patroness—and with this everything is said." On August 6, 1771, Padres Pedro Cambón and Ángel Somera left San Diego with ten soldiers and some muleteers to found the new mission. On September 8, "the day of the nativity of Our Lady," they raised the holy cross by the Rio de los Temblores, the River of the Earthquakes. Padres Palóu and Lasuén waxed poetic in the accounts they sent back to Mexico of "the mission San Gabriel, through villages of heathen, all mild and tractable." All boded well, for "the country is most beautiful, the heathen numerous and very docile," embellished Lasuén, "and by planting crops we may be able to replant our voices, with all assurance that with the favor of God the most abundant harvests for things both eternal and temporal may be reaped."[34]

First Meetings

Both the Europeans and the Indians were given to magical thinking about a number of things. Probably each side felt much in awe of the other's strangeness at this meeting at the River of the Earthquakes. However, the European claim that an image of the Virgin of Guadalupe immediately spiritually transformed the Indians remains unauthenticated. It is clear, though, that disaster soon struck: within a month of this raising of the cross, soldiers displayed the local chief's severed head spiked atop a pole at the gate to the soldiers' and priests' temporary quarters. Serra initially blamed the tensions on Lieutenant Pedro Fages, who, fearful of the threat they posed to his few soldiers, had limited the number of gentiles his soldiers would allow into the mission area. Fages, who later was named governor, became the new scapegoat and suffered blame for all the ensuing problems of the missions. But it seems that the pattern of destruction had already begun. The chief had fired an arrow at some of the soldiers. A soldier blocked the arrow with his shield and then killed the chief with a musket ball. Bancroft and Palóu agree that the original arrow had been fired as retribution for the outrages of the soldiers on Indian women, maybe even the wife of the chief. Serra said that the homicidal soldier was on the prowl at the time of the incident. The father president went on about "that crowd of soldiers [who] became lazy; at once they refused to do any work; they were angry and discontented." These "soldiers, clever as they are at lassoing cows and mules, would catch an Indian woman with their lassos to become prey for their unbridled lust. At times some Indian men would try to defend their wives, only to be shot down with bullets," reported the disgusted and appalled Serra. The Iberian warriors' appetites extended to "even the children [*muchachos*] who came to the mission [and] were not safe from their baseness." This pattern repeated itself at San Luis Obispo in 1772. Serra noted that the founding proceeded "in spite of the Enemy who already began to lash his tail by means of a bad soldier, whom soon after arrival they [the founding priests] caught in actual sin with an Indian woman, a thing which greatly grieved the poor padre." The soldiers had journeyed a long way from their European homes, and they were not Iberia's finest young men, either. They believed it was time for their just deserts.[35]

These sorts of soldier activities often caused the troubles that continually divided the religious and temporal representatives of the crown. Suffice it to say for now that the soldiers made the priests' already-substantial task, in Serra's words, "more and more [difficult] each day, turning away the hearts of the gentiles, and pushing them farther away from where their true happiness lay." Not until November 27 did the first baptism take place at San Gabriel, and that was of a child. In the first two years of the mission only seventy-three Indians were baptized.[36]

The Indians quickly learned that more came with the strangers on horseback than trinkets, colorful pictures, and free food. "The women all along the [Santa Barbara] Channel were timorous," Herbert Bolton remarked, "because of abuses committed by soldiers who had passed to and fro in previous years. When Anza's caravan went by most of the women hid in their huts and peeped out at the strangers through cracks or partly open doors." This narrative commenced with the first meeting of the Indians and the Iberians at what would become Mission San Gabriel. The Scottish ranchero informant who was married to a Gabrieleña heard from his wife that "shortly afterwards they received another visit from a larger party, who commenced tying the hands of the adult males behind their backs; and making signs of their wish to procure women—these having again fled to the thicket, at the first appearance of their coming. Harsh measures obtained for them what they sought." A father historian of the modern era has railed, "With what bitterness of heart must not Fathers Miguel and Zalvidea have informed Fr. Presidente Tapis that between 300 and 400 out of their 1,200 wards were infected with the malady which among decent people is named only in disgust." That the soldiers made the fathers' task infinitely more difficult—and, not incidentally, infected the Indians with syphilis and gonorrhea—is beyond any doubt.[37]

Indian medicine had kept diseases specific to Indian worlds largely under control. However, against these new diseases the shamans and their arts were powerless. The failure of Indian medicine to counteract European infection profoundly demoralized the Indians' faith in their therapies and in those who administered the treatments. For example, California Indians used the sweat lodge, which the Spanish called a *temescal*, for many ailments, likely to some salubrious effect. For the Europeans' measles, mumps, smallpox, and pulmonary infections, the sweat lodge, followed by a plunge into cold water, only intensified the ailments. An important thread was thus pulled from their cultural fabric; their medicine proved useless now. The diseases not only physically demoralized even Indian villages with only limited contact with the Europeans but spiritually enervated them as well. As these villages became less and less viable, their increasingly weakened condition pushed them into the missions for free food and, they hoped, better magic for their diseases. As much as the padres correctly blamed the soldiers for the problems their sexual license caused, the incurable diseases these deserters, philanderers, and rapists spread was a crucial factor in delegitimating traditional native beliefs and bringing the generally demoralized Indians within earshot of the Word of God at the missions.[38]

To Christians true happiness lay with that word. "The Word dwelt with God, and what God was, the Word was" (John 1:1): so it is written in their holy book. Such words come in two forms, written and spoken, and the particular form has important meaning. For Indians, words and story are spoken between and within generations. Naturally, as story is passed on, it changes, or as Indians would say, it breathes. New breaths give story new life. Written story, however, does not breathe; it is not in-spired. The written symbols of human communication withdraw some of the fertility the spoken word includes. Kiowa author N. Scott Momaday believes that European man "has diluted and multiplied the Word, and words have begun to close in upon him. He is sated and insensitive; his regard for language—for the Word itself—as an instrument of creation has diminished nearly to the point of no return." Respiring story can enrich experience, whereas written story cements meaning, though ensuring its precise preservation. Indeed, the Spaniards' word, in its particular written form, became immutable law. Moreover, only the church and its earthly representatives could rule on this law. Now the marks on paper and their interpreters came between the people and the Word; now the Word could be used as an authority against the people. Proudly, the padres brought the (impressed) word in the form of a holy book, printed in Venice in 1588, to the Mission San Gabriel. It was truly a great and powerful book for the Europeans. After all, this Word of God had united the European peoples and structured and defined their lives in the otherwise-disorderly epoch that followed the demise of the imperial city of Rome and preceded the creation of their nation-states.[39]

The padres sought to bring this wondrous and powerful Word of their God to the gentiles, but only through their bellies

could the heathens hear the Word. The padres already knew
from their experience with the Indians of the interior of New
Spain that the heathens would devote themselves to the Word
only if provided with material goods and comforts they did
not already have. Food, beads, trinkets, utensils, and clothes
became the lures these fishers of souls used. Padre Francisco
Pangua, guardian of the College of San Fernando, noted that
the heathens "are attracted more by what they receive from
the missionaries"—what he called "the bait and means for
spiritual fishing"—than by what is preached to them" Anza
recorded in his diary, "Already more than five hundred had
been Christianized at San Gabriel and Carmelo alone, and
there would have been more if food had not been so scarce."
The fathers at Carmel told Anza "that even if atole [a gruel
of corn or grain] alone had been plentiful, they could have
doubled or tripled the harvest, but for this lack of it they
have made their living outside the missions." Pangua's predecessor, Rafael Verger, lamented to the viceroy that "a
hundred who have just been Christianized went to the Mountains to look for their food having not enough in the Mission
to maintain themselves." "It seems," Viceroy Bucareli summed
up the problem in 1774, "that the great progress of the spiritual conquest was only suspended by the lack of foodstuffs
to maintain the Indians in the mission enough time for their
instruction [in the faith]." Indeed, food opened ears to the
word. Moreover, the process was a dynamic one. Once the
missions produced crops in the fertile soil of California, there
was more of the stuff to draw and keep the Indians in the
mission long enough to come to know the faith. "But the more
abundant our crops gathered here," Serra reassured Bucareli
the next year, "the more numerous are the consumers." Though
sometimes a crass and certainly condescending conversion
method, these gifts were largely a sincere and acceptable way
to befriend the Indians and interest them in the words the
padres had to offfer.[40]

After the initial blundering and outrages of the soldiers that
accompanied the founding of San Gabriel and other missions,
a few Indians succumbed to the lures of the padres. San Gabriel got a new officer, Corporal José María Cóngora, who

"changed the whole aspect of affairs," and the Indians "gradually forgot the affair [when the chief was killed] and once more came to visit the mission." The missionaries appealed primarily to the Indian women. Father President Lasuén noted in 1801 that the Indian women "never object or show any dislike for the work we assign. They are not so much given to running away." Lasuén surely exaggerated, but the fact was that at the mission the women had access to "grinding-stones, pans, pots, stew-pots, and even small ovens for baking bread." In other words, moving into the mission compound improved important aspects of their material lives. Here another comparison with the Pueblo peoples of the Rio Grande Valley is instructive. There, where women had more power within their cultures and families, they rarely voluntered for conversion. California Indian women, unlike their Pueblo cousins, had something to escape from, namely the harshness of their patriarchs, and could take advantage of what the padres offered. After all, cooking in a metal pot is far easier than balancing victuals over a fire or dropping heated rocks into a wood container to heat liquids. The free food the padres offered all Indians appealed especially to the women, accustomed to the drudgery of preparing meals without metal pots and having their men devour most of the products of their labors.[41]

The women who went to the mission, trading one patriarch for another, did not betray their people any more than La Malinche, Cortez's Aztec mistress, whom the Aztec men sold to the conquistador in the first place. In each case the women did something that bettered certain aspects of their lives. We see here how the power relations prevalent between women and men in Indio culture contributed to the spiritual conquest of the natives. The Indian women who went and stayed at the missions rejected their harsh fathers. The Pueblo women had much less reason to do so and stayed home. The politics of the hearth figured crucially in the very different histories of the California and Pueblo Indians' relations with the Spanish. This inevitable opposition to the Indian fathers bore fruit, which ultimately rotted, in the missions of California.

The pageantry of the missionaries attracted Indians as well. At the Fiesta de Santa Barbara bullfights and brandy drew

Indians down from the hills and into the mission compound
where they might be baptized. The padres also found brightly
painted pictures an effective aid in their spiritual conquest.
In the words of an Anglo traveler's account of 1831, the paint-
ings exhibited "in the most disgusting manner all the tor-
ments the imagination can fancy, for the purpose of striking
terror into the simple Indians, who look upon the performance with fear and trembling." The padres wore bright red,
gold, silver, and purple vestments for their rituals, colors the
Indians had never seen in clothing. E. B. Webb's description
of a procession in 1771 at Monterey bears repeating:

It was headed by the military resplendent in their dress-parade uniforms, the red coats of the Catalan volunteers contrasting with the
tan of the "leather jackets," or soldados de cuero, as they were
called. Seated on their gaily caparisoned horses, the soldiers fired
occasional volleys from their muskets, as was the custom of the day,
the sound of the firing supplying, no doubt, the lack of musical
instruments. Following the soldiers came three servers, the one in
the center carrying the processional cross while the other two bore
tall candlesticks with lighted candles in them. After the acolytes,
or servers, came the incense bearer, walking backwards and swing-
ing the glittering silver censer before the celebrant, Padre Serra,
who, bearing the Sacred Host, and accompanied by two priests
serving as deacons, walked beneath a silken canopy upheld by four
stalwart men. The Padre President and the other priests were vested,
some in capes and some in dalmatics of several colors and glittering
with silver and gold braid and fringes.

It was an impressive display, to be sure. The Spanish showed
the Indians that their magic, or what the Luiseños termed
ayelkwi (knowledge power), was superior to, or at least fan-
cier than, the Indians'. This preeminence got the Spanish a
few more converts.[42]

These indulgent methods attracted only a few neophytes.
Padre Cambón lamented early on in the history of Mission
San Gabriel that the Indians "made themselves so scarce that
even months later, one hardly saw a single Indio in the entire
neighborhood, except occasionally a boy hanging around and
an adult of some twenty years, who from the start had become quite attached to us. The local ranchería moved away

to another site far away from us." To attract greater numbers than the few who wandered in and were taken into the mission, additional energetic measures were needed to cast more broadly the net into the sea of heathens. Moreover, the situation of the first converts in the missions did not draw in the remaining infidels. The condition of the neophytes had always been a problem for Spain in America. In the 1720s Madrid was warned regarding all of its viceroyalties, "It is shown that how much the converted Indians suffer gives birth to the opposition that we find in the infidel Indians to accept Evangelization, and become reduced to vassalage of the Kings of Spain." Similarly, the California Indian neophytes' apparent rejection of their ancestors' lifeways, settlement into flea-infested missions, problems with the soldiers, and restriction of bodily freedom hardly attracted the mass of Indians, especially the males. About four thousand had been missionized in 1783. By 1790 the eleven missions had grown to seventy-five hundred, a gain of only five hundred a year. (Actually, according to Bancroft, during these seven years sixty-seven hundred had been baptized, twenty-eight hundred had died, and "about 400 had apostatized and fled to the old delights of savagism.") Only those in the immediate vicinity of the mission were entering the process of Christianization. Once the initial attraction of clothing, food, and trinkets wore off, neophytes became scarce. Shortly after the first mission foundings the padres and soldiers began peaceful excursions to Indian villages to persuade the local chiefs to convert, hoping that then some of the tribe would follow. But more likely they would not. As Captain Beechy noted in 1831, "the wild have a great contempt and dislike for those who have entered the missions." Soon some of the Indians started to run away from the missions. Initially the orders of governors Fages and Borica forbade sending soldiers, or even Indian converts, after the apostates. But later, under the rule of Borica and particularly in the last decade of the eighteenth century, soldiers and priests undertook expeditions to recapture apostates.[43]

The Indians remained legally free to choose or reject salvation. However, once having accepted the religion and presents from the representatives of the Catholic king, fealty bound an Indian to lords temporal and heavenly. Thus, the authorities could legally and legitimately arrest and punish those who fled, *los huidos*. "They easily succeed in escaping," noted French explorer A. Duhaut-Cilly, "but they are often retaken by emissaries sent in their pursuit by the missionaries and the commandants of the soldiers. . . . They are generally treated as criminals, and pitiously put in irons." Padre President Lasuén wondered "what food, then, will be able to overcome in these men the hankering after the brutal life they knew? It was free and it was lazy. Who can keep them from murmuring after it?" As all types of fathers too often do, the padres turned to soldiers to resolve such dilemmas. Not only were *los huidos* brought back and punished, but some of their as yet unreduced fellows also got snared in the net. Although the latter were frequently released, the worldly rewards for success in the spiritual (though increasingly physical) conquest tempted the expeditions and the missions to count as novitiates those whom the soldiers incidentally captured. Clearly the reality of what it took to gain converts wrecked the aspirations of Serra and Gálvez for the Indians joyfully to accept the true faith.[44]

In this way conversion gained a new dynamism by no later than 1800. Anastasio Carrillo reported from Mission San Fernando to the military in Santa Barbara that *los huidos* "are very distant," and the troops went in search of them. The results of this particular expedition are unknown, but it is easy to imagine the *soldados de cuera* returning with more than backsliders. Hunting down Indian *huidos* meant entering lands remaining under Indian control, and the Indians defended themselves against what they naturally and legitimately perceived as an invasion. Once fired on, the soldiers were fighting a just war, in accordance with European law and custom, and could punish and capture at will. Sherburne Cook, citing historical documents, describes an episode of 1805 that became all too typical of Spanish practice: "Luis Peralta went on a punitive expedition from Santa Clara. After he had caught up with the Indians the latter began to fight. He fired on them and killed 'five of the bums (*gandules*).' The survivors fled to the brush, where he attacked again and killed five

1. "The way of fighting of the Indians of California" is the caption on this drawing, which gives another view of the conquest. A conquistador, *a caballo*, rousts heathens from their round houses. (Photo of a drawing in the Naval Museum in Madrid courtesy of the Seaver Center for Western History Research, Los Angeles County Museum.)

more. The Spanish then 'beat the bush' and captured 'twenty-five head (*piezas*),' all women. The prisoners were then brought to Santa Clara for conversion." José María Amador, an old Californio, remembered an episode of 1822 in which the troops set out to "castigate the evildoers." When caught, "the women and the children were reduced to the Mission San José to be Christians and the men were put to making adobes for the San Francisco Presidio. When they completed their sentences all were made Christians." He also remembered such methods as having Indian auxiliaries buy all of the heathens' arrows, first inviting them to eat, then capturing them "and putting them all in horse collars." The more Indians captured against their will, the more that ran away; the more that ran away, the more expeditions of soldiers sent out to capture more Indians.[45]

This internal dynamic continued to accelerate the process

of conversion, only more intemperately. We have already seen
the fragility of the native ecosystem. Obviously, the Spanish
disrupted more than a few of the tightly woven interconnections between the people and nature. The Indian food supply
dwindled as the Spanish increased their control of the areas
along the coast. After the turn of the century plenty of cattle
roamed on lands the natives had previously used for foraging.
This situation impelled some Indians toward the food handouts of the missions and others toward the idea of capturing
cattle. Not surprisingly, many gentiles, sometimes in league
with neophytes, raided the cattle. And not surprisingly, the
Spanish responded with counterraids to retrieve the cattle and
punish the increasingly hungry thieves. These forays provided
a fine opportunity to justly capture more neophytes. The
number of Christianized Indians measured the success of the
California experiment for both Spain and Mexico. If the padres
wanted more funds and tolerance for their effort, they had to
demonstrate a substantial harvest for the Lord.

Captain Beechey describes the result of recruitment expeditions of neophytes and their de razón overseers:

On these occasions the padres desire them to induce as many of
their unconverted brethren as possible to accompany them back to
the mission, of course implying that this is to be done only by per-
suasion; but the boat being furnished with a cannon and musketry,
and in every respect equipped for war, it too often happens that
the neophytes, and the gente de razón, who supervise the direction
of the boat, avail themselves of their superiority, with the desire
of ingratiating themselves with their master, and of receiving a reward. There are, besides, repeated acts of aggression which it is
necessary to punish, all of which furnish proselytes. Women and
children are generally the first objects of capture, as their husbands
and parents sometimes voluntarily follow them into captivity.

By the 1830s, the end of the mission period, the means of
conversion had undergone a thorough transformation. Some
have described these methods as proof of the Spaniards' cruelty toward the Indians; others have defended them as necessary in the service of a nobler cause—European civilization
and everlasting salvation.[46]

However, these factors—the sexual-political contradictions

of Indian society, soldier-introduced disease, the appeal of free clothing, food, and clever magic, and the desire for converts captured in "just" wars—explain how Indians were missionized in California. In the case of Mission Santa Barbara the native population was thoroughly reduced (to either Christianity or death) by 1801. By 1812 all the Indians along the coast within a forty-mile radius of the mission had been missionized, and by 1828 those of the mountains and the Channel Islands no longer roamed as they had before 1769.[47]

The Indian Responses
to Missionization

The difficulties of attracting and holding converts bespoke a whole series of problems between the Indians and their ways, on the one hand, and the missions and the ways of the padres, on the other. I will now analyze the varieties of this conflict and arrive at some conclusions about the nature of the culture that the interaction of these two peoples produced, particularly as regards its social structure and hierarchy and as regards work.

We cannot generalize about Indian response to the initial presence of the missions. Sometimes the natives simply avoided them by moving their villages, sometimes the padres could attract a few in, and sometimes the Indians attacked the interlopers. We have already seen how and why the Gabrieleños fought the soldiers at Mission San Gabriel only a month after its founding. Padre Cambón feared that soldier outrages and the very presence of the Europeans had united the previously adversarial locals. "We awoke," he said of October 11, 1771, the day after the impaling of the local chief's head, "to find plumes of smoke signals all along the entire horizon. We investigated and learned that this was a general pow-wow of all the surrounding rancherias, convoked to make peace between those of the sierra and those from the coast, mortal enemies up to this time." The two priests, whom only fourteen soldiers guarded, were nervous indeed. Yet the missionaries at San Gabriel encountered only apathy during their first few years. The warring tribes of southern California could not transcend their squabbles and unite to cast out the Iberians.

More than a decade later, in October 1785, some Gabrieleños, both inside and outside the mission, tried to obliterate the mission. Toypurina, said to have been a green-eyed sorceress, led the Gabrieleños against the Spanish soldiers and priests. At the inquest after her capture Toypurina stated that she had commanded a chief to attack "for I hate the padres and all of you, for living here on my native soil . . . , for trespassing on the land of my forefathers and despoiling our tribal domains." Those inside the mission expressed different reasons for wanting the death of the padres and soldiers. The inquest said that Nicolás José, the neophyte who convinced Toypurina of the necessity of terminating the interlopers, desired the extinction of the padres and Corporal Verdugo because they disallowed him his "heathen dances and abuses." During the night of October 25 a band of Indians from six local villages entered the compound but failed in their mission because Toypurina's special powers failed to kill the padres as planned. The corporal of the command discovered the plot; Fages dispatched in irons the headmen and Nicolás José to the presidio at San Diego and released the others with twenty lashes; and Toypurina suffered banishment to Mission San Carlos in the north.[48] Nicolás José's sentiment produced a variety of forms of Indian resistance, which we will look at shortly. However, Toypurina's view, that the Spaniards should not be there at all, the Diegueños most forcefully expressed.

On the night of November 4, 1775, the Yumans in the vicinity of the first of the missions, San Diego Alcalá, attacked and burned the mission and created the first martyr of the Franciscans' cause in Alta California. Awaking a little after midnight and finding the buildings in flames and the heathens vociferous, Padre Luis Jaume confronted the marauders with the command "Love God, children." Not only were these his last words but they also mark a turning point in Spaniards' attitudes toward, and hopes for, the Indians. It is not thoroughly agreed that both heathens and neophytes participated in the ruin of the mission. Most likely neophytes did participate because, as Rivera y Moncada testified, "they wanted to live as they did before." Nevertheless, this is the first and only major attempt on the part of the Indians to rub out the missions before they had much actual experience with Hispanicization. Once Indians were missionized, the nature of their revolts changed. Now neither religious nor military authorities echoed their initial optimism about their prospects for conversion. "The disaster at San Diego," Serra lamented, "beyond the tragedy that is in itself, is and will be a decided setback for future foundations, especially in view of the attitude of Don Fernando [Rivera y Moncada]." And Anza noted, "The event has filled everybody with terror and caused them to realize what the natives of this region are capable of attempting, which formerly they did not believe." Only a few months before the debacle, Palóu waxed poetic: the two San Diego friars "were both very happy, seeing that they were gathering in abundance the spiritual fruit of that vineyard of the lord, for on the 3rd of October in the same year . . . they had baptized sixty heathen." No longer does one read of the optimism of, for example, Garcés on his journey with Anza from Tubac to San Gabriel in 1774: "Oh! what lands so suitable for missions! Oh! what a heathendom so docile!" The Indians were now fearful creatures in the minds of the Spanish.[49]

The revolt at San Diego emphasized the increasingly apparent failure of the Indians to flock to their priestly shepherds. In his "Report on the Californias" of November 30, 1775, Lieutenant Pedro Fages wrote that "the compliance and meekness of the Indians" in the missions "is the effect of a just fear rather than affability and goodness." Any accomplishments on their part toward civilization proved "in truth very rare." By contrast, he described the rivers and lands of the area that in 1781 would become the pueblo of Los Angeles and imagined how it would be easy to grow fruit, beans, corn, and wheat. The site "offers comfort for some Spanish families to join as neighbors." Whereas before Spain's representatives in California had put their faith in Hispanicized Indians, Fages now saw in these "españoles" (he undoubtedly meant mestizos or Mexicans) "the hopes of an important settlement." In other words, Fages was giving up on the Indians whose conversion was to populate the territory with loyal subjects of his Catholic majesty. Instead, he saw settlers from the interior of Mexico as the hope for a successful colonization of California and the way to hold the land secure from the Russian and English threats. Fages simply did not like Indians. Referring to the Diegueños, who were then revolting in more ways than one, he called them "friends of treachery and very little of the Spanish." Serra still held to the missionizing vision. "Missions are what this country needs," he said faithfully in 1778. "They will not only provide it with what is most important— the light of the Holy Gospel—but also will be the means of supplying foodstuffs for themselves and for the Royal Presidios." Serra concluded his remarks about the missions with a barb aimed at his secular adversaries: "They will accomplish this far more effectively than those pueblos without priests."[50]

Spain's unified view of the continuing colonization of California, with religious and civil authorities pulling together first to Christianize and then to settle Indians and turn them into loyal subjects of the crown, was surely breaking down. Many of the civil and military figures simply did not believe that the Indians could be converted. "They are idol worshippers," Fages concluded. Fages's and Serra's uncannily bitter relationship strained Spanish unity of purpose even further. As we saw in the fatal mishap that accompanied the founding of Mission San Gabriel, Serra held then commander of the presidio Fages responsible for virtually every shortcoming of the Alta California effort. In 1772 Serra founded Mission San Luis Obispo and broached the issue of a mission at San Buenaventura. Both the potential site and the potential of the Indians favorably impressed Serra. Fages was not so moved, however, and refused to send a guard to protect what he considered to be an isolated and dangerous location, thus widening their rift. On his year-long trip to Mexico City in 1773 Serra pleaded with Viceroy Bucareli to remove Fages (who actually belonged to a different branch of the military than the *soldados de cuera*) from the presidial command," a measure that seems to me of special importance. . . . Otherwise there will be no stopping the desertions of soldiers." But primarily Serra blamed him for the halting progress of conversion. "If I were called upon to tell," the father president continued, pouring out his grief, "not of the annoyances he has caused me, and the rest of the religious, . . . but of the damage his conduct has continually done to the missions, it would be a long story." Apparently Serra got his story heard because Bucareli replaced Fages with Rivera y Moncada. As fate would have it, this new commandant, in his zealous persecution of the San Diego insurgents, entered a church, sword in hand, and arrested a wanted Indian. As if relations between the military and padres were not sufficiently strained, now the ruffians were violating sanctuary. Padres Fuster (Juame's luckier partner), Lasuén, and Amurrió declared Rivera y Moncada excommunicated in 1776. (He later repented his act.) In another evil twist of fate for Serra, the viceroy again appointed Fages governor in 1782. In December of that year Serra wrote to Fray Pangua, "Common sense, laws, and precedents mean nothing to him."[51]

The conduct of the soldiers continually exacerbated this division between the religious and civil officials. Too many of them sniggering lunkheads, yet consistently important players in the Spanish California pageant, they largely sat about eyeing the Indians with contempt, fear, and lust—a mix with frightening potential, to be sure. In 1773 the five missions that had been founded by then each had only six to sixteen soldiers protecting them, for a total of only sixty men guarding all of Alta California. By 1800 there numbered 372 military men, though sixty of these were *inválidos*, or retirees. Since such a force seemed unlikely to deal effectively with a concerted Indian revolt, the settlers and soldiers always lived in fear. In spite of their limited numbers these soldiers managed to inflict irreparable damage on the mission effort, which continually enraged the padres. "I am tired," said Padre González de Ibarra of San Fernando, "of telling them that there is a law that prohibits their dealings and contact with the Indians after following them [the troops] to the ranchería." The soldiers paid little attention to the strict regulations prohibiting any interaction with Indian women. Padre Serra's letters back to Mexico consistently complained of the soldiers' taking concubines and raping Indian women. He begged and pleaded for married soldiers, "gente no perversa," to be sent to guard the missions. The father president understood that the soldiers were needed both for the protection of the Europeans, especially after the San Diego uprising, and for the flogging of Indians, "so that it can be carried out without reprisal." Yet "so many men of such low character"—under the command of Fages, no less—proved the padres' primary nemesis. This "plague of immorality," as Serra termed it, caused no end of difficulties between the religious and military actors in Spanish California.[52] Eventually the ranchos, gifts of land to soldiers, would replace the missions and supercede the vision of the Franciscans. At the same time the tiny pueblo of Los Angeles would fill with ex-soldiers and shepherdless Indians and grow into a city without priests.

The Fathers and
Their Indian Children

In spite of the soldiers the priests forged ahead with their variously acquired neophytes. The padres regarded the Indians as children. They were *sin razón* to the Franciscans, people who had not attained the age of reason (about seven years), and thus their dependent little ones. "They are our children," Father Serra wrote to the viceroy, "for none except us has engendered them in Christ. The result is we look upon them as a father looks upon his family. We shower all our love and care upon them." The *llavera*, or woman in charge of keys for the Indian women's *monjerio*, or dormitory, remembered how Padre Zalvidea "cared much for his mission children, as he called the Indians he himself had converted to Christianity." "No matter how old they are," confirmed Padre Juan Calzada, guardian of the College of San Fernando, in 1818, "California Indians are always children."[53] Moreover, by reducing Indians to Christianity and settled agricultural ways, the padres ripped from under them their economic and cultural supports. Traditional hierarchies were apparently destroyed as the Indians, despite their previous status in their clans, all became as children—not only in the view of the European Franciscans but in their physical and emotional dependence on the mission system as well. In trying to wean Indians from the bosom of mother nature and rear them to become civilized Christians, the padres only succeeded in infantilizing them.

The padres had all the obligations and duties of fathers toward children as well as the rights and privileges. They could arbitrarily regulate the activities of their dependents according to their desires for their children's development. As Don José del Carmen Lugo remembered, "The minor faults which the Indians committed, the kind that the father of a family would punish, these padres could correct themselves." Pablo Tac, a Luiseño Indian, recalled his experience at the mission with the padres: "None of the neophytes can go to the garden or enter to gather the fruit. But if he wants some he asks the missionary who immediately will give him what he wants, for the missionary is their father." The padres were to be loving and stern, with love forthcoming when the Indians internalized, or at least complied with, the fathers' wishes. They monitored their children constantly. In the sacristy of Mission San Gabriel one can see a large, round, framed mirror with a sign saying, "Used by the padres during mass to watch the movements of the Indians." The medieval mind generally perceived those who had not reached the age of reason as innately licentious and unconstrained, even more sinful than the adult sons of Adam. Padre Tapis of Mission Santa Barbara punished Indian transgressions of European mores "with the authority which Almighty God concedes to parents for the education of their children." "They are treated with tolerance," affirmed Father President Lasuén in 1801, "or dealt with more or less firmly . . . while awaiting the time when they will gently submit themselves to rational restraint."[54]

The first step in reining in the Indians' unbridled spontaneity and wildness was their reduction and confinement to missions, where they could be parented and taught the Catholic faith. Those "who live dispersed and vagrant in that extensive land," as Viceroy Bucareli perceived them, would have to be settled and clothed on their way to civilization. Recall that in Serra's view the Indians must first be clothed "for decency and modesty," especially the frail sex. Fathers Gil y

2. A modern view of Mission San Juan Capistrano, which displays the classic portrayal of Father Junípero Serra—paternal civilizer making the spiritual conquest of infantilized, unclothed Indians of the California coast. Father Serra actually stood less than five feet tall. (Courtesy of the Seaver Center for Western History Research, Los Angeles County Museum.)

Taboada and Zalvidea of San Gabriel replied to the Interrogatorio that "although they are much addicted to nudity, we make every effort to have them go decently covered. The dress which for the present is given for that purpose is the frazada or blanket, a short tunic which we call the *Cotón*, and a narrow cloth which serves as covering and which we call the *taparabo* or breechcloth for men. For the women, a blanket, tunic, and a skirt." Now that the Indians appeared on their way toward looking like Spaniards, or at least not like naked savages, they would have to sound like Spaniards too.[55]

The missionaries presented the Castilian language to the Indians in mixed ways and with mixed results. The padres largely, though not always, made both a serious effort to learn the native languages and to teach Spanish to the Indians. The adults did not take quickly to the new idiom, if at all, so special efforts were made to teach the children their prayers in Spanish. At the same time, at least at San Gabriel, the mission "has the catechism in the respective idioms of the natives or tribes of which its population is composed; but they are not approved by the Bishops, because not only is it difficult but well nigh impossible for the Bishops to find an interpreter who could revise them; for even composing them the missionaries found it a matter of much labor and patience." Padre Zalvidea, who wrote these words, was probably one of the few with any facility in an Indian language. The llavera of the mission remembered that he taught the Indians to pray "in their own language." In 1811 each mission received an *interrogatorio*, or questionnaire from the Spanish government; the replies about language vary. At San Fernando "there are those who understand Spanish, but they speak it imperfectly." At Santa Barbara "several neophytes understand Spanish somewhat," and at San Luis Rey "many of the Christians, especially the men, speak and understand Spanish, although not perfectly." These are statements of padres with an interest in demonstrating the success of their teaching. The father president summed up the situation: "Some speak Spanish, although with much difficulty." One Indian, whose narrative of mission life survives, did learn Spanish. However, typical of such "successes," he was raised in the mission. On the whole, it would appear that the adult Indians did not learn the language with which to learn the Word.[56]

That the Indians did not learn the language of their acculturators suggests that they probably did not comprehend much of the religion either. The padres required only eight days of instruction in the faith for baptism—eight days of hearing very bad Shoshonean or Chumash, or eight days of hearing Spanish, which the neophytes did not understand. Indeed, the Catholic church had much to offer in the way of visual aids to conversion, and these the Indians genuinely appreciated; but one suspects that a thorough change in the Indians' religious worldview was not forthcoming. The padres so much as admitted that the Indians were not sincerely changing their ways. "The Indian by nature is apathetic and indolent," said Narciso Durán, father president of the missions from 1825 to 1827, "so much so that the Spanish rule of ten years' *neófita* is for him wholly inadequate." The old ways, the ways that had brought success to the Indians for so long, held sway against whatever attractiveness the word of God might have. Father Lasuén lamented:

> On an occasion like that, when some one asked permission for some of this group who get "hungry" to go to the mountains for a week, I said to them with some annoyance: "Why, you make me think that if one were to give you a young bull, a sheep, a fanega of grain every day you would still be yearning for your mountains and your beaches." The brightest of the Indians who were listening to me said, smiling and half-ashamed of himself, "What you say is true, Father. It's the truth."

As should be becoming clear in this narrative, and as will become even clearer in the following pages, the Indians of the coast of California did not—could not—internalize the *razón* of the Europeans. There is simply no evidence that they did to any significant degree. The Spanish effort had succeeded only in making them dependent, not in converting them. A traveler writing in 1836 noted that "some few were civilized"; but generally, they kept much of their old belief system and learned little of Spanish ways.[57]

What Fages called "a just fear" kept the converts at least playing the role of Hispanicized Indian. Noted Eulalia Pérez of Mission San Gabriel, "Several of the Indians learned music, and played instruments and sang in the mass." The Indians made their own instruments—flutes, guitars, violins, drums, and triangles—and played sonatas and religious chants with varying success. To Vicente Lugo these neophyte "minuets" sounded "more or less bad," though "An Intelligent Bostonian" observed, "The Indians are apt learners of a variety of arts; and I can assure you, (not having an ear for music,) I have heard two native Indian bands, with violins and wind instruments, perform some church music, & other pieces, in a pleasant and skillful manner." At Mission San Luis Obispo, according to Encarnación Pineda, "The leader of the band was Joaquín, a neophyte. With a rod he led the musicians, striking with it whomever among them made a mistake. In the course of time the band dressed in blue uniforms

3. A daguerreotype of the last Indian choir at Mission San Buenaventura. (Courtesy of the Seaver Center for Western History Research, Los Angeles County Museum.)

with a red stripe along the length of each trouser leg, [and]
a red cap with a tassel." Outwardly, perhaps, the Indians did
tolerably well at Europeanization.[58]

But the Indians' old spirits still lived and continued to have
some power, at least in 1826 at Mission Santa Inez. There a
neophyte Indian, Tomás, was accused of witchery, specifically
of damaging Angela, the Indian wife of a soldier. This episode
demonstrates the resiliency of Indian religion and, though it
is difficult to discern precisely what happened from the records, the power of the Indian spirits over the gente de razón.
The soldier testified that "Tomás had illicit dealings with a
woman," Angela's niece. Apparently Tomás wanted to move
the woman closer to Angela, but for reasons the testimony
does not include, Angela objected and thus incurred the wrath
of Tomás. As Angela sat in her house, Tomás entered and
touched her on the palm of her hand with a stick. The pain
began immediately on her hand, and within an hour it became "flaccid and useless." Shortly thereafter her whole body
was overcome with pain. As this "chest and body pain" con-

tinued and she thought she was going to die, "out from her mouth came the sound of black pigs, and at the same time some threadlike hairs came from her mouth." The alcalde, Adriano, affirmed the testimony of the soldier and Angela, but Tomás and his wife Eleuteria denied everything. The Indian spirits, or the Catholic demons, were still alive. Three years later another charge of sorcery was leveled at Santa Inez neophytes: "They were found dancing in one of the houses of that ranchería, and bringing to the said dance house those most dangerously ill. To each of the latter they said that it was necessary that every one of the sick who had been dancing should contribute glass beads or some other thing, in order that by this dance which they were making to the Devil they should become cured of their illness." José el Ventureño was the shaman in charge.[59]

As late as 1828 the neophytes journeyed back in time and space to the world they shared with animals. "Their dances," Juan Bandini reported, "consist of an attempt to imitate the coyote, the deer and other animals." The old beliefs, the dancing bodies' old connections with the cosmos, still held sway with the formally Christianized Indians. "The Catholic Indians in everything resemble the gentiles," he noted with an eye toward disparaging the mission effort. Hugo Reid concluded of the Gabrieleños:

They have at present *two* religions—one of custom and another of faith. They don't quarrel with their neighbor's form of worship but consider their own the best. The life and death of our Savior is only, in their opinion, a distorted version of their own life. Hell, as taught them, has no terrors. It is for whites, not for Indians, or else their fathers would have known it. The Devil, however, has become a great personage in their sight; he is called Zizu, and makes his appearence on all occasions. Nevertheless, he is only a bugbear and connected with the Christian faith; he makes no part of their own.

It may well have been desirable for the Indians to gain the new and, often as not, apparently more potent magic of the Europeans and their gods. What the neophytes did internalize of Christianity they simply incorporated into their own indigenous belief system.[60]

Chapter Two

Brutal Appetites

The Social Relations of the
California Missions

The old ways continued to reign in spite of the padres' earnest attempts to inculcate a new form of time and productive discipline in their charges. In the Indian worldview certain spirits, which formed part of a being's essence, animated plants, animals—indeed everything in their small worlds necessary for their subsistence. They had to be assuaged correctly for humans to appropriate them. People produced when they were hungry, and the availability of food and the seasons determined when the work was done. When the Europeans came, they determined that these important attitudes regarding land, work, and animals had to change. This effort at forced assimilation constituted a crucial factor in the evolution of production in California.

When people engage the land, its resources, technology, and human labor in the cause of production, they inevitably produce more than either their subsistence or commodities. They produce a particular structure of human society, which we may best term the social relations. People make their own history but do so within the context, restraints, and supportiveness of these social relations. Usually these forms of human interconnectedness are inherited. But sometimes, as in the case of California during missionization, the interaction of two cultures as well as the traditional ways of each produce the

social relations. So far we have seen what assumptions about
religion, the relationship of fathers to women and children,
land and animals, production, and virtue in society the Spanish and Indios brought to the mix that would become Spanish
California culture. The conflicts and interaction of the two
worldviews, with the Spanish clearly holding the upper hand
in physical force, produced a seigneurial system which the
world market buttressed, based on presumptions of European
cultural, patriarchal, and racial supremacy. When the padres
established that first mission at San Diego in 1769, they set
in motion the social relations that would constrain the future
history of California. Obviously, many people changed and
moved this history, and many of their names have appeared,
and will appear, in this account. However, they were not free
to act in a world of their own making, their claims to the
contrary notwithstanding. As history obliged them, the various peoples of California developed complex inner worlds,
which they then projected outward and refracted through the
social relations that the history of imperial and cultural conflicts had bequeathed them.[1]

I will commence the analysis of this slowly unfolding legacy
of padres and Indians with the meaning of the introduction
of European notions of time, animals, and tools. Unwilling or
unable to despiritualize their customary understandings of
these, the Indians evaded assimilation of European reason.
Similarly, the Indians could not incorporate the priests' efforts
to teach them to discipline their bodies—which, in the Europeans' view, apparently were given over to fleeting carnal
pleasures—for determined work. The missions, nevertheless,
produced magnificent harvests in spite of the apathy of the
Indians. In addition to foodstuffs, they began the production
of the seigneurial ways that would come to characterize the
social relations of Alta California. The Indians, though, did
not prosper. Disease ravaged them, and the punishments which
the padres inflicted to teach them reason only made them
more bewildered. Mostly they died, though sometimes they
revolted, and this outcome ended the padres' dream of reason
for the natives of California.

Discipline and Transformation

The friars at San Luis Rey asserted, with a sureness suspect when considered against other friars' statements about Indian indolence, that "the new Christians regulate themselves by the clock of the mission; and for timing their rest, meals, and work, we sound the bell." Each mission had a clock and usually two bells, the larger one to note the time for prayers and devotions and the smaller one the temporal duties. At Mission San Carlos excavators in the 1920s uncovered a sundial on which "all around the dial, carved in stone, were objects and figures indicating, apparently, the various duties to be performed by the neophytes at the hour marked by the shadow of the gnomon." There came to be, in other words, a new regulator of activities for the neophyte Indians, one they neither comprehended nor internalized.

Time for such people had been rather circular, or more accurately, cylindrical, as we have already seen. The important events were repeatable ones. Time was not linear, with every event leading to some new place in history, nor abstractly represented, with minutes and hours dividing days, or weeks dividing months. The seasons were the important events, and they came, went, and came back again in the same fashion each time. Padre Serra had an alarm clock at Mission San Carlos, and the padres at Santa Clara received "a wooden clock with little bells for hours and quarter hours." These clocks, powerful symbols of European work discipline, did not sound meaningfully in the ears of the neophytes. "They satiate themselves today, and give little thought to tomorrow," whined Padre Lasuén. "If they are put to work, nobody goads them on. They sit down; they recline; they often go away, and come back when it suits them." The strength of the old habits and practices earned the Indians a reputation for laziness in the world of the timepiece.[2] This reputation they would carry with them through the European phase of their history. It would further justify the Spanish view that only force could hold them in the missions because they were brutal (in the Latin sense of the word, that is, irrational and insensible) and the later Yankee Protestant view that they deserved to die.

The Indians had to adapt themselves not only to an entirely new conception of time discipline. Tools have a power of their own, and they press people to transform their sense of, and relationship to, nature. Consider, for example, the making of a plow from a tree. Tree, as the Indians understood it, was a spirit-inhabited being that gave acorns or other fruits, provided fuel, and welcomed birds. The deities had arranged its nature that way and given it a spirit that encouraged it to act in the world with those purposes. To make tools from it, people had to transform their sense of tree. Its mechanical and technical potentialities had to be separated from its literally animated pith. If it became the (or any) tree, simply a thing, then its wood could be used without fear of retribution from any spirits. This is not to say that Christian Europe had cast out thoroughly all the pagan spirits from peasant consciousness by this time. Nonetheless, the European spirit world, embodied and unified in the Christian concept of the one true God, transcended earthly life and objects; it had despiritualized the world. Europeans encountered simply a tree, which they could use without fear of retribution from the spirit world for acting inappropriately toward it and its prescribed function. Making use of technology—or more accurately the Iberians' prototechnology or handicrafts, which had at least the potential to improve the material quality of life for the California Indians—required a metamorphosis of the Indian relationship to nature and all its beings.

The Indian relationship to animals is particularly important in this regard and will help clarify this idea. Animals and humans, their spirits and their flesh, together formed the Indian creature world. All beings, two-legged, four-legged, and winged, coexisted in the spirit part of the world. This notion gave the Indians of California and the rest of the Americas a certain oneness with animals. The oneness was not always harmonious because they often preyed on one another, but it was a oneness the Europeans had lost or transcended. For the latter, the laws of science came to govern all anatomies, which they increasingly perceived as simply mechanical because the influence of the spirits, especially that of the Devil, had become mere shadows in the light of the one true God. Animals, then, came to have otherness for Europeans when they rigorously separated mind and spirit from their own bodies and denied animals a spiritual nature. Christian Europe perceived all bodies as only corporeal, the human soul as ethereal, and animals as having no souls or spirits. Not only does this view divide the self into two sometimes-warring parts, but it also changes peoples' relations to animals. Humans and animals no longer coexisted in the European spirit world as they still did for the people of the California coast before 1769. Animals were no longer companions but others that humans could utilize as they did the trees. (Curiously enough, the founder of the padres' order, Saint Francis of Assisi, in some ways sought to restore human and animal companionship. All were God's creatures to Saint Francis, but he distinguished between "irrational animals" and "human beings made in the image of God." Only the latter had souls, though they all could be "brothers.") In Genesis 1:28 God told humans to "rule over the fish in the sea, the birds of heaven, and every living thing that moves upon the earth." For Indians, though, their essential oneness with these creatures in the spiritual world required that they maintain a certain equality with animals in the material world.

Thus, for Indians to use an ox-driven wooden plow required a tremendous transformation of their orientation toward the cosmos. The ox and the tree lost the old spirits that had animated them and formed part of their essence. The mass production of animals for food and as trade items, such as occurred with the huge mission cattle herds, further alienated people from an interconnected and companionate relationship to animals, except to keep them as dependent pets. Many of the Europeans' tools and skills could well have advantaged the Indians, but they could not find a place in the firmly held Indian worldview. The sacristy of Mission San Gabriel displays cabinets that the neophytes constructed with fantastically carved drawer handles depicting grotesque heads. Though such images were not uncommon in Iberian cathedrals, we cannot help but wonder what spirits still animated these drawers and knobs even after instruction in European religion and wood handicrafts. Such custom, habit, and story, so long in their formulations, could not have been transformed without considerable consequences, including the resistance and destruction of tribal peoples. Indeed, tools only fatally confused and disordered the California Indian world.[3]

Tools developed initially in cultures only when someone, in the words of Lewis Mumford, "performed the stunning act of dissociating" such a function as lifting from its essence as something that only arms performed. Levers could only do lifting when lifting was dissociated from what usually did it, thus allowing something else to fulfill that particular function. The Indian view of nature's beings as animated stood between them and the use of the Europeans' tools. Those without technics could not control and manipulate the environment because it was not separated from humankind but animated with genuinely kindred spirits. Thus the environment, and each of its constituents, were endowed with the same caprices and unruly fears and urges that humans had. Technology, which insists upon arrangement, regularity, and, most important, a sense that humans can work their own productive will on, rather than with, nature, cannot manage a disorderly and inconsistent world. It requires that the body be accessible to manipulation by authority for specified operations and not be susceptible to spirits or desires. In a way, then, Father Peyri was correct when he wrote that "apathy reins over the Indians." At least I think we can understand why he believed this.[4]

The padres brought to the Indians an institution ideally suited to enable them to make the leap to a mechanical mindset. The mission, with its thoroughgoing efforts to restrain the bodily appetites, could have provided the discipline necessary for the separation of the world into physical and animated spheres if the Indians were willing to accept such a division. Loathing and then denying the body reinforced its split from the mind, making it easier to allow machines, in Mumford's words, "to counterfeit this or that action of the body." The teachings of the church about the sinful nature of the flesh, so susceptible to devilish influence, meshed nicely with the demands of technical transformation in which objects must be dissociated from their spirits, desires, whims, and animation. Christianity helped in this regard when it ejected the spirits that animated all things and replaced them with a single omnipotent Spirit. Moreover, though the ways of this new God often proved inscrutable, at least He had a great plan, which His law regulated, and He had created an orderly world. Bringing the Indians the Word, the padres believed, would free them from their animist view of the world and help them understand its regular and consistent essence. Padre Lasuén showed dim awareness of this situation: "Here then we have the greatest problem of the missionary: how to transform a savage race such as these into a society that is human, Christian, civil, and industrious. This can be accomplished only by 'denaturalizing' them. It is easy to see what an arduous task this is, for it requires them to act against nature." But nature and its spirits did prove stronger than the Europeans' earnest efforts—the Indians usually took to neither God nor industry.[5]

Herein ultimately lies the meaning of *de razón* as well. To become like the Europeans the Indians would have to achieve the same split of body and mind that their civilizers accepted. The mind must control the body both for religion and for technology. Reason must control appetite and nature. Padre Venegas stated the problem with the Indians from the de razón point of view thoroughly if not sympathetically: "Their characteristics are stupidity and insensibility; want of knowledge and reflection; inconstancy, impetuosity and blindness of appetite; an excessive sloth and abhorrence of fatigue; an incessant love of pleasure, and amusement of every kind, however trifling or brutal; in fine, a most wretched want of everything which constitutes the real man, and renders him rational, inventive, tractable, and useful to himself and society." Yes, they were as children to the Europeans—not yet grown to the age of reason wherein the mind would successfully (usually) battle the body for control and subjugate its desires to the need both for internally disciplined productive activity and for the appropriately humble relationship to God so that His plan would be revealed.[6]

The resistance or indifference of the Indians to this particular form of reason and European-style maturation were attributed either to their brutish nature or to the workings of
the Devil, or to both. This explanation for their apparent unwillingness to adopt the conquerors' ways produced and justified coercion of the Indians. Padre Lasuén, upset at a failure
to increase troops at the presidios, wrote in 1797 that if the
authorities

withdraw or altogether remove soldiers from the limited garrisons
. . . they may lose everything. The majority of our neophytes have
not yet acquired much love for our way of life; and they see and
meet their pagan relatives in the forest, fat and robust and enjoying
complete liberty.

They will go with them, then, when they no longer have any
fear and respect for the force, such as it is, which restrains them.

Even that most notable of soldier-loathers, Padre Serra, noted
"that the presidio needs more people to contain the uneasy
and pernicious disposition of these natural Christians and
heathens."[7] The first restraint, and likely the most important
one the fathers imposed on their Indio children, was the severe limitation of their sexuality.

In California the priests confronted their antithesis. The fathers were usually sexually restrained, punctual, monotheis-
tic, sedentary, and bent on accumulating wealth for the missions. In their minds, of course, what they did was virtuous,
and what the Indians did, largely the opposite, was sinful.
The Indians were everything the Europeans (with the exception of many soldiers) had been trying to transcend or repress. By terrorizing and generally restricting women who realized Satan's will through their "insatiable lust," the Europeans
conquered "carnal lust." Sexuality was a fearful, if not devilish, issue for these fathers. They confronted primitive and
apparently uncontrolled and infantile beings who represented
that over which their civilization thought it had triumphed.
The California padres, like virtually all European fathers, knew
what to do with people whose alleged sexuality threatened
their sense of restraint and civilization. They controlled them

with seeming kindness, infantilized them, and then coerced them to discipline their sexual relations. The priests unilaterally transferred their role of loving, kind, protective European father, and ruthless castigator of their errant, incontinent, and lesser charges, to the California Indians. Indeed, not only would the subjugation of the Indians' physical intimacy elevate Indians to their standards and inculcate a body-mind duality, but also the padres could overcome any of their own ambivalence about their own victory over desire through the rigorous control of someone else—their Indian children.

The padres enforced sexual restraint with lock and key. Few things were locked up in Spanish California, but an exception was the securing of unmarried Indian women, and sometimes men, in the missions. The model for this practice was the locking up of daughters by their fathers. Class tensions do not seem to have produced sufficient anxiety among property holders that they felt the need to make fast their private property, though the missions secured supplies from the neophytes. There seem to have been enough material goods on the bounteous California coast to supply all and limit the fear of losing goods. Instead, the padres feared too much sex, or at least sex Christian marriage had not confined. The padres divided up traditional Indian families to take control of them. They knew from experience that children raised in the mission were much more likely to become Hispanicized than their parents, who were largely set in their libertine ways. Wives and husbands lived in a ranchería very near the mission with their little children. The llavera at Mission San Gabriel, Eulalia Pérez, remembered how "the girls [*mujercitas*] were brought to the monjerio when they were from seven to nine years of age, and were tended there until they left to marry." Indian girls were socialized to European ways in "what was commonly called the monjerio," as another woman recalled from the era, "under the care of an older Indian woman who was like the matron. She watched them carefully . . . and never lost sight of them." A very few settler women, well-trained Indian women, or, later on, sometimes soldiers' wives served as *la madre abadesa* (abbess). She had the job of keep-

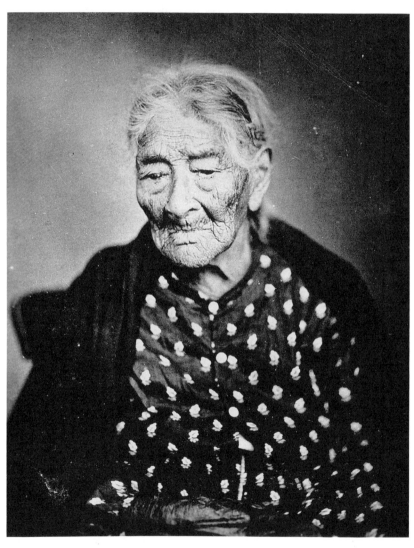

4. Eulalia Pérez, the Hispanicized Indian woman from Baja California who became the *llavera* at Mission San Gabriel. (Courtesy of the Huntington Library.)

ing the young Indias "secure from any insult." They could not come out until the morning; the llavera made sure that the door was locked and then gave the key to the padre.[8]

Because it took some time for the Indians to learn European *razón*, or the mastery of the mind over the bodily desires, the padres locked up the women to enforce Spanish sexual mores. "It is only in a very few of the missions," noted Lasuén, "that unmarried men are kept under lock at night, for it would seem that, with the unmarried women out of the way, adequate precaution against risk is secured." Yet "the men in these missions," according to la Pérouse, made "greater sacrifices to Christianity than the women" because they had to give up polygamy. Sexual control was the primary and initial function of the monjerios. In 1927 Fray Engelhardt wrote, in accord with the ideal mission culture, that "the girls grew up unsullied till they married." Chastity was important within Spanish culture, to say the least. Among the gente de razón, the same practice prevailed with respect to their own children. José del Carmen Lugo remembered how "the boys [slept] in the outside porches, exposed to the weather, and the girls in a locked room, of which the parents kept the key, if there was any key, which was not a common thing." The padres probably kept all the keys to the quarters of their children. The object of the padres' efforts was not, however, the simple repression of Indian sexuality. Rather, as in the case of disciplining the body vis-à-vis productive activity, they hoped that self-government and regulation would replace the expression of desire, which only nature previously delimited or actually encouraged. Sexual relations, after all, produced more neophytes. The priests thus sought not to rid California of sex, only to limit it to Christian marriage where it was genuinely useful. It soon became apparent, however, that the monjerios could serve a related function—to keep the Indias safe from the soldiers, who were busy proving that being born de razón did not necessarily mean that one subdued one's concupiscence. Father Lasuén observed in 1801 that "all possible care is taken so that nothing will be prejudicial to their [the Indias'] health." He is undoubtedly referring here to what San Gabriel fathers called the "putrid and contagious malady

[that] has recently been inflicted on the Indians. It began to show itself after the sojourn which Don J. B. Anza's expedition made at San Gabriel" in 1774.[9]

The monjerio also served to train the Indian women and girls in skills befitting their new life-style. Padre Font, on that infectious Anza expedition, noted that the young women at Mission San Luis Obispo had been taught to sew "and to keep clean; and they already do so very nicely, as if they were little Spaniards." The function of the monjerios was multifaceted but ultimately served the unified purpose of creating Spaniards from Indians. They regulated sex, taught the Indias to work to the clock, and sequestered them in a way proper to Castilian young ladies.[10]

"All these precautions are still inadequate," reported la Pérouse, "and we have seen men in the stocks, and women in irons for having eluded the vigilence." The criminalization of their desire brought the Indians either who knows what nervous ailments, if they did repress the sexual urge, or punishment, if they did not. Spatial restriction in the monjerios was a crucial element of Indian life in the mission as well. The monjerio rooms measured about seven hundred square feet and housed fifty to one hundred women and girls. At best, then, each internee had only about fourteen square feet in the monjerio. Filth and fleas must have accumulated in these overcrowded and minimally ventilated rooms. Obviously, these physical changes in accommodations provoked resentment, which the Indians expressed mainly through apathy but also through running away and outright disobedience. In the mission as a whole, people accustomed to living in seminomadic groups of from thirty to one hundred individuals before 1769 now found themselves concentrated in groups of from five hundred to six hundred neophytes in and around the compound, though aggregates of one thousand were not uncommon and even groups of up to two thousand Indians occasionally lived in a mission. Moreover, it cannot be doubted that such confinement and restriction produced individual and collective psychological afflictions the precise analysis of which is beyond our capacity to empathize with the Indian mind-set before or after missionization.[11]

Life and Labor in the
Missions of California

Properly confined, restrained, disciplined and denatural-
ized—in short, reduced—the Indians could now engage in
actual production in the missions. Unlike in the Rio Grande
Valley, where the natives had evolved a sophisticated agricultural system in which surpluses were produced and stored
and which the intruders could appropriate, in California the
initial Spanish colonizers had to depend on their supply system from San Blas, on the coast of central Mexico, for sustenance until the missions could start producing. Anza's first
expedition to San Gabriel (1774) found the priests and guards
existing on only three corn tortillas and some herbs a day.
On that journey Padre Francisco Garcés, formerly of Mission
San Javier del Bac in Tucson, noted in his diary, "We found
the mission in extreme poverty, as is true of all the rest. . . .
We were sorry on both sides, the fathers at having so little
to give, either of animals or provisions, and we at having
brought nothing to relieve them of their want." By the time
of Anza's second expedition (1776) Padre Font reported milk,
cheese, and butter from "fat cows," a small flock of sheep,
hogs, and some chickens at San Gabriel. "I do not remember
having eaten fatter or finer mutton," he wrote. Nature had
taken its course with the few livestock that boats had carried
from the lower to the upper California missions. Fortunately,
the missions soon started producing a bounty from the hospitable California soil. Once the land could be planted in corn,
beans, and wheat, not only could the missionaries supply
themselves and the neophytes with an abundance of food, but
so too could the presidios partake of the plenty. Now, moreover, food, which was utterly crucial to the conversion effort,
could be offered to the heathens consistently. The Indians
would not wander off when the handouts were over, and the
padres would not have to fear starving the rest of the mission
inhabitants. The generosity of California's coastal soil and
temperate climate compensated for the lack of willing and able
neophyte producers, who were now hesitatingly and falter-
ingly engaging in sedentary agriculture on land over which

the Indians had roamed and gathered their sustenance only a few years previously.[12]

Initially, the soldiers assigned to the missions were to provide both the labor necessary to get the enterprises under way and a model of de razón work habits. Hispanicized Indians from Baja California assisted them in this task and functioned, in Bancroft's words, "as servants of all work in the new missions." One of the military guards also held the position of *mayordomo* (Serra's 1773 trip to Mexico established the right of missions to employ such a soldier) and directed the labors of the neophytes. Under the mayordomo were the *caporales,* who were "selected from the more intelligent Indians who understood a goodly part of the Spanish language." These caporales interpreted and transmitted orders and, once they approached a state of *razón,* "assisted . . . the mayordomo in the policing and the work generally." Besides sowing, tending gardens and fruit orchards, and raising livestock, the Indians had to begin construction of the edifices that would house and train them until they could be settled into pueblos of their own. The first buildings were no more than lean-tos, at least at San Gabriel and Santa Barbara. Then in the 1780s the Indians were directed in the raising of structures with walls made of willow poles filled in with mud and tule-thatched roofs. Sharpened poles formed a stockade surrounding the structures. In 1792 the government in Mexico sent twenty artisans to further train Indians (even those de razón) in masonry, carpentry, tailoring, and leatherworking. Their instruction had some effect on the productive abilities of the missions, though most of the skilled mechanics returned to Mexico in 1800. By 1795 the various artisans and workers of Mission San Gabriel had raised the edifice to half its intended height with stone and mortar, and by 1801 it had a vaulted, albeit cracked, roof. (An earthquake in December 1812, however, knocked all this down.) Learning European skills was a long process for the Indians, one that was never completed.[13]

It is difficult to discern precisely how much work the mayordomos and priests got out of the neophytes. In 1799 investigators for Governor Borica reported that the Indians worked from six to nine hours a day, depending on the season, and

5. A drawing of the early structure of Mission Carmel with Indian ranchería in the background. (Photo of a drawing in the Naval Museum in Madrid courtesy of the Seaver Center for Western History Research, Los Angeles County Museum.)

more at harvesttime. The padres maintained that the neophytes worked only four to six hours a day, with only half of them working at any given time. They soon learned passive resistance to this rudimentary industrial discipline. Father Lasuén noted that "the healthy are clever at feigning sickness, and they know that they are generally believed, and . . . even when there is only a doubt, the missionary will always give them dispensation from work." Generally, the neophytes' workday began about two hours after sunrise, following breakfast and the assignment of tasks. Between eleven o'clock and noon they ate, and then they rested until two o'clock. At five o'clock came worship and the end of work. The Indians worked six to eight hours a day, thirty to forty hours a week, at an easy pace that did not require undue strain. The men herded the "half-wild stock," plowed, tended and harvested crops, and labored in the mission workshops. "The women," la Pérouse observed, "have no other employment than their household affairs, the care of their children, and the roasting and grinding of corn." Though most of these tasks were "both tedious and laborious," in the adventurous Frenchman's words, it seems clear that the quantity of work was not injurious to the Indians.[14]

But the missions produced—ah, but they produced! Simultaneously they introduced the novice Christians to European methods of production and relationship to nature, on the one hand, and assumed responsibility for provisioning the far northern frontier of New Spain, on the other. Once in motion, the missions relieved San Blas from responsibility for supplying the presidios with food, though this interaction generated more friction between the military and religious authorities, as we would expect and about which we shall hear more later. Mission San Gabriel, the "Queen of the Missions," emerged as the largest producer in California under the direction of the tormented Padre Zalvidea. The mission's *obraje,* or workshop, had looms, forges, and facilities for carpentry and the production of bricks, wheels, carts, ploughs, yokes, tiles, soap, candles, earthenware, adobes, shoes, and belts. By 1800 the obrajes wove California wool into clothing for the neophytes, and there was enough soap to keep everyone clean, if they chose to use it. Some leather goods still had to be imported from Mexico, however. The mission ranchos raised cattle, pigs, chickens, geese, and sheep. Fruit trees, grapevines (which yielded a claret and a brandy famous in all of Hispanic America), wheat, corn, potatoes, beans, garbanzos, lentils, squash, watermelon, and cantaloup all grew in abundance. The magnitude and diversity of production, based in agriculture but expanding into light artisanal manufacturing, might lead one to believe that the missions were indeed securing California by successfully occupying and inhabiting the remote territory.[15]

The statistics are striking. According to Bancroft, between 1783 and 1790 the number of mission horses, mules, and cattle increased from 4,900 to 22,000 while sheep, goats, and swine increased from 7,000 to 26,000. Between 1790 and 1800 these numbers trebled. In 1783 the missions produced 22,500 bushels of grain, in 1790, 37,500, and in 1800, 75,000. By 1810, a year of decline, the missions counted 116,306 head of cattle, 16,782 horses, and 1,561 mules. By 1821 there were 149,730 head of cattle, 19,830 horses, and 2,011 mules. In 1819 Mission San Fernando, in the shadow of Mission San Gabriel, had 12,800 cattle. At the time of the disestablishment of the missions in 1834, the Queen of the Missions had 163,578 vines, 2,333 fruit trees, 12,980 head of cattle, plus 4,443 "cattle loaned to various individuals," 2,938 horses, and 6,548 sheep.[16]

Shortly I will analyze the trajectory of the neophyte population. Suffice it to say for now that the harvest of cattle and other agricultural products outpaced that of Christians. For example, in 1785 there was only one and a third head of cattle to each neophyte. Six years later the ratio increased to three to one, and by 1800 four to one. By 1810 there were 6.2 head of cattle to each mission Indian, and by 1820, 7.3, a monumental feat of both nature and the padres. The soil and climate of California produced more than the various inhabitants could consume.[17] This situation created a problem of what to do with the surplus and a context in which there was no imperative for technological innovation.

Although most contemporaries of the missions seemed to believe that the Indians were well fed, there is conflicting evidence about the quality and quantity of nutrition the Indians realized from mission largess. Mission San Gabriel, reported the friars at the turn of the century, "gives them sufficient time so that they have three meals of corn, wheat, beans, and meat a day. Likewise, in their respective seasons is given them an abundance of cheese, milk, melons, peaches, and all other kinds of Spanish fruits." The llavera of the mission confirmed the padres' optimistic estimation of their charges' diets. Breakfast was usually pozole (boiled barley and beans) and meat; lunch consisted of pozole with meat and vegetables, and atole, and meat. On holidays they got chocolate. The rancheros, José del Carmen Lugo, José María Amador, and Carlos Híjar, agreed that they were well fed. "Everything was given to them in abundance, and they always went away satisfied but lazy, for they did not like to go to work," declared the latter. "This sort of food," la Pérouse added, "of which the Indians are extremely fond . . . , they eat without either butter or salt, and it would certainly to us be a most insipid mess." The neophytes supplemented this European-style food with their traditional nuts and berries, which the fathers reluctantly allowed them to gather from the wild. By contrast, Sherburne Cook refers to their diet as "suboptimal, . . . a level of nutrition probably insufficient for ordinary maintenance and certainly below the optimum necessary to provide a high resistance to infection." He estimates a daily intake of only two thousand to twenty-one hundred calories. (In comparison, slaves in the American South consumed about a thousand more calories a day, but this was in 1859, the height of slavery. Moreover, slaves were generally larger and worked harder than the neophytes.) Cook asserts that the missionized Indians foraged because "conversion frequently outran cultivation." In other words, the padres had to let the Indians have their native foods or they would be hungry and run away. E. B. Webb agrees that injections of such food into the diet kept them from fleeing but emphasizes that it was an "occasional vacation." Cook's otherwise brilliant book is here problematic, in my opinion. As we have seen, the quantity of food produced changed over the brief history of the missions. In this matter Cook is ahistorical. For example, his statistics for beef consumption derive from 1796. Only ten years later cattle production increased 50 percent and 15 years later 100 percent. Furthermore, different missions produced different quantities of food, depending on the environment and the fortitude of the padres. Cook does not address caloric consumption in the mature missions, and it actually appears to have differed only insignificantly from that of comparable groups. The point, though, is that the California environment and the diligence of the padres enabled the stabilized missions to adequately feed their neophytes.[18]

The Business of the Missions and Their Social Relations

The missions produced plenty of surplus food, which needed some outlet if production were to continue. Some went to the presidios as early as the late 1770s, and some went to trade. The missions were surely the most successful producers in Alta California by 1800. The fledgling ranchos, the tiny pueblos such as Los Angeles, and the presidial fields did not produce nearly as much. For example, in 1782 Los Angeles could contribute only $15 to support Spain's war with England, whereas Mission San Gabriel gave $134. The year 1810, however, marks an important watershed in mission-presidial economic relations. In September of that year Padre Hidalgo's famous "Grito de Dolores," the call to take up arms for the independence of Mexico, caused such chaos that few or no supplies could make their way north to the far frontier. After that time the presidios thoroughly depended on the missions for food, though it is important to remember that the missions depended on the presidios for a market through which to earn much-needed exchange credits. After all, the wars for independence meant that the Spanish Pious Fund for the Californias could no longer deliver the annual four hundred pesos to each missionary for his work among the heathens. Moreover, once Mexico achieved its independence in 1821, the political and economic tumult of the new nation precluded effective provisioning of Alta California. Provincial governors continually pleaded with the government in Mexico for supplies and pay for the increasingly ragged and resentful troops, but to little avail. Unpaid and unsupplied after 1811, the presidios consistently looked hungrily to the missions through the rest of the mission period. In 1828 Mission San Luis Rey actually sent supplies of maize and beans south to Mazatlán and Fronteras as well as to the San Diego presidio.[19]

These supplies for the presidios, in the words of Governor Solá, came in the form of "donation(s) to the troops in the name of the communities of neophytes." The padres, however, charged cash (which the soldiers did not have, of course), pleading poverty and the needs of the neophytes. Supplying the presidios had important effects on the missions. The institutions now became more concerned with buying and selling (in other words, money) than with souls and concentrated on specialized production. The already touchy relations with the presidios worsened. For example, in 1820 Padre Pascual Nuez complained to Prefect Mariano Payeras about the situation. He declared that the mission

in 1814 distributed to the troops and other vassals of the King no
less than a bit over a thousand pesos worth of various goods, which
at least kept the escort soldiers and their families clothed. . . . In
1816 or 1817 this mission aided not only the inhabitants within the
perimeters of its jurisdiction, but also those of the four presidios of
the Province with more or less 5000 pesos' worth of goods useful
to the country such as blankets from China, etc., with the understanding that the said goods would not be exchanged for the products of the Province, such as seeds, tallow, soap, etc., but only
coin, in spite of its well-known scarcity, and that they would be
used only to dress the unclothed.

As if the troops going naked was not offensive enough, "in
order that the families of the pueblos of Los Angeles would
not be nearly entirely naked and we would have to be the
sad spectators of this misery they were in, their young maid-
servants, nearly adults, went without shirts, having no way to
get them nor finding any way at all to obtain them." Padre
Nuez was clearly disgusted with both civilians and soldiers
and piqued at the demands made on him and the mission.
In his dealings with the presidios he was an earnest, if not
sagacious, merchant.[20]
   The government had established a schedule of prices for
mission sales to the military, linking soldiers' pay to the price
of goods. In theory, low food prices would keep pay rates
down and keep the soldiers contented. Governor Neve issued
the first assize on January 1, 1781, and Governor Fages re-
vised it in 1788. Apparently, the former set of price regulations was intended to keep the padres from exploiting their
monopoly of supply until the pueblos and ranchos advanced
sufficiently to compete. Of the many protests about these price
controls, that of the missionaries was the most vociferous; they
contended that the "just prices," in the medieval concept where
tradition, rather than the market, set exchange values, were
too inflexible and that they could not make adjustments for
bad harvests. Missionaries and presidial commanders both
competed with each other and pleaded with the government
to get prices set in their favor. By 1810 the price lists were
significantly modified, but the missionaries continued to cavil
about not being able to set their own exchange rates. The

padres paid the assizes little attention, with the important exceptions of wheat, corn, and cattle products. Pleading the needs of their neophytes, they manipulated supply and demand and dickered with the presidios about price. When the commander of the Santa Barbara presidio reprimanded the padres for not sending more provisions there, Fray González de Ibarra informed Comandante de la Guerra in May 1825 that his letter "could not be read without indignation." Referring to what de la Guerra apparently called "the sacred obligation" to give "aid to the presidio," the padre countered that "we want the sacred in copper coin." Help for the army should have been forthcoming "to the Presidio as a consequence of its help to the mission in its Spiritual and temporal progress." Apparently, the problems of the military had left "the mission in worsening circumstances than at the beginning of its conquest, because then, if an Indian ran away, the troops were there immediately to apprehend him and bring him back." The soldiers were there to support the work of the missions (catching runaway Indians, for example), not the other way around, in the view of "Los Ministros de esta Misión."[21]

From the soldiers' point of view it was, I imagine, unfortunate enough that they had to be stationed on the frontier protecting a missionization effort that evidently did not produce many gente de razón: they were not about to work. "What is lacking," noted Rafael Verger as early as 1772, "is hands to cultivate and work the fields because the soldiers do not want to help in any way in this task." In 1787 Lasuén noted one result of the soliders' laziness: "It has happened very frequently that Indians are carried off to the presidios because they have killed some beast or animal, or simply because they ran away from the mission. There they are held technically as prisoners, but in reality as peons." Work (and concubinage) came to be for the soldiers the only reasonable use for these Indians, who failed continually at becoming Spaniards.[22]

However, the vast majority of Indians working at the presidios were actually hired from the missions. They received a small wage, usually about two reales a day, credited to the mission account, and food and clothing, in exchange for all types of labor including field work, personal service, adobe making, general repair and maintenance and other construction work, and blacksmithing. Skilled neophytes earned a little more, and sometimes pay was only one and a half reales a day. The first decade of the nineteenth century appears to have been the heyday of the mission as labor contractor for the presidios. There is some evidence of decline in the practice after 1810 in the mission account books, but it may only reflect the increasing inability of the presidios to pay. In 1815 Padre Zalvidea wrote to Comandante de la Guerra, "The governor's letter was received offering [illegible] and the fifty Indians that the Sergeant of the Los Angeles garrison requested are on their way." Indian labor was still crucial to the military after 1810 even if it could not pay for it on a regular basis. The padres initiated a practice of great significance for the history of California after the mission period when they hired out their surplus mission Indians to the gente de razón. By the turn of the century there were few de razón families without an Indian servant. As we will see in the next chapter, the labor of Indians on the ranchos left an indelible stamp on the history of production in California, and the padres facilitated this organization of work. Suffice it to say for now that hiring out of Indians provided an important source of income for the missions close to a pueblo or presidio.[23]

The padres considered such income central to the continuation of their mission. The number of souls saved still measured the success of their enterprise, but the fathers nevertheless sought to save some money too. The crown's laxity in delivering its annual allotments to both the missions and the presidios encouraged them to test out more reliable sources of support. Of course, the events following 1810 intensified this desire for financial independence from the crown—indeed, made it into a requirement. The American and British trading ships that began to appear off the coast, especially after 1796, suited the padres' needs for hard cash and provided an outlet for their surplus production. As early as 1794 Governor Borica was sufficiently concerned about smuggling to wrest promises from the padres that they would not engage in such trade. It became customary for American vessels, especially those involved in the fur trade, to materialize in several ports on their way down the coast to replenish their supplies and see if anyone had anything to sell. William Shaler, a genuine Connecticut Yankee, stealthily appeared in the courts of several missionaries. His journal contains this advice and information:

For several years past, the American trading ships have frequented this coast in search of furs, for which they have left in the country about 25,000 dollars annual, in specie and merchandise. The government has used all their endeavors to prevent this intercourse, but without effect, and the consequence has been a great increase of wealth and industry among the inhabitants. The missionaries are the principal monopolizers of the fur trade, but this intercourse has enabled the inhabitants to take part in it. At present, a person acquainted with the coast may always procure abundant supplies of provisions.

Earnest producers of valuable surpluses in service of the faith, the padres were no match for this son of Calvin when it came to marketing and commerce. Robert Archibald notes that "some twenty or at least one-half of the pious padres were in his debt. Of these, only four had honored their notes."[24]

The missions provided for more than the local economy. The padres brought California into the world market through their trade with New England. Despite their dependence on the paternalism of the Spanish crown for their very existence, the friars itched for freer trade relations with those outside the realm, even though the restrictive trade requirements of Spanish mercantilism were integral aspects of this system that had fostered missionization in the first place. This desire for freedom from such mercantile and colonial fetters is familiar from the American and Latin American revolutions. The friars had a much more amenable trade situation with the end of Spanish mercantilism in 1821; ironically, however, they had remained largely loyal to Spain during Mexico's struggle for independence and had refused to take an oath of obedience to the constitution of 1824. But financially strapped Mexico did impose customs duties, which in turn encouraged the friars to smuggle even by means of ships engaged in legitimate trade. Juan Bandini, a Spaniard who journeyed to Peru where he started his family before establishing himself as a ranchero in southern California, describes how trade generally operated in the 1820s:

The commerce of the ships which resort to this coast is entirely confined to the missions; that with private individuals being of little importance. As soon as a vessel arrives at a port the captain puts himself in communication with the minister of the neighboring mission; the latter asks for a list of the articles for sale, selects those that are needed, such as iron, carpenters tools, dyes, hand mills to grind wheat . . . , cotton clothes, thread as well as gaudy colored bandanas of the cheapest quality, also such articles as may be necessary for the use of churches, stills to make brandy and copper boilers to render the tallow and make soap, kitchen utensils and tableware.

The missionaries brought Christianity to the Indians and the world market to California, especially after 1822. José del Carmen Lugo remembered how "when I was twelve or fourteen years old I used to see carretas loaded with hides and tallow headed for the ships at San Pedro." It was mainly these hides and tallow that the padres exchanged for manufactured goods, at the rate of two dollars (about fourteen reales) for each arroba (twenty-five pounds) of tallow and each cowhide. This trade with the Yankees was seductive indeed. "The missions produced grain in great quantities," Lugo noted, "but they had to feed their numerous neophytes. Later the missions increased production near the ports, because they were in a position to sell their surpluses such as hides and tallow." It is probably impossible to know what proportion of this trade was aboveboard, though Bandini asserted that "the duties collected [at the port] . . . are never sufficient . . . , and as they [the mission] control all branches of business and are exempt from all taxes it is not to be wondered but that the public funds are short."[25]

Some of the produce of the lands held in trust for the Indians was now transformed into commodities. Whereas initially production was only for subsistence, now some was for gain. California previously had a barter economy, but because of the increasing volume of trade with foreigners, money was now becoming the medium of exchange. The missions were clearly the economic mainstay of Alta California. They sup-

plied the military and the townspeople, the trade of their surpluses brought in manufactured goods, and it was they who
were the earnest and vital producers. The priests kept precise
records in their leather-bound account books. They paid close
attention to their transactions with the presidios. Usually the
balance in their books favored the missions over the presidios, and they received a signed warrant for payment from
the *habilitado general*, or paymaster, in Mexico City. When
payment was not forthcoming, the balance was carried over
to the next year. When they could not collect the debts of
persons with whom they had traded, they would often send
a collector and pay him a commission. The missions functioned as banks, allowing one to discharge his debt to another
by having the mission pay out and charging it to his mission
account. The mission paid either from its small cash reserves
or in kind. They protected their monopolies. For example,
Lugo asserted that the fathers would not let the ranchos have
orange and lemon seeds out of egoism.[26] Providing an outlet
for the products of Indian labor, their increasing trade also
strengthened the Indian labor system at the missions, which
brought to California economic independence and security from
foreign intrusion. Lurking in the background, however, were
the decline of the neophyte population and the continuous
unfolding of liberalism, which would bring freedom, if not
equality, to the mission Indians.

Narratives such as the following often give the impression
that events happened quickly: the Indians were baptized, and
the soldiers outraged them; they had to change their relationship to animals, but the old spirits still had some effect;
the padres smuggled, and the capitalist world market em-
braced the missions. Actually, much time passed between
events. It is vital to remember that on most days not much
happened. Although the padres did indeed draw California
into the capitalist market, and that very market encouraged
production for gain beyond the Indians' subsistence, in no way
can we say that the prevailing social relations were corre-
spondingly transformed. What prevailed on a daily basis can
tell us much more about the nature of human interaction at
the missions than can inclusion in the world marketplace. Yes,

6. Mission San Luis Rey "from a painting made during the Mexican sovereignty and published in France in 1840 by Duflot de Mofras." (Courtesy of the Huntington Library.)

the involvement in the world capitalist system had important effects on California society, and this incorporation of mission production even strengthened their system. However, the relationship between the producers, the neophytes, and those who controlled production, the Catholic fathers, remained fundamentally constant. This relationship, moreover, made an indelible mark on the future of California.

Pablo Tac, an Indian raised in the mission just north of San Diego, remembered, "In the Mission of San Luis Rey de Francia the Fernandino Father is like a king. He has his pages, alcaldes, majordomos, musicians, soldiers, gardens, ranchos, livestock, horses by the thousand, cows, bulls by the thousand, oxen, mules, asses, 12,000 lambs, 200 goats, etc." Indeed, Spain had some success in recreating its society in Alta California. Each father had exclusive and thorough managerial prerogative with respect to the land and his Indians. Consis-

tent with this age of household production, the fathers' dominion over his children included both family life and his
charges' labor activities. Whatever regulations were to guide
his actions could not be enforced because of the physical distance between him and any authority in Mexico or Spain.
Though generally far more ascetic than a European lord, aspects of his life-style paralleled that of the European nobility.
"The pages are for him and the Spanish and Mexican, English
and Anglo-American travelers," Tac continued. There were
"the musicians of the Mission for the holy days and all the
Sundays and holidays of the year, with them the singers, all
Indian neophytes." A rigid hierarchy prevailed in which "the
alcaldes are to help him [the Padre] govern all the people of
the Mission. . . . The mayordomos are in the distant dis-
tricts, almost all Spaniards." Tac described perfectly how involvement in Anglo capitalist trade reinforced the mission system: "The Fernandino father drinks little, he who knows the
customs of the neophytes well does not wish to give any wine
to any of them, but sells it to the English or Anglo-Americans, not for money but for clothing for the neophytes, linen
for the church, hats, muskets, plates, coffee, tea, sugar, and
other things." The system was plainly seigneurial in the sense
that El Padre Señor lorded over his charges, within a system
of reciprocal obligations, in the ways Pablo Tac described.[27]
This is not the last we shall hear of this particular set of social
relations.

The padres worked hard fulfilling their obligation to bring
the Indians Christianity. But their seigneurial life was not
without its rewards. Father President Narciso Durán wrote to
Governor Figueroa in 1833:

The best wine which I have found at the various missions are those
of San Gabriel. There are two kinds of red wine. One is dry, but
very good for the table; the other is sweet, resembling the juice
pressed from blackberries and so rather unpleasant. There are also
two kinds of white wine. One of them is from pure grapes without
fermenting. . . . The other from the same juice is fermented with
a quantity of grape brandy. These two make a most delicious drink

for the dessert. The wine from the pure grape juice is for the altar; the other for any use whatever.

That Durán was intimately acquainted with the dryness of the red wine (a claret made from Zinfandel grapes) means we must temper Tac's account of the dryness of the friars. The mission lords apparently enjoyed some of the produce of those 163,578 vines at Mission San Gabriel. The Indians stomped the grapes with washed feet to produce the wine the padres drank, traded, and served at the altar.[28] These Indians' children would know this wine later on, but in a different way, as we shall see. It was an important reason the neophytes would have no grand-children.

"During the time of the missions, neophytes were prohib-ited from riding horseback," recounted another Luiseño, Julio César, born in the mission in 1824; "the only ones permitted to do this were the alcaldes, corporals, and vaqueros." That prohibition has more significance than first appears. A *caba-llero,* or gentleman, was someone who rode *a caballo,* or on a horse. (Spaniards were derisively called *gachupínes* in Latin America because a caballero's *gachupín,* or spur, was what someone saw who was *a pié,* or on foot.) Hence *gente de razón* had a certain social status; they were *a caballo,* literally socially elevated. Don Lugo, certainly a caballero, affirmed that "no Indian who was not a cowherder was permitted to ride a horse. This riding a horse was considered a grave crime from the days of the Spanish government." The state, through the military, enforced this proviso of seigneurial social rela-tions, themselves a key product of the mission system. In 1818, at a time of great political, though apparently not social, flux, Antonio Olivera of Mission San Fernando sent to Santa Bar-bara presidial commander de la Guerra a "list of those who go 'a caballo' at the mission," which included only two cor-porals and twenty-seven vaqueros among the Indians. Three years later Padre Ibarra of the same mission reassured de la Guerra that "besides the 'baquero' not a single Indian goes 'a caballo.'" Could an Indian ever become de razón? There would not be time for the mission system to answer that question one way or another.[29]

Disease and Denouement

Before their gradual termination of the 1830s, the missions were already in precarious straits, their productive success notwithstanding. The year 1805 marks an important turning point in the history of the California missions. The mission population did not again exceed the figure for that year until 1817, and growth tapered off after the latter date. After 1821 only the missions at San Diego (finally), San Luis Rey, San Gabriel, San Jose, Santa Clara, and San Juan Bautista grew in neophyte population, and then each declined, with the exception of San Luis Rey, after 1824. In 1817, for example, San Gabriel had 1,701 new Christians, but by 1825 it could claim only 1,594, and by 1832 only 1,320. San Juan Capistrano's numbers fell from 1,361 in 1812 to 1,064 in 1820 and 926 in 1830. Troublesome Mission San Diego attained 1,829 neophytes in 1824, but this number dropped to 1,544 in 1830. San Luis Rey alone among the southern missions maintained its catch of souls in the 1820s, with 2,869 in 1826 and 2,819 in 1831. Between 1805 and 1821 the mission population grew by only 894, with 31,795 baptisms and 27,590 deaths. The rest presumably ran away during those years. Overall the mission annals from 1769 to 1834 record about 79,000 baptisms, 62,600 deaths, and only 29,100 births. In 1770 there numbered about 135,000 Indians in the areas the Spanish penetrated. By 1832 the missions and the soldiers had reduced the population to about 98,000. As we have already seen with the example of Mission Santa Barbara, by 1828 all of the surrounding Indian villages had been gobbled up for the Catholic faith, effectively ending the supply of potential converts. In other words, the mission labor supply was diminishing.[30]

Actually, the success of the missions at reducing all the Indians did not cause their demise. After all, had the neophytes achieved *razón* and become genuine tax- and tithe-paying subjects of the Spanish king or, after 1821, productive citizens of the Republic of Mexico, historians would have judged the missions a success. The mission ranchos would have been transformed into productive lands that Hispanicized Indians possessed and operated. These fully converted faithful would

have sustained the old mission churches. The greatest problem was the physical weakening of the neophyte population,
which accounts for the fact that the numbers of baptisms and
deaths at the missions were roughly equal. Over the centuries
the Indians had achieved their fragile balance with nature. In
the terms of European science, the longer and more precisely
adapted a species is to its environment, the greater difficulty
that species has accommodating itself to new circumstances.
Yet precisely such adaptation was expected of the California
Indians. In only a few years—ten, the Spaniards planned—
they were to acclimate themselves to new material surround-
ings and internalize an entirely new relationship to the spiritual cosmos—a profound emotional and cultural transformation indeed. The Indians responded in two ways. Some actively
resisted and fled or, on occasion, revolted. Most, however,
undramatically and sullenly went through the movements of
the daily mission routine. This delicately adapted species experienced physical and emotional demoralization.[31]

Into this multiply weakened population came European microbes, the most devastating of which was *Treponema palli-
dum,* which causes syphilis. Fray Englehardt echoed Zalvidea's and Cambón's assertion that Anza's first expedition (1774)
brought the malady, but it is most likely, as Sherburne Cook
points out, that all of the expeditionary forces, including Portolá's of 1769, "were without doubt heavily infected, not to
speak of the early settlers." Not all the soldiers were such
rogues. Padre Serra speaks highly of Corporal José María
Cóngora, who went to Mission San Gabriel after the initial
soldier outrages and "changed the whole aspect of affairs."
Another military commander at San Gabriel, Gabriel Moraga,
earned the praise of Padre Zalvidea, who said that the soldier's "manner" and "comportment" had brought four hundred
converts to the mission in 1810. A number of soldiers legally
married Indian women, *cristianitas nuevas,* as Serra termed
them. (In California the Spaniards repeated their general and
uncanny pattern of conquering the Indians of the New World,
putting them to forced labor, mortally infecting them, and
then marrying those women who remained.) The Spanish crown
took sexual transgressions seriously, especially when the in-

creasingly infuriated priests prodded the civil authorities into action. In 1785 Fages issued the following order: "Observing that the officers and men of these presidios are comporting and behaving themselves in the missions with a vicious license which is very prejudicial because of the scandalous disorders which they incite among the gentile and Christian women, I command you, in order to prevent the continuation of such abuses that you circulate a prohibitory edict imposing severe penalties upon those who commit them." The authorities did punish outragers of Indian women, for example in 1777 at San Gabriel and San Juan Capistrano, "who are those who go by night to the nearby villages for the purpose of raping the native women." Civil law punished severely all sexual relations considered inappropriate—when it could. (In June 1800 two Indian women reported that they had witnessed soldier José Antonio Rosas, a native of Los Angeles, commit an "unspeakable crime" with a mule. Rosas was shot and the mule burned.) Despite the efforts of the civil and military authorities, the pleadings of the padres for married soldiers, "de gente no perversa," and the presence of a few genuinely upright ones, the soldiers brought the Indians syphilis.[32]

Most of those who have written about the mission period in California have mentioned the "immorality of the soldiers" or the "mongrel assortment of convicts and jailbirds inflicted on the Missions of California in the capacity of guards." The soldiers proved a generally loutish bunch to be sure, but we can do better than to understand their attitudes and actions simply as immoral. Some were indeed the offal of society, which "the higher civil and military authorities in Mexico, who persisted in flooding California with the scum of society," in Fray Engelhardt's enraged words, sent to "guard" the missions. However, those on the initial (infecting) expeditions were recently arrived Catalonian volunteers, the famous *soldados de cuera*. Whether those "uniformed degenerates" partaking in the initial scandalizing at San Gabriel came directly from Spain cannot be told from the record. This information is not as important as the fact that these men had renounced (willingly and unwillingly) the comforts and security of domestic existence, denied most bodily comforts, and endured the rigid discipline of military life and the exhaustion of forced marches (trespassing) through fearful territory inhabited only haphazardly by people they considered barbarous. Throughout Western history most men have felt some entitlement to women's bodies, which they have been acculturated to believe exist for their pleasure. Couple this belief with the soldiers' deprivation for what they must have considered the dubious cause of civilizing savages, who were themselves profligate, and we have the so-called immorality of the soldiers. In this context the Europeans did not civilize but rather syphilized the Western Hemisphere.[33]

This "immorality" existed soundly within a context of imperialism as well. Conquest and the pursuit of a glorious state required submission to regimentation and discipline. "Civilization originates in conquest abroad and repression at home," in Stanley Diamond's words. In ancient farming or hunting-and-gathering cultures the female moon equaled the male sun in importance. But in Europe and Aztec Mexico, for example, repression at home was a necessary factor in achieving the will to conquer. When a culture moved to conquer, it worshiped the male images in the church or temple. Members of the society had to discipline bodily desire to achieve sufficient regimentation for conquest. The male war gods, Mars and Huitzilopochtli, achieved dominance over the female goddesses of love and fertility, Venus, Coyolxauhqui, and Tlazolteotl. When the foot soldiers had completed their initial duty, there usually followed an explosion of repressed desire, which the women of the conquered culture suffered. Weaponry and physical force provided only one means of conquest. The domination of people's most intimate activity was another integral aspect. Sexual terrorizing of women boomed a message to all of the natives: you are totally powerless. Such was the consequence of the rape of slave women in the American South as well. Conquest of intimacy effectively created despair of resistance, which enabled the conquerors to continue to dominate and exploit after the guns were put away. It was hard for vanquished men to resist or transcend conquest when losing control over "their" women rendered them powerless.

In the Spanish conquest of California the priests and the soldiers, otherwise adversaries, both controlled native sexuality.[34]

The first soldiers were not the unusually incontinent ones. Soldier morale generally declined over the years. Father President Durán remonstrated to Governor Figueroa in the Mexican period, "It is said that prostitution, drunkenness and gambling with the Indians are continuous." Some soldiers virtuously married Indian women and proved not to be *perversos*. But there can be no doubt that soldier sexual violence against Indian women stands as a consistent and continuing aspect of mission history. Indeed, certain Indian men may have used Indian women to soften the conquest for themselves: "We have positive proof," wrote Serra to Neve in 1780 in regard to Mission San Gabriel, "that their alcalde, Nicolás, was supplying women to as many soldiers as asked for them." These soldiers, moreover, were carriers of venereal diseases.[35]

The microbes had a life of their own. The Scotsman Hugo Reid continued on about the events at San Gabriel: "The women were considered contaminated, and put through a long course of sweating, drinking of herbs, etc. They necessarily became accustomed to these things, but their disgust and abhorence never left them until many years after. In fact every white child born among them for a long period was secretly strangled and buried." That these measures restored the Indian communities physically and spiritually seems unlikely. That they killed the microbes is impossible. Soldiers, usually because their commanding officers mistreated them, deserted on numerous occasions. They went to live with the Indians, "carrying their venereal diseases to spread among their hosts," as Cook says. On Anza's 1774 expedition Father Garcés heard from a Spanish-speaking Indian from Mission San Luis Obispo about nearby deserters, some of whom the Indians killed and one of whom had married into the local tribe. Opportunities abounded for infection even outside of the mission compounds.[36]

These various new diseases sped through a vulnerable populace. José María Amador recalled that syphilis "became so common that the majority of the men and many of the women were contaminated. This was mainly in the Indians, but it was not absent among the gente de razón." Reduction into the mission more rapidly spread the diseases because of the far larger aggregations of people than the Indians had known previously. Traditionally living in villages of no more than one hundred people, disease struck several hundred at a time dwelling in crowded buildings that were no longer burned down regularly. At Mission San Fernando a padre responded to the Interrogatorio of 1813 that "among the more prominent diseases are the *gálico* [syphilis] from which a considerable number die." At San Gabriel the padre responded that "many children at birth already manifest the only patrimony which their parents give them. Hence it is that of every four children born, three die in their first and second year while those who survive do not reach the age of twenty-five. If the government does not supply doctors and medicine Upper California will be exhausted of its Indian inhabitants." The monjerios did not contain Indian sexuality nor protect the young women effectively. "The diseases that the Indians suffered," recalled Apolinaria Lorenzana, "besides headaches and simple fevers, were syphilis and sores." Sir George Simpson noted the universality in all the mission Indians of "an hereditary syphilis [which] ranks as the predominant scourge alike of old and young."[37]

Indians who did not die from syphilis were so weakened by it that they were left susceptible to more immediately fatal illnesses. The suffusion of the disease throughout the Indian population produced the collective and individual physical and spiritual degeneration of the mission neophytes. The situation of "so many sick Indians," as Zalvidea put it to the governor in 1832, was tragic. Prefect Mariano Payeras, in his biennial report of 1819, described the situation:

The Missions of San Gabriel, San Juan Capistrano, and San Luis Rey have built chapels in their hospitals, in order to administer the sacraments there to the sick more conveniently. I say hospitals, because, as the Fathers observed that the majority of the Indians were dying exceedingly fast from dysentry and the *gálico*, they took energetic steps to arrest the rapid spread of such a pernicious malady by erecting in many [missions] said hospitals in proportion to their knowledge and means, and also by procuring such alleviation as was available. In spite of all this, we see with sorrow that the fruit does not correspond to our hopes.

A year later Payeras wrote back to the College of San Fernando in Mexico:

The Indian population is declining. They live well free but as soon as we reduce them to a Christian and community life they decline in health, they fatten, sicken and die. It particularly affects women. It is the sorrowful experience of 51 years that the Indians live poorly in the missions. Even when they remain healthy, the women lose fertility, and their sterility can scarcely be determined from annual reports because in most areas of the province where they are still baptizing gentiles, one is confused with the other and the total [of neophytes whether fertile or sterile] always increases.

The relationship between the imperial ethos, men's sense of entitlement to women's bodies, the unleashing of desire repressed in the cause of civilization, conquest, and production, and death is indeed complex. The missions started dying from the moment the soldiers assisted in their birth.[38]

Indian Bodies

The padres knew well the origin of the *gálico*, but they blamed Indian promiscuity for its spread. In 1801 Lasuén declared that "they shamelessly pursue without restraint whatever their brutal appetites suggest to them. Their inclination to lewdness and theft is on a par with their love for the mountains." Only twelve years before, Lasuén had noted that after they had been proselytized, "their hardness tends to soften, and they begin to realize that they are human beings and to appreciate the happy status they have attained after leaving the barbarism and brutality in which they grew up." Padre Gerónimo Boscana of Mission San Juan Capistrano wrote in 1825 that "they are careful to select vice, in preference to virtue. This is the result, undoubtedly, of their corrupt and natural disposition." The missions were degenerating and the padres at least sensed it. Gone was their optimism about the prospects for conversion, which accompanied their initial mission foundings. As the syphilis-weakened Indians died and died, the padres were all the more impressed with the power of Indian paganism and the Devil's work. They fought sexuality, and there can be no doubt that Indian sexual license spread disease. The padres did their best to regulate Indian desire; they earnestly sought to deny the demons that aroused it. From the Indians' viewpoint the padres inexplicably and futilely battled the earth spirits, which brought life from the sexual act. Whatever carnal desire was, it came back to haunt them all in a perverted and deadly guise.[39]

This battle for discipline and encouragement to internalize European ways revolved around physical punishment; after all, the Indians were *sin razón* and could not be rationally convinced of much of anything. Only through the senses could the Indians, like children, be reached. "The spiritual fathers," Serra noted, "castigated with whips their Indian children." Since reason had failed to convince the Indians to master their bodily impulses in conformity with European ways, only force could socialize them. Moreover, because it was bodily appetites that the padres disciplined, it followed that the chastisements were acted out on the body. Violence had to be used "in order that they could be reduced without forgetting that they were Christians." One padre termed physical punishment for an Indian "giving them spiritual aid." Padre Zalvidea, in many ways the most successful missionary, instilled industry and European morality with the lash. Hugo Reid noted that "he seemed to consider whipping as meat and drink to them, for they had it night and morning." Running away, drinking alcohol, engaging in pagan practices, "taking things," consistent tardiness, "neglect [of] the exercises of piety," gambling, and, of course, fornication earned an Indian a whipping. The Indian alcaldes, which the neophytes somehow annually elected, both brought transgressors of the Europeans' rules to justice and administered most of the punishments the padres imposed under the direction of the corporals of the guard, who occasionally did some flogging on their own initiative. "These *caciques*," noted la Pérouse, "are like the overseers of a plantation, passive beings, blind performers of the will of their superiors." These punishments, performed publicly, reinforced and reactivated the sovereignty of the padres. In the wounded body of the neophyte their power was reaffirmed.[40]

There can be no doubt, however, that more operated in these whippings than paternal chastisement and spiritual aid. "I am willing to admit," confessed Serra, "that in the infliction of the punishment we are now discussing, there may have been inequalities and excesses on the part of some Fathers." Although the Spanish perpetrated limb-hacking chastisements on the Puebloan Acomas as a people in 1598 for failing to appreciate or even comprehend that they were on their way to becoming Castilians, such mutilations did not happen in California. But Julio César recalled, "When I was a boy the treatment given to the Indians at the mission was not at all good. . . . We were at the mercy of the administrator, who ordered us to be flogged whenever and however he took a notion." Another Indian, Lorenzo Asisara, asserted that "the Spanish fathers were very cruel with the Indians—they mistreated them often." He recalled a neophyte having his belly whipped and children receiving twenty-five lashes for such transgressions as missing work. Such punishment surely appeared utterly gratuitous to those who suffered it, and this lack of legitimacy explains why it never achieved its desired effects. There were many types of padres, to be sure; Asisara mentions several, and Angustias de la Guerra Ord said of Padre Ripoll of Mission Santa Barbara that he "loved his neophytes as a devoted mother." One should not get the impression that a mission was simply a sort of prison. Missions were a lax and disorganized home to many more neophytes than the soldiers and priests could watch closely. "At San Gabriel," wrote Fray Francisco de Ibarra y González to Comandante de la Guerra in 1823, "from here to there, some were going, and others were coming, mainly without registering in the mission." But goodly numbers of Indians experienced flogging or imprisonment. "The punishments that were imposed," recalled the llavera at San Gabriel, included

stocks and confinement—and when the misdeed was serious the delinquent was taken to the guard house, and there he was fastened

to a cane or a post, and given 25 lashes and upwards, according to
the offence.

Sometimes they were put in the head stocks—other times they
put a bayonet through the scalp and fastened him this way, and
sometimes the hands were fastened this way—this punishment was
known as the law of Bayonne, and was very painful.

"But," she added, "Fathers Sánchez and Zalvidea were always
kind to the Indians."[41]

Such punishment, moreover, was entirely legal and justified in the Spanish worldview. When Indians became members of the church and a subject of the Catholic King, they
were no longer free to act; they entered into the system of
reciprocal obligations that was part of becoming de razón. The
state stoutly guarded the mission enterprises and accepted the
task of returning the stray sheep to the flock. Padre Estevan
Tapis of Mission Santa Barbara explained in his response to
the Interrogatorio:

A man, boy or woman either runs away or does not return from
the excursion until other neophytes are sent after him. When he
is brought back to the mission, he is reproached for the transgression of not complying with the obligation of hearing holy Mass on
a day of obligation. He is made to see that he has freely subjected
himself to this and other Christian duties, and he is then warned
that he will be chastised if he repeats the transgression. He again
runs away, and is again brought back. Then he experiences the
chastisement of the lash or the stocks. If this is insufficient, as is
the case with some, seeing that a warning is useless, he is made
to feel the shackles, which he wears for three days while he is kept
at work.

Legal and rational to the Europeans, bewildering and tyran-
nical to the Indians, "the same practice is observed for those
who are caught in concubinage." The control of women proceeded in a time-honored European way, for as Tapis noted,
"The stocks in the apartment of the girls and single women
are older than the Fathers who report on the mission." Those
in the monjerios could spend one to three days in the stocks,
according to the seriousness of their offense against European
ways. They could also suffer flogging in the monjerio "if they

are obstinate in their evil intercourse, or run away. . . . Sometimes, though exceedingly seldom, the shackles are put on." The shackles, the lash, and the stocks were integral aspects of the missions. "Such are the chastisements which we inflict in keeping with the judgment with which parents punish their own beloved children," concluded Tapis. Only in these ways did the priests sustain their harvest of souls.[42]

Experience taught the fathers that a runaway, an *huido*, rapidly lapsed back into her or his old ways. "We have begotten the neophytes for Christianity by means of our labors for them, and by means of Baptism in which they received the life of grace. We rear them by means of the Sacraments and by means of the instruction in the maxims of Christian morals." Tapis and his comrades had worked hard for their yield from the rocky heathen soil, and they were not about to let the seeds scatter in the breeze. "We therefore use the authority which almighty God concedes to parents for the education of their children, now exhorting, now rebuking, now also chastising when necessity demands it." Tapis did not exaggerate about necessity here. Indians who fled were a poor advertisement for Christianity and the missions to neophyte, heathen, and land-hungry gente de razón alike. Taking flight disrupted the productive workings of the enterprise and further involved these soldiers in the process of missionization. Most important, apostates were the ones most likely to inflame anti-Spanish feeling among those gentiles still in Satan's grasp and provoke an attack such as the one at San Diego, of which every priest was all too conscious. The gente de razón obviously could not tolerate such a situation. In this context, of the Spaniards' own making, some sort of action to curb running away was absolutely a "necessity."[43]

Outsiders, however, generally perceived the penal system as brutal. Alfred Robinson noticed that "it is not unusual to see a number of them driven along by alcaldes, and, under the whip's lash, forced to the very doors of the sanctuary." Even granting that there may have been a greater good awaiting them in that church (San Luis Rey), they had to be hurt to get there. When they escaped from San Luis Rey, the mission that had raised Tac and César to reason, they were caught and flogged and had an iron clog attached to their leg, as Robinson intimates was routine. Duhaut-Cilly observed that captured escapees "are generally treated as criminals, and piteously put in irons." La Pérouse and his men had "seen both men and women in irons, and others in the stocks; and lastly the noise of the whip." The Frenchman was taken aback at the quantity of punishment because "corporal punishment is inflicted on the Indians of both sexes . . . , and many sins, which are left in Europe to the Divine justice, are here punished by irons and the stocks." "Women are never whipped in public," he added, "but in an enclosed and somewhat distant place, that their cries may not excite a too lively compassion, which might cause the men to revolt. The latter on the contrary, are exposed to the view of all their fellow citizens, that their punishment may serve as an example." At Mission San Diego, Padre Panto—"a rigorous disciplinarian," in Bancroft's words—gave his neophyte Nazario more than two hundred lashes in a twenty-four-hour period in November 1811. Padre Quintana whipped his neophytes at Santa Cruz with a cat-o'-nine-tails flecked with short pieces of wire to punish fornication and theft. Excesses abounded, and yet, often as not, the Indians did indeed "forget that they were Christians."[44]

The psychodynamics of the usually celibate, sometimes-venereal, apparently often-tormented fathers and their relatively promiscuous charges is bewildering to unravel. A mission was, at any rate, something of an "emotional hothouse," in Karen Horney's words, in which the padres required abstinence, all the while suspecting depravity. It is unlikely that the Franciscans naively acted to elevate the Indians to their grade of civilization. Human motivation is inevitably more complex. Punishing Indians for sex, the Devil's nefariousness, undoubtedly enhanced the fathers' righteousness. They restrained the Indians and appeased God's wrath; they gained status in heaven by purifying society of people whose actions affronted Him. These ideally, if not actually, gloriously abstinent men often punished Indians with a severity that bordered on sadism. Although by such punishments the padres thought to justify the righteousness of their civilizing mission, whipping Indios with a wire-flecked cat-o'-nine-tails for sexual transgressions conjures up an image of a powerfully ambivalent sexuality expressed as pious and paternal corporal punishment. The power of paganism and the Archfiend impressed the padres all the more as they unremittingly and ferociously battled lust and Indian liberty—and yet the neophytes continued to fall to syphilis and to run away. This general context of the padres' confronting their opposites in matters of moral convention, work discipline, and general worldview, and the Enemy's frustration of their efforts, helps explain these "excesses" in the interaction of the two increasingly estranged cultures.[45]

Rebellions

Not surprisingly, the padres' actions to discipline the Indians to enhance production and instill faith provoked resentment and rebelliousness. Sherburne Cook calculates that 10 percent of the neophytes ran away at one point or another and that 40 percent of the runaways made good on their efforts. Fleeing was only one sign that many Indians did not take to their new environment. A social scientist may incline toward abstractions and generalizations about why an Indian would take flight, but it is important to remember that Indians reacted in concrete ways to concrete situations; they did not philosophize about, and then respond to, their situation. A number of *huidos* from Mission San Antonio de Padua, south of Monterrey, were questioned after their capture about why they absconded. The most typical response was that they "had been flogged for leaving [including simply wandering off] without permission." Many left when a loved one died. The comment "Twice, when he went out to hunt food or to fish, Father Danti had him whipped" exemplifies nicely the dynamics of punishment and flight. This neophyte most likely just wanted something of his customary food to eat. He could understand no reason why he should not hunt or fish. To the padre, his action was treason and apostasy. Freely accepting baptism and subjecting himself to the king of Spain, the former heathen had accepted certain obligations, which he was now fleeing.

Punishment seemed entirely appropriate to the padre and confounding or despotic to the Indian. Thus, the chosen forms of chastisement could never have their intended effect of deracinating the natives, who perceived them as arbitrary. The Indian decided to decamp in response to his baffling situation. Returned to the fold, he was, of course, whipped.[46]

On occasion neophytes attacked the fathers. The initial revolts at San Diego and Toypurina's efforts at San Gabriel attempted to expel an unwanted interloper and restore the old ways. Later struggles revolved around the already-established social relations between the feudal and Catholic fathers and their neophyte Christian charges. Events at San Gabriel in late 1810 illustrate a transitional form of revolt containing aspects of both sorts of insurrection. As many as eight hundred men, mostly gentiles, poised themselves to strike at the mission in November. Had they attacked, they easily would have wiped out Mission San Gabriel. Yet the new ways had by this time irrevocably altered Indian life. The raid intended not only to end the mission but also to redress grievances of the Franciscan entrada. It seems that both neophytes and gentile Indians cooperated in the pilfering of the mission storehouses. Some had been caught and imprisoned for what the Indians likely considered just expropriation of goods. Besides, they were probably hungry, given the interlopers' pressures on their food supply. Thus agitated, instead of eliminating the productive mission they made off with three thousand sheep (which were recaptured). Two contradictory impulses motivated this action: to eradicate the Spanish priests, and to appropriate the mission as a source of food. This sort of rebelliousness, existing within the mission structure, now prevailed. Acts of revenge took place within the mind-set of an institutionalized mission. Nazario, for example, Padre Panto's cook, used *cuchasquelaai*, an herb, to poison the "rigorous disciplinarian" of Mission San Diego, who died six months later in 1812. He was not the first priest to be so afflicted either. In 1801 at Mission San Miguel, north of San Juan Capistrano, Padre Francisco Pujol died of a violent illness. His two companions, padres Carnicier and Martínez, survived their seizures, for which several Migueleños claimed credit.[47]

One striking episode provides a window (somewhat opaque, given the lack of records and the passage of time) into the dynamics of the padres' discipline and punishment of Indians. In 1812 several of the neophytes plotted revenge on Father Andrés Quintana (of the cat-o'-nine-tails), who had journeyed from his home in Álava, Spain, to California, where in 1805 he assumed his duties at Mission Santa Cruz. It is unclear whether the Indians responded to fears of a new iron strap to punish fornication and theft, which the padre had ordered, or were getting even for his brutal whipping of the neophyte Donato. What is clear, though, is the dynamic of the punishment spectacle. The ritual, intended as a lesson for the group, this time catalyzed the neophytes' solidarity, and the violence this time boomeranged. Between nine and sixteen Indians conspired to smother the padre so that the death would look natural. They began their revenge by first crushing one of his testicles after ambushing him on his way to administer the last rights to the Indian gardener, who was feigning death. They shut him in his rooms, squeezed out his breath, and unlocked the monjerio. Then "the young people of both sexes gathered and had their fun," as one Indian recalled. The essential castration of the padre was the first step toward the superabundant restoration of the Indians' sexual mores. From the Indian point of view the padre received a punishment befitting the crime he committed against them.

The denouement of the story is also interesting. One of the Indians, Lino, took a break from his diversion with one of the women to make sure the father was actually dead. Lino found him recovering and then with some of the others "crushed the Padre's other testicle," finally killing him. The death of the priest raised suspicions. In the investigation, according to some accounts, the padre's stomach was cut open to see if he had been poisoned, but "because of modesty they did not discover" his altered condition. A few years later several Indian women, squabbling, were overheard accusing one another's husband of the deed. The assassins were arrested and tried in 1816. Though the authorities in Mexico took Quintana's cruelty into account (testimony was given that he had beaten two neophytes almost to death), five of the culprits received two hundred lashes and sentences of two to ten years at hard labor at the Santa Barbara or San Diego presidios. Lino died in 1817, and only one of the convicts is said to have lived through his punishment.[48]

Such patricide occurred infrequently, yet Quintana's case best illuminates the underlying tensions of the Indian-padre relationship. (The Indian informant about these events at Santa Cruz reported, however, that the neophytes stoned Quintana's successor, Padre Alba.)[49] Does the uniqueness of the Indian actions toward the unfortunate, but unconsciously trouble-seeking, cleric relegate the instance to footnotes or anecdotes about Old California? No; such episodes isolate, clarify, and condense the fermenting tensions that everyday activities and Indian apathy concealed. These stresses characterize most societies and historical epochs and seem to move history. Remaining generally submerged, they flare up at rather random moments in events worthy of note.

What the Indians at Santa Cruz did after emasculating the father was included in an event in 1824, this time to the south, at Mission Santa Barbara. In February of that year Chumash neophytes directed a revolt against the soldiers of missions Santa Inez, La Purísima, and Santa Barbara. The trouble started at Santa Inez when Corporal Cota ordered a neophyte flogged. The ritual of chastisement reversed itself again when the oneness of the Indians, rather than the reassertion of the European's power, emerged from the violent ceremony. The transgressors' companions attacked the soldiers and padres, and while the soldiers successfully defended themselves and the ministers, the neophytes burned mission buildings. The revolt quickly spread to La Purísima and Santa Barbara but remained confined to actions against the soldiers, who retaliated viciously, at least at Santa Barbara. The soldiers sacked the Indians' houses and killed indiscriminately. The various tensions of the soldiers of Mexican California that had been simmering since 1810, especially the loss of a steady payroll and supply system, now erupted. There seems to be little doubt that the revolt happened in a context of soldiers' increasing demands for Indian-produced necessities and their escalating abuse of Indians. Padre Antonio Ripoll of Santa Barbara cried over the news of the rebellion of his children. Though the target of the Chumash revolt differed from that of the Santa Cruz episode, both insurrections disclosed tensions that existed within the social relations of mission society. At least one incident of the Chumash revolt was similar to events at Santa Cruz. During the revolt, Father Ripoll reported, the neophyte Andrés "separated the exchanged wives and returned them to their proper husbands." Five witnesses testified after the revolt that carnality reigned. The official report states, "When the Christians arrived in the valley they exchanged their women for those of the gentiles without distinction as to married and unmarried women, for they were all mixed up among the Indians." As difficult as it may be to discern precisely what happened, clearly two different understandings of conjugal relations existed at Mission Santa Barbara.[50]

In other words, at both Mission Santa Cruz and Mission Santa Barbara the neophyte Indians associated insurrection against the Europeans with rebellion against the sexual discipline the missions had instituted. Revolt encompassed restoration of the sexual license their culture validated. The imposition of European productive, spiritual, and sexual ways, together with the introduction of European diseases, produced various Indian responses. They responded with apathy toward the clock and labor, apostatized and fled the Word of God, and occasionally revolted against punishment for such flights and sexual transgressions. They emerged thoroughly diseased from this harsh and bewildering journey. These Indian adaptations, defiances, and ruinations distill for us the significant social tensions of California mission culture and society. Not only were the neophytes diseased and, in the eyes of the padres, incapable of discipline and indolent, but they were now genuinely threatening too. It is only in hindsight that we know that these instances of revolt did not portend general insurrection. Californians orally relating their memoirs to one of Bancroft's assistants in the 1870s attributed the Chumash revolt to a carefully planned conspiracy. The con-

tinuation of the mission effort proved more and more doubtful, regardless of the increasing population pressures on the
land.[51]

The end of the missions was contained in their beginning,
when the soldiers brought diseases and the priests sought to
upset the Indians' delicate balance with nature and replace it
with their particular notions of subduing and replenishing the
earth. Formally, however, the mission period came to a close
during the years of the secularization, 1833 to the early 1840s.
The social relations that mission California produced in those
few years derived from many factors—Iberian political and
religious imperialism, patriarchal relations between Spanish
fathers and Indian children, the conflict over the relationship
of humans to labor and nature, and disease. Clearly, production in California entailed much more than providing (converted) producers with tools to work the landscape and then
markets for the products of their labor. We see here how a
culture emerges as well. The sometimes explosive, sometimes
degenerating interplay of conquering proselytizers and native
heathens, the efforts of each to adapt to or force the other's
acquiescence, and the unfolding of history produced this curious syncretic culture of Alta California. The further alteration of this nascent culture in succeeding generations will be
the subject of the following chapters. The Spaniards had the
best of intentions; they meant to bring reason and salvation
to the Indians. Instead, they shredded their native culture
and infested them with fleas and microbes. Then the padres
buried the Indians.

Part Two

Of Cows, Dons, Indians, Cholos, and Peddlers

"They are a strange breed, these Yankees," Tercero said. He felt the hard gaze of his superior, Father Gallegos. "I have read of the independence, the liberty that they treasure more than life. At times I think a little of that would not hurt us. . . ."

"But crude, hard men," Don Francisco added. "There is no tradition with them. No respect for family and church. As if every man were a government unto his own who owed nothing to anyone."

Father Gallegos' eyes glistened. "But they know how to make money. They do things. They work hard. And profit by it."

"Work is for peons and Indians," Carlos said. "Not for hidalgos."

Nash Candelaria, *Not by the Sword*

Any race under the sun would have been to the Señora less hateful than the American. She had scorned them in her girlhood, when they came trading to post after post. She scorned them still. The idea of being forced to wage a war with peddlers was to her too monstrous to be believed.

It gave her unspeakable satisfaction, when the Commissioners, laying out a road down the valley, ran it at the back of her house instead of past the front. . . . Whenever she saw, passing the place, wagons or carriages belonging to the hated Americans, it gave her a distinct thrill of pleasure to think that the house turned its back on them. She would like always to be able to do the same herself; but whatever she, by policy or business, might be forced to do, the old house, at any rate, would always keep the attitude of contempt,—its face turned away.

Helen Hunt Jackson, *Ramona*

*The manifest injustice of such an act [the Land Act of 1851] must
be clearly apparent to those honorable bodies when they consider
that the native Californians were an agricultural people and that
they have wished to continue so; but they have encountered the
obstacle of the enterprising genius of the Americans, who have assumed possession of their lands, taken their cattle, and destroyed
their woods, while the Californians have been thrown among those
who were strangers to their language, customs, laws, and habits.*

Petition of the California landowners to
the United States Congress, 1859

*It has been impossible to hire anyone since Friday—every laboring
man seems to be on a grand spree; to send their souls to Heaven,
or some other place.*

Manager, Lake Vineyard Ranch
(San Marino), 1869

*Despotism is a legitimate form of government in dealing with bar-
barians, provided the end be their improvement and the means justified by actually effecting that end.*

John Stuart Mill, *On Liberty*

Chapter Three

To Join as Neighbors
Pueblo Life in Los Angeles

A priest presided over the ceremonial founding of El Pueblo de Nuestra Señora la Reina de los Ángeles, but the friars would never have much regard for the place. The civil authorities, though, considered this founding to be a key event in the settlement of this northern frontier. Four years after the establishment of San José, Governor Felipe de Neve sojourned in the south of Alta California for several months to supervise and celebrate this occasion. The eleven families, twenty-three adults and twenty-one children, all recruited from Mexico, waited at Mission San Gabriel to settle on the site he had already selected. The place, close enough to the river for irrigation but on ground high enough for safety from floods, had willows, cottonwoods, alders, and a few wild grapes and roses. The founding families had suffered smallpox during its march from the interior, and did not all arrive at the same time. During the summer of 1781 the families in several groups settled the lands near the Río Porciúncula and next to the village of Yabit. On September 4, 1781, the governor led a ceremony formally establishing the pueblo named for the Virgin Mary, Queen of the Angels. Father Palóu's story confines the process to that single day. According to him, Neve led the *pobladores*, or settlers, in procession to the site; they marched slowly around it and, after a speech by the governor, received the blessing of the mission fathers for their un-

dertaking. In this enshrined sketch the settlers acquired their
solares, or house parcels, and drew lots for their *suertes,* or
fields. Either way, the settlers—all mestizos, mulattos, and
Indians (one may have been a Spaniard)—received recompense for their journey from the interior of Mexico, where
the *hacendados* (large property owners) and the church controlled most of the land, to this far northern frontier. Within
a few months only eight of the patriarchs remained on the
town list; the others, including the reputed European, were
sent away as useless.[1]

By the end of the Mexican era, however, from these in-
auspicious beginnings of civil society a seigneurial culture had
evolved in which California rancheros were as lords. Ever since
the debate over Eugene Genovese's notion that seigneurialism dominated the social relations of the American slave South,
contemporary historians only gingerly have applied feudal terminology to phenomena outside medieval Europe. Certainly,
the padres had brought California into the capitalist world
system when they engaged in trade with Great Britain and
New England; and the rancheros traded hides and tallow with
North Atlantic capitalists for consumer goods, particularly cloth
(for clothing that helped distinguish them from undressed Indians).[2] Nevertheless, the worldview of the rancheros fundamentally differed from that of the men on the ships who sold
them manufactured commodities, though perhaps not so much
from that of the cotton producers.

Each Californio, as the mestizo settlers of Alta California
came to call themselves, produced only enough wealth for an
ostentatious and generous life-style that would establish his
social position; the relationship between those who possessed
the productive means—land in this case—and those who,
possessing none, had to labor for those who did was as personal as it was hierarchical and binding. Traditions of kinship
and mutual obligation ideally and actually bound them socially. Though the ranchero system had certain characteristics
in common with other socioeconomic systems in North America, neither chattel nor market structures adequately describe
the way the Californios organized production or their social
relations. Geopolitical concerns about the Russian threat, mis-

sionization and its destruction, European diseases, the transformation of certain soldiers into the economic elite, ideas about who was and was not civilized, the capitalist world market, and liberalism all produced this system and this culture. These relations of power and production derived from the efforts of the padres to discipline the body vis-à-vis labor and sexuality, to alter the native people's relationship to nature and its spirits, and to gain access to land, among others. This mix produced seigneurialism, a term that perhaps most precisely characterizes the social system of Spanish and Mexican California. The trade of the California coast of the early nineteenth century may well have been a part of the world market, but the territory was not capitalist—the market did not mediate between persons or things. Many travelers compared the Indians' plight to slavery, and indeed both rancheros and slave owners aspired to seigneurial gentility; but the Indians were not chattel bound by the law. The system of reciprocities recalls the feudalism the Iberians tried to establish in the New World, but the social relations that bound the Indians and the rancheros were more indirect, if not very subtle, than those that bound serf and lord.

Rancho Cañada de Santa Ana, provisionally granted to Sergeant Antonio Yorba in 1809 and then confirmed to his heir, Bernardo Yorba, in 1834, illustrates this seigneurialism. By the end of the Mexican period the rancho engaged on its lands and small manufactories wool combers, tanners, shoemakers, seamstresses, washerwomen, and more than a hundred "lesser employees." Bernardo and his mayordomos supervised the Indian laborers who waited on him and produced for him. In return he guaranteed their subsistence: "Ten steers per month were slaughtered to supply the hacienda." Recalled a descendant, "The Indian peons lived in a little village of their own." The rancho was a strikingly self-sufficient undertaking and "the social and business center of the Santa Ana Valley" (now Orange County). All the while, Yankee clippers transformed the hides, tallow, and wine into commodities in the North Atlantic market. The system obviously bears a resemblance to that of the plantations of the American South. Carey McWilliams makes the comparison: "The Indians were the slaves, the gente de razón were the plantation owners or 'whites,' and the Mexicans (Yorba's mayordomos and artisans) were the 'poor whites.'" Indeed, both systems were seigneurial in that appearances, racial and sartorial, distinguished those who owned land and those who labored on it. Yet neither a chattel nor a market arrangement (the Indians were neither sold nor fired) but a relationship of mutual and personal dependency with the Yorbas attached the laborers to the rancho.[3]

Economic and social systems, feudal, slave, or capitalist, cannot be transferred to some other place where power relations are different from those that gave rise to those systems originally. As Michel Foucault argues, "Relations of power are not in a position of exteriority with respect to other types of relationships (economic processes, knowledge relationships, sexual relations), but are immanent in the latter." In other words, those relations of production—to nature and to sexuality—that marked California history in the eighteenth and nineteenth centuries created a set of economic and social relations that bear characteristics of several classic systems (especially as regards seigneurialism) but cannot be categorized usefully and accurately as feudal, slave, or capitalist. "It seems to me," writes Foucault "that power must be understood in the first instance as the multiplicity of force relations immanent in the sphere in which they operate and which constitute their own organizations."[4]

I will now proceed to analyze these relations to see how the seigneurial culture of the Yorbas developed. First I will outline the plans for the secular pueblo of Los Angeles and then examine the way in which the Californios' relations with the heathen natives affected assumptions about who should work. Next I will discuss the founding of the first ranchos in the 1790s and their successful challenging of the missions for the land of California. The Indians, after secularization freed them, attached themselves to the ranchos, where the seigneurial culture generally referred to as California Pastoral flourished. Once established, this culture, which the elites forged on this frontier, dominated the lives of those who worked—Indians, then cholos, Chinese, and after 1900, Mexican immigrants. Finally, I will investigate the many impor-

tant consequences of the arrival of Yankee and British merchants who brought the market and commodities and then
took the daughters and the lands of the rancheros. I will show,
in other words, how all of these people produced a seigneurial culture and explore the consequences of their doing so
within the constraints of history, particularly as regards who
should work.

Civil Settlement

At the end of the eighteenth century the Spanish empire,
nearly three hundred years after Columbus, made a concerted effort to settle Alta California. Journeying from Loreto
in Baja California in 1777 to Monterey, the new capital of the
Californias, Governor Neve advised Viceroy Bucareli with regard to the area around the Rio Porciúncula that he had

gained the idea that no other service could have so much importance as to encourage sowing, planting, and raising of cattle of all
sorts at the three presidios, as well as to aid settlers, giving them
all possible assistance applicable to agriculture and the raising of
cattle, so that a few sites may produce the necessities to make these
new establishments self-supporting, thereby avoiding the growing
costs occasioned the Royal Treasury for the forwarding of grain, fruits,
and cattle and the obvious risk to which they must be exposed by
being dependent for all subsistence on the risks, losses, and other
incidents which befall the ships which transport them.

The governor had a plan, which he articulated in his *reglamento,* "Fundamental Laws of California," for establishing the
king's sovereignty in the land by making it prosperous. Whether
as an expression of true faith in the Franciscans or as an attempt to allay their fears, his *reglamento* set the duty of the
settlers "to attract the Indians joyfully by the practice of true
justice and good example by the knowledge of our Sacred Religion." Ultimately pessimistic about Hispanicized natives fulfilling his plan, he encouraged settlers from New Spain, including a number of soldiers and their nominally Christianized
wives. Neve was admirably competent in attracting settlers,
garnering support from Mexico City, designing the commu-

nity, and organizing the immigrants into the pueblo, but the idea to start the community was not his alone. His predecessor, Pedro Fages, noted that the area along the Rio Porciúncula "offers a hospitable place for some Spanish families [no doubt mestizo families from the interior of Mexico] to join together as neighbors." It had "fertile soil, good places for all kinds of cattle where they would subsist comfortably, [illegible] in them the hopes of a genuinely significant settlement," Fages reported in 1775. "Three leagues from that mission [San Gabriel]," Neve tantalized his superior by reporting six years later, "is found the Porciúncula River with much water easy to take on either bank and beautiful lands in which it all could be made use of." The Indians too had situated Yabit and Yangna, their largest village in the area, at that river. As all agreed, and would continue to agree for more than two hundred years, it was a place that promised comfort and prosperity. From Sonora the comandante of the Interior Provinces of New Spain, Teodoro de Croix, issued the instructions to carry out Neve's recommendations in December 1779.[5]

Neve wisely planned the little pueblo in advance of settlement. Journeying from Monterey in the spring of 1781 to meet the prospective pobladores upon their arrival at Mission San Gabriel during the summer, the governor completed his designs for land distribution, irrigation, and positioning of the pueblo and issued his instructions on August 26. This *instrucción* follows closely Neve's *bando* of March 8, 1781, and displays clearly what the governor had in mind for a town in the south of Alta California that would "be formed as prescribed by the laws of the kingdom." In addition to the solares and suertes "there shall also be designated for the pueblo a suitable *ejido* [common lands which also later could be divided and given to new settlers] and *dehesas* [common pasturage] with the sowing-lands needed for *propios* [lands rented to pay municipal expenses]. . . . From the rest grants shall be made by the governor in the name of his majesty to such as may come to settle later, especially to discharged soldiers."

The solares and suertes functioned in the traditional feudal way. A person was entitled to land in return for fulfilling his obligations to the crown, in this case by settling and securing the frontier. Possession became permanent in 1786 when Governor Fages granted titles to the land, which all the illiterate grantees accepted by signing their names with a cross. The lands could not be taken away, though they could be forfeited because of abandonment, failure to cultivate, or noncompliance with pueblo regulations. (Settlers were also fined for failing to do their required sweeping in front of their houses every Saturday.) The lots could not be sold or mortgaged. Hispanic America had not yet adopted private property as the guarantor of freedom and prosperity but was for now apparently granting entitlement to land that could be passed on to descendants. How each settler listed himself in the town records is significant: "queda avezindado en el Pueblo."[6] *Avezindado* (the infinitive, *avecindarse*, Fages used in his report on the Californias) derives from *vecino* and means "joined as neighbors." These words indicate the most essential social relation in the new pueblo.

According to Neve's plan, these original neighbors would have the skills necessary to maintain a viable pueblo. Such artisans, however, could not easily be recruited for such a perilous and arduous undertaking, and only a tailor and a gunsmith arrived in the group. The settlers do appear to have been competent farmers, and the census list suggests some had construction skills. The neighbors received from the government pay and rations, which were to be phased out as they achieved self-sufficiency. Ominously, however, three of the families disassociated themselves from the others the following March. As Neve left California the following year (he accepted a promotion to a post in the interior), he warned his successor, Pedro Fages, about the settlers' need for closer supervision—the wheat crop had come up short and the corn had failed because they did not irrigate.[7]

Governor Neve ruled that the people of the pueblo elect the alcalde and eventually the *regidores*, or council members. Together they formed the *ayuntamiento*, or town government. Eventually there would be a *síndico*, who functioned as city attorney, collector of taxes and license fees, and treasurer. In the early years of the pueblo of Los Angeles the *comisionado*, usually a corporal or sergeant whom the presi-

dio commander appointed, had most of the power in government policy matters. The alcalde, because of his varied duties, was often referred to as the father of the village. The
ayuntamiento settled the myriad squabbles that arose in the
town and had to deal with the endless difficulties of variously
unruly individuals. The alcalde typically apprehended a cul-
prit, presided over the trial, and then passed sentence. Similarly, people brought their disputes to him, including marital
and family troubles. With so many delicate decisions to make
it is hardly surprising that alcaldes were often unpopular.
Turnover was high, and there were few volunteers for the
job. Whenever the ayuntamiento could not decide an issue,
the growing pueblo established the tradition of sounding the
public alarm, whereupon the gente de razón assembled in the
council hall and after debate arrived at a decision. Hispanicized natives did not figure in any of these plans for the pueblo,
though the so-called Indian problem would take up much of
the energy of the ayuntamiento later on.[8]

Indians and Settlers

As was generally the case in California, the Spanish authorities never sought simply to get rid of the Indians of Los Angeles. They were considered to be future Spaniards, a source
of labor, and more: the wives of some of the settlers were
Indians, and after 1820 a very few neophyte men married
Spanish women. In other words, at the same time as Indians
(both gentile and neophyte) and gente de razón were polar-
izing, they were also amalgamating. In 1784, for example, the
Rosas brothers, Carlos and Máximo, who were of Indian and
mulatto descent, both married gentile Indian women (who had
to be baptized for the occasion). The two women, from Yang-
na and Jajamóbit rancherías, were both probably familiar with
pueblo life. In 1796 another Rosas married a neophyte from
San Gabriel, as had a number of other settlers. A few soldiers
from Santa Barbara and San Juan Capistrano, encouraged by
Spanish policy, married Indian women. Two of the couples
from San Juan Capistrano moved to Los Angeles before 1800.
After forty years of missionization a few Indians were selected

to leave, marry other new Christians, and join the pueblo. As William Mason points out, Indian and Hispanic culture interacted in important ways in early southern California, not the least of which was intermarriage. We begin to see here what happened to those few Indians who did not die or were not Europeanized: many of them were drawn into Mexican culture. Their children were essentially Hispanic American, neither Indian nor Iberian in culture but a hybrid, a mestizo. Today there remains only a small number of pure-blooded southern California Indians. Their ancestors, those whom the missions did not ruin but partially transformed, helped develop a southern California Hispanic culture distinct from that of Mexico.[9]

It is perhaps emblematic of the complexities of this fusion that Captain Rivera y Moncada, who led the recruits to the north, died at the hands of Indians (much of whose food supply had been trampled and devoured by the immigrating settlers' cattle) after sending the families to San Gabriel on the Colorado River. Recrossing the river in July, Yuman Indians attacked and killed him, two priests, and nearly all of his ten men. The event effectively cut off the fledgling pueblo from any overland provisioning from the interior and thoroughly terrified the vulnerable and isolated settlers. Indeed the military and civilian authorities had less and less cause to be optimistic about, or even content with, the priestly plans for converting heathens to a life of reason.[10]

All the time Governor Neve was laying plans for his new pueblo, he was feuding with Father President Serra. Sometime in mid-1779 Neve challenged Serra's right to administer confirmation into the Catholic church on the appropriate grounds that no one could perform the act without royal approval. Neve insisted that Serra show his papers from the Royal Council granting him the right or cease offering confirmation, though Serra assumed he had papal approval for doing so. Either because Serra, who had recently confirmed about twenty-four hundred largely neophyte adherents, did not have the proper papers or because he understood that, in Bancroft's words, "secular authority in the province was something to be used rather than obeyed," he refused Neve's request. Neve forbade Serra to perform any more such rites, but Serra continued to grant the neophytes what he considered to be a privilege and a promise of their initial conversion. By March 26, 1781, the exasperated governor was writing to Croix about the friars' general "immeasurable and incredible pride" and Serra's particular "unspeakable artifice and shrewdness." No wonder that in May of the same year, when the governor journeyed from Monterey to San Gabriel to establish the pueblo, the ambitions of the missionaries were conspicuously absent in the plan he produced.[11]

Although the fears of the missionaries about competition with their own enterprises eventually came true, Neve's vision of self-sustaining settlements never materialized in the little pueblo on the Río Porciúncula in either the Spanish or Mexican periods. Travelers usually passed up the town, prefering Mission San Gabriel as a way station. In 1793 George Vancouver, exploring the Pacific coastline, could not see from his ship the place he called "the country town of the Angels." The landed residents of Los Angeles, however, did not concern themselves much about their town's obscurity. They squabbled incessantly with one another and with town officials about vagrants and scandalizers and about the alleged misconduct of public officials. But the settlers lived lives of relative ease, which could be, and was, perceived in different ways. "The two towns founded twenty years ago have made little progress," gloated Fray Isidro Antonio Salazar in 1796. "The residents are a group of laggards." The friar may hardly be an unbiased source of information on "those pueblos without priests," whose inhabitants sought primarily leisure and what were all too often undignified pleasures, yet there is plenty of evidence that he was recording what he saw. Moreover, he had some understanding of, and complicity in, the reason the pioneers did not bustle about productively. "The Indian is errand boy, cowboy and manual laborer for them— in fact general factotum," Salazar continued. Some of the male townsfolk maintained the presidial culture of Indian relations. "Confident that gentile Indians are working," Salazar added, "the young men ride on horseback through the Indian villages, soliciting the women for immoral acts." Punishments, however, awaited some of those caught violating gentile women.[12]

We cannot know much about the eighteenth-century settlers of the pueblo of Los Angeles beyond their names and caste. They were usually illiterate, and no one took down their story. Later generations often celebrate their pioneers and in the process idealize them. The portrait of such immigrants as hardworking, heroic, adventurous, brave, and stoic belies the certain truth that they were beings with a full range of human emotions, including fearfulness, anxiety, loneliness, and a desire for some pleasure. We cannot know for certain how these various traits combined in the first Angeleños, but we do know that the New Spain from which they came endured drought, frost, bad harvests, and epidemics, especially after 1770. The elites in Mexico took advantage of these hard times to further monopolize land. The rural masses, by contrast, suffered grievously; nonetheless their population greatly increased. Whether by migrants from the interior looking for a better life or, as Bancroft believed, "by the growing-up of children and the aggregations of invalids [retirees] from the different presidios," the de razón population of Los Angeles increased from 140 in 1791 to 315 in 1800. Many of these pioneers worked hard both in their own fields and cooperatively on the pueblo's *zanja*, or irrigation ditch. Others lacked the work ethic and the attendant self-discipline.

The civil authorities sought to attract to California a mix of artisans and farmers as well as women to raise families. Governor Borica requested in January 1798 "young healthy maids" for California. As Antonia Castañeda has pointed out, such a migration promised not only to further the establishment of family life but also to produce offspring who might confine the disruptive desires of the soldiers to marriage. However, few women actually arrived, and the artisans who did travel to California, on discovering that the promises the authorities had made to them about rations and a bounteous life for them and their families were hollow, left this isolated frontier. Thus, permanent nineteenth-century settlers included much riffraff as well as earnest families. Even before 1800, however, *presidiarios*, or convicts, came north, such as the twenty-two (some

of them merely vagrants) who arrived on the ship *Concepción*
in 1798. After that time such arrivals were a frequent occurrence. But families who made the arduous and emotionally
and physically challenging journey to Alta California, virtually
always from a lower caste, could expect to have a house. The
patriarch petitioned for an unoccupied lot and usually got it.
By 1790 the initial settlers had replaced their pole-and-mud
huts with adobes with roofs tarred from the local pits. The
town had a granery, a town hall, barracks, and twenty-nine
houses. They produced more grain than any of the missions,
except for San Gabriel, and three thousand horses and cattle
grazed on the ejido and dehesas. Life was not affluent or sophisticated by any means; in fact, it was a hot and dusty—
and occasionally muddy—existence much of the time. Fleas
were everywhere. Prosperity was modest; neither San José
nor Los Angeles in any way seriously challenged the missions
for economic preeminence. (A third pueblo, Branciforte, near
Santa Cruz, failed completely.)[13] The pioneers came from the
hard life of the socially stratified and increasingly land-
monopolized interior of Mexico or from the ranks of the soldiers stationed on the frontier. In this new place these otherwise diverse settlers had someone to do their work, what
little there was, for them.

For it was the Indians who built the adobe houses and made
the bricks too. Many of the local Indians who avoided the
missions probably went to work for the pobladores right away;
certainly they sowed and harvested the wheat and were a key
factor in pueblo production by 1784. "Spaniards," Bancroft
declared, "showed an undiminished willingness to have all work
save military service performed by Indians. . . . At the pueblos a large part of the settlers were content to be idle, giving
the Indians one third of one half the crop for tilling their
lands, and living on what remained." Three years after the
founding of the pueblo Lieutenant Francisco Ortega noted, "I
feel that only with the aid of the gentiles have [the settlers]
been able to plant the . . . crops of wheat and corn." Concerned that what he called this "pernicious familiarity" between the Indians and townspeople might produce a revolt,
Governor Fages in 1787 issued an instruction to the military

guard in Los Angeles that the Indians were not to be allowed into any houses, not even to grind corn. Itinerant Indian laborers were to reside near the guardhouse, where they could be watched, and permission was needed to hire Indians. A poblador could not mistreat or deceive an Indian about the terms of employment. Although the extent to which the settlers obeyed is not clear, Fages's directive nevertheless manifested the emerging relationship between the townspeople and the local gentile Indians. Similarly, regarding the Santa Barbara presidio and the town that was growing around it, Duhaut-Cilly noted in the late 1820s, "Around the fortress are grouped, without order, sixty to eighty houses, inhabited by the gente de razón and the Indians working as servants to these rational people. . . . The creole population, too lazy and too proud to devote themselves to agriculture, would have become utterly wretched. They live only by means of the Indians who work for them." Fray Durán noted with disgust in 1831:

If there is anything to be done, the Indian has to do it; if he fails to do it, nothing will be done. Is anything to be planted? The Indian must do it. Is the wheat to be harvested? Let the Indian come. Are adobes or tiles to be made, a house to be erected, a corral to be built, wood to be hauled, water to be brought for the kitchen? Let the Indian do it. . . . But what about the other class that calls itself "gente de razón"? Nothing. With them it is walk about, play the gentleman, eat, be idle, . . . generally at the cost of the Indian's hard labor, so that in reality it seems as if nature had destined the Indian to be the slave of the "gente de razón."

Observed Richard Henry Dana in 1834, "The Indians . . . do all the hard work, two or three being attached to the better house; and the poorest persons are able to keep one at least; for they have only to feed them, and give them a small piece of coarse cloth and a belt for the men, and a coarse gown, without shoes or stockings, for the women." Whether or not this was meaningful prosperity, we see here the remarkable way in which the settlers both worked the local Indians and amalgamated with them (in vulgar and virtuous ways), all the while living in fear of those still ranging free to the east.[14]

Among the landed pobladores of eighteenth-century Los Angeles there seems to have been little class or caste distinction. They generally had houses and gentile Indians to serve them. New unsettling forces influenced the natives. "The Indian for his labor is given his meals and a blanket," lamented Padre Señan in 1796. "With this garment he then struts around prouder than any one, unwilling to trouble himself about religion." The little pueblos prospered in this lumpen seigneurial way. Regardless of whether they arrived in the pueblo with such aspirations, by the turn of the century there were few de razón families without an Indian servant. As early as 1800 the Mission San Gabriel padres were complaining about the laziness of their parishioners because of the ease with which they could obtain Indians to do their work. The pueblo of Los Angeles never meaningfully competed with the missions for the presidial market, only with the presidios for crude indecency. The pueblo came to join the presidios as the cause of the priests' troubles with their missionization efforts. The committed Padre Zalvidea of San Gabriel fumed in 1816, "That [pursuit] to which everyone dedicates himself is to go about on horseback, put in grapevines, hiring a few gentiles for this purpose, teach them to get drunk, and then take jars of aguardiente to Christian Indians to exchange for the clothing that the latter receive in the mission, and with this same clothing they exchange to hire more gentiles for their work." Nor did the settlers strive to produce any surpluses, there being no markets for them anyway. They did succeed, however, in irritating and subverting the priests' efforts with the residents of Yang-na and the other villages. The baser of those activities often affronted the padres' sense of respectability as well. Whereas the missions confirmed the civil authorities' view of the fruitlessness of trying to make Spaniards of the Indians, the pueblos confirmed the predictions of Serra, who could "not see or recognize any advantage . . . whatever, either on the temporal or spiritual side," of secular settlements. Moreover, the situation would worsen as the decades passed, and the pueblo would fill with both earnest settlers and more and more of the offal of frontier and mission California and the interior of Mexico.[15]

The First Ranchos

A year after the founding of Los Angeles Pedro Fages, the nemesis of the California Franciscans, assumed the governorship. In 1784 the old captain of the San Diego presidio (the Catalonian also marched with Portolá in 1769) granted several tracts of land to three or four veterans of his old command. He thus transformed elements of the military into the economic elite and initiated the rancho era of California history. The governor wrote back to his superiors:

The cattle are increasing in such manner, that it is necessary in the case of several owners to give them additional lands; they have asked me for some 'sitios' which I have granted provisionally, namely to Juan José Domínguez who was a soldier in the presidio of San Diego and who at this moment has four herds of mares and about 200 head of cattle on the river below San Gabriel, to Manual Nieto for a similar reason that of la Zanja on the highway from said mission . . . and to the sons of the widow Ignacio Carrillo that on the deep creek contiguous to the foregoing.

In the usual two years it took to send a letter to the interior and receive a response, Fages's action gained approval. As long as the grants did not encroach on the lands of the mission, the common lands of the pueblo, or any Indian rancherías, the fledgling dons would be entitled to their lands. Entitlement entailed certain obligations, of course. The rancheros would have to build a stone house, maintain at least two thousand head of cattle, and arrange for sufficient vaqueros to manage the herds. The grant of a rancho was ample reward for a soldier's service to the empire. Those soldiers who had won and then protected the frontier would now settle it for the king of Spain. Nieto received about 150,000 acres after the initial grant was pared down so as not to conflict with the domains of Mission San Gabriel; Domínguez received approximately 75,000 acres; and José María Verdugo, one of Fages's soldiers since 1769 and captain of the guard at Mission San Gabriel, secured 36,000 acres, apparently replacing the Carrillos as grantees. Verdugo had been grazing cattle near the mission to supplement his meager and unreliable pay from the mission, and the other grants preempted his space. Fages conceded to Verdugo only "the permission which he solicits to keep his cattle and horses at the Arroyo Hondo"; he did not give title. The precise status of these grants remained vague until Governor Borica, fearing for the right of the converted Indians to the best lands, reluctantly confirmed them ten years later. By 1795 there were four such ranchos in the possession of ex-soldiers and another briefly rewarded to a civil servant of the king. The earnest and experienced sergeant Mariano de la Luz Verdugo received a small but fertile grant, and Alcalde Francisco Reyes acquired Rancho Encino, which he had to relinquish for the founding of Mission San Fernando in 1797.[16]

The indeterminate boundaries of these ranchos is yet further evidence of the generally imprecise terms of the grants. This vagueness was not a problem, however, at least for the time being. Most of the deeds in both the Spanish and the Mexican period included the words *mas o menos,* "more or less" in describing the boundaries. A grant was given for so much land in a certain area bounded by this or that landmark. Robert Glass Cleland describes one such grant:

The boundary lines of the Rancho San Antonio, far-famed home of the Lugos' adjoining the Pueblo of Los Angeles, were marked by . . . a bullock's head on a bluff, a place where two roads crossed, a spot "between the hills at the head of a running water," a spring surrounded by some little willows, a brush hut on the bank of the San Gabriel River, a clump of trees on the same stream, a large sycamore, a ditch of running water, and an elder tree blazed in several places with a hatchet.

Such delineations sufficed. Everyone knew where the Lugos' rancho was, and any boundary conflicts with other ranchos could be resolved with a handshake and another cartographical *mas o menos.* Cattle from both mission and ranchos freely roamed the land anyway.[17]

In the thirty-seven years between Fages's initial entitlements and the birth of the Mexican republic in 1821 fewer than twenty ranchos were granted in California. There were few residents of the territory worthy of such entitlements, but most important, the authorities refused to compromise the preeminence of the missions with respect to land. Of these ranchos about half were situated within one hundred miles of the pueblo of Los Angeles, and a few lay near Monterey. In the Spanish period, and before 1828 when the trade that the padres initiated with New England began to flourish, the ranchos, later mythologized as outposts of grace, honor, and pastoral affluence, were remarkably rough. The ex-soldiers had not yet taken on the material comforts or the genteel manner of their fabled heirs. A descendant of Antonio María Lugo, grantee of the convivial Rancho San Antonio on the outskirts of Los Angeles, recalled some beds made of poplar twigs and leaves, with hides for blankets and with only a few sheets. Their two-room adobe, a *sala* (living room or parlor) and a sleeping room (divided if the family was large), had a stick-thatched roof.[18]

The ranchos of the 1820s were not yet as important to California production, society, and history as they would become after secularization, when their numbers increased spectacularly. In the decade after Mexican independence the number of ranchos in California doubled, from about twenty-five to about fifty. Even these early ranchos established crucial patterns of social and economic relations in large part borrowed directly from the mission model. Their humble beginnings notwithstanding, the ranchos profoundly influenced the course of California history. The rancheros had some success in forcing the civil authorities to shut down the missions. The ranchos, in precisely the same way as the pueblos, depended on Indian labor and reinforced the seigneurial patterns being established at the missions and pueblos. They interfered with missionization, and their example of seigneurialism brought pressure on the missions to cede lands for what the rancheros considered to be the more practical effort to settle the territory with gente de razón instead of Hispanicized natives.

Contemporaries were quick to notice these emerging patterns. In 1795 Fray Vicente Santa María journeyed from his own Mission San Buenaventura to San Gabriel to scout out a site for a new mission. Two years later the founding of this mission, called Mission San Fernando, would swallow up Francisco Reyes's rancho, on which Indians did the planting

and tended the cattle. His comments on the tour are illu-
minating:

On this expedition I observed that the whole pagandom, between
this mission and that of San Gabriel, along the beach, along the
camino real, and along the border to the north, is fond of the Pueblo
of Los Angeles, of the rancho of Mariano Verdugo, of the rancho
of Reyes, and of the Zanja. Here we see nothing but pagans passing, clad in shoes, with sombreros and blankets, and serving as muleteers to the settlers and rancheros, so that if it were not for the
gentiles there would be neither pueblo nor rancho.

Initially, nonmission Indians worked these new ranchos for
minimal recompense, usually payment in kind. On this base
developed the ranchos' legendary genteel existence to which
so many settlers aspired throughout the nineteenth century.
The Peruvian-born Spanish sea captain José Bandini could not
help but notice that Indians did the work on the ranchos when
he visited in 1828 and that "most [of the rancheros] live in
idleness; it is a rare person who is dedicated to increasing his
fortune. They exist themselves only in dancing, horseman-
ship, and gambling, with which they fill their days." Duhaut-
Cilly concurred: "It is to be regretted that this duty should
be entrusted to a kind of slave, whilst men and vigorous youths
pass their life in horseracing or in squandering in gambling
the little they have." Richard Henry Dana called this aversion
to work "the California fever."[19] The rancheros' relatively easy
life spawned that most complex and sensitive of issues in the
relations between Latinos and Anglo-Saxon Protestants—lei-
sureliness regarded as indolence. The desirability of this life-
style created a demand for more entitlements in a territory
where the missions monopolized the best pasture and tillage.
    European goods drew Indians to the ranchos to work, as
they had to the missions; but the rancheros did not insist on
the European spiritual and bodily discipline that attended
missionization—a more attractive situation for many local Indians. William Mason reports that Santa María, an old Indian
woman, told Padre Sarría that the employed gentiles at Santa
Ana would prefer being eaten by coyotes to being mission-

ized. "Finally," she explained, "these pagan Indians care neither for the mission nor for the missionaries."[20]

At least some of the missions could not refrain from as-
sisting in their own demise. After becoming accustomed to
renting Indian labor to the presidios, a few of the missions
bolstered the work force of local ranchos by hiring out Indians. "It is not the Californios who till their lands," noted
Captain Duhaut-Cilly in the late 1820s. "For this work they
obtain Indians, whose wages they pay to the missionaries."
K. T. Khlebnikov, head of the Russian-American Company's
Pacific operations, said that "the men do practically nothing
and, if they can get Indians from the mission to work, walk
around with arms folded, telling the Indians what to do."[21]
The missions, presidios, and pueblos, for all their jealousy and
squabbling, shared intimately in a collective history.

The End of the Missions

The Indians are the central players in this common saga of
the missions and ranchos of Hispanic California. (The presidios existed primarily to protect these institutions from the
Indians.) The Indians were at once the key to the emerging
rancho labor demands and, as the technical holders of the
vast mission lands, the barrier to the expansion of the ranchos. The missions had the best lands, which in theory they
held in trust for the day when the Hispanicized Indians would
take possession of them. San Gabriel, the largest of the missions, had twenty-four ranchos extending from the ocean to
the San Bernardino Mountains, about 1.5 million acres. It was
becoming more and more apparent to many gente de razón
that the Indians would never regain the land held in trust for
them. Even Father President Narciso Durán admitted "that
the Spanish rule of ten years' 'neófita' is . . . wholly inadequate." The padres always defended holding the Indians in
the missions, asserting that they were not yet ready to become citizens regardless of how long the neophytes had ap-
prenticed to Christianity and European ways. Justifying the
ongoing retention of the neophytes put the padres in a bind.

To defend continuing the missionization efforts, they had to admit that they were failing in their designed task of turning savages into gente de razón. To those outside of the institutions, the missions and their diseased, profligate, lazy Indians were clearly in the way of progress. Governor Borica said in 1796, "According to laws the natives are to be free from tutelage at the end of ten years . . ., but those of New California at the rate they are advancing will not reach the goal in ten centuries." Don Juan Bandini, son of José Bandini, concluded, "The Indians are naturally dirty and lazy; their heritage is misery, ignorance, and stupidity, and their education is not calculated to develop their reason." Indeed, the Indians were far from de razón but instead were "weak and without vigor" and were never going to improve themselves, according to Bandini and others. "The pneumonia and rheumatism common among them are consequences of their habits of life and the *gálico más refino* [venereal disease] among them is very natural."[22]

The Indians in the wild—*bestias* they were often called—further alienated many Californios from the cause of elevating them to European ways through missionization. Their food supply continually shrinking, Indians began raiding some of the ranchos and missions for cattle and horses grazing on lands over which they had previously foraged for their subsistence. The gente de razón perceived numerous threats of Indian insurgencies—raids for cattle or in revenge for outrages the gente de razón perpetrated. For example, in 1819 the inhabitants of Southern California lived in constant fear that the various Colorado River tribes would attack them. In that year a party of Amajavas, or Mohaves, had journeyed to Mission San Buenaventura to trade. A fight broke out, and a number of Indians were killed. Those directly on the route that avengers might take to attack and destroy the settlements, particularly in the area around San Gabriel, trembled in their houses throughout that summer, in spite of the dubious nature of the rumors. In 1831 Indian raiders from the desert burned the *asistencia* (a mission extension near San Bernardino) of Mission San Gabriel. It was rebuilt, but Paiutes, under the leadership of a former neophyte called Perfecto, attacked it again

three years later. In early 1833 a rumor spread in the San
Diego area that neophytes and gentiles were about to rise up
and seize the mission property. Coupled with the actual rebellions at Santa Cruz and Santa Barbara, it made the Indians
into fearsome beings in the minds of the gente de razón. Such
desperate actions, real and imagined, only further convinced
many that Hispanicization was a quixotic, if not utterly futile,
cause.[23]

There was simply not enough land as it was. "The clamor
for land is greater than ever," David Weber quotes a for-
eigner as saying in 1831. "Many soldiers . . . do not know
how they are going to settle with their growing families."
Mariano Vallejo concluded that "it is just [the case] that twenty-
one mission establishments possess all the fertile lands of the
peninsula and that more than a thousand families of gente de
razón possess only that which has been benevolently given
them by the missionaries." Don Juan Bandini, destined to become one of the grandest rancheros, said, "The missions extend their possessions in one continuous line although not
needing the land for their crops and herds and in this way
they have appropriated nearly all this territory. . . . This is
a system which the gente de razón should reform, taking op-
portune means to reconcile all interests."[24]

But what was to be done with the Indians? The Chumash
revolt of 1824, assumed to be a coordinated effort to rid the
territory of gente de razón, and the various rumors of treachery and insurrection made this question all the more terrifying and confounding. Thus, in thinking about the issue the
gente de razón mixed some philosophical worldliness and legitimate fear with a bit of nonsense about Indians. Juan Bandini, whose low opinion of Indians has already been noted,
realized that "they cannot be depended on away from their
missions. Indeed the system of these missions is the most appropriate to retard their mental development, but to change
it suddenly would cause serious disturbance." Indians had been
largely apathetic and only intimidating; they were now palpably dangerous. The civil authorities occasionally flirted with
ideas about freeing up the Indians from their monastic constraints. According to la Pérouse, Neve believed that "the

progress of faith would be more rapid, and the prayers of the Indians more agreeable to the Supreme Being, if they were not constrained. He was desirous of a constitution less monastic, affording more civil liberty to the Indians, and less despotism in the executive power of the presidios." But freedom was a dilemma. Comandante de la Guerra's daughter recalled how her father and Governor Echeandía (1826–30) "several times discussed the effects of imbuing the neophytes with the ideas of citizenship and liberty. My father counseled moderation in his enthusiasm and that he should try to curb the Indians because many of them were treacherous and any day might uprise and kill the whites." It is worthy of note that these recently rebellious neophytes outnumbered the gente de razón by six to one.[25]

The geopolitical threat from without mounted as well. The Russian threat subsided in California when Spain allied with its erstwhile rival against Napoleon in 1812. But in 1821 a Russian settlement at Bodega, just north of San Francisco, caused excitement in the new nation of Mexico. By the early 1830s Anglo-American expansionary impulses joined the threat of Russian encroachment into the northern frontiers of Mexico. In 1835 Ignacio Zúñiga, a military officer recently stationed in Sonora, warned of the "two great colossuses who will seize them [Sonora, New Mexico, and California] if they are left in their present abandonment." Thus, there was increasing incentive to settle California. Yet civil and military authorities continually asked how settlers could be drawn to California if the missions, with their indolent and intransigently sin razón Indians, controlled all the best lands and the labor supply. Indeed, in an effort to maintain dominion over the mission lands, an administration so large and thorough that it was virtually unrivaled in New Spain and Mexico, the obstinate Fernandino fathers opposed any settlements that might even potentially threaten their terrain. At the same time there was less and less reason in the minds of the civil authorities to keep these extensive and fruitful lands in trust for people who remained stubbornly Indian. The slow progress of missionaries and Indians toward Hispanicization disturbed both Fages and Neve in the eighteenth century; now in the nineteenth century the pressure from Californios intensified. Energetic, or at least avaricious, gente de razón were eager to make those rich lands serve more than this evidently foolish missionization effort.[26]

Even in the Mexican republic in the 1820s and 1830s there must have been no doubt that a serious problem existed in California with the missions and the Indians. As was to be the case all too often, Mexico looked to the model of its prosperous northern neighbor for solutions. Life, liberty, and property brought success to England and the United States; it made sense for the new nation of Mexico to emulate these exemplars of affluence and political stability. Some youthful members of the Creole elite in Latin America had been to Paris, where liberal revolutionary ideas were more than passing fads. The ideas of the French Enlightenment excited all of the Latin American universities, from which came the revolutionary leaders of Latin America. It was in this context that Mexico viewed and tried to solve the dilemma of California. In 1823 Secretary of State Lucas Alamán reported to the Mexican congress:

It is necessary to consider other interests than those of the missionaries in the vast and fertile peninsula of California. The rich commerce of which it is one day to be the centre, the multitude and excellence of its agricultural products, and the aid it can lend to the formation of a national navy, and the ambitious views respecting it shown by certain foreign powers, should claim the attention of congress and the government.

Understanding these problems and potentials of California, Alamán proposed a solution borrowed from the Lockean and Jeffersonian tradition:

If the mission system is that best suited to draw savages from barbarism, it can do no more than establish the first principles of society and cannot lead men to its highest perfection. Nothing is better to accomplish this than to bind individuals to society by the powerful bond of property. The government believes, therefore, that the distribution of land to the converted Indians, lending them from the mission fund the means for cultivation, . . . would give a great impulse to that important province.

People in the Mexican government made the decision to end
the most flourishing, though seriously decaying, institutions
in Alta California. Never mind that the concept of private
property flew in the face of Indian views of the land, or even
of Spanish ideas about entitlement to use land: it had apparently worked in Massachusetts and Virginia. Besides, the missions smacked of Spanish feudalism, and Mexico was a modern nation born in the age of the liberal revolutions. The
missions were temporary institutions anyway, designed to equip
heathens for rational life as Spanish subjects, now Mexican
citizens. The powerful bond of property would accomplish the
goals of the new nation vis-à-vis the sin razón where previously the word of God had failed for Mexico's parent country.
Now private property would bring prosperity and stability to
Mexico, including its frontiers. The notions of personal liberty
and equality propagated in the French and American revolutions were the way of the future, not reciprocal obligations
and servitude. Liberal elites in Mexico solved the problem of
what to do about the Indians solidly within the restraints of
their belief system and an abiding faith in the ideals of the
Age of Reason and the liberal revolutions, of which the Mexican republic was genuinely a product.[27]

Thus, the pressure on the mission lands derived from internal as well as external factors. Mexico's romance with liberalism (which the powerful landowners and the church often
successfully countered) and its geopolitical concerns regarding
Russia and the United States combined with land pressures
within California to threaten the hegemony of the mission effort on that frontier. The Colonization Act of 1824 sought to
stimulate immigration to the Mexican frontiers by liberalizing
land policy. That legislation, together with the supplementary
Reglamento of 1828, provided the legal framework for the
subsequent granting of ranchos in California. The act seems
to have had little immediate effect in California, however. More
important, the year 1825 saw the arrival of Governor José María
de Echeandía. De la Guerra Ord observed that "when he
[Echeandía] arrived in California in 1825 he came speaking of
the republican and liberal principles which filled the heads of
Mexicans in those days." In 1826 Governor Echeandía led a

group of influential Californios in pressuring the Mexican government to open the mission lands for settlement. In August 1830 he sent to Mexico City his formal plan to convert the missions into pueblos of Indians. The padres got a reprieve, however, when in 1831 Colonel Manuel Victoria assumed the governorship and put an end to these plans of liberty for Indians.[28]

At this crucial moment the political history of Mexico came to bear heavily on the events in California. As the new nation struggled with the question of whether a strong central government or a federalized system would best bring the benefits of liberty to its people, personal jealousies, intrigues, and revolts reigned over California politics in the Mexican era. The *abajeños*, or southerners, two-thirds of California's population, fumed at the political control of the *arribeños*, or northerners, who exercised disproportionate power over the military, customs revenues, and politics simply because of their proximity to the capital at Monterey. But they shared frustration with the often chaotic central government and with the governors that distant government appointed to rule them. In 1831 the Californios, railing against his subversion of federalism, rose against the arbitrary and authoritarian governor Victoria, who refused to convene the *diputación*, a junta of five members representing each presidial district. Led by Pío Pico, José María Echeandía (who would succeed Victoria after squabbling with Pico over who would hold power), José Antonio Carrillo, Juan Bandini, and probably the Yankee businessman Abel Stearns, the insurrectionists defeated Victoria's thirty-man army just north of Los Angeles. (Eulalia Pérez claims to have treated the wounded Victoria at Mission San Gabriel.) Bandini shipped Victoria to Mazatlán on an American ship.[29]

In January 1833 Governor José Figueroa arrived with explicit instructions from Alamán to revoke Echeandía's order, but only because he had exceeded his power. The new governor was to study the situation and put forth a prudent plan to secularize the missions. To Figueroa, who ruled until 1835, the missions represented "monastic despotism." He issued a reglamento in 1834 directing the reordering of the mission system. Article 5 of the secularization orders gave land to the neophytes: "To each head of a family and all who are more than twenty-years old, although without families, will be given from lands of the mission . . . a lot of ground not to exceed 400 varas in length, and as many in breadth, nor less than 100. Sufficient land for watering the cattle will be given in common." Secularization, with its promise of liberty and property, would realize the original dream of the padres, only liberalized. Instead of pueblos made up of faithful subjects of the crown who were entitled to use lands, private property would give birth to Mexican citizens free to prosper and make contracts.[30]

Yet the authorities clearly depended more on faith than on reason in effecting these schemes. Father Durán described the situation accurately in a letter to Echeandía in 1833:

May God grant his blessing, which is so necessary, because the ideas of the Indians, of the non-Indians, and of the government are so very different. The latter wants that the Indians be private owners of the lands and other property, which is very just. The Indians want the freedom of vagabonds, and the rest want the absolute emancipation of the neophytes and without the order of townships formed according to the manner of civilized settlements. . . . I do not understand how such opposite interests can be reconciled.

Bancroft relates the narrative of Juan B. Alvarado, one of the commissioners responsible for carrying out the secularization, who tried to convert the Indians of Mission San Miguel (north of San Luis Obispo) to the new "new ways" in 1831. Alvarado stood on a cart in the mission courtyard and "vividly pictured the advantages of freedom to the Indians; then requested that those who wished to remain under the padre to stand on the left and those prefering freedom on the right. Nearly all went to the left at first, where they were joined by the small minority who had not the courage of their convictions." The commissioner reported that the neophytes of San Luis and San Antonio expressed similar views.[31]

Some few Indians born and raised in the missions became freeholders, as the secularization orders decreed. An Indian named Simeon operated a small rancho in what was formerly the San Gabriel lands. Victoria of San Gabriel, who owned a small tract, married Hugo Reid, a Scot, one of the largest rancheros in California. Ramón, Francisco, and Roque owned the four-thousand-acre Rancho Encino, once part of Mission San Fernando. A former neophyte of that same mission planted his tract in the far north of the valley in pomegranates, pears, and oranges. Most Indians, however, did not comprehend Spanish land tenure or land use. They could not comprehend the concept of private property or know how to negotiate it, but they could make contracts. These citizen-Indians sold their land for pittances to insistent gente de razón or the businesslike Yankees, who came to California in increasing numbers beginning in the late 1830s. Virtually all of those few Indians who got some land were immediately dispossessed of it.[32]

The padres, of course, considered secularization to be an outrage against themselves, the neophytes, and God. They saw secularization as a nefarious plot the lazy gente de razón perpetrated so that they could reap the material harvest of the padres' spiritual sowing. Everyone agreed that the Indians, sixty-two years after the founding of the first mission, remained unready for independence from the priests; but to give the mission lands over to the rancheros, whose minds and bodies lay as fallow as much of the mission lands, would be a scandal. "Let the latter [the gente de razón] begin to work, to found establishments and schools, and to practise arts and industries; then will be time to lead the Indians to follow a good example," railed Father Durán against Echeandía's plans. "Truly, I know not from what spirit can proceed such a policy, or rather I know too well. Why not write what all say? . . . What all believe is that, under the specious pretext of this plan, there was a secret plan for a general sack of the mission property." The padres acted quickly to turn as much of the mission lands as possible into cash. They ordered the slaughter of much of the cattle, chiefly in 1834, dividing evenly the hides between themselves and those with whom they contracted for the job. But vengeance was not theirs. In her memoirs Eulalia Pérez, the llavera at Mission San Gabriel, retold the death of Padre Sánchez, the friar of that mission and president of the missions from 1827 to

1831. (Whether she witnessed the actual incident or only recalled the story of witnesses is unclear.) The neophytes, on receiving their freedom, verbally and physically accosted Padre Sánchez, and he died of grief a month later.[33]

The missions were to have been secularized with careful consideration for the rights and needs of the neophytes. But the various decrees and laws guaranteeing Indian entitlements were paid little attention as a consequence of the intermittent political confusion that prevailed in California and the interior of Mexico. In July 1835 Governor Chico sailed from Monterey fearing for his life. According to de la Guerra Ord, he "had sworn to support the principles of the new regime of centralism which had been inaugurated in Mexico [by Santa Ana's coup]—a regime that was never acceptable to the Californios." Another revolt in 1836 tossed out Chico's easygoing but besotted and womanizing successor, Nicolás Gutiérrez. Juan B. Alvarado, the Californio who had tried to convince the neophytes to become citizens, assumed the governorship. Alvarado's federalist revolt coincided with federalist ascendance in Mexico and essentially achieved self-rule for the Californios who had been "desirous for a long time to have a native son of the territory as governor." The yoke of the central government effectively was eliminated.[34] Now Californios were free to rule themselves (ever squabbling over such matters as the location of the capital), the land, and the Indians.

What remained of government during Alvarado's rule, particularly after he was replaced in 1842 by Manuel Micheltorena, whose rule touched off even more chaos, was now firmly in the hands of the elite gente de razón. The various governors after 1833 appointed commissioners and mayordomos to manage the remaining mission lands. Typically, the recipients of such appointments were cronies and cohorts of the political intriguers. Between federalism and periods of chaos Mexico could not check the actions of its frontier rulers. The fledging elite Californios thus thwarted the plans of such Mexican liberals as Vice President Gómez Farías to settle the former mission lands with Mexicans from the interior and even Indians. According to Angustias de la Guerra Ord, "Of the administrators of the missions, some were incapable, others without morality, and some, a very few, were men of good faith who did everything possible to conserve the properties."

The governors gave the guard of the chickens over to the foxes. Juan Bandini, for example, became mayordomo of San Gabriel in 1838. The mayordomos gained control of the mission lands and ruled over the former neophytes, who did the work and became *peones*, landless laborers. In 1841 Duflot de Mofras declared, "Those now in control are the rancheros . . . who have grown rich by plundering the missions and who, under the Franciscan regime, served as mayordomos, cowboys, and servants to the Fathers." As the Yankee invasion loomed on the horizon, Governor Pío Pico sold off the last of the mission lands in 1845 and 1846 to his compañeros. The missions were transubstantiated into ranchos, Indians and all.[35]

Shepherdless among the land-hungry wolves, mortally wounded by disease and alcohol, and free to make contracts for their labor, the neophytes who had moved to Los Angeles became "servants of white men who know well the manner of securing their services by binding them for a whole year for an advanced trifle." "All in reality are slaves," declared Narciso Durán. Probably five thousand died during the disarray of secularization. Most, however, merely went someplace else and then aimlessly dawdled when they got there. Reported Hugo Reid in 1851 from his rancho, which was once part of San Gabriel, "Nearly all of the Gabrieleños went north while those of San Diego, San Luis and San Juan overran this country." By 1840 nearly one thousand neophytes had fled Mission San Gabriel, leaving about four hundred on the old grounds. A similar number stayed on at San Fernando. At Santa Barbara there were 711 neophytes in 1830, 556 in 1834, and at most 250 in 1840. San Diego had 1,382 on the eve of secularization and 800 in 1840, "nominally under control of the ex-mission authorities, though there were only 50 at the mission proper," according to Bancroft. At least into the 1850s there were "a number of these old Indians, with families, who have been sufficiently civilized at the mission, to command considerable respect with the whites who know them well,"

7. Ex-neophyte Indians living outside San Diego. Alienated from their original lands and estranged from their traditional means of gaining subsistence, Indians had to scrounge a meager existence from the towns. (Courtesy of the Seaver Center for Western History Research, Los Angeles County Museum.)

reported Anglo ranchero Cave Couts. These, however, were the exceptions. The Indian population of Los Angeles tripled in the decade after secularization, "filling Los Angeles and surrounding ranchos with more servants than were required," Reid noted; "Labor in consequence was very cheap." The town, not known for economic dynamism, could not soak up the missions' discharges. Alcohol cornered the attention of these now-legal huidos who came to live an utterly debased existence on a tract of land the city ayuntamiento granted them in 1836. "The different missions," lamented Reid, whose wife was a former neophyte, "had alcaldes continually on the move, hunting them up and carrying them back, but to no purpose; it was labor in vain."[36]

Ultimately Spain's efforts in Alta California yielded not Hispanicized vecinos of the king's realm but thoroughly disorganized Indians who were displaced from their lands along the coast and concentrated into degraded villages. The Indians either scrounged an existence literally from the offal of the pueblo or did itinerant work for low wages as ranch hands on land they themselves had occupied only a short while earlier. The former Indian lands now produced hides and tallow for the North Atlantic market. This trade was both a cause (private producers wanted the mission land) and a consequence (there was more land on which to produce cattle cheaply) of the Indians' displacement.

Secularization marks the end of an era, to be sure, but it did not suddenly put earnest and promising neophytes at the mercy of aguardiente and avaricious and lazy gente de razón. As we have seen, the missions and the Indians were already long in decline by 1833. The Indians remaining outside the missions were hungry too. Military excursions and the expansion of mission (and later rancho) lands continued to disrupt the food sources of the gentile Indians. Raids on the missions and ranchos became more and more frequent as the Indians grew more and more desperate. In the decade of the Mexican struggle for independence neophytes and gentiles operated in league to pilfer the mission cattle and storehouse at San Gabriel. In 1821 Comandante de la Guerra received a report that "at Bartolo Tapia's Rancho . . . some Indians were damaging the cattle and stealing horses." An Indian was captured with "some horses belonging to various individuals" and sent to Mission San Gabriel. Juana Machada, the daughter of a soldier, remembered that "when the padres were still at Mission San Diego, Indian robberies of horses and cattle were fairly common."[37]

Before the arrival of the Spanish, Indians foraged widely for their food. This unintensive means of procuring subsistence required a good deal of land. The Spanish settlement of their customary foraging lands meant that there was no longer enough area to support those Indians who remained outside the missions. Moreover, cattle and horses now grazed on much of the ground that had previously supplied them their food. Hence it is not surprising that mounted Indians raided those cattle and horses. Secularization intensified this situation.

The horse previously had symbolized the Indians' lower-caste status. Now as they used it for raiding (and developed a taste for horse meat), the horse became their means of gaining a subsistence. As we might expect, the San Diego area experienced most intensely the Indians' desperate fury. In the spring of 1837 Indians attacked Rancho Jamul, killed Mayordomo Leiva and three others, and took Leiva's two daughters, who were never seen again. In 1839 few of the San Diego area ranchos escaped plunder, and most of the rancheros had to flee to the town at one time or another. In the same year Señor Arguello wrote from Los Angeles to Governor Alvarado in Monterey that "the number of Indians who have run away [since secularization] to take up criminal pursuits is so great that the entire southern district is paralyzed. Particularly the cattle hands run away, taking a great many cattle with them."

These erstwhile neophyte vaqueros often returned with their gentile confederates. In the late 1830s rancheros settled in San Bernardino, where the Mission San Gabriel asistencia had fallen to raiders a few years previously. Their stock became the displaced Indians' food. English voyager Sir George Simpson noted that secularization and political turmoil in the north "aggravated the evil by turning loose into the woods a multitude of converts, whose power of doing mischief, besides being increased by knowledge and experience, was forced into full play by a sense of the injustice and inhumanity of the local government." No area of California escaped depredations, of which only a few examples have been given here, though obviously the frontier ranchos were in the most danger. Although there were numerous terrifying episodes, the gente de razón sensed more of a menace than actually existed. The strife in southern California cannot compare with the so-called Indian wars that raged in the late nineteenth century on the Great Plains with the Lakota or along the border of the United States and Mexico with the Apaches and Yaquis.[38]

The market also stimulated the Indians' raiding. The Anglo trappers, often as not a seedy bunch who had little or no respect for Mexicans or their laws, and occasionally New Mexican traders bartered southern California horses with tribes of the plateau and Rocky Mountain regions. Sometimes they took half-wild horses that roamed the region, and other times they stole horses that clearly belonged to a rancho. These mountain men induced the mounted Indians, after plying them with liquor, to raid the herds and then trade the horses at a rendezvous, usually the southern tip of the San Joaquin Valley. In 1839 the resolute and bold Ute chief Walkara led one of the most remarkable raids. The Indians federated with several American mountain men. One of the mountain men ingratiated himself with the rancheros at Rancho del Chino, enabling the raiders to know the location of the herds. The associated Indians and whites gathered five thousand horses, though they lost at least two thousand in the ranchero counterattack. The market for horses impelled Indians to raid for horses beyond what they needed for food.[39]

The gente de razón genuinely perceived a terrible threat; they numbered relatively few, and the Indians were now *a caballo*, not to mention allied with treacherous gringos who were as without reason as the savages. Mexico could not afford to dispatch many troops to settle the Indian problem. "Repeated complaints [to the authorities] have had no effect," lamented Señor Arguello. When this thievery for subsistence passed the limit of the Californios' tolerance, they exploded with vengeance. As Simpson noted, "the Indians of all tribes are, from day to day, rendered more audacious by impunity. Too indolent to be always on the alert, the Californians overlook the constant pilferings of cattle and horses, till they are aroused beyond the measure even of their patience, by some outrage of more than ordinary mark." The gente de razón followed in the tradition of retaliation that the mission guards had established in California. Sometimes the avengers managed to track down the brigands: they found Walkara and five thousand horses and killed several raiders. But other times they did not. The cagey pilferers would make off into the mountains, leaving other defenseless Indians on the fringe of the frontier to suffer the rage of the gente de razón. "Then," continued Simpson, "instead of hunting down the guilty for exemplary punishment, they destroy every native that falls in their way, without distinction of sex or age." The Indian for-

ays, genuine or rumored, kept the Californios in a constant
state of tumult and fear. Thus, they intermittently took leave
of their reason and practiced their particular form of savagery.[40]

More confirmation that the Indians as a people were genuinely unsalvageable came from their degraded status in and
about the pueblo of Los Angeles. The compulsion to work
was gone. Complained Captain Pablo de la Portilla, after taking charge of Mission San Luis Rey, "these Indians will do
absolutely no work nor obey my orders." The Russian Or-
thodox priest John Veniaminov noted in 1836, "Only this Mission [San José] and another very close to it enjoy the old right
of ruling and managing the Indians as their slaves for from
the others the Mexican government took away the Indians,
having given them the freedom of citizenship or, to say more
correctly, the freedom to loaf." The inappropriateness of European notions of liberty clearly manifested itself to many observers. Angustias de la Guerra Ord explained, "Echeandía
made the Indians of the Missions know that they also were
free men and citizens. This produced a harmful effect in the
Indian mind. They began to demand the practice of these
rights. At once a relaxation of discipline became apparent and
the Indians did not obey the missionaries with their accustomed submission." The sources all agree that after secularization a superabundance of licentiousness commenced immediately. Vicente Guerrero, a síndico, said before the
ayuntamiento of Los Angeles in 1840, "The Indians are so utterly depraved that no matter where they may settle down
their conduct would be the same, since they look upon death
even with indifference, provided they can indulge in their
pleasures and vices." By the mid-1830s the sale of liquor to
Indians had become a significant retail activity of the pueblo.
Episodes of Indian drunkenness, though hardly new, accelerated dramatically, and the physical ravages of syphilis kept
pace. Records of the ayuntamiento meetings of Los Angeles
show the extent of the problem as local politicians perceived
it: "Taking advantage of their isolation they steal all neighboring fences and on Saturdays celebrate and become intox-
icated to an unbearable degree, thereby resulting in all man-

ner of veneral diseases, which in a few years will exterminate this race." Liberalism thrust on a culture that had no desire or means to assimilate it, or even understand it, translated into libertinism.[41]

The nature of the Indians' chaotic and tragic lives should be readily apparent. Max Horkheimer, writing in 1941 about the expansion of Christian European ways generally, neatly summed up the essence of the Hispanicization effort of the missionaries:

The individual has to do violence to himself and learn that the life of the whole is the necessary precondition of his own. Reason has to master rebellious feelings and instincts, the inhibition of which is supposed to make human cooperation possible. Inhibitions originally imposed from without have to become part and parcel of the individual's own consciousness—this principle already prevailed in the ancient world. What is called progress lay in the social expansion of it. In the Christian era, everyone was to bear the cross voluntarily.

The Indians already had mastered those instincts necessary for the functioning of their bands and clans, particularly those necessary for their interaction with nature and its spirits. But their taboos were the wrong ones for the padres, who then had to force on the gentiles European patterns of discipline, which they did in the name of progress and civilization.

Horkheimer then speaks to the outcome of Christianization for those, such as the Indians of California, on whom it was imposed:

For those at the base of the social pyramid, however, the harmony between the universal and the particular interest was merely a postulate. They had no share in that common interest which they were asked to make their own. It was never quite rational to them to renounce their instincts, and as a result they never were quite reached by civilization, but were always made sociable by force.

The neophytes (an odd term still to be using at this point in the narrative—they were not even genuine novice Christians) were then freed from their constraints, in the name of progress and civilization. The missions, the soldiers, the pueblos, and the diseases rent asunder their old system of social control. As a whole the Indians never internalized the ways of the Europeans. Once the missions were gone, they had little left of either their original cultural ways or the new discipline that made them social beings.[42] Alcohol easily overpowered any remaining restraints. Culturally unraveled and physically brutalized in a nominally liberal world, the Indians approached their final end. But in spite of—indeed because of— their condition, they would still figure crucially in the evolution of regional practices of production and various dominant peoples' ideas about race and about who should work.

Ranchos, Indians, and the Social Relations of Rancho California

Certain attributes a culture takes on as it journeys through history can be explained, as Horkheimer says, simply as the "habitual forms of the individual's adjustment to the social situation." Although the gente de razón confronted circumstances partly of their own making, it is important to remember that their estimation of the Indians derived not only from their daily contact with the natives but also from their position as the socially ascendant people of the region.

The period after secularization saw an explosion in the number of concessions of land. The governors granted approximately seven hundred ranchos in California, with neither the territorial nor the Mexican government receiving any form of payment. Grantees were required only to build a house, settle on the land, and stock it with cattle. Because of the trafficking in mission lands on the part of the well-connected, most of the grants in southern California went to such familiar names as Nieto, Pico, Yorba, Sepúlveda, Figueroa, Bandini, Domínguez, Lugo, de la Guerra—a sort of Homestead Act for those who were already rancheros.

There were many exceptions, of course, among the seven hundred grants. A grantee still had to find favor with the authorities, however, and high status was the most usual, though not the only, way to do so. For example, Manuel Garfias, who served in Micheltorena's army, was "poor, handsome and brave." One Luisa Ábila took an interest in the man; so she would not have to marry down, his former commanding officer gave Garfias Rancho San Pascuale just north of Los Angeles in January 1843. (This rancho had originally been given to the widow Eulalia Pérez, whose great benevolence toward the neophytes as llavera at San Gabriel earned her a grant of fourteen thousand acres from Padre Zalvidea on the eve of secularization. She lost San Pascuale because she could not stock it.)[43]

These rancheros were surely the grandees of the area; they controlled the dominant economic and social institution of the California coast. But they were new hidalgos. In Spanish the word *hidalgo* derives from *hijo de alguién*, "child of someone." But these landed gentlemen were the children of soldiers or were themselves retired military men. Thus, they were of dubious lineage with respect to status, and to acquire social standing befitting their landed domains became their primary ambition. The Indians were absolutely central to the realization of this aspiration.

A brief history of one of the most famed and illustrious families of Hispanic California will help us picture the situation. Santiago de la Cruz Pico came to California as a soldier recruit in the Anzà expedition of 1775. He was of mulatto and mestizo lineage. His eleven-year-old son, José María Pico, accompanied him, along with the son's future wife, María Eustaquia Gutiérrez. (Her widowed mother is said to have disturbed Padre Font with her flirting and ribald songs.) Santiago had intended to stay at the San Francisco presidio but was transferred to the San Diego company in 1777. In the next decade he finished his term of service and joined the Los Angeles pueblo. In 1795 Fages granted him Rancho San José de García de Simi, though he had to remain in the pueblo. José María Pico enlisted at the San Diego presidio in 1782 at the age of seventeen and had a brief sojourn at Santa Barbara in 1785. Four years later he married Señorita Gutiérrez in San Diego. In late 1800 José María was transferred to San Gabriel as corporal of the guard; the next year a midwife at Mission San Gabriel assisted at the birth of Pío Pico, their fourth child. In 1805 he went back to San Diego, where the wife of a sergeant educated young Pío. José María died in

1819 at San Gabriel. Pío Pico and María Ignacia Alvarado married in the Los Angeles church in 1834. The Pico brothers, Andrés and Pío, were two of the most influential and fabled Californios. Their ranchos included the sprawling Rancho Santa Margarita y Las Flores, made up of former Mission San Juan Capistrano lands, from which Indians took five hundred horses in 1850. Pío Pico was the last Mexican governor of California. His grandfather, a soldier recruit of mixed blood, brought the family to California. In only two generations the family amassed terrific wealth in land and eventually epitomized those with the title of don in the pastoralist imagery of rancho California.[44]

In the same manner that missionization entailed more than bringing heathens to Christianity, more prevailed in these relations between rancheros and Indian laborers than work. For the gente de razón, a class in search of social standing and elite self-definition, the conception of the Indian as their opposite played a central role in the formation of their social personalities. On a frontier where brutal appetites seemed to reign, Califorios lacked the benefit of the formal and at least mildly scholarly education that enabled the priests to reassure themselves of their rational nature. They had no positive role models for eminence. Whereas the priests concerned themselves with the heathenism of the Indians and not their physical features, now race came to be an operative force in demarcating the peoples of California. To be de razón meant not to be like Indians, who drank to excess, had sex, worked at a pace bound to nature, had a demonic religion, and were generally "wild." But in fact the gente de razón were mestizos who also drank, had sex (with Indians, no less), were not known for dedication to hard work, and, between the Holy Trinity, the saints, and the revered Virgin of Guadalupe, had something of a pantheistic religion. This bind, of which the gente de razón were vaguely aware, kept them searching endlessly for meaningful distinctions between "us" and "them." "They" served not only as a work force but also as a contrast to "us." Violence against Indians allowed the gente de razón not only to obliterate threatening similarities but also to realize the forbidden fantasy of wild and unrestrained brutality

8. Don Pío Pico, the son of a soldier and last Mexican governor of California, and his wife, María Ignacia Alvarado. (Courtesy of the Huntington Library.)

against an other. Racial ideology was replacing reason and the alleged lack thereof as the divider of the peoples of nineteenth-century California.

The Indians, whose service as the degraded other was expanding, did not wear many clothes. "In those times," affirmed Juana Machada, "female Indians did not clothe themselves except for a cover of rabbit skins that covered their shameful parts." Indeed the Indians were *sin vergüenza*—without shame—in matters of the body. The rancheros, by contrast, dressed thoroughly and lavishly. The *chaleco,* a men's silk or calico jacket, and the short-sleeved gowns of the women continue to symbolize Californio elegance. The rancheros produced neither for the sake of producing nor to accumulate wealth: they traded hides and tallow with the Yankees and British, particularly after the liberalization of trade policy in 1828, for luxury goods. Their expensive clothing indicated their seigneurial status most apparently. Rich waistcoats, gilt-laced velveteen pantaloons, brightly colored sashes, and necklaces and earrings for the hatless and long-haired women sought to establish the prestige and social leadership of the wealthy gente de razón. After 1840 they even had available to them European fashions. Social status was the goal of their productive efforts, and they were not indolent in pursuing it; they diligently endeavored to elevate themselves to grandeur and aristocracy.[45]

The mirror facilitated this way of appearing. The mirrors unloaded from the trade vessels not only allowed the Californios to assure themselves of their sartorial distinctiveness but enabled and encouraged a new awareness of self born of preoccupation with one's image. Dressing in front of a mirror, family members could decorate themselves in a way they imagined would inspire authority and awe.[46]

The horse expressed the gentility of the Californio elites. "Californians are excellent horseback riders," noted the Russian Khlebnikov: "From childhood they begin to ride horses and grow up to be skillful horsemen. They deftly throw the lasso over the horns of bulls and heads of horses. . . . Children also go around with lassos and become trained in this practice from youth, throwing the loop over pigs, chickens and, from sheer mischief, often on horses." Yet another European impressed with the apparent lack of Californio productive ambition sneered in 1861 about the remnants of ranchero society: "The only thing they appear to excel in is riding." Sir George Simpson agreed with the negative estimation of California equestrian culture: "With such painted and gilded horsemen, anything like industry is, of course, out of the question; and accordingly they spend their time from morning until night in billiard-playing and horse-racing, aggravating the evil of idleness by ruinously heavy bets." Simpson's statement reveals something about what his own culture perceived as appropriate activity as well as what the rancheros valued. Racing indeed produced trouble for the Californios, as we shall see in the Yankee period. "The Spanish Californians are passionately fond of horse-racing, and the extravagant bets which they make upon them contribute not a little to their ruin," concurred the French traveler Duflot de Mofras.[47] An elite ranchero did not simply idle about but rode *a caballo*, showing the common folk and the Indians his *gachupín*.

In their own estimation they were honorable men, not idlers. Elites referred to one another as *mi valedor*, "my defender"; the idea of the self-interested individual had not yet come to California. They sought personal riches, to be sure, but maintained a sense of reciprocity and obligation, at least with respect to other gente de razón. These were vecinos—neighbors, not citizens. José Antonio Rocha of Rancho La Brea and Juan Antonio Carrillo referred to "vecinos of the said Pueblo [Los Angeles]," and Juana Machado discussed "vecinos of Los Angeles and San Diego." Vecinos lived in relation to other vecinos. They were not independent citizens who lived in relation to a state. All people in such cultures feel an interconnectedness and a restraint that is absent in liberal society. Governor Figueroa's calling card had on it the motto *honor y lealtad*.[48] In spite of Mexico's newfound liberalism, *vecindad* and *lealtad* still reigned in the culture over citizenship and liberty. The amount of *honor* one had made a reputation, not the amount of money. (Of course, material wealth gave one the wherewithall to act graciously, honorably, and generously.) An acquisitive person who acted without regard for other gente de razón was aberrant. Indians (allegedly) and Yankees acted that way toward their own people.

Fealty to the true church was a central aspect of being de razón. The reciting of prayers helped strengthen ties among family members. Family patriarchs asserted their appropriate leadership role by enforcing proper attention to church ritual. They led their wives and children in their morning devotions and evening rosary. Church attendance was obligatory on Sundays and holy days. Education meant learning church doctrine; de razón elites made confession and received the sacraments regularly. Much of their extensive social lives revolved around mass and church fiestas. Religion was a serious matter for the elites. It underpinned their status, provided the rationale for the control of women and children, and kept the elites confident that, even on this frontier, they remained de razón.[49]

These family fathers locked up their unmarried daughters at night. José del Carmen Lugo remembered how "the boys [slept] in the outside porches, exposed to the weather, and the girls in a locked room, of which the parents kept the key, if there was any key, which was not a common thing." Locks primarily functioned to regulate sexuality, maintain sexual propriety, and control and protect girls. Liberal social relations did not take hold in the elite families with respect to marriage. "These [marriage] arrangements," Carlos Híjar recalled of the 1830s, "took place only between the fathers of the children, and they tried to keep them from learning of their plans." Parents may well have considered the wishes of their children and probably headed off disastrous liaisons with marriage bargains when they noticed dangerous flirtations at the Californios' frequent fiestas.[50] Lust and love could not be permitted to inspire de razón social relationships. After all, passion could not be allowed to run its subversive course with so much property at stake. Instinct enslaved the lower classes and Indians; and love, a rather fleeting emotion anyway, could not provide a stable basis for a marriage. To the gente de razón it seemed better that paternal reason should prevail.

The fathers reigned over families of occasionally as many as a dozen children and usually three or four. "Implicit obedience and profound respect are shown by children, even after they are grown up, towards their parents," reported Simpson. Duhaut-Cilly concurred: "Fathers exact from their children great submission, and this dependence is frequently maintained after marriage." Angustias de la Guerra Ord (one of thirteen children, she herself gave birth to a dozen) noted "the respect and obedience of children towards their parents in those times, because paternal authority was unlimited and did not cease even after the children married or even when they had their own children." José Sepúlveda asserted that "at the death of the father it was customary for the younger brothers to respect the elder, who stood in the position of father to the family."

All the sources agree on the rigidity of the children's relationship to their parents, especially to the fathers. The quality of such relationships is hard to gauge, however. Formality prescribes behavior but hardly precludes affection. The traditional Hispanic value of honor and respect for one's parents provides a reasonable and proper model for how one should treat other people—indeed all life and the earth. Honor and respect assumes reciprocation as well. Fathers must treat their charges respectfully and considerately; and although disrespect for elders remained outside the parameters of appropriate behavior, so too did corporal punishment. Yet it is unlikely that de razón fathers were exceptions to the dictum that power corrupts and absolute power corrupts absolutely. Even married sons could not smoke or sit in the presence of their fathers without permission, and physical punishment could follow grave transgressions. Duhaut-Cilly may have exaggerated when he declared that "seldom does one see a child of either sex sitting at the table of his father who, more often, eats alone, served by his wife, sons and daughters"; but his statement does not call forth images of familial conviviality. Moreover, when, as Horkheimer states, "the individual has to do violence to himself" by submitting to authority and mastering rebellious feelings and desires, there are inevitable consequences, especially for the young, to whom such au-

9. Don Juan Bandini and his daughter Margarita. (Courtesy of the Huntington Library.)

thority appears arbitrary. The parents too were subject to the transforming powers of filial love. Historian Gloria Miranda notes that fathers-to-be built toys and furniture for their infants, that parents made note of their children's first steps and first teeth, and that relatives exchanged locks of their children's hair. When a mother gave birth to a child, she rarely abandoned it, and the death of a child was a tragedy.[51] The family generally is a source of security, sadness, pleasure, affection, oppression, and pain. Surely Californio families were no exception, and these dispositions were present in most families in widely varying mixes. Nonetheless, this particular model provided the patterns of submission, hierarchy, and obligation that prevailed between patriarchs and their women, children, and Indian laborers in the golden age of the ranchos.

This system did supply certain protections. The institution of *padrinos,* or godparents, while doubling the number of fathers to which a child had to submit, ensured that children would not be orphaned. Sepúlveda maintained that godparents were "always treating each other with respect and affection, and having the child as a living token of their esteem, it was rare to see these pleasant relations disturbed." *Compadrazco* "no doubt added much to the harmony of society." The padrinos accompanied the parents to church for the baptism with music. Afterward came a fiesta lasting one or two days. The de razón, few in number, frequently intermarried. Most everyone was related, if not by blood, then by marriage or compadrazco.[52]

While their rule went largely unchallenged, the patresfamilias did not arbitrarily lord it over de razón women, at least in the ideal culture. Women had legal protections against abuse. Men could be punished for maltreating their wives and pressured to marry or fined for "ruining" a woman; in 1821 the authorities "condemned [a soldier] to two years' work in shackles for rape of a child." The many instances of such punishments indicate that such violations happened regularly, that the culture considered them deviant, and that the perpetrators were castigated, however inconsistently. The civil law enforced sexual morality. Living together without benefit of marriage got the man and woman sentenced to hard labor, banished, and subject to public humiliations. Bancroft described an errant couple in Monterey in 1829 or 1830 who "were compelled to kneel near the presbytery, in full sight of the public, bound together by the neck with a thick hempen rope, and having before them a washtub filled with green grass, representing the manger of a stable, to signify that the man and woman had been living like beasts." The ascendant frontier culture, through the civil law, made sure that this couple lived like reasonable humans rather than *bestias*, animal or aboriginal humans. José María Amador describes what before the 1830s was more probably the ideal culture than the real, but his words are still instructive:

In the years before 1830, the men were of good habits with few exceptions—without prejudice there were cases of prostitution, drunkenness, games of chance, and abandonment of families—these things existed but scarcely.

After 1830 the better sort in the society began to slacken as people (who were not all good) from outside came, mainly because of the ease of obtaining their subsistence, and the political convulsions began to introduce those customs, making them fairly common amongst our men. Gambling, prostitution, vagrancy, and drunkenness became very common.

In this recollection of halcyon days the men behaved themselves until outsiders broke down the restraints that had previously checked men's propensity to sin. Women and de razón society were left without their traditional protections. What we know of Hispanic California society before 1830 belies the assertion that the men generally were "of good habits." But we see here expressed the notion that the culture obligated men to treat others decently, despite the tendency of male power to corrupt those values.[53]

Regard for others expressed itself most famously in the Californios' legendary hospitality. According to José del Carmen Lugo, "The traveler could go from one end of California to the other without it costing him anything in money, excepting gifts he might wish to make to the Indian servants at the missions or on the ranchos." Being respectable—and having Indians about to labor generously—enabled one to partake in the abundance of the region. Said Salvador Vallejo, "Formerly our cattle roamed by thousands, yet not one was stolen, for the unwritten law of the land granted to the weary traveller the privilege of killing cattle whenever he wanted beef, so long as he placed the hide where the owner could easily find it." Californio informants, recalling rancho life in the Mexican period twenty-five years after the Yankee conquest, undoubtedly embellished their stories of gracious entertaining for effect. "Selfishness was foreign to them to such an extent that they were completely ignorant of it," declared Carlos Híjar of his fellow gente de razón. A group of travelers "would hardly arrive at the ranch where they were to spend the night when the men would proceed to kill a calf to eat, a calf which they had run down and lassoed from the road, without noticing whether or not it was theirs," he elaborated. But foreign travelers corroborate these tales. "The virtue of hospitality knows no bounds" declaimed George Simpson. "They literally vie with each other in devoting their time, their homes, and their means to the entertainment of a stranger." (Simpson added an essential truth about California hospitality, however. It was the fleas who were "decidedly the best lodged, and, as we found to our cost, not the worst fed denizens of California.") "Every rancher's house was open to everybody, free," marveled an Anglo traveler in 1841. Another had previously noticed the restriction on the type of person to whom such generosity was extended, but basically agreed: "Any decent person might arrive at any hour of the day or night at a mission or ranch house, and though, entirely unknown, be sure of being entertained without charge." In this historical and cultural context a man increased in social standing if he gave away, rather than hoarded, his wealth.[54]

These gente de razón acted from neither foolishness nor pure generosity. They acquitted themselves admirably within the context of their aspiring seigneurial culture. A spirit, in this instance one of social ascendance and caste solidarity, animated this material graciousness. A human being, in this case a don, "does not act so as to safeguard his individual interest in the possession of material goods," Carl Polanyi points out. "He acts so as to safeguard his social standing, his social claims, his social interests."[55] The gente de razón earnestly endeavored to be successful; they were not simple idlers. But success derived not from producing and accumulating; rather, the rancheros valued material goods only insofar as they allowed

10. A drawing from 1865 of Don Andrés Pico, hero of the battle of San Pascual, at his rancho in San Fernando. A romanticized depiction of the seigneurialist life-style of the Californios. (Courtesy of the Los Angeles Public Library.)

genteel openhandedness—a sure mark of seigneurial status. The bestowal of some of their surplus through ritualized generosity safeguarded the social standing of the elite gente de razón. This gracious form of disaccumulation became part of their individual and collective characters.

Generosity also expressed and reinforced elite de razón caste solidarity. "It is fitting to observe here," noted one of the informants on hospitality, "that all the rancheros regarded their interests as though they were communal." "They all treated one another as cousins," Híjar recalled, "even though there existed no relationship whatsoever." Sharing in the practice of hospitality enabled the gente de razón to affirm who they were or at least who they were striving to become. Again defining themselves as they distinguished themselves from others, they were genteel and benevolent, whereas others were groveling or stingy. "They considered themselves as members of a single family," Híjar concluded.[56]

Like all families, they squabbled. Certain members were temporarily banished and then welcomed back. Some became jealous of others and refused to remain on speaking terms. Sometimes they came to blows, though their social conventions prescribed the limits of violence. Altercations of this "single family" erupted in politics as well. These relations were the cultural content of their incessant political spats and revolts which culminated in the dual governorship at the end of the Mexican period.

In order for them to exercise this seigneurialism, the elites could not sequester themselves. Their epic and illustrious fiestas allowed them to display their affluence and demonstrate their generosity by redistributing some of their bounty to those of lower status. As distinct as they sought to make themselves from others, the gente de razón did not recoil from social mixing, at least in the years of their emergence as a class. This is not to say that the gente de razón danced and chatted with the rest of the people. Richard Henry Dana noted that "there is always a private entertainment within the house for particular friends." Surely, when everyone assembled in the yard of a ranchero, or in the plaza, the boundaries between gente de razón and servants and laborers remained. But the few elites could not make a whole fiesta, and they could reassert their superior position on the social ladder through community celebrations. At the de la Guerra wedding in Santa Barbara in the 1830s "all the town was invited to participate, when old and young, rich and poor, lame and blind, black and white, joined in the feast," observed Alfred Robinson. In spite of the undoubted social distinctions between rancheros, local militia, and the ex-neophyte vaqueros taken with this new pageantry, he found disturbing "the want of distinction observed between those of virtuous and those of immoral habits." José Arnaz recalled that when he arrived in Los Angeles in 1840, "society . . . was mixed up—rich and poor, honorable women and prostitutes, participated equally in the amusements." It is likely that caste distinctions were suffi-

ciently evident, even at aguardiente-laced fiestas, that the gente
de razón did not need to sharpen them further by means of
complete segregation.[57]

The apparent democratic sociability of these weddings hid
their class nature and function. Socioeconomic factors determined marriages. Intermarriage was rare in the Mexican era.
Gloria Miranda notes that "in the Spanish era Santa Barbara
officers and enlisted men stationed at Los Angeles frequently
married daughters of soldiers or inválidos rather than wed
women from the pueblo's lower strata." The wedding celebrations included everyone; the ceremony, however, "produced an elite social-political group who perpetuated their
newly acquired privileged standing in the community by way
of continued intermarriage among themselves." By 1840 careful intragroup marriage prevailed among the increasingly seigneurial gente de razón: recall that "poor, handsome and brave"
Manuel Garfias had to be elevated to landed status by his old
commander Micheltorena before he could marry Luisa Ábila.
There came to be much at stake in Californio weddings. Love
could too easily interfere with the weighty matters of status
and land.[58]

But they all danced, "for on such occasions it was customary for everybody to attend without waiting for the formality
of an invitation." People danced until dawn and then resumed
the next night. A wedding festival could last up to a week if
the bride's family could afford it. At such a fiesta it could take
a calf a day to feed the guests, and "wine was served in abundance." Another Californio remembered fondly wine and
brandy "without limit." Days of religious celebrations inspired
not only serious devotion but also joviality. Several days of
preparation preceded the holy day of the patron saint of Santa
Barbara. In the morning a solemn mass was said; then followed a bullfight (that is, people and a bull chasing each other
around an arena), a bear fight, and a dance that would last
two or three days, well fueled by wine and brandy. Toward
morning the singing became "boisterous and discordant."

The fiesta was a momentous part of Hispanic California life.
On a day-to-day basis not much actually happened. People
looked forward to the celebrations. Californio informants de-

scribed them at great length, in great detail, and with great fondness. José del Carmen Lugo could remember eight of the dances well enough to describe the steps in 1877. He recalled how the *jóvenes* had to wait for the old folks to dance before they could start. It appears from the sources that the completion of most everyday tasks called for singing and music. The women, de razón and servants, sang after finishing the wash. Guitars and song often greeted the end of the workday. Such was the desired end of labor and production.[59]

The gente de razón had taken only a tiny and naive step into that liberal world of freely associating individuals for whom personal freedom was the greatest virtue. The rancheros maintained many of their traditions of reciprocity with those from whose labor they extracted wealth. The fiesta affirmed the social relationships of Spanish and Mexican California by serving to spotlight the big man giving it. At the same time it softened the relationships of domination because at the fiesta the produce of the land was shared with those who worked it and because it was an opportunity for the two groups to rub elbows—figuratively, of course. Thus, the fiesta ritually incorporated different elements of the population into a single society at the same time as it accentuated that society's hierarchy.

People ate very well whether there was a fiesta or not. A relatively small population and plenty of pasture coupled with the fecundity of nature produced more than enough beef to feed everyone, even marauding Indians. Later in the century an Anglo visitor saw at San Gabriel "herds of cattle, lying down, as if oppressed by surplus food." The wealthy had an admirable diet. Their Indians served them through the course of a day chocolate with milk, corn pinole (cereal), bread, roast beef or veal, beans, garbanzos, cabbage, vegetables (especially squash), and potatoes (introduced into California by the irrepressible la Pérouse in the 1780s) mixed with chile, cheese, and corn tortillas. In the afternoon was tea with milk for the women and tea with brandy for the men. Dairy products were not easy to obtain. To milk a cow took three people: one held the cow by the head, another kept a tight grip on a rope around the hind legs, and a third milked the cow with one hand and steadied whatever receptacle could be found with the other.[60]

In all of Europe and the Americas people were poor if they did not have access to sufficient land to provide a family subsistence. Without land breadwinners had to attach themselves to someone who had land or productive capital to work for wages or payment in kind. This pattern prevailed in nineteenth-century California, but with the notable difference that there was more food than there were people there. A rancho was unlikely to miss a cow; but just in case, the hide was left behind to appease the owner. If Indians or lower-caste persons were hungry, it was easier to give them a cow from the profuse grazing lands than to intensify the sorts of conflict that raged between the haves and the have-nots in places of scarcity. Anyway, a cow's worth was in its hide and tallow since no value could be realized on the meat in those days before packinghouses and refrigeration. When, for whatever reasons, the rancheros slaughtered cows, they customarily distributed the meat. (The packs of dogs present on every rancho and in every pueblo consumed the offal.) The ranchero laborers received from their patrón a ration of beef, butter, corn, beans, garbanzos, squash, and chile; they also grew some of these victuals on small plots of their own. Beef, which was extremely tough, tortillas, and beans were the most common donations, which the laborers ate from *cajetas de barro*, or clay dishes. The poor had a regimen of meat and more meat, but at least they ate.[61]

And they drank—the employed ones to excess, and the unemployed ones to destruction. "Intemperance, too," Dana noted, uncharacteristically understating the matter, "is a common vice among the Indians." Misery and degradation existed alongside the plenty and festiveness. Indian social organization continued to unravel, and Indian drunkenness and vice did not abate. Many of these Indians were permanently unemployed, a ready pool of itinerant labor, although inefficient and lethargic. Convicted Indians inevitably wound up in a chain gang, pressed into service for petty misdemeanors and drunkenness. As early as 1836 the ayuntamiento of Los Angeles authorized the use of arrested drunken Indians to clean the irrigation ditch. Thus, the law turned the decaying Indians into the city public-works force through the penal system. That the Indians, ever more apparently sin razón, should do all the work was public policy, too.[62]

Those attached to the ranchos labored like peones, not free workers. They lived on their patrón's land in houses made of tules or sticks stuck vertically in mud and then thatched. Some inhabited the *indiada*, or quarters, near the main casa, and others lived in the thatched huts of the rancherías by the water holes and corrals where the herds were. They awoke at daybreak, sometimes joining their patrón in morning prayers, and then got to work. "Throughout all California," observed Dr. John Marsh, visiting in 1836, "the Indians are the principal laborers; without them the business of the country could hardly be carried on." Commented Juan Bandini in 1828, soon to become a ranchero, "Riding on horseback and lounging lazily is the gamut of their days and the women bear all the responsibility of the house."[63]

"While the men are employed in attending to the herds of cattle and horses, and engaged in their other amusements," noted an Anglo traveler of the 1840s, "the women (I speak of the middle classes on the ranchos) superintend and perform most of the drudgery appertaining to housekeeping, and the cultivation of the gardens." "These beautiful creatures," Bandini wrote in 1828, "are without doubt more active and industrious than the men." The patrona worked hard setting the host of Indian women attached to the rancho to work sweeping, sewing, cooking, washing, and gardening. The de razón women supervised the milking of the cows and the making of cheese to ensure that the milk was clean and strained. Making bread, candles, and soap and cutting wood for cooking was their responsibility, as was the planting and tending of small gardens. The embroidery of clothes took much of their time. Some few of the girls from prominent families learned to read at the home of one of their mothers, and certainly they mastered the social graces, but what little formal education existed in Spanish and Mexican California was for boys. The tediousness of the interminable work both of the Indias and the patrona is striking. Both had exhausting jobs: the disinclined Indias were responsible for most of the work but could not comprehend de razón ways and tastes, and the patrona had to coax household production from her muddling charges. A ranchero patriarch fondly, if not wishfully, recalled that the women "were virtuous, industrious, and constantly devoted to the needs of their families, which were never neglected."[64]

The rancheros and the mayordomos supervised the Indian vaqueros. Their job was largely restricted to riding after the cattle—a fair amount of work, but at this time there was not the intensive agriculture such as was emerging in the mission era or would prevail towards the end of the century. The rancheros were content to let the grass grow and the cattle breed without husbandry. This way they could ride *a caballo* and be genteel while the Indians did their work.

Unlike their recent ancestors, however, these Indians now routinely tended and then slaughtered thousands of animals. How thoroughly were the old attitudes toward animals altered? Since the cattle came from outside the Indian world, did it make a difference that they killed so many in the *matanzas?* Was beef such an attractive and easily obtainable food source that the Indian ranch hands readily adopted the cattle culture? There can be no doubting the profundity of this cultural transformation, given the traditional Indian regard for animals. Because we have little or no information on the ex-neophyte or gentile Indians' perceptions of these changes, informed speculation on the quality of this transformation is impossible.

This Indian labor produced not only the subsistence of rancho California but a fundamental part of its seigneurial social relations and ideology as well. The gente de razón built on this base their remarkably new seigneurial status. There was some fusion of Indian and de razón cultures. Material goods and alcohol, together with the supply of food after the disruption of the ecosystem, drew the Indians, gentile and nominal Christians, into the rancho productive and cultural system. Of course, the fusion went only one way—the gente de razón adopted only a few Indian herbal medicines. It would be fascinating to know what sort of relationships prevailed when members of the pueblo married Indians, but the historical record is silent about this matter. It does not appear, however, that any Indian ways came into Hispanic California culture through intermarriage. The Indians served only the old soldier families' efforts to achieve their elevated social position. Perceptions and the reality of relations between the two groups were dissonant. The patrona of the influential Vallejo family declared:

All our servants are very much attached to us. They do not ask for money, nor do they have a fixed wage; we give them all they need, and if they are ill we care for them like members of the family. If they have children we stand as godparents and see to their education. If they wish to go to a distant place to visit a relative, we give them animals and escorts for the journey; in a word, we treat our servants rather as friends than as servants.

An Anglo traveler with an aversion to the grammatical period observed in 1834 that the stock was "herded by the indians, who cost them but a trifle more than they eat, in fact they always contrived to keep the poor indian in debt, or at least to make the poor devil think so, they were seldom paid more than two or three bullock hides per month or six dollars in goods, this they always drank in Arguadiente [*sic*] on Sunday."[65]

As incongruous as these two views of the same relationship may seem, they are not contradictory. Yes, the Indian servants were very much attached to the gente de razón, but not because of affection. Rather, after the unraveling of their old way of life and the thorough intrusion on their lands the Indians had no choice but to bind themselves to the ranchos. Fiestas, cloth goods, and aguardiente smoothed over the grimy bond. In this personal and seigneurial relationship the patrón took care of his charges' fractured needs for subsistence and conviviality. There was no place for a fixed wage, a concept foreign to the Indians anyway. An easy familiarity between the two peoples may well have characterized much of their day-to-day relationship, given their powerful mutual dependence, in spite of the vast difference in social position. Indian laborers drank to excess, paid no apparent attention to their health, and did not try to advance from their lowly condition, not because they suffered deracination, but because they remained, like children, sin razón. This situation not only suited the labor needs of the gente de razón but made them feel more confident about their socially ascendant and reasonable selves as well.

José Antonio de la Guerra wrote verse explaining what it meant to be de razón: "The Holy Father, when He made man, says a Christian prayer, gave him reason in order to understand, appetite in order to love, liberty in order to work with merit, . . . He gave faith to govern reason, charity in order to guide and balance his appetite, and grace in order to strengthen his liberty."[66] This felicitous worldview surely led rancheros to perceive Indian life and culture, inside or outside the missions, as aberrant, if not grotesque. Through this prism the gente de razón saw themselves as rational, as God's worthy ones: the Holy Father had not given the Indians any of these qualities, and they would not learn them in the missions. This verse also shows how de la Guerra defined human nature for his culture. The gente de razón, to whom the virtues of native culture were incomprehensible, considered the hopelessly sin razón Indians to be fit only for servitude.

Peddlers

Despite rancho self-sufficiency California entered into trade. In some ways engagement with the North Atlantic market altered Mexican California, and in others it reinforced the existing economic and social patterns. The essentially barter trade with the clipper ships—a cowhide bought about two dollars' worth of goods, and an arroba (twenty-five pounds) of tallow bought one dollar and fifty cents' worth—had consequences far beyond this simple act. International trade played a crucial role in the unfolding of the history of California as it neared mid-century. Like the flies around the cow pies in the rancho fields, energetic traders from the United States and England swarmed wherever there were goods capable of being transformed into commodities. "Any part of the earth," boasted

Thomas Jefferson Farnham, an early Anglo settler in California, "with its forests, its native grasses, herbs, flowers, streams and animals, unmolested by the transforming powers of that race which derives a livelihood from agriculture, commerce, and their attendant handicrafts, is a spectacle of great interest." Yankees brought from California hides for the shoe factories of Massachusetts and tallow for candles and soap, mostly under the auspices of Bryant Sturgis and Company, which was headquartered in Boston. When their boats appeared off the California coast, the gente de razón set out to greet the traders with their carretas full of hides and beef fat. They desired the cloth, silk, lace, tableware, furniture, and other goods befitting their status that the ships carried. Max Weber understood that within this ethic "they make tallow out of cattle and money out of men."[67] The boats also brought cheap cloth, which the rancheros used to attract and keep Indian laborers. This trade encouraged and strengthened the seigneurial system. Commerce provided an outlet for the products of the ranchos and materially benefited the area in ways that reinforced the apparent differences in dress and possessions between different elements of the society.

As rough as the rancheros' beginnings may have been, they came to enjoy the physical comfort and status these goods provided, especially after 1828, when liberalized Mexican trade policies took full effect. They could now have glass in their windows, fine fabrics, metal knives and forks. They replaced their cowhide furniture with wood (the fleas living in the hides were quick to find new abodes). Moreover, they could now supply the meager wants of the Indians more cheaply and conveniently. For example, in February 1836 José Antonio Pico ordered from a prominent Yankee merchant two dozen "of the cheapest blankets for the Indians, four pieces of the cheapest calico." Maintaining their seigneurial Indian labor system further involved the gente de razón in the capitalist market. They had to trade mainly in hides and tallow, there being no money to speak of in Mexican or Spanish California. In this situation people who had little affinity for business produced essentially raw materials to exchange for the manufactured consumer goods they so powerfully desired. Onto this stage strode a number of merchants who would play a key role in the fundamental alteration of Mexican California.[68]

The most famous and important of these characters in the south was Massachusetts-born Abel Stearns. Orphaned at the age of twelve, he went to sea. As he approached thirty, he decided to settle in Mexico to seek his fortune. After becoming a naturalized Mexican citizen, he journeyed to California in 1829 and set up shop in Los Angeles. He bartered hides and tallow for the groceries, dry goods, and liquor he acquired from the ships. Life was not without misfortune in California, though. In 1831 Governor Victoria ordered him out of the territory, and later a knife-wielding American permanently disfigured his face in a dispute over a cask of brandy. Then in 1834 he bought from the mission fathers of San Gabriel their *"casa en la playa,"* which they had used as a warehouse for the hides they sold to the ships before secularization ruined the missions. Stearns—or Don Abel, as he came to be known—now did the rancheros' buying and selling for them. Paying him a commission in those plentiful hides, the rancheros no longer had to worry about missing a ship with their slow and creaky carretas. Either Don Abel would send his own carts full of merchandise to the ranchos, or people could select their goods from his adept displays in his tienda in the town. The greater efficiency that this centralization brought attracted more ships to the port.

Stearns' papers, at the Huntington Library, show clearly the thriving business he developed by inserting himself between the rancheros and the Yankee traders. He made a small fortune in this enterprise, sometimes paying the customs charges that the Mexican government required, sometimes not. Money proved powerful stuff in a land where there was little of it. Stearns maintained a ready supply of cash, which enabled him to buy advantageously. When people needed money, they had to go to Don Abel. He thereby came to have a number of influential gente de razón in his debt. Thus, in 1840, when customs officers found him to have a large amount of contraband and dubiously branded hides at his warehouse, which he renamed Casa de San Pedro, they did not jail, expel, or even fine him but instead made him the administrator of customs.[69]

Stearns represented not only a specifically Yankee influx of businessmen but also the general penetration of market-oriented individuals. Mexico had liberalized its immigration laws, allowing foreigners to settle in 1824. The naturalization law of 1828 required that one reside continuously for two years, be useful and moral, and be a Catholic. The foreigners, at least nominally, joined the Roman Catholic church. Most of those who settled from outside the Hispanic world were indeed Yankees. A few trappers wandered as far west as the Pacific and stayed on in California. Some settled into respectable ways, but most trappers lived as *sin razón* as many Indians. Some immigrants were genuine traders, some were fortune seekers, and others simply wound up there. John Temple arrived in Los Angeles in 1827 and formed a partnership with fellow New Englander George Rice, opening the first general store. (Temple, the second Anglo to settle in the area, came after Joseph Chapman, a pirate who was caught, convicted, and paroled in 1818 and lived with his wife, Guadalupe Ortega, at Mission San Gabriel as a general handyman.) Not only Yankees arrived. Harris Newmark, a Prussian Jew, came to Los Angeles in 1835, unable to speak Spanish, and set up shop when he was only twenty years of age. The family of Englishman John Forster selected him to go to Guaymas to assist in his uncle's business. After staying for two years in Baja California, he came to Los Angeles in 1833 and opened his store in 1834. In 1840 he took charge of Stearns' import-export and smuggling operation in San Pedro. These outsiders dominated local business, which remained lethargic between ship arrivals. Richard Henry Dana wrote of those English and Americans who, "having more industry, frugality, and enterprise than the natives, . . . soon get all the trade into their hands."[70]

The presence of other immigrants could not help but get the attention of the gente de razón as well. Mexico continued to use California as a dumping ground for its unwanted elements. Others with less pretension, or even aspiration, toward respectability or industriousness also migrated to California. A number of trappers, indifferent to work and the law, settled there. More numerous were the unfortunate citizens of the interior of the new nation who migrated north. These *cholos*, as they were known, could find barely enough itinerant labor to keep them in aguardiente. Like the soldiers stationed in California, especially those Governor Micheltorena brought with him in 1843—"consumate rascals," de la Guerra Ord called them—many of the cholos nearly matched the Indians in social degradation. The gente de razón needed to find a way to distinguish themselves from these migrant Mexicans, who were of the same race as they. Consequently, they began to identify themselves more as Californians than as Mexicans. They came to associate their very name, gente de razón, with Europeanness and ceased to view themselves merely as Spanish-speaking Catholics. The arriviste gente de razón naturally gravitated toward respectable Anglos to counter the threat that the Mexican immigrants, whose numbers they correctly perceived as growing, posed to their shallowly rooted status and culture.[71]

The Anglo presence, then, had a variety of reverberations. Skilled in the manipulation of capital and goods and bent on accumulating wealth to gain status and power, these men further integrated California into the world market. They were, moreover, genuine white people. Their color appealed to the gente de razón because it was so distinct from that of the Indians. Nonetheless, we can imagine that genteel Californio society was hesitant to welcome those whose purpose in life was to make money. Thus, the Anglo merchants both compelled the rancheros because of their whiteness and threatened them because of their business acumen. Intermarriage between the two groups emerged from this context.

It is a brave, or foolish, soul who pretends to understand precisely what produces a marriage, much less a successful one. Different family members at different times in history have had a central role in such decisions. Since a divorce was nearly impossible to obtain in the nineteenth century, children may well have appreciated their parents' involvement in the risky undertaking of acquiring a mate, at least in retrospect. With the family's material wealth and social prestige at stake, propertied parents took active part in their children's selection of a spouse. This was particularly true in California, where women as well as men inherited property. Certainly, de razón parents believed they had their childrens' best interests at heart, though just as surely those interests reflected their own authoritarian set of concerns. Locking up the daughters exemplifies their anxieties about dubious paternity. Nonetheless, it remains difficult to generalize about the motivations behind Californio marriages. Some parents arranged a felicitous marriage for one of their children if they saw her or him courting an acceptable member of the opposite sex. Others pressured a child into a marriage that served family interests. Some fathers gave their daughters away to male friends or associates. As mentioned earlier, marriage agreements among the upper class seem to have taken place "only between the fathers of the children," as one ranchero remembered. One historian, all too enamored of the pastoral image of the Spanish Arcadia of California, asserted that the señoritas took a fancy to the *ojos azules,* or blue-eyes. Intermarriages, along with resentment on the part of de razón young men, followed. But the fathers still determined who would inherit the family hearth with its mantel of patriarchy when they unlocked their daughters and delivered them away. Marriages in these social settings amounted to an exchange of women among men, which bolstered the kinship networks that organized society. But by the gifting of women, fathers also gave away some of their future by more or less giving over control of their line of descent to the patriarchs of another culture.[72]

Marriages between Anglo merchants and *hijas del país* created important social linkages. The inclusion of these ascendant and acquiring men into the rancheros' kin networks apparently mollified any threats to California's wealth. By marrying their daughters to the whites, the Californio fathers improved their family's racial standing and social aspirations. Such alliances further distanced the gente de razón from the cholos and Indians as well as from their own pasts.

The historical sources do not provide details of the marriage negotiations between parents and brides, grooms and fathers-in-law, or the betrothed themselves. We do know, however, that Abel Stearns and Juan Bandini had extensive business dealings beginning in the 1830s. They always addressed one another warmly in their frequent, sometimes daily, correspondence. At the age of forty *Cara de Caballo*, or Horseface, as Don Abel was known after the knifing, "made formal suit" for the hand of Don Juan's fourteen-year-old daughter, Arcadia Bandini. "Don Juan gave his permission to the proposed marriage," and in 1841 Abel Stearns joined one of California's premier families. Cave Couts married another Señorita Bandini, as did James B. Winston, and John Forster married Pío Pico's sister, Isadora. Alfred Robinson, whose account of California informs this narrative, married one of Captain de la Guerra's daughters, and Angustias de la Guerra became Mrs. Ord. John Temple married Rafaela Cota from Santa Barbara, B. D. Wilson married Ramona Yorba, and William Wolfskill and Stephen Foster (who would become the first mayor of Los Angeles in the American period) both married daughters of Antonio María Lugo. These men ignored their own culture's proscriptions about such racial mixing and entered into Californio society through kinship ties.[73]

These marriages brought good fortune in other ways too. Now better connected to de razón society, Stearns purchased ex-governor Figueroa's Rancho Los Alamitos from his brother Francisco, who administered it for him. This acquisition began Stearns's 200,000-acre empire in southern California. When John Temple married Rafaela Cota, he came into possession of Rancho Los Cerritos, which Governor Figueroa had granted her mother in 1833–34. John Forster profited by his marriage to Isadora Pico. First, his ready cash allowed him to buy portions of Mission San Juan Capistrano when Governor Pico put it up for sale to the highest bidder. Later, loans Forster made to his brother-in-law enabled him to acquire Pico holdings. The Kentuckian Lemuel Carpenter, who arrived in California in 1833 on a fur-trading expedition, married María de Domínguez and acquired Rancho Santa Gertrudes. Hugo Reid, the son of a Scottish storekeeper, married the San Gabriel neophyte Victoria. Through the efforts of Eulalia Pérez the llavera of the mission, Doña Victoria, as she was known, received Rancho Santa Anita from the disbursement of the mission lands. Not only did this Celtic wanderer learn from his Indian wife stories of her people, which he told in the form of newspaper letters (which have significantly informed this narrative) but he acquired the substantial dowry of a rancho.[74]

The sources speak clearly and unanimously about the English and Yankee domination of commerce in mid-nineteenth-century California. Noted Bancroft, "They have married Californians, have joined the Catholic church, and have acquired considerable property, owing to their possessing more industry, frugality, and enterprise than the natives, and these qualities soon bring the whole trade of the town into their hands. They usually keep shops, in which they retail to advantage the goods purchased in large quantities from vessels arriving in the port." But the cultural influence was not simply in one direction. Observed Alfred Robinson, "While here [in San Gabriel] I met with a Yankee—Daniel A. Hill [from Santa Barbara] . . . who had been a resident in the country for many years, and who had become, in manner and appearance, a complete Californian." He commented similarly on the Yankees in Los Angeles and San José. Added Richard Henry Dana, as usual grossly mistaking Californio aspirations toward gentility for indolence, "The Americans (as those from the United States are called) and Englishmen, who are fast filling up the principal towns, and getting the trade into their hands, are indeed more industrious and effective than the Mexicans; yet their children are brought up Mexicans in most respects, and if the 'California fever' (laziness) spares the first generation, it is likely to attack the second." Still, people can reject their culture but cannot escape it. "One peculiarity, however, he [Hill] retained," continued Robinson, "the spirit of trade—which had lost none of its original power."[75]

These new Californios knew how to dance as well. The home Stearns built (purportedly for his socially conscious wife) on property he purchased in 1834, El Palacio, soon emerged as a social center for the elite. But the gatherings that took place at El Palacio differed from the old fiestas. As the hide and tallow trade increased the wealth of the area and more outsiders came in—both cholos and *"gente decente,"* as one who arrived in 1840 called his group—elites began to segregate themselves from the rest of society throughout California. Interclass mixing hardly ended abruptly in 1840, but the mass of folk was no longer as often included. Though there had always been terrific social distinction in California, now the physical separation of those who owned and did not own land broadened the gap between rich and poor even on fiesta days.[76]

On Dieciséis de Septiembre (September 16) Mexicans celebrate El Grito de Dolores, the day Padre Hidalgo declared independence from Spain in 1810. Whereas criollo conservatives dominated the outcome of the revolution, liberal ideas of this age of revolutions—liberty, equality, and fraternity, and life, liberty, and the pursuit of happiness—competed with traditional notions of hierarchy and obligation. Curiously enough, on Dieciséis de Septiembre in 1840, celebrating Mexico's independence and emergence into the liberal world, two fiestas were held. One was at the plaza, for "the greater part of the population," José Arnaz recalled, and "on the other side, the most outstanding families attended at the house of Abel Stearns." A minor episode compared to the political turmoil that raged in Mexico, this relatively trifling event marked and illuminated an important watershed in history. Mexico's liberal trade policies opened California to commerce and then brought to California the market, a widening gap between social classes, and the Anglos. Those very processes and ideas of liberalism brought forth formal and physical class segregation in Los Angeles in the important matter of the fiestas. The old feudal Spanish ways allowed for a hierarchical corporate society in which notions of reciprocity bound persons and classes. The social distinctions that de razón elites, increasingly freed from obligations of reciprocity, made prevail between themselves and everyone else were manifested on Dieciséis de Septiembre, not incidentally at the home of a Yankee merchant. No longer did everyone rub elbows at the fiestas. The *populacho*, now excluded from the elites' fiesta and undoubtedly consuming titanic amounts of aguardiente on the holiday, became furious and began throwing stones, breaking windows. There would be no more such riots at the Stearns-Bandini house for another decade, but "since then," stated José Arnaz, "there have remained established two societies in Los Angeles."[77]

Chapter Four

Heaven, or Some Other Place
A Conquered Los Angeles

The more the Anglo presence made itself felt, the more the Californios sensed what they were up against. Pío Pico saw the threat clearly, though late: "We find ourselves threatened by hordes of Yankee immigrants who have already begun to flock into our country and whose progress we cannot arrest. . . . Whatever that astonishing people will next undertake I cannot say, but on whatever enterprise they embark they will be sure to be successful." Californios perceived a difference between the first Americanos, as they called Yankee immigrants to Mexican California, and those who came after the early 1840s. "Many settled among us and contributed with their intelligence and industry to the progress of my beloved country," stated Governor Alvarado. "Would that the foreigners that came to settle in Alta California after 1841 had been of the same quality as those who preceeded them!" In 1846 Subprefect Guerrero wrote to Manuel Castro, "Friend, the idea these gentlemen have formed for themselves is, that God made the world and them also, therefore what there is in the world belongs to them as sons of God." In their spirit world (uncomplicated with saints and the deification of the Virgin Mary), their one true God had made everything but then transcended worldly existence and left management entirely up to the men, who could, and usually did, act without restraint toward His creations. Mexicans observed, but did not always grasp, this sentiment. Before his country experienced American military might, General Manuel Mier y Terán noted:

The department of Texas is contiguous to the most avid nation in the world. There is no Power like that to the north, which by silent means, has made conquests of momentous importance. Such dexterity, such constancy in their designs, such uniformity of means of execution which always are completely successful, arouses admiration. Instead of armies, battles, or invasions, which make a great deal of noise and for the most part are unsuccessful, these men lay hands on means, which, if considered one by one, would be rejected as slow, ineffective, and at times palpably absurd.

Mexicans, and much of the rest of the world where American capital and its representatives penetrated, felt repulsion and attraction, envy and resentment, admiration and anger, and bewilderment and a desire to emulate these industrious and sermonizing people. Divined Manuel Castro before a junta at Monterey, "These Americans are so contriving that some day they will build ladders to touch the sky, and once in the heavens they will change the whole face of the universe and even the color of the stars."[1]

In the convulsive years immediately following the conquest, the different peoples that have entered this narrative would have different stories to explain the same phenomena, each according to its own worldview. People do not simply fabricate stories to mislead, though that is sometimes the case and often the consequence, but rather they reflect reality through their cultural presuppositions. Such premises rarely include empathy; in fact, convoluted notions of other, fear, presumption of superiority, and other such factors predominate in the making of the story. This narrative, then, shall reflect some of the chaos of the decades following the conquest. To approach the truth, we must know as many of the stories of the time as possible. I shall now proceed to analyze the Anglo-American view of the inhabitants and the land of southern California and of the conquest. Americanos would now control the productive means of the area, and Mexicans' and Indians' history would develop in relation to theirs. What they brought, particularly notions of liberalism and land law, both of which they enforced with violence, proved problematic to Indians and Mexican Californians of all classes. Such ideologies contributed powerfully to the ultimate demise of the Indians and the Californios. I shall analyze in greater depth the Mexican and Indian experience of these same ideas and events—the desperate rebellions of the Indians, Mexican ambivalence about liberty, and the Californios' response to their criminalization and exclusion from the productive opportunity of southern California. Anglo culture reigned supreme within a few decades, and this fact had profound consequences for the ways in which Mexicans, whose thin stream of migration to California continued throughout the nineteenth century, would have to adapt to the demands that Americano industrial culture would put on them.

Anglo Views of Californios and Indians

The Americanos of the later migrations expressed little ambivalence toward the Indians and the Californios. After all, they carried their cultural baggage of industriousness and sermonizing along with them when they encountered such peoples as those who inhabited the coast of California in the nineteenth century. Those people, those "others," appeared to them to be not only indolent but also sinful in their ways. Just as when the Indians' refusal to adopt Catholic ways convinced the gente de razón of their savagery, the smiling stubbornness with which Hispanics greeted the market and its ways convinced the business-minded Yankees of their inherent inferiority, whether cultural or biological.

The tales and writings of many of the same travelers who have contributed this narrative enchanted these later settlers, who began arriving in 1840–41. They sought not to join Californio society, as had Stearns and his ilk, but to fashion American settlements within California.[2] As had been the case with Anglo settlers in Texas, they soon came to resent the fact that people whom they considered to be inferior governed them. The Americans saw that Californio society was not as materially successful as it could be or as the Yankees themselves were, and they judged it to be not only of poor quality but also ungodly.

In his widely read *Two Years before the Mast* (1840) Richard Henry Dana declared, "In their domestic relations these people are not better than in their public. The men are thriftless, proud, extravagant, and very much given to gaming." Dana did not lie, only condemn. The Californios behaved indeed thriftlessly and extravagantly; they gave away to achieve status. They felt proud of the gentility they were fostering on this frontier. And the Californios did not simply ride their horses—they bet on them too (though they "pay their losses with the most strict punctuality"). "The men," Alfred Robinson believed, "are generally indolent, and addicted to many vices, caring little for the welfare of their children, who, like themselves, grow up unworthy members of society." The Englishman George Simpson wrote of the "men who do not avail themselves of their natural advantages to a much higher degree than the savages whom they have displaced, and who are likely to become less and less energetic from generation to generation from year to year!" This estimation was not unique to Anglo Protestants. The Russian K. T. Khlebnikov noted in 1829, "The Californians are in general a lazy, untidy people, of limited capacity; and their simple humor evidences their seemingly infantile state."[3]

To contemporaries, the Californios' relationship to nature and production smacked of the sin of sloth and demonstrated their worthlessness. Edward Bryant observed, "With his horse and trappings, his sarape and blanket, a piece of beef and a tortilla, the Californian is content, so far as his personal comforts are concerned. But he is ardent in his pursuit of amusement and pleasure." Colonel Philip Edwards noted about the San Francisco presidio after Mexican independence, "It is now inhabited by a half dozen families, too indolent to do anything to arrest the progress of decay." Such "ruins, however diminutive," he continued, "are melancholy momentoes [*sic*] of human blindness and folly."[4]

Somehow the Californio women escaped such opprobrium. Dana asserted that "the women have but little education, and a good deal of beauty, and their morality, of course, is none

of the best; yet the instances of infidelity are much less frequent than one would at first suppose." But famed chronicler
of the West Francis Parkman graciously referred to the women
he saw in California in 1846 as Spanish, whereas the men he
called simply Mexicans. Alfred Robinson, who actually lived
in California and whose censorious comments on the men we
have just seen, proclaimed about California women that "perhaps there are few places in the world where, in proportion
to the number of inhabitants, can be found more chastity,
industrious habits, and correct deportment, than among the
women of this place." Within the power relations of Californio patriarchy the women adorned and deported themselves
so that men would see them positively, something that the
Anglo men could not help but notice. An enterprising Yankee
or Englishman would look on a genteel Californio man and
see, aside from an able horseman, an enervated person of
limited capacity for production—a feeble presence, to the Anglo mentality. "One might simplify this by saying," according
to John Berger, "*men act* and *women appear.*" By the standards of the Protestant ethic the men were indolent, but the
industrious women appeared "correct" because both patriar-
chies agreed on the way women were supposed to act.[5]

In their productive and accumulationist frenzy these economic men of the great trading nations left something behind.
Norman O. Brown reminds us that "the apparent accumulation of wealth is really the impoverishment of human nature,
and its appropriate morality is the renunciation of human nature and desires—asceticism. The effect is to substitute an
abstraction, 'Homo economicus,' for the concrete totality of
human nature, and thus to dehumanize human nature." Inevitably, then, some of these Anglo travelers to California were
drawn to aspects of this Californio life-style to fulfill other parts
of their being. The trapper J. B. Dye extolled Californios in
1832: "The Californians were the happiest people on earth.
Their time was spent in one continued round of feasting and
pleasure, gaiety and happiness. If any person was so poor that
he had no horse to ride, some friend, relative or compadre
would give him a splendid charger, another a saddle, bridle,
reata, and spurs; a third a milk cow, another a bullock for

beef, and so on, leaving no want unsupplied." Contrary to
the demands of the ideal culture from which Dye came, the
Californios not only worked the Indians but enjoyed themselves as well; they gave things away to ensure status instead
of accumulating them. This attitude toward production and
goods invited both disapproval and attraction. The former
sentiment prevailed in ascetic cultures (such as mission culture) whose quest for material wealth and the triumph of discipline over desire truncated their humanity.[6]

Like the gente de razón and the Indians, the Yankees compared themselves to the Californios to congratulate themselves on the material accomplishments and self-discipline of
their culture. Environmentally congenial California presented
a special trial for "men with the blood of ancient Normans
and Saxons in their veins—with hearts as large as their bodies
can hold," as American settler Thomas Jefferson Farnham referred to the trappers. Eliza Farnham declared that "nowhere
else have the indomitable energies, the quick desires, and the
wide reaching purposes of the Saxon nature been submitted
to so severe a test of their self-regulating power."[7] Usually,
though certainly not always, this "self-regulating power" prevailed.

To so many Anglo-Americans seigneurial Mexicans lacked
such energy and self-regulation. Colonel Philip Edwards, after surveying the scene at the San Francisco presidio, explained Mexico's troubles thus: "These humble ruins, thought
I, vie not with those more extensive and magnificent found
in the old world, but are equally indicative of debased pro-
pensities. . . . A little circumspection and industry would have
averted all." Edwards went on to compare the reasons for the
success of the United States and the failure of Mexico at the
presidio: "One American colony, supposing itself aggrieved,
has dissolved its connection with its transatlantic parent, and
assumed a 'separate and equal station'—[and] has risen to
grandeur and happiness; another, without the same causes of
complaint, and without the essential qualifications in itself,
ventures upon the same experiment, and sinks down into anarchy more abhorrent than despotism."[8] Ignorant of the cultural and intellectual achievements of Mexico City, frontier

Mexico thus became the paradigm for the whole of the new and struggling republic of Mexico. Moreover, each culture, American and Mexican, got what it deserved. Anglo America used these "others," described in widely read travel accounts, to help define itself and thereafter came to have more confidence in itself.

Anglos and the California Landscape

American and British settlement did not alter the labor relations that prevailed on the Californio ranchos. For example, Abel Stearns's account books of the early 1840s for Rancho Los Alamitos contain lists of servants whom he paid in goods. These *sirvientes los alamitos* were obviously Indians. Hugo Reid, the Scot who married the Gabrieleña, "set Indians to work making adobe bricks" for his house and used Indian workers generally on his Rancho Santa Anita; the Hispanicized Doña Victoria herself trained the domestic servants. Jonathan Trumbull Warner, who came from Connecticut in 1831, received a grant in 1844 near San Diego, on which he continued the mission practice of Indian labor. John Temple married into Rancho Los Cerritos; Indian laborers, of course, were included in the deal. In 1844 John Forster took control of the grazing lands around Mission San Juan Capistrano and the twenty or so Indian families on that land. These Anglos, Hispanicized except in financial matters, assumed the Californio suppositions about who should work. From San Pedro, N. Pryor wrote to his employer Stearns about a shipment of goods that "if he [the customer] wants it put in the house he will have to send some Indians with bags to pack it up." The Indians, conveniently, were temporary workers as well. "I have discharged my Indians as I have no further use for them at present," wrote Pryor in 1839. In other ways, however, such Indians proved to be not the perfect workers a Yankee would like. On another occasion Pryor complained to Stearns that "my Indians want to take a paseo."[9]

Sharing with the Californios their assumptions about who should labor on the land, the Yankees proceeded more vigorously to accumulate parcels of land. The American view of land is contradictory. On the one hand, it assumes the family farm to be the mainstay of democracy and liberty and reflects a fear that without such independent freeholds the country and its people would sink into unemployment, dependence, mob violence, and demogogic politics. On the other hand, Americans also cherish the freedom to accumulate, and even monopolize, as much land as possible; thus, it becomes more difficult for the common folk to become autonomous tillers of the soil. The status-hungry Californios greedily accumulated land too; witness the spoilation of the missions. But they also gave land away as a means of increasing their status, a tendency of which their Anglo sons-in-law took advantage. Again Abel Stearns serves as the archetype of the Americano accumulationist personality. Building on the initial acquisition of Rancho Los Alamitos, in the twenty years after his marriage Stearns came to own two hundred thousand acres of the best land in the Los Angeles area as well as lay claim to immense tracts of land in Baja California. He combined his ready cash with an intimate knowledge of the financial troubles and foibles of Californio rancheros, bailing them out of trouble, loaning them money, and ending up with their land.[10] The salvation, however brief, of his indebted father-in-law notwithstanding, Stearns brought to California a new way of dealing with land. To him, it was above all a commodity, its value measured in money. In the presence of men like Abel Stearns the disaccumulationist ways and personalities of the rancheros often proved disastrous. Profligacy in the granting of ranchos after secularization meant that many received land who were genuinely not capable of prospering on it. Their lands were easy prey to the clever and the well connected. Stearns, however, not only planned, strategized, and shrewdly calculated how to get land away from others but also assessed the future impact the monopolization of that land would have on him. He achieved his goals through the manipulation of the market and money. He held no discernible sense of reciprocal obligation to the people on the landscape with respect to his entitlement to what was to him mere property. California was changing because of the ascendancy of market forms of organizing production and was ceasing to be merely the site of small-scale trade, as had been the case previously. Increasingly in charge of the means of production—land, in this case—the Anglo-American presence produced new tensions that would propel history in new directions.

This narrative should demonstrate clearly that the manner in which people organize their societies to produce subsistence, exchange surplus goods, relate to people they consider alien, and arrange their households is culturally and historically specific. Few cultures realize this singularity about themselves, and the Americans were no exception. Americans have always understood that it is natural for them to trade whatever to whomever they pleased. Transforming everything into commodities, even labor, North Atlantic capitalists mediated their relationships to goods and people through the market, which they considered to be value-neutral. Patently the Hispanic and Indian peoples of California did not fully share these views, despite their attraction to the commodities. In the same manner that the Indian refusal of the true word of God led the Spanish to disgust and frustration with the Indians, the Anglos have usually deemed the rejection of their allegedly natural liberal ways as indications of cultural or biological inferiority and subversion.

One Anglo fur trapper, harvesting pelts and traveling without proper immigration papers in New Mexico, put the matter nicely in the *Missouri Gazette* of October 9, 1813, regarding some men who were detained in Santa Fe: "We are asstonished [*sic*] at the barbarity exersised [*sic*] by the officer who commands at Sta. Fe towards these men; for we know that they bore letters and other evidences of their pursuits being purely commercial." Only barbarians did not adhere to notions of free trade, just as only the sin razón did not adhere to the true word. The Yankees proceeded to trade freely in spite of restrictive laws that first Spain and then Mexico passed to protect their own commerce. Obviously, the Yankees did not invent smuggling in California. This practice always requires two parties to buy and sell or to exchange. Californians, including the Franciscans, consistently have been eager to trade for goods that they otherwise could not obtain or for which they would have to pay much more through sanctioned channels.[11]

The situation of Mexico after independence intensified the dynamics of smuggling. The new nation had genuinely liberalized trade but needed the money from tariff duties. The predicament was apparent to Captain Duhaut-Cilly in the late 1820s. "On the one side," he noted, "the Mexican government held strictly to the execution of the . . . laws of its severe customs tariff; on the other, it gave no assistance, in money or equipment, to the commandant general." Mexico could not afford to have diligent American and British traders siphon off its wealth. At the same time, it could only implement its customs laws sporadically, thus presenting the appearance of ineffectualness and capriciousness in its enforcement procedures. Smuggling increased dramatically in the years following Mexican independence. In the Los Angeles area Yankee ships met Californios, from the missions and the pueblo, along the many stretches of beach along the Malibu coast, whose many hidden canyons facilitated their misdeeds. In 1821 Captain de la Guerra apprehended Antonio Briones and Máximo Alanis, who had led a smuggling conspiracy, made them pay a heavy fine to support the chapel in Los Angeles, and condemned them to six months' labor in chains. Padre Sánchez of Mission San Gabriel felt greatly aggrieved to be charged with smuggling in 1828. Yet the traffic in contraband continued.[12]

Bancroft describes the situation in the 1830s and 1840s: "So large a portion of the inhabitants, native and foreign, of all classes, were engaged in contraband trade, that there was slight risk of detection. Customs officers were the only ones who were at all dishonored by smuggling." By the 1840s the methods had changed slightly. Rather than use coastal rendezvous, traders influenced the local authorities and brought the goods directly into port. Bancroft estimates that on three-quarters of California's imported goods in 1843 no duties were paid.[13] The point here is that the Americanos had already thoroughly penetrated California in the years before 1846 with their capital and seductive commodities. Their particular culture of land tenure, social relations, and trade was ascendant, if not already dominant. Significantly, however, the Americans adopted the labor system of their Hispanic predecessors.

California Conquered

The same fate that Texas has suffered a decade earlier now confronted California, and Mexican officials sensed trouble. In 1831, as American settlers moved into Texas, Governor Victoria of California complained that he could not prevent illegal hunting at the offshore islands and that lawless foreigners infested the interior. Juan Almonte, the Mexican minister to Washington, toured Texas in 1834 and presciently warned his government of the danger there. In 1840 he communicated from California to the minister of war that in spite of the apparent and stated intentions of the Anglo settlers to be "peaceful and friendly, your excellency should remember that this is no different than language used by Austin's colony and other immigrants who occupied Texas."[14]

Still stinging from the humiliation of Texas independence in 1836 at the hands of white-supremacist Americanos disrespectful of Mexican law, especially as regards slavery, Mexico showed reasonable concern about American aims. More and more Yankee illegal aliens filled California, and their disregard for Mexican passport regulations convinced the locals of their general disrespect for Mexican law. In 1842 Commodore Thomas Ap Catesby Jones, the commander of the United States fleet in the Pacific, believing rumors that war had been declared, attacked and easily took Monterey. He raised the American flag as well as Mexican suspicions of American designs. Wrote Edwin Bryant shortly before the start of hostilities, "Indeed it seems to be a settled opinion, that California is henceforth to compose a part of the United States, and every American who is now here considers himself as treading upon his own soil, as much as if he were in one of the old thirteen revolutionary states." George Simpson noted on his 1842 visit that "the English race . . . is doubtless destined to add this fair and fertile province to its possessions. The only doubt is, whether California will fall to the British or the Americans." The once remote and obscure California was now a coveted prize.[15]

Bryant likens the Yankee experience in California to that of 1776 because in both cases—the 1770s in New England and the 1840s in California—his people verged on joining in what they perceived (retrospectively regarding 1776) as a perfect union. Anglo-Americans, convinced that they lived in a society that represented the culmination of Western world history, assumed their conquests to be progressive. "Wherever the Anglo-Saxon race plant themselves, progress is certain to be displayed in one form or another," added Bryant. "Laying hands on means," or sending the troops, saved the indigenous people from their indifference toward production and their inability to govern themselves wisely. In short, it saved them from their general backwardness, which Anglo-American standards of enterprise and electoral democracy gauged. In 1831 Abel Stearns received a letter from Alex Forbes, who wrote concerning California that "by all accounts it is worthy of more wise and more enterprising masters than those to whose rule it is subjected." The Americans, still planted atop the "city on a hill," the moral beacon of their Puritan forbears, would save the area from Hispanic sloth. "This opinion is heightened," Forbes continued, "by the description you give of it, and confirms me that if populated it would be perhaps the most delightful country in the world. How many Countrymen of mine who are jostling one another for room at home might live happily in those fertile but uncultivated plains you [Stearns] describe." Since the nonwhite peoples on the Americanos' frontier, the boundary of which always moved further and further west, could be dismissed, Americans carried with them an image of entering an empty landscape. "California is an incomparable wilderness," intoned Thomas Jefferson Farnham. After sharing with his readers the usual descriptions of indolent Mexicans in California, Richard Henry Dana primed his countrymen for another progressive push:

Such are the people who inhabit a country embracing four or five hundred miles of sea-coast, with several good harbours, with fine forests in the north; the waters filled with fish, and plains covered with thousands of herds of cattle; blessed with a climate, than which there can be no better in the world; free from all manner of diseases, whether epidemic or endemic; and with a soil in which corn yields from seventy to eighty-fold. In the hands of an enterprising people, what a country this might be!

"What a splendid country," echoed the Englishman George Simpson, "whether we regard its internal resources or its commercial capabilities, to be thrown away on its present possessors." It is likely that many Americans came to California with the idea of both fulfilling the expectations of its natural wealth and taking possession of the territory for the United States. Stephen Smith, after the dismissal for lack of evidence of charges that he conspired to declare California independent, wrote to John C. Calhoun, "We only want the Flag of the U.S. and a good lot of Yankees and you would soon see the immense lot of natural riches of the country developed, and her commerce in a flourishing condition." There could be no question as to the happiness such an expansion would bring: "To see that Flag planted here would be most acceptable to the Sons of Uncle Sam, and by no means repugnant to the native population." Thomas Oliver Larkin wrote to Stearns that "events will and must take their natural course."[16]

This Anglo-American view of the native population's acceptance of the inevitable mixed the Yankee sense of mission with the Californios' actual predicament. In 1842 a new centralist government in Mexico sent General Manuel Micheltorena and a convict army of three hundred to upend the essentially rebellious rule of Alvarado and to reassert control over California. As the threat from the United States appeared to mount, Micheltorena's army supported itself by theft, and its seedy demeanor disgusted the locals. The Californios planned another revolt. At the battle of Cahuenga Pass, in February 1845, their cannon fire forced the withdrawal of Micheltorena's army; remarkably, no human blood was spilled. The hapless governor was put on a boat; Los Angeles was made the capital of California, and Pío Pico was named governor. By 1846, however, the situation had sufficiently deteriorated so that Pío

Pico, governor in the south, and José Castro, the military leader of 1836 and comandante general in 1845, who claimed control at Monterey, threatened to face one another in battle.[17]

As had happened in New Mexico, Mexico had lost the allegiance of its frontier citizens. Disorganized and unable to defend the locals against Indian depredations, yet meddling in local affairs and trying to collect taxes and tariffs, the Mexican government brought down Californio hostility against it. Obviously, Mexico had given birth to these mestizos, but now Californios felt angry at their inconsistent mother. Thus, many Californios began to consider withdrawing from Mexican sovereignty and forming some other allegiance that promised protection and stability.

Juan Bandini sympathized with the American cause. Others argued for declaring independence. Such sentiment accompanied the revolt against Micheltorena; but as war threatened, Mexico increased its military presence, and the Californios feared retribution. Cognizant of their military weakness, most of them also feared annexation by the United States. (Micheltorena, knowing "the probability of war with the U.S.," could only respond with "a hundred laboring Indians" to fortify San Juan Bautista in 1844. The Yankee juggernaut would encounter little military resistance.) Though some supported the American cause, Californio elites probably would have preferred some sort of independence under British or French protection. In the north General Castro had planned for separation in 1847 or 1848, once there had arrived sufficient foreigners to steer allegiance away from Mexico and garrison the place. Confirming and encouraging news came from the south on this matter as well. However, the famous Bear Flag Revolt of June 1846 (after the United States had declared war on Mexico but before the news had arrived in California) made them leery of this plan. "Seen in California as a mortal enemy," wrote José María Amador, the bear flag and the presumptuous revolt it symbolized showed the Californios that independence would likely translate into Yankee domination in one form or another.[18]

In California the elites remained disorganized and continued squabbling, unable to defend effectively their territory.

In Mexico the debate raged over how to respond to American belligerence and American designs on Mexican lands, especially California. Fearful that the same fate that befell America's Indians or Africans would be theirs too if defeated, the Mexican people girded for war. In Washington President James K. Polk contemplated how to win himself a place in history. "There are four great measures," Polk claimed, "which are to be the measures of my administration: one, a reduction of the tariff; another, the independent treasury; a third, the settlement of the Oregon boundary question; and, lastly, the acquisition of California."[19]

The war came, of course. The Americans had already laid their hands on a good deal of the means of California—much of the land, that is; now the military conquest formalized what had already been transpiring in subtle, but no less important, ways. In the transference of one-third of Mexico's territory to the United States, in which California was the primary objective, the diplomatic and military aspects are important, to be sure. For our purposes, however, a brief review of events will suffice. John C. Frémont's forces landed at San Diego on July 29, 1846; Commodore Robert Stockton sailed from Monterey on August 1 and, touching first at Santa Barbara, landed at San Pedro five days later. Shortly thereafter Stockton arrived in Los Angeles, meeting only insignificant resistance from the fractious and demoralized forces, the "pastoral dragoons," of José Castro and Pío Pico. Pico signed over other mission lands to his associates, and on August 10 both he and Castro fled to Mexico.[20] The United States now had its Pacific coast prize; its borders, through military conquest, extended from sea to shining sea.

The reaction to, and the impact of, the war will not escape analysis here, however. The previous profound ambivalence upper- and lower-class Californians felt toward the Anglo-Americans vanished with the invasion. Moreover, their rivalries, particularly between *abajeños* (southerners) and *arribeños* (northerners), turned to nearly unanimous animosity toward the common enemy. "Such an action is infuriating [and] is an insult to the dignity of the nation," the newly patriotic Pío Pico wrote to his cohorts on hearing of the declaration of war. Soon these caballeros would take to their horses for a brief and ritual victory over the avaricious foe. Meanwhile, in September 1846 the local inhabitants of the pueblo of Los Angeles under the leadership of Sérbulo Varelas issued a proclamation: "Citizens: For a month and a half, by a lamentable fatality resulting from the cowardice and incompetence of the department's chief authorities, we see ourselves subjugated and oppressed by an insignificant force of adventurers from the U.S. of N[orth] America, who, putting us in a condition worse than that of slaves, are dictating to us despotic and arbitrary laws." Now came the Americans' turn to try and subdue the *populacho,* and, not surprisingly, they would find them revolting in more ways than one.[21]

In August 1846 Captain Archibald Gillespie, commander of the American occupying force in Los Angeles, responded to the usual Angeleño rumpus by declaring a curfew, closing the stores, and banning most public and social assemblages. Gillespie and his men looked down on the vanquished Californios as an inferior and cowardly people. Assuming their own racial and cultural superiority, the conquerors of Los Angeles acted to keep the errant locals in line, as they may well have learned to discipline Indians and blacks, their alleged inferiors, through seemingly arbitrary regulations and punishments. In this way activities (with and without aguardiente) that did not fall precisely within the spirit and letter of the laws of the ayuntamiento, but were tolerated before the occupation, were now criminalized. Gillespie assumed that his mestizo charges were a lawless bunch (indeed many were) acting in rebellion against his authority. Many, branded as rebels perhaps before they themselves even thought of revolt, were jailed.

To these regulations and arrests Varela's people responded with their pronunciamiento. While the statement had some political content, one wonders if trouble would have started at that moment if Gillespie had allowed the *populacho* their usual tawdry pleasures. Now an outlaw, Varela attracted a number of followers, who in turn commanded the allegiance of smaller groups of locals. Varela's force succeeded only in antagonizing Gillespie and his men, though they began to fancy raising enough men to attack the garrison and drive out the invaders. Many Californians thus perceived that the war had broken out anew and responded by allying themselves with Varela's corps, now grown to three hundred men. The markedly more sober elites prevailed in the organization of the patriotic uprising. They chose Captain José María Flores to lead them, a paroled officer of the Mexican army who had escaped arrest by remaining neutral in the conflict. Antonio Carrillo and Andrés Pico were second and third in command. They had few weapons but scrounged enough from their houses to give them at least a military appearance, and Juan Temple's wife, the former Rafaela Cota, sent some arms to their camp from her husband's store.[22]

The guerrillas won some victories against the invaders. Encouraged by their victory at Chino in late September, their fight at Rancho Dominguez on October 8 cast Gillespie and his men out of Los Angeles. But the major battle occurred at San Pascual, north of San Diego, on December 8, 1846. Actually a rather small affair if measured by casualties—the Americans lost 18 men and the Californios none—it is important for its symbolism. In this battle of sabres and lances the Americans, led by Kearney and including Gillespie (both of whom received serious wounds), proved no match for the Californios, who were among the best, or at least most practiced, horsemen in the world. At best the Californios might have hoped to hold the territory until they could force a peace treaty giving them some power in whatever new government would rule their homeland. The wisest of them knew, though, that ultimately they could not win a permanent victory. And they squabbled again. Some wavered in their commitment to the cause, and others—including Pico, of course—resented the leadership of the Mexican Flores. They had accomplished what they wanted at San Pascual. There the Californios, *a caballo*, had shown the sneering conquerors their *gachupines*. They were caballeros again. Their honor restored, Andrés Pico, who assumed command from Flores after the latter fled back to Mexico, could graciously surrender to the vastly superior American reinforcements under Frémont at Cahuenga Pass on January 13, 1847. The Californio combatants were pardoned for their hostile actions and were permitted to ride home, which most did, after surrendering the weapons of their army—two cannons and six muskets. Now the American military unequivocally had completed its conquest of California.[23]

In some ways the Mexican War marked a dramatic juncture of history, as California ceased to be part of Mexico and became part of the United States of America. The former country now felt further wounded and weakened, and the latter felt more confident, having fulfilled what its leaders considered its providentially inspired imperial mission.

The gold discovered at Sutter's mill in 1849 represented another such dramatic juncture, as it catalyzed the entire territory. Actually, the discovery of gold had more to do with the Anglo presence than is first apparent. Because they preferred houses of wood rather than adobe, they diverted streams to run mills to cut lumber. On one such stream James Marshall made his famous strike. Gold had been discovered north of Los Angeles in 1843, but without much consequence. The Gold Rush of 1849 in the north drew hordes of wealth seekers, who, when frustrated in the mines, laid claim to plots of land as squatters. The fervent migration of miners and clever lawyers obliterated the Hispanic social and political order in the areas around the gold strikes.

In the south the impact of the Gold Rush was entirely different, though the transfiguring power of the yellow metal that drives white men crazy (as the Sioux called it) still worked its magic. There the new and sudden demand for beef to feed the hordes of miners and others whom the dream of quick wealth had attracted brought a terrific, but ultimately dangerous, boom to the cattle counties. In the days of trade with New England a cow hide brought two dollars and an arroba of tallow one dollar fifty cents; the meat itself had no market value. Now, in the seven years after 1849, the price of San Francisco beef cattle soared to between fifty and sixty dollars a head and could reach as high as seventy-five dollars. It cost a ranchero twenty dollars or less to raise and transport a steer north. On the ranchos of the south a full-grown steer now brought from thirty to forty dollars, a tenfold increase in price over the hide and tallow days. It was as if wealth had been forced on the rancheros, Anglo and Californio alike.[24]

One description, albeit an embellished one, of cattle-boom Los Angeles tells why the Californios delighted in the inflation. "The fact was, they were all getting rich," exclaimed Horace Bell. "The streets were thronged throughout the entire day with splendidly mounted and richly dressed caballeros, most of whom wore suits of clothes that cost all the way from $500 to $1,000, with saddle and horse trappings that cost even more than the above named sums. Of one of the Lugos, I remember, it was said his horse equipment cost over $2,000." José del Carmen Lugo led fifteen to twenty men against the Americans at the Chino battle during the revolt José María Flores led in late 1846. Now the Lugo family's experience of Yankee rule, if not their estimation of it, undoubtedly changed. What caballeros they were when the market for beef brought them undreamed-of wealth![25]

It should go without saying that the market brought even more wealth to those who brought it to California in the first place. "The business of the place was very considerable," Bell observed, "and all seemed to be doing a paying business." Their cows were herded north to feed miners too. A few Americans even began to plant oranges. William Wolfskill started an orchard in 1841, the year his daughter Juana was born. By the 1850s he grew two-thirds of the state total. Benjamin D. Wilson, who faced José del Carmen Lugo in battle at Rancho Chino, there expanded his orange groves, which the mission fathers had originally planted when his rancho was part of Mission San Gabriel lands.[26] The Yankees did well with this sudden influx of money, but, curiously enough, they caught California fever—a love of leisure.

Twenty years after the formal conquest of Los Angeles even Abel Stearns would earn the derision of his associates for "fussing with horses" and not paying enough attention to business. Now perhaps he was truly a don. John Forster, the Englishman who started with Stearns and came "to live in regal splendor" on former Mission San Gabriel lands, raced horses and gambled on them like the Californios. This is a

11. Don Vicente Lugo, a consummate caballero, in the finery that the inflation in the price of cattle during the Gold Rush has enabled him to buy. (Courtesy of the Seaver Center for Western History Research, Los Angeles County Museum.)

difficult matter, the relationship between environment and human activity. Richard Henry Dana, who coined the phrase *California fever*, acknowledged it as such. Sir George Simpson in his voyage of the early 1840s repeated Dana's sentiment when he wrote that "neither Dutchman nor Scotchman could retain their laborious habits, and still less could they communicate them to their children, in California." Wrote William Brewer of his trip in the early 1860s, "This is the climate for a lazy man, that [of New England] for labor, this for *dolce far niente*, that for action." Marveled a visitor from Chicago in 1939, "The climate has made me lazy—I'm still in a daze over the whole thing." Although there is certainly a relationship between climate and life-style, we must stop short of espousing meteorological determinism. Max Weber surely missed a variable in his analysis of the Protestant ethic and the spirit of capitalism, however. The conduct of business here differed indeed from that in New England. In the old days "a merchant sometimes entertained a neighbor with a game of cards, the host sitting on a chair at the window sill [the windowsills of the adobes were three to four feet wide] which served as the card table, and the guest on a box or barrel outside." Storekeepers had no compunction about closing up for a few hours for meals or "to meet in a friendly game of billiards." It is easy to see how those with California fever, an apparently widespread malady, would not act in a thrifty manner, especially in a time of massive influx of money.[27]

"The Yankee demand for beef made the cattle owners suddenly rich," noted Charles Nordhoff, "and they made haste to spend what they so easily got." Few people save money for the future during boom times, and the disaccumulationist Californios were the least likely to do so. Their present situation was rosy and they had no reason to look to the future with pessimism. After all, they had been joined to the United States, with its fabled prosperity. In response to the terrific demand for their cattle both Californio and Anglo rancheros added to their land and stock by going into debt, about which we shall hear much more shortly. These expanding ranchos needed more Indians to do the work. The racial labor system was thus perpetuated and even strengthened.[28]

Indians and the Despotism of Liberty

All the while that Anglo businessmen were marrying *hijas del país* and that Californios and Americans were warring over control of California, the rancho labor system remained fundamentally unchanged. Abel Stearns's account books after 1848 still listed *Sirvientes los alamitos* or *sirvientes pagados*. At the

Domínguez family's Rancho San Pedro some of the Indians worked for forty years, that is, through the Spanish, Mexican, and United States periods. Charles Nordhoff noted that "about San Bernardino the farm laborers are chiefly Indians." Henry Dalton's Rancho Azusa provides another example. In his diary he monotonously recorded "Indians hauling," or "Indians making a fence." His biographer acknowledged:

Of course there was always work to do, but the hired hands took care of most of the ranch chores. Even harvest season presented no labor problem, for Dalton obtained help for harvest seasons in a unique way. Ever since 1846 he had maintained a friendly relationship with the Cahuilla Indians near San Bernardino and Temecula. Beginning in the 1850s, every time wine making approached in October he would send a messenger to a chief of the Cahuillas with presents, sometimes a stovepipe hat adorned with red ribbons, or a blue coat with pants trimmed in red, and a few yards of brightly colored calico cloth for his spouse. The messenger would advise the chief that it was time to commence the vintage and that he was in need of help to pick the grapes and make the wine. In a few days the chief with twenty or thirty of his people would arrive at Azusa where the people would go to work in the fields while the chief received a royal welcome as guest of the Daltons.

We see from this description that not only did the assumptions about who should work—Indians—remain unaltered after United States annexation but so did the means of attracting Indian workers. The result was the same at American ranches as it had been at Californio ranchos and at missions— a seigneurial life-style: "This left the Dalton family plenty of time for social and recreational activities."[29]

Most account books still extant are from Anglo ranches; in keeping with the accumulationist personality, Anglo ranchers saved old records. The story of Manuel Domínguez provides a telling comparison with Anglo ways. According to the chronicler of Rancho San Pedro, "It is said that Manuel Domínguez, even when well advanced in years, personally supervised the loading of the stock." He was, however, no double-entry bookkeeper: "Family records indicate that Don Manuel always carried a chamois money pouch, and as each animal came up the ramp into the cattle-car, the agent was required to drop a twenty-dollar gold piece into the pouch." This way of doing business, though not without charm, does not leave behind records. But there is no reason to believe that the labor system on Rancho San Pedro, or any other rancho still under Hispanic control, differed in structure from that revealed in the account books and letters of the Anglo ranchers. The Indians received payment in kind as well as some cash. Stearns's account books for the 1850s show that he paid such people as "Luis Yndito," "José Angel Yndito," and "Nicolas Yndio Baquero" in shoes, pants, sugar, cinnamon, and some cash (his account books for the 1840s and 1860s show similar payments). Indians like "Nasario de Temecula" and "Juan de Dios" received similar goods in exchange for their labors at Rancho Santa Ana del Chino. Cave Johnson Couts of Rancho Guajome paid his "servants" largely in money but also in aguardiente. A bond that was not chattel nor feudal (Indian workers were free to come and go) nor typical of a free labor market attached these Indians to the various ranchos.[30]

In fact, this system was anything but a free labor market. In the first place, the continuing destruction of the Indians' traditional cultural and productive ways, not to mention destruction of their native environment, left them no choice but to attach themselves to someone else for their subsistence. Beyond this basic reality of virtually all Indian peoples on the continent, however, lie the specific mechanisms that bound the Indians to the ranchos in the decades following the annexation of California. As we have seen, many Indians lived semipermanently on the ranchos in their rancherías. Others lived in town or on land set aside for them by the ayuntamiento or came down from the hills to work on an itinerant basis. But in April 1850 an act of the California legislature changed the form, though certainly not the substance, of the relationship between Indian laborer and rancho employer. "An Act for the Government and Protection of the Indians" gave rancheros several new tools to bind their workers to the newly prosperous cattle ranches. Article 6 stated that "Indian testimony [is] not allowed when against a white person." Closing all legal recourse to Indians freed the whites and gente de razón to use the rest of this act for their own benefit. The reader should have no problem visualizing the bonanza that articles 14 and 20 of the act of government gave the rancheros:

ARTICLE 14: When an Indian is convicted of an offense punishable by fine, any white person may by consent of the Justice of the Peace give bond, conditioned for the payment of said fine and costs, and in such case the Indian shall be compelled to work for the person so bailing, until he has discharged or cancelled the fine against him, providing the persons bailing shall treat the Indian humanely, clothe and feed him, [etc.].

ARTICLE 20: Any Indian able to work, and support himself in some honest calling, not having wherewithall to maintain himself, *who shall be found loitering and strolling about, or frequenting public places where liquors are sold, begging or living an immoral or profligate course of life* shall be liable to be arrested on the complaint of any resident citizen of the county and brought to any Justice of the Peace . . . and . . . satisfied that he is a vagrant . . . he shall make out a warrant . . . authorizing and requiring the officer having him in charge or custody, to hire out such a vagrant within twenty-four hours, to the highest bidder . . . for any term not exceeding four months [emphasis in original].

These articles were both a remarkable description of the condition of the Indians of California, and, through the criminalization of their quotidian activities, a solution to the labor needs of the rapidly expanding ranchos. The words of this legislation are rather astounding, particularly in the light of the free-labor ideology the Americans brought with them: the old peonage system of the Californios was giving way to a forced-labor system of the conquerors. That August the Los Angeles City Council passed an ordinance laying out the manner "that such a number of prisoners will be auctioned off to the highest bidder for private service."[31]

If we accept that after the secularization of the missions the Indians were left in a shepherdless condition, then the old peonage system of the ranchos had some benefits for the ex-neophytes. Whereas the mission system relied as often as not on force, the Indians attached themselves to the ranchos more freely. They could leave at any time, unlike at the missions, from which most of them fled after secularization. Between the rancheros' seigneurialism and the interdependence of all persons on the ranchos, this form of peonage could, and sometimes did, provide the Indians a transition from their aboriginal state to the dominant ways of the Spanish and the Hispano-Americans.

The old rancho system was not complex; it gave immediate, concrete, and comprehensible rewards of commodities. (Of course, the most craved commodity, alcohol, proved utterly destructive.) In both the mission and Anglo free-labor systems, discipline had to come from within the individual Indian. But in the usual course of events, force had to be used on the Anglo ranches. George Harwood Phillips quotes one visitor's description of the Warner ranch: "The labor is performed by California Indians, who are stimulated to work by three dollars per month and repeated floggings." On the old ranchos no new social consciousness or worldview had to be forced on them and internalized. No soldiers or priests stopped their indigenous cultural, religious, and sexual practices on the rancherías. Their families and clans could remain more united there than at the missions, which purposefully broke them up. Old or feeble Indians could remain on the rancho until they died; at least such was the case at the Vallejo rancho. For the women, the household tasks they had to perform differed more in form than in content from the old tribal ways. This system was easier for the Indians than what had come before in the missions and came later on the Anglo ranches. The proof lies in the fact that keeping them on the ranchos required neither a military guard nor an "Act for the Government and Protection of the Indians."[32]

The ambivalence of the Anglo-Americans toward the Indians differed from that of the priests and Californios. The priests felt both optimism that the savages could be made reasonable as well as disquietude over their apparent inability to do so. The dons derived both psychic benefits and cheap labor from the Indians at the same time as they feared and hated these people, whom they perceived as beasts. Both priests and rancheros needed the Indians, despite the contribution of each to their destruction, to maintain their social and economic institutions; and both accepted a notion of reciprocity towards their vassals.

The Anglo-Americans, with their particular conception of liberty—each man a government unto himself—were "much more engrossed with our private interests and concerns than with any of a public character," as Eliza Farnham noted. The natural law of the marketplace, rather than reciprocal obligations, would take care of things. Given their conceptions of manifest destiny and progress, the Anglo-Americans envisioned a new fate for the Indians: they would have to be kept under guard until the natural unfolding of history relegated the Indians to the dustbin or exterminated them. The Los Angeles *Star* of March 13, 1852, in a remarkable combination of racism, laissez faire, and gunboat diplomacy stated:

To place upon our most fertile soil the most degraded race of aborigines upon the North American Continent, to invest them with the rights of sovereignty and to teach them that they are to be treated as powerful and independent nations, is planting the seeds of future disaster and ruin. . . . We hope that the general government will let us alone—that it will neither undertake to feed, settle or remove Indians amongst whom we in the South reside, and that they will leave everything just as it now exists, except affording us the protection which two or three cavalry companies would give.

This attitude derived from the combination of the American sense of mission and its racism.[33] Because Indian history bears such a crucial relationship to the Hispanic history of California, we must now turn to an analysis of Indian-Anglo relations to see how the Indian story further evolved.

D. A. Shaw, a forty-niner who stayed on in the Golden State, saw the providential errand of his nation clearly: "To wrest an extensive domain from semi-barbarism; to reveal its unlimited treasures; to open up new avenues of commerce; to form a progressive, enlightened and liberal government; to herald the advent of new social and religious conditions; these made a commendable field for noble endeavor." The Indians from Massachusetts to California had either proved incapable of joining, or simply gotten in the way of, this progressive

juggernaut. "Our flag," Shaw continued, "the emblem of freedom, floats over millions of our fellowmen in distant lands
and islands of the sea, to lead them on and up to a better
and nobler condition of physical and intellectual life."[34]

Yet the Indians, the first over whom the flag flew, stood
at the brink of doom. Those whom Shaw and other Anglo-
Americans saw in California were clearly beyond help, destined to vanish one way or another. Traveler D. L. Philips
observed in 1876, "The women are very much like the men,
almost wholly given to a vagabond life, swarming about the
towns and, as generally and openly stated, utterly oblivious
to the obligations of the marriage relation. The Indians . . .
are simply doomed, by their laziness and vices, to early extinction." "They will disappear from the face of the earth as
the whites extend over the country," stated the United States
Indian agent for California, T. Butler King, in 1850. Again
combining progress with violence, King added that "a very
considerable military force will be necessary, however, to
protect the emigrants in the northern and southern portions
of the territory." Governor Peter H. Burnett in his annual
message of January 1851 to the California Senate summed up
the American attitude: "That a war of extermination will continue to be waged between the two races until the Indian
race become extinct, must be expected; while we cannot an-
ticipate this result with but painful regret, the inevitable destiny of the race is beyond the power and wisdom of man to
avert." Sometimes they lamented it and sometimes they did
not, but the Anglo-Americans assumed the inevitability of the
Indians' demise.[35]

Whereas the priests had the Devil to blame for the Indians'
failure to grasp European civilization, the Anglos relied on
racist conceptions of Indian inferiority to account for the ob-
stinacy of Indian ways in the face of progress. The next governor, John Bigler, wrote that "the acts of these Savages are
sometimes signalized by a ferocity worthy of the cannibals of
the South Sea. They seem to cherish an instinctive hatred
toward the white race, and this is a principle of their nature
which neither time nor vicissitude can impair." Let us turn
to D. L. Phillips to neatly conclude this discussion of Anglo-

American attitudes toward the California Indians with a rhetorical question: "Why, then, make such an outcry about ejecting a lot of worthless Indians from lands which they never owned and never intended to own?"[36]

Indians may have been worthless in his enterprising estimation, but somebody had to do the work, and it was not going to be any of those people quoted in the preceding paragraphs. Government policy, Anglo-American assumptions about culture and race, and the need to find a tractable and cheap supply of labor meshed and reinforced one another. Hence Anglo-Americans perceived no contradiction between their professed ideology of liberty and the law they concocted legalizing, facilitating, and even encouraging servitude. In *Common Sense Applied to the Immigrant Question* the California Immigrant Union stated in 1869: "Let us leave them [the colored races] to the workings of the law of laissez faire. Our work is to try and fill this vast empty territory with the men and women of those liberty-loving races *whose descendants we are ourselves* and in whose hands, those of their children, can be safely entrusted the custody of American institutions" (emphasis in original). In the meantime, however, the "liberty-loving races" would accustom themselves to having other races do their work for them.[37]

The California legislature of 1850 did not originate this sort of servitude, of course. I previously noted the old practice of putting Indians arrested for drunkenness to work on the zanja or the church. Now, however, "Los Angeles had its slave mart as well as New Orleans and Constantinople," as Horace Bell declared. When the Indians finished work on Saturday, the ranch laborers would be paid in aguardiente or in cash, which they exchanged for the swill. They then drank themselves into a stupor and spent that evening and all day Sunday in complete debauch. Then the town marshal and his special Indian deputies ("The deputies were sober because they had been kept in jail all day for that very purpose") literally swept them off the streets and into the jail. On Monday morning, in accordance with article 20, the marshal auctioned off the now sullen and sick Indians to the local rancheros, both Anglo and Californio. "They would be sold for a week," Bell continued, "and bought up by the vineyard men and others at prices ranging from one to three dollars, one-third of which was to be paid to the peon at the end of the week, which debt due for well performed labor would invariably be paid in aguardiente, and the Indian would be happy until the following Monday morning having passed through another Saturday night and Sunday's saturnalia of debauchery and bestiality." The crusading ideology of liberty and prosperity of those who brought market capitalism make the contradictions between liberalism and racism all the more apparent and profound.[38]

Local authorities attempted to curb liquor sales. According to the Los Angeles *Star* of January 4, 1853, "It does not appear that the Liquor Ordinance has done much good so far. It went into effect . . . over one month ago, and still the Indians get their liquor the same as ever. Negro Alley is the principal resort of these Indians, especially on the Sabbath, when the little money they have been able to get the rest of the week, is spent for liquor." In a not unusual occurrence Vicente Guerrero and Birardo Sunega were arrested and fined for selling alcohol to Indians in March 1855. Very few other business opportunities were available to Mexicans in Anglo Los Angeles. A habit had been formed that was not to be broken, and hardly anyone genuinely served as a model of more temperate behavior: "It has long been a practice of the Indians of this city to get drunk on Saturday night. Their ambition seems to be to earn sufficient money through the week to treat themselves handsomely at the close of it. In this they only follow the white example."[39]

Indeed, it was a remarkably besotted town, this City of the Angels. Plenty of scummy whites had come west in the years following the American conquest, and they mixed their drunkenness with violence. When it came to behavior while inebriated, the Indians were "seldom quarrelsome," reported the *Star*, "and, more especially, and unlike some white men, whom the Marshal is too discreet to arrest, they do not[,] when drunk, brandish knives and pistols through the streets." The Indians did not remain completely passive about this "slave mart," as the following incident in September 1853 attests: "[The] worthy Marshal and his energetic assistant last Sunday opened the ponderous gates of the prison and locked up twenty five Indians, all supposed to be drunk; but he had no sooner turned his back than, crash! went the door, and the Indians scattered in every direction, up every street in town. Jack swore, and the Marshal, utterly confounded at the impossibility of heading off so many fugitives, stood solemnly silent." Far more typically, however, the *Star* then reported that "an Indian named Bacilio, was found dead near the zanja . . . this morning. Justice Dryden and a jury sat on the body: verdict, 'death from intoxification, or the visitation of God.' Bacilio was a Christian Indian." "Many are aged and infirm," reported the *Star* of January 18, 1855, "and are left by the government to drag out a miserable existence, living on roots and acorns when they can be obtained, but who are fast disappearing to the silent grave for the want of food and clothing."[40] To their final demise we shall return later.

Indenture more permanently attached Indians to the ranches and their owners. For example, Cave Johnson Couts petitioned the county judge to " 'bind and put-out' to me by indenture, the said Indians, the males as apprentices to husbandry, and the females as apprentices to housewifery." All he had to show was that "said Indians are vagrant Indians having no settled habitation or means of livelihood, and have not placed themselves under the protection of any white person." This not being difficult, he and his wife, the former Ysidora Bandini, had some more indentured servants. In 1854 two Indians, "Jesus Delgado and Paula, his wife, or woman," stated that they had "of their own accord, turned over a small Indian girl named Sasaria, to Doña Ysidora Bandini de Couts, to serve as her servant until . . . the age of 18 or 21 years. Said girl . . . is an orphan child, and mother has the right to dispose of her. This is intended for the benefit of the child (now six years old) and for and in consideration of the sum of fifty dollars to therein have paid." Another petition reads, "An Indian woman named Jacinta . . ., of her own free and voluntary will hereby turns over and binds her son José Antonio, to Doña Ysidora Couts, for the period of three years . . . to take care of, and teach to work: he is to be clothed and fed, and Jacinta to receive thirty dollars each year." On another occasion, in 1858, Couts successfully petitioned the court to return "Francisco, an Indian boy" whom his wife "had the care and control of" and had been "enticed away by others"; the court returned him. We cannot know how widespread this practice was. Couts no doubt tried to make a difficult social situation into a mutually rewarding work system through these indentures. "My only object, as you know," he reported to the Indian agent, Benjamin Wilson, "was to regulate the San Luis Indians." Probably no one objected to this method, despite the child buying and family breaking, because, as Couts asserted, "they are well regulated."[41]

All this prosperity seemed simply for the taking in bounteous California, even to wage laborers. Yet in the view of Protestant Anglos the Indians did not do anything about it except lie around and engage in dubious pleasures. Customarily Indians worked strenuously, as the seasons, the cycles of nature, and their needs demanded. To succeed as a laborer, however, one had to regulate one's work daily by the calendar and the clock or else save up enough money and goods to tide oneself over during times of idleness. The Indians did not make this transition; instead, they transferred their old work habits to the new situation. Those who had been missionized, Sherburne Cook explains, "came to confuse economically valuable labor with duress and punishment, an effect which further intensified Indian aversion to labor per se." These ways all the more firmly convinced the prosperous and enterprising Yankee Protestants of the Indians' cultural and racial inferiority. "The Indians generally are well made and of good stature," acknowledged Edwin Bryant. But "they appear to be indolent and averse from labor of any kind, unless combined with their sports and amusements, when they are as reckless of fatigue and danger as any class of men I have seen." "They use the bow and arrow, but are said to be too lazy and effeminate to make successful hunters," reported Indian agent T. Butler King to the secretary of state in Washington. To him, they "seemed the lowest grade of human beings. . . . They do not appear to have the slightest inclination to cultivate the soil, nor do they even attempt it."[42]

Occasionally the quality of Indian labor found favor with

Anglo-Americans. "These people, of whom California has still several thousand, are a very useful class," wrote Charles Nordhoff. "They trim the vines; they plough; they do the household 'chores'; they are shepherds, and trusty ones too, vaqueros, and helpers generally." However, with the notable exception of the skilled vaqueros, the American ranchers and travelers generally regarded them as miserably indolent, tediously inefficient, and frustratingly unreliable. They apparently had achieved neither reason nor discipline. King reported that "many of those now attached to families seem to be faithful and intelligent. But those who are at all in a wild or uncultivated state are most degraded objects of filth and idleness." The Indians were troublesome but not mystifying because of the way the Anglo-Americans neatly fit them into their worldview: they would die out, but in the meantime Indian shiftlessness, which, "being brought into competition with that class of labor that would prove most beneficial to the country, checks immigration, and retards the prosperity of the country," would have to be suffered.[43] Fear, however, combined with frustration and anger at the Indians' unwillingness to accede to the new ways that the conquering American mission brought to California.

Desperate Indians

Nearly one hundred years of foreign intrusions and attempts to assimilate the Indians of California had succeeded only in breaking down their traditional forms of social organization, mortally infecting them, and addicting them to alcohol. Moreover, beginning in 1769 the various settlements of California choked their food supply. The Indians had to rely on activities that the new landholders perceived as criminal simply to eat, unless they joined the labor market. A letter from Cave Couts to John Forster, both married to *hijas del país*, nicely displays the fearfulness that Indian social disorganization produced in the minds of the whites and the Californios: "When I arrived home the other night I found that there was a general drunk[;] and the family were in such a grand scare I found some difficulty to induce them to open the doors to let me in . . . and the following night under the same wine cellar influence the smoke house was burnt up with all the bacon."[44] However, the battles over food—raiding, in other words— brought the most pervasive fear to the non-Indians of all of California.

Many residents of California had looked forward to having the Yankees deal with the Indians. The United States Army had already established a reputation for proficient, and bloody, repression of native peoples. The Indian reservation, a key aspect of government policy and strategy, came to the Pacific Coast with the formal transfer of California to United States jurisdiction. With the reservation the Indians' territory would be reduced, thus giving more land over to settlers; the provisioning of Indians with food and clothing would expand the market for the white settlers' products; and the natives supposedly would be trained in sedentary farming and in handicrafts. This program would both replace their old ways of hunting and nomadism, which brought them into conflict with the whites, and prepare them for eventual entry into the conquerors' world.

More often, though, the segregated reservation only accustomed the Indians to dependency—the model ultimately adopted, through ghettoization, for virtually all resourceless people of color in the United States. The system involved both force and adaptation. The destruction of the Indians' ecology and the United States cavalry forced Indians onto reservations. But as Sherburne Cook points out, "If the native population can in any way maintain itself in conflict with the new civilization by forcing that civilization to support it, then the native population has succeeded measurably in adapting itself to its altered environment." In other words, it may be cheaper to feed them for a year than to fight them for a week. The establishment of the Tejon reservation near Santa Barbara, for example, seems to have solved the problems the de la Guerras had with raiding. Responding immediately to Indian attacks, the federal government organized several such reservations in the interior of southern California in early 1852.

The state legislature, however, fearing that such reservations would take up valuable land, prevailed on the two senators from California to stall ratification.[45]

There had been conflict over food between Indians and the various interlopers in California since at least 1769. Consistently the settlers most desired the fertile valleys and rich river bottoms the Indians occupied. Now the Anglo-Americans who sought prosperity on California soil or whom the Gold Rush had frustrated pushed into Indian habitats in the interior of the state, not solely on the coast, as the Spanish had done. The Indians naturally resisted the incursions, and the ensuing violence concomitantly pushed them further and further into the barren lands of the interior. Some estimate that fully one-half of the remaining California Indians died in this brief frenzy of greed and violence against the land and native peoples. To rid the land of Indians, all of the interlopers since 1769 had resorted to destroying the Indians' foodstuffs. Hunger pushed them to greater desperation. Then came the cattle, which grazed on the grasses from which the Indians had previously gathered seeds, and hogs, which ate their acorns. (One wonders whether or not this intrusion of hogs had anything to do with Cave Couts's bacon getting "burnt up.") Both on the reservation, where the government provided food, and on the ranchos, as payment in kind for their labor, sometimes the Indians made this forced transition from consuming their traditional foods to eating the whites' flour. Other times they stalked the ranchos on their old lands for cattle. This situation as regards food is the fundamental context of California Indian history in the 1850s.[46]

Thus, various pressures from interlopers broke down the old linkages that had united Indian societies, particularly among Indians thrown together in the missions and then released to the rancho jacales or to the squalor of Los Angeles. Battles with soldiers over land or the capture of neophytes, shrinking food sources, and disease continually disrupted those Indians who remained outside the formal control of the interlopers. New forms of social organization arose from the scattering of the old lineage systems. Especially on the coast, but in the interior as well, remnants of old groupings united under the leadership of new headmen. Sometimes even ex-neophytes, these new chiefs were usually men of some importance in the old times or descendants of leading lineages. There emerged, in other words, new social and political organizations.

These new leaders seem to have had an impact primarily on the affairs of the interior. They exercised dominion over the people of particular territories rather than over kin groups, though many clans still survived in fragmented form. These chiefs negotiated with other Indian groups and with the whites, as we saw at Rancho Azusa; organized their villages and appointed other officials; and heard and judged the disputes of their followers, including delivering punishment. Now the new outsiders had to treat with powerful headmen who were increasingly familiar with the white man's ways. In comparison with the diffuse political organization the Spanish had engaged, this new structure allowed the Indians to defend their land more formidably.[47]

Juan Antonio of the Cahuillas and Manuel Cota of the Luiseños rose to such leadership positions. Juan Antonio, and each one of the twenty village captains under him, ruled strictly over the approximately three thousand Cahuillas. Juan Antonio, not a hereditary chief, assumed power through his own political strategizing among the Cahuillas, the Californios, and the whites. Many of the Cahuillas lived on and around the Lugos' Rancho San Bernardino, and they allied with these Californios against other marauding Indians. They were exceptional, however, with respect to their relations with the Californios. Having formed into larger tribal units once their traditional bands had collapsed, these people maintained their resentment of those who had displaced them from their lands. Especially the Cupeños and Luiseños continued to raid ranchos and missions. These ex-neophytes looked favorably on the Americanos until they met with the army, and until San Diego County ruled in 1850 that they should be taxed. To the Indians, this action was as gratuitous as it was inexplicable.[48]

The most famous, or notorious, of these chiefs was the Cupeño Antonio Garra, an ex-neophyte of Mission San Luis Rey. According to George Harwood Phillips's narration, the taxation of Garra's people and the increasing number of avaricious whites heading to the goldfields by the southern route provoked Garra to attempt the annihilation of the American [but not Mexican] trespassers at San Bernardino, Los Angeles, and San Diego. In 1851 Garra, seeking a grand confederation, began contacting the leaders of ex-neophyte communities and area chieftains at San Pascual, Santa Isabel, San Luis Rey, Temecula, and as far north as Tulare and as far south as Baja California. Juan Antonio seems to have considered joining but did not. The Luiseños remained generally loyal to the Americans, though the Los Coyotes Cahuillas, led by Chapuli, joined the insurrection. Warner's rancho was shot up, but not much else actually came of the uprising except for an increase of fear on the part of the whites. In December Juan Antonio asked Garra for a meeting, at which the rebel leader was treacherously taken prisoner. A small skirmish at Los Coyotes canyon on December 20, at which Chapuli was killed, marked the end of this rebellion. Garra was executed in January 1852.[49]

The revolt, an unthreatening episode in retrospect, terrified the residents of southern California, who understood their own vulnerability but exaggerated the Indians' military strength. Garra claimed to have commanded no more than thirty or forty men with guns, but it was assumed that at least four hundred to five hundred well-armed, vengeful Indians, with thousands more in reserve, targeted the poorly garrisoned whites. "It is supposed," declared the *Star* of December 6, 1851, "that all the southern Indians are in a plot to massacre the whites."[50]

Continuing Indian raids after the Garra revolt accounted in part for their fears. The treaty with the Cahuillas, Luiseños, and Serranos that formally ended hostilities and initiated their relocation into reservations promised the Indians food. Provisions were not forthcoming, however, and the Cahuillas and virtually all the tribes with any vitality commenced raiding to feed themselves. "It is quite likely," Cook notes for all of the California Indians in the 1850s, "that on many occasions whole villages and tribes were saved from literal starvation by the livestock which they were able to steal from the whites."[51]

The whites, however, thought another uprising was at hand.

The local papers were filled with the news of Indian raids. Tulare Indians got thirty horses from the remains of Mission San Gabriel, reported a typical *Star* article of June 26, 1852, though a posse got them all back. Another Juan Antonio, a former neophyte of San Fernando who according to reports almost magically could break out of jail, was alleged to have stolen many horses from the area around his old mission. "Most of the horses were used for food," Cleland points out; "in some instances, however, the stolen animals were sold to Mormon settlers or even California-bound emigrants." In sum, those approximately five thousand Indians whom neither the labor market and its alcohol nor the ranchos had ensnared— those still "in the wild," as the local whites would have it— faced hunger, more white encroachments, and then more hunger. They managed as best they could under the leadership of Juan Antonio and Manuel Cota, who tried to accommodate and get what they could for their people from the United States government. Most of the time that strategy failed and, simply to stay alive, they purloined cattle and horses to supplement what the meager soil they were given would grow. Disease continued to ravage all of them. (In February 1863, after having sweated in a *temescal* and then plunging himself into cold water in an attempt to rid himself of the affliction, Juan Antonio died of smallpox.)[52] Obviously, the American conquest did not solve the tensions between Indians and Anglo-Americans. Conflict over land and lifeways intensified as it persisted in different, but no less tragic, forms. Leaving the story of the Indians for a while, let us now examine the consequences of the American invasion of the Californio lands.

Land and the Conflict of Legal Cultures

The war and the formal transference of sovereignty had a profound effect on Hispanic society in California. After all, Americans had waged war against Mexicans. Americans inside and outside the government coveted the wealth of California. The Gold Rush only further encouraged Anglo-American visions of bonanza capitalism. They considered the territory to be their just reward for bringing liberty and prosperity to the once-slumbering northern lands of troubled Mexico. "When I came," recalled one of the city's first businessmen, "Los Angeles was a sleepy, ambitionless adobe village with very little promise for the future. . . . We possessed however, even in that distant day, one asset, intangible it is true, but as valuable as it was intangible—the spirit popularly called 'Western,' but which, after all, was largely the pith of transferred Eastern enterprise." The editor of the *Semi-Weekly News* opined in 1868, "As we stand on the bank of the river and gaze over the fine fields with their teeming population, we cannot but wonder at the goodness of God and the power of man to redeem and civilize a country. A few years ago, the vast tract of land we now so much admire, was only a little Rancho, uninhabited save by a few vaqueros." America, for those of the enterprising spirit and the accumulationist bent, represented a place not merely to live in but also to get rich in. This new, far western region was to be no exception.[53]

America needed open land to maintain its vision of individual liberty and thus its uniqueness. Without it its eastern cities would crowd with unemployed, who might turn to demagogues and mob action for redress. Then the nation with the special mission would become like authoritarian Europe, where in the revolutions of 1848 the unemployed rabble took to the streets. With land available in the West, though, resourceless people could move there and set themselves up as independent freeholders. "How many Countrymen of mine," wrote Alex Forbes to Abel Stearns about California, "who are jostling one another for room at home, might live happily in those fertile but uncultivated plains you describe!" Open land, in other words, guaranteed not only prosperity but also social mobility and, in turn, political stability and liberty.[54]

This compelling idea never came to much for the underclasses. The urban unemployed had neither the agricultural skills nor the material wherewithal to establish themselves as farmers in the West. (For this reason, the Homestead Act of 1862, which embodied this concept, largely failed.) Moreover, the liberty to speculate in real estate usually meant that all the good land was monopolized. Those who controlled capital at the start often wound up with all the wealth, while army soldiers, recruited from the underclasses, pacified the natives, who resisted the appropriation of lands. But these notions did motivate people in the state and the culture as a whole to acquire lands. Bancroft describes what I have termed *bonanza capitalism*: "The fever was raging in Washington as well as Sacramento. It was not of 500 or 1,000 rancheros, living on stock-farms owned by themselves and their fathers, and of little value by American standards, that the senate was thinking, but of a marvellous land of gold-mines, great towns, and limitless prospects; not of a quiet, pastoral people, but a horde of speculators, hungry for gold and power and land." In California pastoral dons with Indian vaqueros inhabited huge tracts of land on which they did not do much other than supply hides and tallow, feed themselves, and maintain their seigneurial life-style.[55]

The Californios soon found themselves and their ways placed outside the new Anglo-American laws. The conflict between Spanish law, based in Roman law, and United States law, based in English common law, derived not only from juridical philosophy. When one culture, assuming that its own laws ensure justice and social tranquility, imposes them on another culture, the latter sees that very same legal structure as the mechanism that excludes its people from justice and the material rewards of the newly dominant society. The law, in other words, has been for many the means not of justice but of oppression. In 1850, for example, the California legislature passed a bill establishing the so-called foreign miners' tax so that the state could pay off its debts by regaining some of the wealth that "foreigners" (obviously a vague and relative term at this moment in California history) took out in gold. It also provided physical protection from attack for "foreigners" once they had paid the monthly fee of twenty dollars for a license. Those at whom the lawmakers aimed this legislation perceived it as a discriminatory and arbitrary action and objected strenuously—usually privately but sometimes publicly. The act had the effect of giving license to American miners to eject Mexican (including Californio), Chinese, and Chilean miners through mob action. The reason for this expulsion goes beyond xenophobia. One Californio miner, the most renowned citizen of Hispanic Los Angeles, Antonio Coronel, recalled that "the reason for most of the antipathy against the Spanish race was that the greater portion was composed of Sonorans who were men accustomed to prospecting and who consequently achieved quicker, richer results—such as the Californios had already attained by having arrived first and acquiring understanding of this same art." T. Butler King railed that "more than fifteen thousand foreigners, mostly Mexicans and Chilenos, came in *armed bands* into the mining district, bidding defiance to all the opposition, and finally carrying out of the country some twenty millions of dollars' worth of gold dust." King knew for whom this gold was destined: "[It] belongs *by purchase* to the people of the United States." (The United States formally paid Mexico $15 million for California, Arizona, New Mexico, and much of Colorado, Utah, and Nevada.) "If not excluded by law," thundered King, "they will return and recommence the work of plunder." The legal formality of payment enabled King to put Mexicans outside, and his culture inside, any norms, as laws, regarding "plunder."[56]

Coronel described how, in anticipation of such legislation, "one Sunday, notices appeared in writing in Los Pinos and in several places, that anyone who was not an American citizen must abandon the place within twenty-four hours and that he who did not comply would be obliged to by force. This was supported by a gathering of armed men, ready to make that warning effective." Such armed groups, "the major part under the influence of liquor," terrorized "foreigners"; in one case a mob falsely accused two unfortunates of theft, tied their arms behind their backs, loaded them on a cart, and publicly hanged them. After many others had fled or been chased out, merchants who had initially favored the act found that the gold the "foreigners" were alleged to have removed they actually spent in their stores. The odious act was repealed only a year after passage, though the consequences of expelling nearly everyone except white Americans from the goldfields of the north continued. "Daily, though," Coronel continued, "the weakest were dislodged from the digging by the strongest." The law never protected miners of color; it

only supported efforts to exclude everyone from economic opportunities except the conquerors. The ultimate result, in other
words, was the expulsion of non-Americans—Mexicans and
Chinese especially were singled out—from the mining opportunities of California through apparently state-sanctioned
mass violence against people of color. The Mexicans ejected
from the goldfields either headed south, where they merged
with their compatriots in the so-called cow counties, or crossed
the new border into Mexico. They carried with them, along
with the few belongings with which they escaped, a profound
hatred and fear of Yankees.[57]

Different notions of land tenure produced the most consequential disputes between Californios and Anglos. Let us
recall the mechanism by which Californios received grants and
their notion of what entitled one to land. Such markers as a
"bullocks head on a bluff," a "clump of trees," and so on described the boundaries of the old grants, such as the Lugos'
Rancho San Antonio. The validity of the land tenure of such
ranchos derived as much from occupancy and tradition as from
written documents. Entitlement (granted sometimes to women
as well as men under Spanish law) to the land came from
living, working, and maintaining, if not extending, the royal
domains of the Spanish king. In the Mexican period, when
most of the land was granted, the conniving Californios acquired the former mission lands in spite of the desire of many
liberal Mexican officials to encourage small freeholds. The
governors did sign legal deeds to the Californios converting
the land into private property. Vague boundaries, however,
still predominated. This situation framed the Californio rancheros' encounter with United States land law and indeed with
the whole culture of Anglo land tenure.

The Land Act of 1851 wreaked havoc on the rancheros'
claims. It created a three-person commission to which all titles of the Spanish and Mexican eras had to be submitted for
validation. The problems for the rancheros lay less in any biases
against them on the part of the commissioners than in the
biases of the law itself. The commission proceeded from the
assumption that all titles were invalid until proved otherwise.
This policy put an enormous burden on the Californios, who

did not understand the workings of a system based on common law or even the language in which it was implemented. Claims often rested on long-forgotten or misplaced written deeds. Usually the courts did not allow the recollections of eyewitnesses to entitlement; but even when they did, claims could be thrown out on technicalities, and there were successful court challenges to boundaries established only by custom. Even a claim that was perfectly in order could cost a Californio a good deal of land. Except for merchants, Californios had little cash on hand and had to sell land and cattle, or mortgage land, to pay legal fees. That the hearings took place in San Francisco only increased the difficulties of the cow-county rancheros. The Land Act effectively dispossessed Californios of approximately 40 percent of their lands held before 1846. In the contradictory American tradition of liberty, speculators with cash and shrewdness, not small farmers usually, grabbed the lands.[58]

Article 9 of the Treaty of Guadalupe-Hidalgo declared that Mexicans "shall be maintained and protected in the free enjoyment of their liberty and property." Secretary of State James Buchanan said to those nervous about the protections Mexicans would have for their property, "It is our glory that no human power exists in this country which can deprive one individual of his property without his consent and transfer it to another." The massive alienation of Californio lands, and their transfer to others, obviously fell outside the letter and spirit of the treaty and American respect for private property.[59]

A number of factors produced this ruination of many of the ranchos. One was greed. Americans fought the Mexican War to get some of Mexico. Once the Americans won the war, they were not about to allow Mexicans to remain on land they believed now belonged to them. They saw it as their manifest destiny to bring progress and civilization to this land held by indolent Catholics of a different and inferior race. Many came west as forty-niners, and they generally found disappointment in the goldfields; only a few struck it rich. These Americans, believing they had a right, as the yeomanry of a noble democratic tradition, to a farm and to prosperity, looked to acquire farms in bounteous California from the Californios, who indeed monopolized the best tillage with relatively unproductive cattle ranches. Particularly in the north, they squatted on lands they knew were in difficult litigation, compounding the troubles of the rancheros. Out of this situation the lawyers and speculators got much of the land in the areas that had drawn the most immigrants. The earnest efforts of frustrated democratic fortune seekers to gain a freehold proved only slightly more fruitful than their labor in the mines and goldfields. This greed for land, inflamed by the lawyers, would catch up to the rancheros in the south, though there their own profligate ways led in part to their undoing, as we shall see shortly.

To say the least, Anglo-American land law did not work for the Californios in the way that Secretary Buchanan extolled. "The practical working of the law was oppressive and ruinous," stated Bancroft. "They were virtually robbed by the government which was bound to protect them."[60] The accuracy of his description of the effects of the Land Act of 1851 and his condemnation of it do not replace the need to analyze why the law worked as it did. Having discussed the motive of greed, we need to follow through with a fuller analysis of the conflict of legal cultures. In so doing, we will better understand, in particular, the land and labor situation and other legal matters affecting Hispanic and Indian peoples and, in general, the way that the legal system reflected and illuminated, and framed and affected, Anglo ascendancy in their newly won Southwest. The history of the Mexican War and the transfer of territory and wealth did not end with the signing of the Treaty of Guadalupe-Hidalgo. Because the legal system figured so prominently in this phase, it is important to analyze that factor thoroughly.

The Criminalization of
the Mexican People

The legal system helped the Americans exclude Mexicans from economic opportunities, thus forcing them into dependency on wage labor and then forcibly pacifying them if they resisted. Generally criminalizing them provided the means to this end. The functioning of the law ensured that the growth and development of southern California's productive wealth would be an Americano affair. This is not to say that Los Angeles was an orderly, law-abiding town before the Yankees arrived, but the situation did change, not necessarily for the better, after 1848. A variety of newcomers came from the east and the south to Los Angeles in the years immediately following the conquest, and they did not like each other. Fired up by the war sentiment, contemptuous of Mexicans so easily defeated in 1846–47, and carrying with them Anglo-American notions about people of color, the Yankees saw no reason not to dispossess Mexicans of what little they had. Those who had been cholos in the years before the conquest now were called greasers and bore the brunt of Anglo animosity toward things Mexican. Moreover, many Sonorans had come to California seeking gold and bringing with them hard feelings toward Americans developed when the latter invaded their homeland. Then they were unceremoniously cast out of the goldfields. Many of those few who did not go back to Mexico went to Los Angeles, where the barrio became known as Sonoratown. Many of the northern California Mexicans also fled their homes before the onslaught of the rapacious interlopers. They took their families and anti-American sentiments and settled in the southern counties, which would now be home to two-thirds of the state's Mexicans, who increasingly blended together in Sonoratown regardless of their origin. All this hostility was a dangerous mix especially in a place like Los Angeles known neither for its decorum nor for its sobriety.[61]

In this potentially explosive situation the status-conscious Californios, especially those in the circles of Andrés Pico, Tomás Sánchez, and the other gente de razón, continued to seek to ally themselves socially and politically with the influential Anglos. Californio elites increasingly called themselves Spanish to distinguish themselves from the disparaged lower classes, whom everyone began calling derisively Mexicans regardless of their origin, economic condition, or moral quality. This ef-

12. Sonoratown and Los Angeles in 1857. (Courtesy of the Seaver Center for Western History Research, Los Angeles County Museum.)

fort to protect their property and status and generally insulate themselves from the opprobrium and consequences of American bigotry initiated the "Fantasy Heritage" of Spanish California. People and things deemed Spanish (food, music, horsemen, and so on) were acceptable to Californians, whereas those deemed Mexican carried negative connotations, a pattern that has persisted to this day.[62] The Americanos allowed them their social prestige, included them (unlike the mestizo cholos) in white society, and did not threaten their wealth. Thus flattered, these Spanish Californios paid allegiance to the Americans, rode horses with them, and further distanced themselves from Mexicans. This accommodation helped pacify the area, which was still simmering from the tensions of the war. The Spanish-speaking population was divided: the elites were joined in various ways with the Anglos, and the lower classes, without sponsors or protectors, were left to bear the brunt of the Anglo frenzy against "dirty" and "lawless" Mexicans.

Before 1846 no one really stole cattle, except marauding Indians. The southern counties had plenty of cows, which were valuable then only for their hides and tallow. If someone was hungry, they got some beef because it was plentiful and had minimal exchange value. They received plenty of (rather tough) meat: the poor's bellies did not push them to desperation in order to eat. Public morality was none the best—surely alcohol muted discord between property owners, laborers, and the underclass—but there were few crimes against persons or property. Occasionally a sensational case excited the populace, but for the most part people were safe on the highways and in their homes. Besides, where would one sell or otherwise dispose of stolen goods in old California? But when the Yankees came, full of contempt for Mexicans, conditions changed. During times of war the public and the government disparage their enemy to enable themselves, or their soldiers, to kill. Permission to kill the "others" derives from these careening feelings of hatred, which do not suddenly disperse after the armistice. Mexicans throughout the new American frontier painfully experienced the results of this hostility.

In the decades following 1848 the most common items in Los Angeles newspapers were about murders. For the most part Indians murdered Indians, Mexicans murdered Mexicans, and Anglos murdered Anglos (usually after consuming prodigious amounts of aguardiente). In 1853 the editor of the Los Angeles *Star* concluded, "There is no country where nature is more lavish of her exuberant fullness and yet with all our natural beauties and advantages, there is no country where human life is of so little account. Men hack one another in pieces with pistols [*sic*] and other cutlery." But the newly dominant Anglos usually blamed Mexicans for the violence and came to believe that they threatened organized and armed insurrection. "The assertion has been often made," said another *Star* of the same year, "that Sonorenian [*sic*] thieves and murderers are harbored and assisted in our midst." The *Star* did not state explicitly by whom they were assisted, but obviously their compatriots were the prime suspects.[63]

Proceeding from the example set in the gold mines, the inflamed citizenry righteously and violently punished those they assumed responsible for the turmoil—Mexicans. Unlike in the north, in Los Angeles all of the spectacular lynchings involved Mexicans, as did most of the minor episodes. A number of Texans settled El Monte, which was east of the pueblo and formerly part of the Mission San Gabriel lands. All too many Texans had learned the art of taking care of unwanted Mexicans beginning in 1836. Now they brought those skills to Los Angeles. An "important function that engaged these worthy people," recalled Harris Newmark, "was their part in the lynchings which were necessary in Los Angeles. As soon as they received the cue, the Monte boys galloped into town; and being by temperment and training, through frontier life, used to dealing with the rougher side of human nature, they were recognized disciplinarians."[64] They dispatched the "Sonorenian thieves and murderers," and anyone else who got in the way. Lynching was a public ritual performed on the body of the prisoner. That body was of the same flesh and blood as the bodies of those who watched or at least knew what was happening even if they avoided the spectacle. The execution thus warned Mexicans against transgressing the boundaries which the dominant group had established. Lynching manifested and asserted juridical and political power. The "Monte boys" sought to become the "recognized disciplinarians" of all Mexicans, who they assumed "harbored and assisted" criminals and therefore encouraged criminality. This process tended to criminalize all of *la gente mexicana.*

These criminals were literally outlaws, or people outside the law. Therefore, normal standards of behavior were considered to be unnecessary in dealing with them. The Spanish-language weekly *El Clamor Público* expressed outrage at both the general level of violence and robbery and the officially tolerated brutalization of the Mexicans. One episode of February 1857, as dramatic as it was common, will suffice to illustrate these points. A Mexican robber had been apprehended in the vicinity of Mission San Gabriel:

The "great number of suspected persons" [quoting the *Star*], it is said, were all Mexicans or individuals of the *raza española* who were in San Gabriel. All were taken prisoner and assembled in front of the church. There they were when the body of the Mexican who had been killed in the marsh was brought. One of the Mexicans who was arrested, in whose truthfulness we have the greatest confidence and whom we have known for a long time, has given the following information: "When they brought the body, a justice of the peace of the mission took out his knife and cut off the head (even though some Americanos opposed him in this) and rolled it around with his foot as if it were a rock; then he thrust the knife into his chest several times, with a brutality rarely seen even amongst these very barbarians."

The Monte boys caught this thief, a desperado named Miguel Soto, and proceeded to do with him as their culture prescribed. They also rounded up the usual suspects—nearly all of the Mexicans of San Gabriel—most of them to watch the spectacle, but two of them to serve as further illustrations of the dangers of being Mexican or at least of the need to remain in one's proper place. These two, criminals only because of their *raza,* were killed as well.[65]

Those who similarly criminalized lower-class Mexicans perceived the Monte boys, like the Texas Rangers, as champions of law and order. The Los Angeles *Star* described the very same events as follows: "Now, a general search took place, and a large number of suspected persons were taken prisoners. . . . A jury of twelve persons was appointed by the citizens assembled, among whom were some natives, and a fair and impartial trial was given them, in proof of which, a large number were released. . . . Each of the men was sentenced to die and they were executed." To one side of what *El Clamor Público* called "la guerra de las razas," justice and public morality had been reaffirmed. Justice, in this particular case, had been done only when the whole *raza* was punished or at least had been exposed to the message of the public executions. The fact that "a large number were released" hardly qualifies the executions as a clean judicial proceeding. The two innocents were, in the words of an *El Clamor Público* article of three months later, "hanged as suspects." It was a frankly terrorist act.[66]

Sometimes the violence cut across cultural and racial lines. In December 1853, Jesus Senate, a Mexican, killed Jack Wheelan, a Los Angeles constable trying to arrest him. "There was much excitement and many threats were uttered against the whole mixed race," reported the *Star,* "but we are glad that our order-loving citizens have not added another blot to the unenviable annals of the city." (This danger of effecting arrests helps explain why the city continually offered a whopping yearly salary of ten thousand dollars for sheriff but had trouble finding takers. In January 1857 thieves killed Sheriff Barton and three others who had hunted them after they had murdered and pillaged at San Juan Capistrano.) In July 1855 the *Star* reported another incident: "A serious fray occurred at the Mission San Gabriel, on Sunday afternoon, consequent upon the consumption of too much bad liquor, in which pistols were drawn and freely used as is usually the case, and which resulted in three men being shot and severely wounded. . . . We are informed that it was a free fight in which Americans, Mexicans and Indians were mixed up in glorious confusion." Some besotted Irishmen murdered one another in January 1855, and a gathering of drunken Americans in Sonoratown ended in fatal carnage in May 1854. Indeed, it seemed that "this country is in a state of insurrection, clearly and plainly so. A large gang of outlaws, many of them expelled for crime from the mines, are in open rebellion against the laws, and are daily committing the most daring murders and robberies." When these crimes were perpetrated by Mexicans, it was a "terrible outrage," but when two Monte boys got drunk and killed one another in January 1855, it was a "terrible tragedy."[67]

This terror explains something of why the Mexican community of Los Angeles generated relatively few leaders for nearly a century after the conquest. This criminalized population did not dare to organize an opposition to such well-armed and fanatical defenders of white supremacy. The Mexicans of Los Angeles responded, however, in two ways. First, a very small number took to the hills and began a life of crime against the white Americans. Such actions further convinced the Americans of the criminal nature of Mexicans. The Mexicans themselves looked to these bandidos as avengers, materially supported them, and gained vicarious revenge through them. Second, the newspaper *El Clamor Público* and its young editor, Francisco P. Ramírez, overcame intimidation and voiced the outrage of the Mexican and Californio communities.

In *The Splendor and Death of Joaquín Murieta* Pablo Neruda calls that most fabled of the bandidos "the murderer who murdered the murderers and died for our honor." That phrase aptly characterizes the possibly sociopathic young man from a respectable family who journeyed from Sonora to work the goldfields of California. The story of Joaquín Murieta has "breathed." We cannot know precisely what took place in his short life, let alone know his own perceptions of outlawry. But the story goes that he and his woman friend Rosita Feliz settled into the Stanislaus mining district in 1850, when Murieta was only eighteen years of age. There he was told in no uncertain terms that he had to leave because he was not "American." He and Rosita met the same fate when they tried to farm in Calaveras County. Racism and the threat of violence denied Murieta the productive wherewithal of California, so he turned to dealing monte, a card game. Did the Americans further outrage him with more taunts and indignities? Did he tire of such monotonous methods of supporting himself and Rosita? Both humiliations and boredom must have motivated Murieta, whose race denied him access to redress of his grievances. At any rate, by 1851 a band of highwaymen terrorized the countryside. The young Murieta, who had been joined by Reyes Feliz, Rosita's sixteen-year-old brother Three-Fingered Jack, and several others, robbed and murdered white American travelers.

At first it was generally thought that only Americans suffered at the hands of this fabulously notorious outlaw gang, though in actuality Chinese seem to have been favored targets. Mexicans protected Murieta, or at least they never betrayed his whereabouts, whether out of solidarity or out of fear. But later Murieta started robbing Mexicans, and he shot [not fatally] the disloyal Rosita. Then his own people, one version goes, disclosed his position to Captain Harry Love, a bounty hunter, who stalked and killed Murieta in the summer of 1853. Whether this version is true or apocryphal, Love did receive the reward of five thousand dollars from the legislature and, it is said, a further thousand dollars from the Chinese community of San Francisco. According to another version of the story, the fatally wounded Murieta said to Love, "You have taken me by surprise, but it does not matter; I die con-

tented; I have already avenged myself enough." Those in the
south, however, did not accept that Love had actually killed
Joaquín Murieta because the Angeleños were certain that the
bandido had been in their vicinity the night he was alleged
to have been killed; they believed that Love had cut off the
head of some other Mexican and presented it for the reward.
Murieta's or not, the head was preserved in a jar and exhibited in San Francisco until the earthquake of 1906 destroyed
it. Now this exposition of Joaquín Murieta, whoever he actually was—highwayman, murderer, avenger—brought him
to life again in the imaginations of many Mexicans, this time
as a hero, a symbol of American injustice toward their people.
"I call the rage of my countrymen just," concludes Neruda,
who transformed him into a Chilean immigrant to California,
"and I sing of Joaquín Murieta."[68]

None of the many versions of this story genuinely can claim
accuracy in relating the history of Murieta. His importance
lies in the perceptions of that history, which expose the depth
of racial antagonism both sides felt. To the Americans, the
same man symbolized both the violent nature and the criminality of Mexicans in general. The *Star* reported the story of
some desperados who were hanged in October 1853. The three

were condemned to be hung for horse stealing etc. . . . by our
citizens, then reprieved and sent to San Luis Obispo. . . . [The
locals] were assembled on the beach, and . . . took them to the
first tree and hung them. The prisoners uttered no complaints, made
no confessions, and scorned the services of the padre, and were
game to the last. They were asked if they had any requests to make;
to which Higuerro replied, that he would die happy if he could be
freed long enough to flog one Yankee. His request was not granted.

La Estrella, the Spanish language edition of the *Star*, reported the case of Felipe Alvitre, who atoned for the murders
of a Chilean and an Americano. "The reason he gave for having killed Ellington was 'because he was an American,'" noted
the paper, concluding, "This amply proves the feud that exists between the two peoples." Harris Newmark retold an episode of the 1850s in which bandidos approached and "it was
reported that some of the outlaws were on their way to Los

Angeles to murder the white people. As soon as possible, the
ladies . . . were brought together for greater safety in Armory Hall, on Spring Street near Second."[69]

The boundaries between Californio and Mexican continued
to collapse in the minds of the Americans. No Mexican could
be trusted. Salomon Pico "was a young man of good family,
and until the American conquest, bore a good reputation."
(Cleland calls him the "dubious offshoot of a famous family.")
But after 1848 "he decided to lead a life of crime, concentrating his efforts on the hated gringo." His actions resonated
in the sentiments of his people—"he was protected and almost revered by a great part of the native population" during
his ten-year career. Yet it is the careers of Juan Flores and
Tiburcio Vásquez that most eloquently illustrate our points
here about how a people as a whole come to be outside the
law, and the consequences of that relationship to the law.[70]

A number of factors show clearly that the Mexican War
continued to sizzle for at least a decade after the peace treaty.
The people of the times generally perceived themselves to be
engaged in bloodletting. The sympathy that Mexicans felt toward their countrymen, whom they believed the Yankee invaders drove outside the law; the outright material and emotional support the bandidos received from their compatriots;
the general criminalization of Mexicans; and the increasingly
sharp racial consciousness on the part of both Mexicans and
Anglos are all important both in and of themselves and as
they bear on economic and social history. These matters are
dynamically interrelated, particularly with regard to the transfer of the labor force and capital to those who followed the
United States military into California.

The most fearsome desperado of the southern counties, Juan
Flores, was the man who, together with his gang, killed Sheriff Barton and forced a group of ladies into the armory. In
late 1856 the horse thief and San Quentin escapee and his
lieutenant, Pancho Daniel, attracted more than fifty Mexicanos (not all of them cholos, according to Leonard Pitt) from
the southern counties to their standard. Holed up in the San
Juan Capistrano area, these aggressive and energetic men appeared to threaten general insurrection. The upper-class Cal-

ifornios opposed them (Andrés Pico, Juan Sepúlveda, and Tomás Sánchez all helped hunt down Flores and his men), whereas many of the lower classes abetted them. They robbed and plundered for a variety of reasons, some tenuously political. This brigandage, particularly when perceived as a response to (Protestant) Yankee political, legal, and economic injustice, expressed, in the words of Bancroft, "political privateering, religious crusading, and race revenge." Each man joined Juan Flores for his own reasons, but the factors Bancroft identified contributed to each man's decision. One is said to have joined to get revenge on Sheriff Barton, who had jailed him in a quarrel over an Indian woman. Nearly 120 armed men, comprised of rangers under the leadership of General Pico, the Monte boys, other Americans, and Indians all pursued the bandido army.

Lower-class Mexicans were guilty by association. Leonard Pitt describes how the Monte boys—"a drunken and bloodthirsty mob," according to a victim's father—rounded up the usual suspects in San Gabriel and lynched three innocent Mexicans. The Californio leaders rummaged through the county where the people, asserted Newmark, "either from sympathy or fear, aided the murdering robbers and so made their pursuit doubly difficult." But they captured some fifty of the desperados, including their compelling leader. The citizens of Los Angeles lynched Juan Flores on February 14, 1857, and "practically every man, woman and child in the pueblo was present."[71]

The *Star* of May 16, 1874, printed an interview with the legendary Tiburcio Vásquez, a classic social bandit: he experienced the oppression of his people, but took to the hills and became a symbolic avenger to the relatively pacific masses. "My career grew out of the circumstances by which I was surrounded as I grew to manhood," he explained after his capture. The encroaching Yankees pushed Californios not only away from the land: "I was in the habit [about 1852] of attending balls and parties given by the native Californians, into which the Americans, then beginning to become numerous, would force themselves and shove the native-born men aside, monopolizing the dances and the women. . . . A spirit of hatred and revenge took possession of me. I had numerous fights in defense of what I believed to be my rights and those of my countrymen. The officers were continually in pursuit of me." Vásquez took a herd of cattle inland from his comfortable home in Monterey County, but "even here I was not permitted to remain in peace." Ever a man of traditional Mexican virtue, he consulted his mother: "I went to my mother and told her I intended to commence a different life. I asked for and obtained her blessing, and at once commenced the career of a robber." He and his companions rustled cattle, distributed a few for food to unfortunate Mexicans, and sold the rest to finance his expensive penchant for women and gambling. His compatriots gave him refuge. In 1857 he was arrested in Los Angeles for horse stealing and sent to San Quentin Prison. "After my discharge from San Quentin [1863] I returned to the house of my parents and endeavored to lead a peaceful and honest life," said the sincere caballero. But in the classic pattern of the social bandit, Vásquez was falsely accused of confederacy with other desperados and "was again forced to become a fugitive from the law-officers." He returned to the penitentiary for three years in 1867. In August 1873 his band's robbery of Snyder's store in Tres Pinos brought this previously inconsequential criminal statewide notoriety. For a year he captured Mexicans' imaginations, just as he captured the Americans' cattle and money. The doors of many homes in the areas surrounding Los Angeles opened to him. Just beyond the Mission San Fernando, "at Lyons Station . . . Vásquez sometimes attended the dances and with no lack of partners, as there was always competition among the ladies because, as they said, he was a wonderful dancer and always a gentleman." One of his men, whose wife Vásquez had seduced, probably betrayed him; after a desperate search, Vásquez was finally captured in May 1874, ten miles west of Los Angeles. He was transported for trial to San José, where thousands of people visited him in prison. Some were merely curious, but many supported him. He sold cards with his picture and a short biography and appealed for defense funds through the newspapers. Convicted in January 1875, he was hanged in March of that year, to the glee and relief of the

13. A poster celebrating the capture of the legendary Tiburcio Vásquez, a scourge to the Anglos and a hero to the Mexicans. (Courtesy of the Seaver Center for Western History Research, Los Angeles County Museum.)

Americans and to the sorrow of his many Mexican support-
ers.[72]

Obviously, much meanness prevailed in California in the
decades following the Mexican War. A race war seemed always threatening to break out because both Mexicans and Anglos believed these stories, of which only a few have been
told here. Violence exploded whenever the bands of desperados came down from their retreats to terrorize property
owners. Indian attacks proceeded apace, also contributing to
the atmosphere of violence that pervaded southern California
at the time. More was going on than mere frontier turbu-
lence, however. The legal culture had coordinated the general assault on Californios and Mexicans. The roughest and
most ignoble of the Americans, whose numbers, baseness, and
firepower far exceeded those of the cholos, enforced the exclusion of Hispanic Californians from the emerging society
through officially tolerated violence. Law and violence in a
given culture usually act not only to privilege members of
that culture but to exclude others from it. The legal culture
accomplished this aim all the while proclaiming in universal
terms the virtues of equal protection and justice through the
rule of law.

Salvador Vallejo, after recalling the old tradition of killing
someone else's steer when hungry but leaving the hide behind for the owner, stated, "Since the transfer of California
to the United States many native Californians have been hanged
for stealing cattle, and I firmly believe that some of the vic-
tims did not know that under the new government it was a
crime to kill a steer for which they had not a bill of sale."
Vallejo may well have been correct, but his comment does
not provide sufficient insight into the new situation. The violence against, and lynching of, Mexicans was not a simple
misunderstanding, as Vallejo suggests, nor frontier lawlessness, as Robert Glass Cleland asserts, nor xenophobia on the
part of racist whites, as Leonard Pitt implies.[73] The cultures
of law and mob violence worked in a dynamic relationship to
finish the task Polk had begun when he promised his constituents the acquisition of California. The conquest started
with the Anglo desire for the Spanish and Mexican lands of

the Mexican northern frontier, proceeded through diplomatic blustering, and climaxed in military victory. The culmination of the conquest, however, was the actual transfer of land, begun before 1846 and continued after 1848, when extralegal violence ruled Mexicans' lives in southern California. The resources and opportunities of the new state were reserved for Americans; Mexicans were excluded.

Mexican Liberalism and the Opposition Newspaper

Short of taking to the hills in merely personal and symbolic protest, there was little that the lower classes could do to respond to Anglo harassment. The conquering Americans outgunned them. The weekly newspaper, *El Clamor Público*, however, voiced the outrage of the Californios of Los Angeles. Its editor, owner, and factotum, the remarkable Francisco P. Ramirez, was only twenty years old when he began the paper in 1855. For four years it ran news and editorials, often indistinguishable from one another, and some undistinguished fiction. In form it did not differ from most other California papers, but in content it certainly did. The vigilantes, the reign of the *linchocracia*, and the everyday discrimination against Mexicans earned the righteous condemnation of the crusading editor. Schooled in Mexico and thus exposed to revolutionary liberal ideology, Ramirez asserted that liberalism was a sham in California "if one had the misfortune of being born in Mexican territory." The experience of his compatriots with the new legal culture showed him clearly that "it is truly curious this idea that one has liberty in the United States." He wrote that for Mexicans "this often-praised liberty is imaginary." Vehement denunciations of the bloody actions of the Monte boys and other enforcers of white supremacy peppered the pages of *El Clamor Público* every week.[74]

Its coverage of *la guerra de las razas*, in spite of the bombast, was hardly one-sided. In true liberal fashion *El Clamor Público* railed against the general lawlessness of Los Angeles—"so many robberies have been committed with impunity"—regardless of the race of the perpetrators. Ramirez lamented, "A week does not go by without us having news of some murder. Last Monday, a quarrel was stirred up among two Mexicans, and as is the custom, the matter was resolved with one of them dead in a field." The dastardly deeds of Juan Flores found no sympathy in the pages of *El Clamor Público.* The weekly counseled reason with respect to the Indian scares: "The Indians have lived peacefully, and since the memorable insurrection of Antonio Garrú [as the chief's name was occasionally spelled], which was instigated by unprincipled men, have shown only the slightest disposition to initiate hostilities against the whites. The Indians of these parts do not resemble those of Oregon—they are friends of peace and cowardly in the extreme." Only 40 percent of Spanish-speaking men and 18 percent of Spanish-speaking women were literate. Nevertheless, *El Clamor Público*, through the printed word, reassured those who could read, or could have the newspaper read to them, that even though "many of its [the *Star's*] compatriots hate our race, . . . we are better and more peaceful citizens than them."[75]

A profound headiness accompanied the ideas of liberalism in the nineteenth century, something of which we have seen with Mexico's solution to the problem of the California missions in the 1830s. Francisco P. Ramirez fell under the spell as well. He knew that "certain people had no type of liberty—this liberty, we have said, is that which is denied in the Courts to every individual of color." But the answer for this lonely voice of reason in Los Angeles in the 1850s was a "textbook liberalism" in which the blessings of liberty would be extended to all regardless of race, creed, or color.[76]

What, however, has been the relationship between race and ideas about liberty? To people of color in the United States, racism marked the fatal flaw of liberalism. Indeed, the two may be related. Edmund Morgan suggests that in colonial Virginia and during the American Revolution whites may well have been able to articulate ideas about individual liberty in a cavalier fashion because they did not have to worry about their effect on the lower or laboring classes. Chattel slavery based on race bound and controlled those who worked. It was much easier to propound such values as life, liberty, and the pursuit of happiness if one was sure that the poor could not hear them and would not start agitating for their inalienable rights. In any case, the formal bonds of racial slavery would make sure that the poor, even if they heard about liberty, would never assemble into the mob and threaten private property and class privilege.[77]

White Texans fought their war of independence for liberty and freedom—but freedom from rule by people they assumed were racially inferior, and liberty to own slaves. Explaining the unrest of the forty-niners to the secretary of state, T. Butler King stated that they "had never been accustomed to any other than American law, administered by American courts. There they found their rights of property and person subject to the uncertain, and frequently most oppressive, operation of the laws written in a language they did not understand, and founded on principles in many respects new to them." They wanted their freedom from the oppression they suffered at the hands of Mexican law and administrators that remained in California. "In no State in the Union," extolled D. A. Shaw, "can it so truthfully be said that every one can sit under 'his own vine and fig tree' and enjoy the fruit of his labor, as in California."[78] To Shaw, California provided the individual with the blessings of liberty. It is clear that the Indians (and later the Chinese and the Mexicans), who tended those vines and trees, did not figure in Shaw's ideology, although it was the labor of people of color that procured those blessings of liberty for the whites. Moreover, the blessed farmer's wife could neither vote nor easily hold and control property, rights that guaranteed the liberty of the men. Francisco Ramirez crusaded to extend liberty and its blessings "to every person of color." But liberalism was never meant for them. Indeed, liberalism prospered not in spite of but because of people of color, bound by slavery, the labor market, or alcohol to work. In their condition the ideals of life, liberty, and the pursuit of happiness could never be realized and thus did not endanger the supremacy of those who articulated that often-praised ideology.

In the courageous figure of Ramirez we see how liberalism

was a praiseworthy, if quixotic, venture in mid-century Los Angeles. Yet liberalism was a dynamic ideology that motivated people, even people of color, to combat their oppressive situation. Its ideals inspired Frederick Douglass, W. E. B. DuBois, and Martin Luther King, Jr., as well as Francisco Ramirez, Benito Juárez (whose struggle for power in Mexico succeeded in 1855, the same year as the founding of *El Clamor Público*), and Ricardo Flores Magón, the Mexican exile to Los Angeles who would popularize ideas of anarchy in the early twentieth century. The ideology of liberalism, if not its ideals in practice, had come to stay in southern California.

The Final Decline of the Californios and the End of the Ranchos

The elite Californios had difficulty adapting to liberalism—a mainstay of this new, often perplexing culture. They continued to mix substantially with the whites through the 1850s and 1860s. Their daughters married Yankees and even a few British; people of color labored in their fields; and they joined Anglos in a chorus of indignation against the horrid Indians, outlaw cholos, and the gringo riffraff. In February 1853 these united elites, consisting of Californios and Americanos, suffered again the consequences of their exclusionary social culture. To celebrate Washington's Birthday at Abel Stearns's house, "several gentlemen saw fit to give a ball . . . to which they invited such individuals as they believed would form an agreeable company." The *Star* continued the story; events resembled those of Dieciséis de Septiembre, 1840, when "certain persons took umbrage, because they were left out, and resolved to break up the ball." The largely white mob expressed its resentment at being excluded from the elites' fiesta, which included Californios celebrating the birthday of the father of their new country. A cannon was fired, to the annoyance of the dancers, but the rabble remained. "About 11 o'clock it [a revolver] was discharged, and the mob numbering some fifteen or twenty, commenced ringing gong, tin pans, bells etc., and burned Chinese crackers," reported the *Star*. "Several gentlemen wished to go out to attack the mob, but were

14. Anglo Angeleños attempted to re-create the fiestas of the Californios. This first "Los Angeles Fiesta" (1875) took place in the plaza
where the Californios held their celebrations, including the riotous
episodes of 1840 and 1853. El Palacio, the home of Abel Stearns
and the scene of those riots, is in the upper left portion of the
photograph. (Courtesy of the Huntington Library.)

restrained until the ladies could be retired from the room."
When the debarred throng rushed "El Palacio" a second time,
shots were fired from within, killing two.[79]

Once admitted (or, more accurately, believing they were
admitted) to Anglo society, Californios failed to adapt. They
experienced some surprises and suffered outrages. In January
1851 three young Lugos were accused of the murder of an
Indian and an Irishman. They narrowly escaped lynching,
protected on one occasion by sixty armed Californios and on
another by their Cahuilla friends. An Anglo lawyer got them
exonerated in October 1852. Manuel Domínguez, a mestizo

signer of the California constitution and a respected ranchero, could not testify in court because of the law forbidding testimony from Indians, and he looked more Indian than European. Many of the more rabid anti-Mexican whites lumped all the Spanish speakers together no matter how they looked. Race war, in which most Anglos would include the Californios on the side of the cholos, constantly threatened. This threat, coupled with the Americanos' manifestly superior lethality, added potential and actual grave injury to vile insult. To redress these grievances, elite Californios resorted to legal and formal protest, and they did their best to adapt to the new environment. They intensified their efforts to identify socially and politically with those who could offer them some protection, namely their sons-in-law. The Californios naturally gravitated toward the forces of property and order. They were, however, outgrowing their usefulness there. Immediately following the conquest, Mexicans—Californios and cholos—outnumbered the Americans. The Californios' alliance with the conquerors helped to reduce the threat that lower-class Mexicans might have posed to Anglo dominance. As Anglo control of southern California solidified, Californios increasingly found themselves lumped with the "greasers."[80]

The new legal culture, it should be clear by now, functioned as regards economics to include Anglos and capitalists and to exclude Californios, Mexicanos, seigneurial rancheros, and those with a dose of California fever. We have already seen the damage that the Land Act of 1851 wreaked on Californio land holdings. The economic culture of markets acted in a similar fashion. The delightful exaggeration in the demand for, and price of, cattle brought on by the Gold Rush played a clever trick on the ingenuous and unsuspecting Californios. Namely, it shrunk back to normal and left them calamitously in debt. During the boom, loans for expansion were made freely and could be paid back. Soon after the Land Act did its damage, however, the market began to contract when new and better breeds of cattle were brought from the plains. Immigrants began to settle on farms in the fertile valleys of central and northern California, supplying both themselves and the miners with food. A drop in the price of cattle ensued,

15. At the home of Pío Pico behind his store, probably in the 1880s. (Courtesy of the Huntington Library.)

and the rancheros increased their herds to make up for the lower return. This all-too-typical response of farmers everywhere produced only greater supply, relative to the falling demand, and overgrazed pastures.

The Californios' culture socialized them for the concerns of family and status and not for the details of the market and production. They were accustomed to financial dealings based on honor and kin ties rather than the rigors of the contract and the impersonality of the market. Yet they fancied so much the beckoning things that cash money could buy in that market. Unfortunately, they could not fathom the demonic qualities of compound interest rates. Thus, the vicissitudes of the market, together with the accumulationist desires of those businessmen and speculators who followed the United States military, operated to cast out the rancheros from the land-based productive wealth of southern California. All of these processes were well in place by 1856, the year marking the end of the golden age of rancho southern California.[81]

Pedro Domínguez, whose Indian-looking family owned vast lands just to the south of Los Angeles, went north to the goldfields in 1849 seeking his fortune, or at least enough to pay his debts. He borrowed his two-thousand-dollar stake from

16. A drawing of 1878 depicting the bustle after mass at ex-Mission San Gabriel. Indians, caballeros, and the common folk all freely mixed here, though the indications of hierarchy are clearly maintained. (Courtesy of the Seaver Center for Western History Research, Los Angeles County Museum.)

Juan Temple at 100 percent interest for six months and offered his share of Rancho San Pedro as collateral. Young Domínguez got no gold, and Temple got the land. (Rancho San Pedro, however, remained in Californio hands longer than any other rancho.) "Poor, handsome and brave" Manuel Garfias, whose old commander, Governor Micheltorena, rose to landed status with the grant of Rancho San Pascuale, borrowed cash to build his hacienda from Dr. John S. Griffen at 4 percent per month. Then he went to Mexico to fight with Benito Juárez. It was impossible for him to pay his debt when he returned in 1858. Griffen actually gave Garfias the fair price of two thousand dollars for Rancho San Pascuale, which is now Pasadena. (Doña Eulalia Pérez de Guillen, the llavera to whom Father Zalvidea originally granted the land, was then living in poverty in San Diego.) José Sepúlveda was a colorful

presence in Old California, with his unstinting hospitality, el-
egant dress, and passion for racing and betting on his horses.
The Los Angeles *Star* of September 18, 1852, reported that
he and Andrés Pico bet one thousand dollars on their horses,
which raced "upon the course near the church"; Sepúlveda
won. The next month he won again—sixteen hundred dollars
and three hundred head of cattle. Soon, however, Sepúlveda
came to owe seven Anglos a total of seven thousand dollars
at 4 to 7 percent interest, compounded monthly. The tales of
debt continue on in the 1850s. José Ramón Yorba signed a
mortgage for seventeen thousand acres with the largest holders of Sepúlveda's debt, James P. McFarland and John G.
Downey, for five thousand dollars at 5 percent per month.
Julio Verdugo borrowed $3,445 dollars from Jacob Elias to build
a house, buy provisions, and pay taxes in 1861. Three years
later Verdugo owed Elias three times that amount, though a
lawyer, Alfred Chapman, later bought his Rancho San Rafael
at auction. Money and banking were not these caballeros' forte,
especially as they confronted accumulationist and land-hungry
speculators practiced in driving a sharp deal. "I had the misfortune," lamented José del Carmen Lugo, "of putting my
signature on the debts of others in whom I had confidence."
Andrés Pico and Pío Pico, the former governor returned from
exile in Mexico, still possessed substantial lands. But their
Rancho Santa Margarita y Las Flores, largely old Mission San
Juan Capistrano lands, was pledged to Pioche and Bierque of
San Francisco, who lent them forty-four thousand dollars at
3 percent per month. (Part of this enormous amount, one pre-
sumes, briefly bouyed Sepúlveda.) Their brother-in-law, Juan
Forster, paid the moneylenders but soon took over the rancho. The Picos' other creditors, such as Abel Stearns, took
what little remained.[82]

The last Mexican governor now depended on family and
friends for his unpretentious subsistence. General Andrés Pico,
who routed the Yankees and then the bandidos of the Flores
gang, lived for a long time at Mission San Fernando. There,
decades later, "people [were always] coming and going, for
General Pico was the most hospitable of men . . . smiling

and bowing and saying in his broken English 'I am de gentleman always'—and such we always found him to be," recalled
the daughter of the developer who made a fortune subdivid-
ing what came to be known as Rancho Ex-Mission San Fernando. Those in whom Lugo had so much confidence "for one
reason or another have left me, as we say vulgarly, 'en las
hastas [*sic*] del toro' [in a jam], and I have had to give up
my possessions and the house in which I lived to cover these
obligations." Harris Newmark told of Francisco O'Campo, a
"man of means whose home was on the east side of the Plaza.
. . . He was very improvident, like so many natives of the
time," and he "died . . . a poor man." "In his later years,"
Newmark continued, "he used to sit on the curbstone near
the Plaza, a character quite forlorn, utterly dejected in appearance, and despondently recalling the by-gone days of his
prosperity." "It breaks my heart," lamented Ygnacio Sepúlveda,
"to think of so many of our countrymen suffering so greatly."[83]
A few Californios held on to some of their land and continued
to provide some Hispanic flavor to the region. But on the
whole the Californio rancheros had been dispossessed of their
lands.

The perils of the market brought the initial Anglo rancheros
difficulties but usually did not ruin them. Abel Stearns lost
his first rancho, Los Alamitos, to falling cattle prices and
droughts, but tens of thousands of prime acres remained in
his domain. Then, too, from his cultural and environmental
association with the southern coastal region he caught a case
of California fever. He devoted more and more of his time
to his horses until his death in August 1871. Meanwhile his
business affairs languished. Juan Forster liked horses and
gambling too. Lemuel Carpenter, a Domínguez son-in-law,
fared less well. Interest rates and beguiling loans befuddled
the Kentuckian; a small debt ballooned, and the court ordered the sale of his land in December 1858. A year later,
almost precisely as the sheriff sold Rancho Santa Gertrudes
to McFarland and Downey, Carpenter fatally shot himself.[84]

The seigneurial era was coming to an end, though its legacy would live on in various ways. Robert Glass Cleland quotes
a poignant and powerfully symbolic advertisement placed by

17. Don Antonio Coronel, the leader of the Mexican community of Los Angeles in the decades following the Mexican War, at home with his family. (Courtesy of The Colorado College Library.)

Don Vicente de la Osa in the *Southern Vineyard* of March 22, 1859: "I have established at my Ranch, known by the name of 'The Encino,' situated at the distance of twenty-one miles from the city, on the road to Santa Barbara, a place for affording the accommodation to the people traveling on this road. . . . I hope those wishing to call at our place will not forget to bring with them what is necessary to defray expenses." According to Harris Newmark, de la Osa stated that it was now "an essential part of the arrangement that visitors should act on the good old rule and—pay as one goes." A new "good old rule" replaced the unbridled hospitality of the old days. "This bounteous provision for the wayfarer continued until the migrating population had so increased as to become something of a burden and economic conditions put a brake on unlimited entertainment," Newmark explained.[85]

The Californios protested, but concerted and assertive action was no more their forte than calculating the marketplace. Antonio Coronel knew that Los Angeles had too many lawyers and that this surfeit was a problem. Ygnacio Sepúlveda mused regarding some legislation that "in the abstract, and in a good community, [that is] to say where there were not

so many speculators, a similar law would have a good effect."[86] Resolutions and petitions poured forth, but they had
little effect on the state government and less on the workings
of the market. The Land Act of 1851 clearly violated at least
the spirit of the Treaty of Guadalupe-Hidalgo, though the Supreme Court ruled that it was within the letter of that document.

The "Petition of the California Landowners" to the United
States Congress of February 1859 calmly and accurately described the inequities of the new land laws and policies. The
forty-nine signers, "some of us citizens of the United States,
previously citizens of the Republic of Mexico," assured the
American government that "very few of the inhabitants of
California opposed the invasion; some of them welcomed the
invaders with open arms; a great number of them acclaimed
the new order with joy." The petitioners then detailed their
complaints against the swarms of frustrated and avaricious gold
seekers, the confounding Anglo-American legal structure (particularly as regards the Land Act of 1851), and the ruinous
interest rates. They concluded their veracious and guileless
analysis of their situation with words that suggest that perhaps
our narrative has not given them sufficient credit for astute-
ness: "The manifest injustice of such an act [the Land Act of
1851] must be clearly apparent to those honorable bodies when
they consider that the native Californians were an agricultural
people and that they have wished to continue so; but they
have encountered the obstacle of the enterprising genius of
the Americans, who have assumed possession of their lands,
taken their cattle, and destroyed their woods." The Californios now found themselves excluded from the industrializing
economy those enterprising strangers would develop. They
also noted a matter of even greater moment for these people
of kin ties and culture consciousness, one that has characterized all of California history since 1769: in their petition they
declared that the Californios "have been thrown among those
who were strangers to their language, customs, laws, and
habits."[87]

The weather, of all things, brought to an end the cattle era
of southern California. The rainy season of 1861–62 produced

unparalleled flooding. Torrents of water killed hundreds of thousands of cattle and horses. The opulent pastures so fattened the remaining cows that the market became glutted. In the spring Juan Forster reported back with optimism from San Francisco that "the prospect is very promising for a good market." He could not understand what he called "the badness of the market" that the fat cows now oversupplied. The flooding was followed by drought. Famine ravaged the cow-county pastures during the years 1863 and 1864. No feed would grow on the parched soil, and a million animals starved to death while the interest rates fattened unpaid loan balances. "Here everything is going badly, if you can call it only that," Juan Bautista Bandini wrote to Cave Couts. "Cattle and horses are dying" was everyone's rancho news. "The poor rancheros have had a *damned* bad string of luck these last two years," the now-pessimistic Forster emphasized, "and if it is going to continue I don't know what will become of us." In Los Angeles in 1860 cattle numbered seventy thousand; ten years later there were only twenty thousand.[88]

Sheep raising provided an interlude between cattle raising and farming. There were a few sheep at the time of the American conquest and about a million in the state by 1860, half of them in the south. The demand for Union army uniforms propelled the California wool clip from 5.5 million pounds in 1862 to 22 million in 1871. Another drought in the mid-1870s finished forever grazing of any sort as an important industry in the southern—no longer cow—counties.

Viticulture continued in importance after the demise of the missions. The forty-niners thirsted for wine (sometimes even for fresh grapes). In 1854 Los Angeles County had 400,000 vines and 3 million in 1866, or about one-sixth of the vineyard acreage of the state. William Wolfskill started an orange grove in 1841 and expanded it dramatically after 1850 when his crop amounted to two-thirds of California orange production. Benjamin Wilson acquired San Gabriel mission lands and mission orange trees in 1852, thereby increasing his crop. However, the lack of transportation precluded much expansion of the market for perishable produce.

This situation changed dramatically in 1876 when the

Southern Pacific Railroad arrived. The mere promise of the railroad connection attracted the attention of accumulationist speculators, as well as settlers in need of yet another second chance for prosperity, to the potentially lucrative land of southern California.[89] The opening of the national market would transform the southern California economy and history. What would not change were customary notions of who should work.

Chapter Five

At Considerable Less Wages

Mexicans and the Labor Crisis of Southern California

The ending of the rancho era presented the Anglo-American actors in our narrative with several choices. In the case of several of the junctures already examined, events could have unfolded in any one of several directions. Regarding the future of the missions and the pueblos in earliest Spanish California, the outcome of the secularization of the missions, or the handling of lands and Indians after the American conquest, people had more than one option of roads to take. I have already tried to explain why they took the paths they did, even though another choice might have been smarter or more humane. People's actions can only be satisfactorily understood when seen in the light of their culture and social relations. What transpired after the cattle era will prove no exception.

The subsequent utilization of the land would have a profound impact on Mexican southern California. We have been following the history of the people on the land, from the primitive communal orientation of the natives, to the notions of trust and entitlement that prevailed in the mission and rancho periods, to the commodification of the land with the advent of the Anglo-Americans. In this chapter we will view the consequences of the conquest and of the inundation of southern California by the conquerors for the remaining Indians of the area. It would be their ultimate demise. We will see how agribusiness came to southern California and how this process increased the demand for unskilled labor. Mexico appeared as the solution, and we will investigate the forces that pushed Mexicans out of their homeland to work in American factories in the cities and in American fields. Next we will see how the Anglos changed Spanish California history to meet their emotional needs and attempt to understand some subtle but important changes in the Anglo attitude toward Mexicans. The simultaneous rise of what I call *California Pastoral,* or the fanciful re-creation of Spanish and Mexican Californian history, and of a sense of entitlement to use Mexicans for onerous work generated by the objectification of alleged inferiors will round out the analysis of Anglo attitudes toward Mexicans. Just as production on the mission lands entailed more than simply giving the Indians tools, so too did the industrialization of Los Angeles prove more complex than the uniting of capital, labor, and markets. Most important, the consequences of these changes for those who labored, whether Indians or Mexican immigrants, would prove profound. We will end with a look at Mexican southern California in the later decades of the nineteenth century. Excluded from the developing economy, segregated into so-called Sonora Towns, and institutionalized as unskilled workers, Mexicans and the making of Mexican culture in frontier California had come a long way since the first meetings of Spanish priests and Indians, the era of great ranchos, and the founding of the little mestizo pueblo on the Porciúncula.

Land in Late Nineteenth-Century Southern California

This decline of the ranchos that the debt and drought of the 1850s and 1860s brought put the land in flux. Some of the ranchos, such as Stearns's Los Alamitos, were subdivided. Perhaps, then, the Jeffersonian ideal of independent freeholds would materialize in southern California. A young San Francisco typographer and philosopher, Henry George, revived the producer ideology into which he was born in Philadelphia. A Jacksonian yeomanry waited to emerge in California from the chaos of the demise of the old ranchos. According to this vision, small producers—white-skinned ones, of course— would replace both the cattle barons and the Indian laborers. Those who produced on the land would be those who owned the land. But there was no capital to loan the fledgling free- holders either to buy land or to stake the crops. What little was available came at exorbitant interest rates. Land titles were still confused. Water was limited. Not until 1876 did the rail- road arrive to transport the produce of the land to market. And there was no one to work the land.[1]

Nevertheless, there ensued a boomlet in southern Califor- nia real estate in the late 1860s. Speakers, pamphlets, mag- azines, letters to newspapers, and travel accounts attracted farmers from northern Europe and the eastern United States, especially from the war-devastated Confederate states. One book in particular drew attention, the professional railroad publicist Charles Nordhoff's *California: For Health, Pleasure, and Profit.* Visions of untold prosperity in the twelve-month growing season and the fertile soil of southern California were dangled before the eyes of struggling farmers hoping finally to succeed on the land. In only one year, 1868–69, the value of real estate transactions in Los Angeles County increased by 500 percent. The price of ranch land reached ten dollars an acre. This real-estate boom would hardly be the last that this curious little city of adobes, orchards, vineyards, and winter flowers would experience. Nor would it be the last to inspire dubious dreams of riches. Cotton, corn, tobacco, and even silk would bring permanent prosperity to the sleepy, but in- creasingly sober, City of the Angels.[2]

The bubble burst in 1873, however, with a national finan- cial panic. Once the worst was over, southern California ex- perienced a quieter and steadier period of growth through the 1880s. In particular the arrival of the Southern Pacific Rail- road in 1876, opening the national market to the area, facil- itated the expansion of production. Richard Gird wrote that he had "leased a dairy of 100 to 120 cows to Collins Bro who are shipping butter to Arizona making some money out of the business." Citrus and vineyard production increased dramat-

ically. The former flourished with the introduction of the
seedless navel orange from Brazil in the mid-1870s, which
produced more consistently and profitably than deciduous fruit
trees.

The town was calming down again. Once the wildness that
the Americans typically brought west with them subsided—a
taming for which they always congratulated themselves—
schools, Protestant churches, stores, roads, and medical treatment became increasingly available on a regular basis in Los
Angeles. A telling exception to the settling down of Los Angeles, however, was the riot of October 1871, in which hostile
whites looted Chinatown, killing at least twenty people. The
total population rose from an estimated 8,700 in 1866 to 17,400
in 1872, though the Mexican population remained steady at
about 2,100. Then, after the panic of 1873, came another boom,
this one mightier than any previous one.[3]

The completion of a rival railroad in 1886, the Santa Fe
line, ignited the boom of the late 1880s. The Southern Pacific
dropped its fare from the Missouri Valley to southern California from $125 to $100. By March 1887 because of a rate
war the cost of migrating to the area had plummeted to one
dollar. The Southern Pacific brought 120,000 people to Los
Angeles that year, and the Santa Fe unloaded three or four
passenger trains a day. In Glenn Dumke's words, the rate
war "stimulated the migration of hordes of people who would
otherwise have confined their interest in California to reading
about it." Tens of thousands of strangers to the land, its inhabitants, and certainly to one another got off the trains hoping to acquire a small farm on the rich land in the warm
climate. What the Gold Rush did for the north, the publicity
and the railroad rate wars did for the south. Anglo-Americans
now thoroughly inundated the territory once ruled from faraway Madrid and once peopled with priests, Indians, and a
remarkable biological and cultural blend of old and new world.[4]

The contradictory Anglo-American attitude toward liberty
and the land again came to the fore during the boom. The
small farm represented liberty to the common folk and an
opportunity for riches to speculators. Land agents, veterans
of the midwestern booms, swarmed over southern California.

The hoopla of brass bands, circus performers, barbecues, and promises of either speculative or residential prosperity in real estate captured the imagination of most whites. Millions of dollars' worth of real estate changed hands every month. In the two and a half years, beginning in January 1887, more than sixty new towns were founded. In spite of, or perhaps because of, the magnitude and ebullience of the boom, everything fell apart again in 1889. Of course, many held on and even prospered on farms of different sizes. But most of the new towns faded away.[5] If prosperity did not always follow the United States flag for Anglo-Americans, it most certainly did not for Indians and Mexicans in southern California. The Indians, so long in spiritual, cultural, and physical decay, approached extinction. The Spanish and Mexican periods initiated their destruction, and the American era quickly finished them off.

The End of the Indians of Southern California

Except for the padres' initial optimism about the prospects for the conversion and assimilation of the natives, the various intruders maintained a remarkably consistent disdain for the Indians of California. But in several important ways the Americans differed. They brought with them to the Pacific Coast a long history of fighting determined and vigorous Indians on whose lands they had encroached. By contrast, the California tribes were diffident gatherers who had already lost most of their cultural vitality. Their condition further diminished what little respect Anglo-Americans had for their lives or territory.[6]

The Americanos, armed with a liberal worldview as well as guns, swept away the traditions of reciprocal obligation, including those toward inferiors, which had characterized the mission and seigneurial periods. Spaniards and Californios had disrupted the Indians' environment, a process against which the Indians had rebelled or fled. There had followed a close, but not thorough, association—a profound, but unequal, attachment—between the two alien cultures in both the mission and rancho periods. Spain looked forward to the mixing of the two races (in marriage, of course). In the Spanish system Indians' souls could achieve salvation; they could testify in court; theoretically, their property was inviolate; and assimilated Indians could participate in civic and political activities. Indeed, Mexico made them citizens when it gained its independence from Spain.

Certain aspects of the American ethos, however, boded greater ill for the Indians of California than even the calamities they had experienced at the hands of the Spanish and Mexicans. Rugged individuals took responsibility for their own welfare, and such people judged the outcome of actions against the yardstick of personal gain. They attached little importance to the effect of their productive or expansionary activities on digger Indians, as the Anglos termed those who lived literally and figuratively close to the land. White Americans loathed and feared miscegenation (though the men often took Indian mistresses and temporary wives). They felt that divine providence and the marketplace, not personal bonds, would deal with the Indians. And the Americans' technologically advanced weaponry proved more lethal to the California Indians than that of either the Spanish or the Mexicans.

We have already analyzed some of the causes and consequences of the meanness toward Indians of many, if not the majority, of the Americans who came to California. In addition, the Bureau of Indian Affairs did little to protect or support either the ex-mission Indians or the tribal Indians, who had by this time largely amalgamated with one another. This policy left these atrophying and despised people to compete with the presumptuous and aggressive Americans for land and subsistence. Whites filed claims for lands that a few Indians held, and the aboriginal peoples could find no redress in either the courts or the bureau. For example, Helen Hunt Jackson tells of "Chrysanto, an Indian, put off his farm two months ago by [a] white man named Jim Angel, with certificate of Homestead from Los Angeles land office," and of "Antonio Douro, another, put off in the same way from his farm near the schoolhouse." Even those few former neophytes who had adapted to the ways of farming and private property found no

18. Simon Cilimovat and his grandchildren in American dress. He is spinning yucca at Warner's Ranch c. 1900. (Courtesy of the Huntington Library.)

protection. Douro "had built a good wooden house; the white man took that and half his land." An Indian agent told Jackson of a white settler who filed a claim for some land farmed by ex-mission Indians living near old Mission San Luis Rey in 1873. "He owned, the agent says, that it was hard to wrest from these well-disposed and industrious creatures the homes they had built up; but, said he, 'if I had not done it somebody else would; for all agree that the Indian has no right to public lands.'" Many of those Indians who escaped alcohol and disease tried to farm, but "from tract after tract of such lands they have been driven out, year by year, by the white settlers of the country, until they can retreat no farther; some of their villages being literally in the last tillable spot on the desert's edge or in mountain fastness." Where the Indian village of San Pascuale once contained those "well-disposed and industrious creatures," there was now "a white settlement numbering 35 voters. The Indians are all gone—some to other villages, some living nearby in cañons and nooks in the hills, from which, on the occasional visits of the priests, they gather and hold services in the half-ruined adobe chapel built by them in the days of their prosperity."[7]

The Indians continued to work on the ranchos. "In California parlance," Nordhoff related, "a man 'has' Indians, but he 'is in' sheep, or cattle, or horses." The few remaining Californio and Anglo rancheros still "had" Indians through the 1860s and 1870s. The chronicler of Rancho Azusa de Duarte describes in 1872 the "jacales . . . still aligned along the water ditches and near the fields the Indians helped cultivate." At the same time Indians still did the work at Stearns's Rancho Laguna. Many of the Indians worked itinerantly: "Considerable numbers of these Indians are also to be found on the outskirts of white settlements," Jackson reported, "where they live like gypsies in brush huts, here to-day, gone to-morrow, eking out a miserable existence by day work." In the San Diego area Juan Bautista Bandini, the leisured son of Juan Bandini and brother-in-law of Stearns and Couts, referred to "the Indians who sheared Ysidora's sheep." In his diary for 1880 he recorded, "Today I plant wheat with a boy José." Five days later "José went off to the hills." The "hills" provided both a temporary escape for the Indians and a source of labor for the rancheros. "I arranged with an Indian who went back to the hills to come and gather the hay," he recorded for May 28, 1881; and for March 1880, "Cueva's [Cave Couts's] little Indio came to gather the hay." The actors in this intercultural kin network agreed on who should work, even around their homes, in spite of their servants' erratic work habits: "The girls went to Las Posas to see an Indian to wash clothes," wrote Bandini on August 3, 1881. "I brought a sheep for the little Indian who is caring for the house, to eat," he noted that September. On November 15 he recorded, "They brought an Indian maid for the girls," but two weeks later he noted that "the Indian girl ran away this morning."[8]

The difference between market-oriented Anglo and seigneurial Californio in their labor relations with "their" Indians corresponds to the broader cultural differences mentioned above. As Max Weber put it, "The more the world of the modern capitalist economy follows its own immanent laws, the less accessible it is to any imaginable relationship with a religious ethic of brotherliness." Gone from the Anglo ranches was the seigneurial sense of reciprocity and personal association that rancheros had even with those whom they considered to be inferior. The Californio ranchero acted in the world so that he would be perceived as a big man. To this end he engaged in ritualized generosity. In his journal Richard Gird, owner of Rancho Santa Ana del Chino, recorded in 1881 that he acted only if "I find it profitable." Gird gauged his success by the increase of his capital. He calculated the exchange value of everything rather than valuing how useful something might be to him or how much prestige it might give him. He remarked about his wife's abilities around the house: "She is a most capital manager of such things." No doubt a new measure of worth prevailed on the commercial ranch. Juan Forster wrote to Cave Couts just after Christmas in 1863 that the latter's Indian mayordomo "may want to leave you on his return from the mountains. In which case I have a man that I can recommend for his place at considerable [*sic*] less wages." Both of these men married *hijas del país* and thus acquired rancho land with Indian laborers. They assumed the labor force from the old ranchos in the same way that the Californio rancheros assumed the mission lands and those Indians who were the forebears of Gird's, Couts's, and Forster's laborers. They simply changed the formal connection binding those who produced the wealth on the land and those who owned that wealth.[9]

A new sense of virtue as regards work and leisure accompanied such market calculation. "Sunday is a very disturbing day in the routine of one's affairs," lamented Gird. "Everybody must stop work[;] most of your help must go to town and indulge in some sort of foolishness," he inscribed in his diary. One did not work to enjoy oneself (however disgracefully) later; one worked because "indolence is the foundation of misery to the good as well as mother of vice to the bad."[10]

The spirit of Poor Richard spoke through Gird's journal: "God helps those who help themselves." Having helped themselves to the Californios' land (the Californios had, of course, helped themselves to the neophyte Indians' lands), these Protestant capitalists could absolve themselves of any responsibility toward the Indians. The Indians did not help themselves, but drank and "engage[d] in . . . foolishness." In the view of the Americans, they deserved nothing of God's favor or bounty and so were justly left to die away.

Still, there was work to be done. Charles Nordhoff put the situation bluntly:

The Indian of these southern counties is not a very respectable being, but he is of some use in the world; he works. It is true that he loves strong grape-brandy; that he gets drunk; that he lives poorly; that he does not acquire money; and has even fewer notions of what we call comfort than his Spanish, half Spanish, Pike, and American neighbors. But he does not assassinate like the brutal Apache, and he has wants enough to make him labor for money.[11]

In other words, these were near perfect workers despite their laxity on the job and the moral disgust they engendered in the ranchers. These Indian workers—paid little, nonviolent except toward their own, dependent on employers but needing only small remuneration (all of which the business class got back at the grog shops), and too narcotized to protest—set the standard for labor. To this ideal the southern California employers became addicted.

To bind people to the free-labor market sometimes required even more than the devilish allure of money and dependence on wages for subsistence. For Indians, the additional link was alcohol. "Indians all drunk," recorded Henry Dalton in his diary for November 24, 1861, "stole aguardiente from the still, all sobered off this evening, weather fair and pleasant." The entries drone on through the 1870s: "Indians drunk"; "Indians merry"; "Indians all drunk, broke into the store and stole two gal whiskey."[12] Dalton watched from his porch, wrote in his diary, and assumed that God's will was being done as the Indians drank themselves to death.

The Indians not only pilfered liquor; Dalton paid them in

it. He figured the wages of his Indians at fifty cents a day but paid them little in cash. His "Indian Books" show that his laborers received shirts, sugar, calico, cigars, soap, hats, brandy, wine, and aguardiente. Benjamin Wilson, proprietor of Lake Vineyard Wine Company on old Mission San Gabriel lands near present-day Pasadena, disbursed to such Indians as Antonio, Manuel, Ramón, Dolores, and Pancho what the account books referred to as "cognac and wine." On some ranchos the Indians were not paid in aguardiente, but there is no evidence that many, besides those few living at the now-crumbling missions, escaped alcohol. Their addiction kept them bound to their employers and bound to die. Volume 2 of Dalton's "Indian Books" begins with the heading "Indians in Debt."[13] In the remarkable conjuration characteristic of debt peonage, those who worked came to owe money to those who received the product of that labor, and this debt kept them working. In the particular incarnation of this institution in southern California, alcohol forged the chains that held the Indian workers on the ranches until they so deteriorated that they died. These account books not only chronicle the finances of the ranches and their labor costs. They also served as one of the instruments of the death of the southern California Indians.

The Indians had now become "a people more than half civilized, but now exhibiting such signs of retrogression and decay as must be deplored by every humane heart," lamented even the *Star* in 1853. Several liquor ordinances were passed, but "still the Indians get their liquor the same as ever." Addicted to a new ritual, they could not stop drinking, "especially on the Sabbath, when the little money they have been able to get the rest of the week, is spent for liquor." There was no disagreement on their condition: "Many are aged and infirm," reported the *Star* in 1855, "and are left by the government [they could only be fed if on a reservation] to drag out a miserable existence, living on roots and acorns when they can be obtained, but . . . are fast disappearing to the silent grave for the want of food and clothing." Alcohol produced their social disintegration. "No one will deny that the murders that are committed with such great frequency in our streets originate with liquor," noted *La Estrella,* the Spanish-language version of the *Star* in 1855. "So it is the case that during last week," read a frighteningly typical notice in *El Clamor Público* of 1855, "two Indians succumbed beneath the assassin's knife."[14]

Diseases intensified their physical disintegration. In the 1850s smallpox epidemics "ravaged the town almost regularly every other year." Sherburne Cook, without "violating any canons of epidemiology or commonsense," calculates the "death rate among those infected with these contagions to have been 20 percent." Thus, "if 50 per cent of the population was annually infected, the net annual death rate due to disease would have been 10 per cent." The smallpox epidemic of the winter of 1863 took a particularly appalling toll, depopulating the poorer Mexican and Indian areas of town. It is no exaggeration to say that venereal diseases infected nearly all the Indians. One long series of uninterrupted epidemics, rather than physical violence, accounted for most of the Indian deaths.[15]

Still, a great many died because of Yankee guns. Cook estimates that "somewhat more than 4,000 Indians lost their lives in physical conflict with the Americans and that this number denotes approximately 7 per cent of the entire population decline up to 1880."[16] Most of these killings occurred in the northern part of the state, where the American inundation was greatest. Nevertheless, Anglo-Americans, like the Spanish Americans, routinely slaughtered those on whose lands they intruded throughout California. The Spanish and Mexican periods had some institutionalized restraints, but the American conquerors swept them away.

The estimated figures speak for themselves. The Spanish missions and soldiers reduced the Indian population in the areas they settled from 135,000 to about 98,000 between 1770 and 1832; secularization caused the death of five thousand more; and the Gold Rush years produced the quickest and most devastating destruction of nearly one-half of the remaining Indians in California. By 1860, before the worst smallpox epidemic, at most thirty thousand Indians survived. Maybe twenty thousand remained in 1880, most of them in isolated places. Those persevering at the decaying missions often married lower-

19. Four generations of Indian women living near ex-Mission San Gabriel in 1883. The two seated were ex-neophytes and over one hundred years old. (Courtesy of the Colorado College Library.)

class Mexicans. In the tradition of Spanish-Americans the few remaining mission Indians merged with the general Mexican population through marriage. "It is doubtful," according to Cook, "whether among these assimilated natives any tribal custom whatever exists." One hundred years of efforts to bring progress, Christianity, and civilization to the Indians resulted in their destruction. What began as faith, farce, and tragedy in 1769 now ended simply as tragedy and genocide. A Los Angeles newspaper reported in February 1872 about several Indian women gathered before a saloon: "With disheveled hair, foaming mouths, and disordered and dilapidated garments, they present a disgusting but pitiable sight, while their discordant voices join in some Indian song."[17]

The Crisis of Labor

The eagerness with which the new settlers took to the speculative mentality tells something profound about the attitudes they carried along with their railroad trunks. They did not come all the way to California and risk so much to become as slaves to the soil. Most of them—whether Northerners or Southerners, operating large farms or small, commercial or subsistence—knew that having someone else on the farm to do all or part of the physical labor contributed to their prosperity; yet their countrymen were not about to hire themselves out in significant numbers. Immigrants were eager to work for themselves rather than for someone else. They came for liberty—an independent freehold that would keep them from falling into dependency on wages.[18]

Demand for the agricultural products of these new Californians continued to grow. But for once in this narrative the Indians are notable for their absence. A manager of Lake Vineyard Ranch wrote in 1869, "It has been impossible to hire anyone since Friday—every laboring man seems to be on a grand spree; to send their souls to Heaven, or some other place." By April 1876 Henry Dalton had to go "in search of Indians to work." Juan Bautista Bandini had a similar problem. He "couldn't find a sheepherder in San Luis" in 1881 and even had to tend the sheep himself. The great national depression that began in 1877 might have brought to California Anglo workers displaced from the farms and factories of the East. "Bobby brought me an American to be sheepherder," noted Bandini in August 1881. But California landowners were accustomed to a particular type of laborer. "The sheepherder, Preston," whined Bandini, "doesn't want to sleep in the oaks and told me to find another sheepherder."[19]

Many Mexicans in Los Angeles certainly did unskilled work, but there were far too few of them to meet the labor needs of the area. Nevertheless, they started to replace the disappearing Indians. "These Indians I shall discharge today, they being desirous of leaving," reported the foreman of Lake Vineyard Ranch in July 1854. However, he could "do without anymore having engaged 4 Sonorineans [*sic*] to make joints." Bandini and Couts could not find enough Indian vaqueros for their ranchos, so the former went to Tijuana to hire some Mexicans in April 1864. Though his trip proved unsuccessful, a crucial precedent of looking south for labor was being set. "I was not able to find any Mexicans to take the horses,"

20. Indians and Mexicans assembled for work in Pasadena, probably in the 1870s. (Courtesy of the Los Angeles Public Library.)

Benjamin Wilson's manager reported to him at Lake Vineyard in March 1874. "All the Mexicans are off shearing and you cannot procure any here."[20] Indians were still expected to do the work.

"They [wine growers] are now paying twice the amount for day laborers paid a few years ago, when Indian labor could be had as required," wrote a resident of San Gabriel to the *Star* as early as 1868. "Now their branch of business has increased to such magnitude that it requires other kinds of labor," he added. "Any persons who have lived in the interior portions of California," reported the *Pacific Rural Press* in 1874 on a statewide problem, "must have had some experience in the difficulty of getting hired help for either out-of-doors or in, particularly household help."[21] Obviously, a labor problem existed, a condition of paramount significance as a new era of Hispanic California history dawned. Those who controlled land and capital would solve this issue in the way that the history of Spanish and Mexican southern California prescribed—with a racially identifiable group of workers who would have to acculturate to new lifeways. This situation would call forth a new wave of migration that would populate California with Mexicans who came to work in jobs Anglo capitalism generated. The swallows were now alone at the crumbling Mission San Juan Capistrano—but not for long.

There appeared another solution on the western horizon, however. "The large immigration of Chinese to our shores," prophesied a writer to the *Star*, "will furnish an inexhaustible supply of cheap labor for those who can give constant employment, although it would hardly pay to transport them from San Francisco for a month or two." (One reason many advocated silk farming is that it is not seasonal.) In some ways employers perceived the Chinese to be as good as Indians, in other ways more problematic. Juan Bautista Bandini mentioned Chinese sheepherders in 1879, 1880, and 1881. "In the morning," he reported in March 1880, "[I] took the sheep to the other side [of the rancho] with the Chino." The old ways had not yet completely gone, though, because he "then set the indito to harrow and plow." The next year, after a futile search for some Indians, he recorded, "I arranged with a Chinese to help me handle the sheep." Arcadia Bandini Stearns (now Baker) had a "Chino" who would come on the train to Santa Monica where Bandini lived after 1883, "and the little Chinaman was put to cleaning the house." The Chinese, at least the ones Bandini employed, came and went like the Indians to the mountains. "Before I left," he noted with his

21. Mexicans dipping sheep at Rancho Los Cerritos. From south of the border and from the remnants of Californio society, such workers replaced the vanishing Indians as the rancho labor force. (Courtesy of the Los Angeles Public Library.)

usual languor in April 1885, "I discharged the Chino for rudeness and in the afternoon another one arrived." All through the 1880s one Chinese or another did most of the household chores—cooking, washing, cutting the grass, and cleaning the windows.[22]

The labor crisis, however, loomed in the fields. By the late 1870s, when the decline of the Indian population accelerated, Chinese began to trickle into the San Gabriel Valley to work the former mission lands. Wearing basket hats for protection from the sun, they picked citrus and carried the fruit to packing sheds on bamboo poles. In the early 1880s they laid the railroad ties to transport the oranges to the national market. Elsewhere, though, the *Pacific Rural Press* reported in 1874, "much of the grain goes to waste for want of help to cut it." The same publication exclaimed on July 30, 1881, "It is difficult to see how the present fruit crop, which is bringing such fine prices, or the immense grape crop now ripening, could be handled at all without Celestial aid." Faced with catastrophe, the growers took "measures . . . to secure Chinese help in the fields." Yet the Chinese did not prove to be the answer to the growers' prayers. They received a pittance in wages, but, according to one farmer, Chinese labor, "as far as any experience of it goes, is anything but cheap." Others complained in letters to the *Pacific Rural Press* about the poor quality of work got from the Chinese "as a natural consequence of working with 'brute force and stupidity.' "[23]

White labor proved utterly worthless. White workers expected too much money and, as we saw with Bandini's sheepherder who did not "want to sleep in the oaks," too many luxuries. Those "tramps" who took to itinerant labor in the panic of 1877 "will not work," wrote a grower in 1879. "You must admit," he stated, "that the character of the white labor which has been available for harvest work has been anything but reliable." Some things were said equally about all agricultural workers. In a statement reminiscent of those made about alcoholic Indians on the auction block, one grower ranted against white laborers in the *Pacific Rural Press* in 1879, "The only way the community can force them to earn their own living is to make them criminals and their occupations an offense against the law." Said another grower in 1881, "I have no sympathy to waste on him [a hired white]. His place is on the chain gang." "There can be no doubt that the chief cause of trampdom is laziness," reasoned another agricultural employer in 1883, and concluded, "All savage people are lazy."[24] The growers looked to colored labor. If all laborers were lazy, racism at least allowed the coercion of nonwhite workers by means impossible to use against white ones.

Chinese otherness continued to prove complex. On the one hand, the Chinese neatly replaced the racially distinct Indians in both the fields and in the historical flow of Californian ideas about who should work. On the other hand, they were of yet another different race in this white man's country. The so-called yellow peril added social costs to the price of these workers. "Far better it is," railed an exclusionist grower, "that every orchard and vineyard in the State should go to destruction than that we should continue to import the Mongolian and ruin our children." Both sides of the dispute agreed, however, that the market left the growers little choice. The growers "are afraid of being ruined if the Chinese teat is pulled out of their mouths," argued a Pajaro Valley farmer on the side of exclusion. "If nobody had Chinamen nobody else would need Chinamen. . . . It is only where one fruit-raiser uses heathen labor that another fruit-raiser is compelled to use it so as to compete." The antiexclusionists faced the fact that competition was not merely local. Even if Chinese labor disappeared from the California fields, the problem remained that the Chinese were "mainly employed in those branches of industry which can only be successfully prosecuted by a constant and certain supply of labor at such remunerative wages as will enable the employer to put the products of his industry on the market successfully in competition with the products of cheap labor in the older centers of labor in the world." In other words, the free market gave growers no freedom to choose who would work in their fields. If one farm used extremely cheap labor, then they all had to do so or else that first grower would have the competitive advantage. Even if "every heathen [were] banished from the state . . . it might be a benefit to the working classes left. But still the question presents itself as to who would be found to do cooking and washing then."[25] The Exclusion Act of 1882 involuntarily weaned them from the "Chinese teat," but growers continued to crave the cheap labor on which they had become thoroughly dependent.

In spite of having insufficient workers to make their agricultural products competitive—no one to do their "cooking and washing"—and in spite of the busts destroying both large and small fortunes, many of those caught up in the booms stayed on in California. Los Angeles was now an emerging metropolis as a result of the boom. As the railroad terminus this urban center dominated southern California. From 1880 to 1890 the population increased from 11,183 to 50,395 in Los Angeles and from 73,000 to 201,000 for the southern counties as a whole; the turn of the century would find the city with 100,479 residents. In the 1880s the land value increased from $7 million to $39 million in spite of the drop from the dizzying heights of 1888. The growth chart showed a jagged line, but demand for the goods of southern California generally climbed upwards. In matters of finance optimism prevailed, a legacy of the general incline and of the booms.[26] Demand for southern agricultural goods dominated production, and railroad transportation was developed to connect supply to that demand. But too few people worked in the manner to which those who controlled the California lands had become accustomed.

Los Angeles was now fully an Americano city. The boom of the 1880s had erased what remained of the rancho culture. Remarkably, only a century after the founding of the little pueblo on the Prociúncula, only a trace of the original settlers' descendants or lifeways survived, hidden away in the city. The Mexican community was segregated in Sonoratown and excluded from the spasmodically developing economy. The few remaining Indians lived on reservations or married Mexicans. Although a few Californio families persisted, this period marks a definite break in the history of Spanish and Mexican California. However, the unfolding history of the industrializing city would draw hundreds of thousands (ultimately millions) of Mexicans to be "thrown among those who were strangers" in Los Angeles in the next century. Curiously, though, these later arrivals from the south would inherit the historical legacy of the now-scattered Indians, gente de razón, and cholos. The new immigrants, usually not cholos, had few contacts with their compatriots who preceded them in California. But they would be successors to—actually, they would fill in—many of the patterns of life and labor established in the past decades. They too would acculturate and retrench their ways, resist and adapt. But before turning to their story, we must journey to Mexico as well as visit the imaginations

22. Nigger Alley, Sonoratown. (Courtesy of the Huntington Library.)

of the Anglo-Americans who would breathe new and fantasmagorical life into the story of the missions and ranchos and then retell it in writing.

Mexico

It has been a salient feature of California history in the eighteenth and nineteenth centuries that so much of it was made in faraway places. Madrid, Saint Petersburg, Boston, New York, and Mexico City all affected profoundly what was then a distant place to all of them. Now we must turn to the interior regions of Mexico to understand more about the people of Hispanic southern California. For more than two hundred years—from the founding of the pueblo of Los Angeles to the emergence of the megalopolis of today, which draws so many north to toil at unskilled jobs—people have been journeying from the interior of Mexico to California.

It has become a truism that Mexico has been a land of contradictions, its land rich yet its people poor. But in fact a causal relationship has existed between Mexico's riches and its poverty. Hernán Cortés conquered the Aztecs for their fabulous gold; Spain colonized Mexico for precious metals mined by its remaining human resources; and, in the nineteenth century, British and American businessmen purchased much of Mexico's resources, including oil, as Mexican political elites opened the door of free trade to attract capital for modern industrial development. Mexico was, in other words, desirable in the eyes of more powerful nations, especially if those capital-rich countries needed natural resources and an outlet to invest excess capital. Capitalist expansion and the market replaced the military as the method of imperial conquest in the late nineteenth century. Development from without has been the consistent pattern for Mexico.

These penetrations, however, only intensifed the prevailing situation in Mexico. The contradictions of Mexican society enabled, or even encouraged, the entry of the foreigners. Cortés defeated Montezuma by uniting behind him those whom the Aztecs had subjugated. Until 1810 the Spanish crown maintained its hegemony by carefully balancing and playing off against one another the church, the military, the aristocracy, and the criollo merchants so that no united opposition could emerge. After independence both conservative and liberal political elites looked outside of Mexico for their policies and programs. Liberals, as noted in the case of the secularization, looked to the model of the United States and England to propel them into the rationalist and economically developed modern world. Conservatives looked to France, which captured Mexico in 1862, and to that bulwark of feudal relations in Mexico, the Roman Catholic church, to save them from liberal reform, which threatened their haciendas. The nineteenth century saw repeated the story of La Malinche: Cortés's mistress, who was handed over to him by her Aztec patriarchs and gave birth to the first mestizo, has been labeled a traitor for giving in to the conquistador and abetting the destruction of indigenous Mexico. Mexico was as violated as La Malinche when elites gave over its productive capacity to foreign capitalists during the regime of Porfirio Díaz, or the Porfiriato, as it was known (1877–1910). By the time of the 1910 revolution Americans owned 78 percent of the mines, 72 percent of the smelters, two-thirds of the railroads and rubber business, and more than half of the oil. In both cases short-sighted elites (and, in the era of the Porfiriato, corrupt ones) surrendered bounteous prizes to avaricious outsiders whom they hoped to propitiate. M. Guggenheim Sons' American Smelting and Refining, the Southern Pacific Railroad and the E. H. Harriman family, the Inter-Continental Rubber Company, and Standard Oil owned the lion's share of Mexican resources, though the list of those who participated in this bonanza includes many other familiar names of Gilded Age capitalism. Remarkably, Americans had greater investments in Mexico than Mexicans. Capitalization also meant that many, such as pickmen and carriers in the mines, lost their jobs when machinery replaced them. The peasantry was already desperately poor in the nineteenth century; now they would have new troubles as capital flowed into the country and brought with it the market.[27]

The acquisition of so much of the natural wealth of Mexico by North Atlantic capital thrust the country into the stormy waters of the world market. Of course, a silver-producing region such as Durango had always suffered the effects of fluctuations in the world price of precious metals, which intensified the harsh conditions of work. During the sixteenth and seventeenth centuries silver production in Durango and the surrounding area witnessed some of the most vicious and destructive labor practices in the Spanish empire, stable prices or not. Thousands of impressed laborers, largely Indians, died painful and miserable deaths on account of their work there, particularly from mercury poisoning. Exploitation was nothing new in the mines of Durango. However, in the late nineteenth century the market, in the context of changes in Mexican land law, made both workers' and farmers' subsistence terrifically erratic. In 1892 inflation accompanied a crash in the price of silver, which further lowered most every Mexican's consumption, not merely that of the newly unemployed miners. Then, in the crisis of 1906–07, in which the world demand for silver again fell precipitously, fully one-half of the 10,481 silver-mine workers in Durango lost their jobs.

The Mexican congress enabled massive expropriations of *ejidos,* or common lands, when it passed new land tenure regulations in 1883. Hoping to open territories to more productive foreign investment, the new land law of the Díaz government allowed companies to buy land previously reserved for the common use of villagers in subsistence production. For example, the granting of a near monopoly in quayule, a rubber plant, in Durango and Chihuahua to the Rockefeller-Aldrich interests robbed many villagers of access to their traditional common lands. During the Díaz administration up to 5 million Mexicans lost access to the lands that produced their subsistence. The population increased from about 8.7 million in 1874 to more than 15 million in 1911, and the new agriculture could not adequately feed them. As the power of the church grew under the Díaz regime, its landholdings increased terrifically as well. Their farming no longer viable, many of the people of central Mexico either migrated to the mining and industrial centers, which were receiving new infusions of foreign capital, or labored on the lands of the haciendas owned by joint-stock companies.[28]

It might seem as if capital penetration was bringing progress to Mexico. Production, and sometimes even wages, increased. However, whereas before people worked for their own subsistence, with the often-crushing burden of payment in kind or in labor to the *hacendado,* they now worked for wages in a capricious market. These dismal wages, inadequate to buy enough food for a family, gave a firm push to migration. Unemployment always loomed as a frightening possibility. Before, people were poor and had to work hard, but they were stable socially and geographically. Now, with the advent of the market, they became poorer because their wages could not keep up with inflation. Their subsistence was less dependable because of the loss of common lands and the fluctuations in demand for their products, which resulted in unemployment and underemployment; they worked harder and longer because of the new time discipline of industrialization; and the variability of the market uprooted them from the land and their customary social relations.

The vast majority of those who vacated the lands moved

within Mexico usually to towns or places where industry was emerging or concentrating. But observers and scholars both then and now, in Mexico and the United States, have emphasized the movement north. Most of the Mexicans who emigrated north after 1890 came from the central states of Jalisco, Michoacán, and Guanajuato. In Los Angeles, however, Chihuahua, Zacatecas, Durango, and Jalisco replaced Sonora as the home state of most Mexican immigrants. Ricardo Romo has perceptively analyzed this migration. Life and labor proved difficult for most Mexicans of the lower classes in the late nineteenth century, but their plight was not uniform. Laborers on the haciendas of the north earned more than their counterparts in the south by as much as 50 percent. The limited economic opportunities of northerners still surpassed those in the central and southern regions of Mexico. Northerners had significantly better sharecropping terms as well and could supplement their earnings with seasonal work in the mines of the north or across the border. The common folk of the north were poor but remained deeply rooted in the land all the while their less fortunate compatriots in central and southern Mexico found their bonds to land and community loosening.[29]

The number of Mexicans who moved to the United States trebled during the Porfiriato, though it was relatively small compared to the number that would come in the 1920s. Texas was still the favored place to go, but during the late nineteenth century southern California gained rapidly on Texas as the intended destination of migrants. Initially, they came to replace the Indians, who were dying off, and the Chinese, who were being excluded from railroad, mining, and especially agricultural labor.[30] Migrants fled Mexico to find work first in the burgeoning agricultural enterprises of the Southwest but later, increasingly, in the urban industries of the area. I suspect, however, that we cannot rely on the usual explanation of immigration. Romo posits the typical view that "the lack of economic opportunities and poor material conditions within his [a Mexican emigrant's] rural environment as well as . . . the promise of favorable circumstances in other areas" drew Mexicans north. This view, though true in some cases, conflicts with the peasant worldview in which retrospection and prospect are quite different than for linear-minded people. Peasants, that is, those who engage in subsistence farming or who produce on the land for those who control land and economic power, have looked forward only to survival, not to a new and affluent life somewhere else.

For the peasant, time is essentially circular. Certainly, peasants act for the future, planting trees in the hope of getting fruit, or raising heifers in the hope of getting milk and more cows; but these results, which the seasons regulate and define, are annular. Risks and dangers—pestilence, thieves, landlords, weather—threaten the future constantly. But there can be no "arrival point of assured security or well-being," in John Berger's words. "The only, but great, future hope is survival," which the subsistence farmer hopes to ensure by doing what has always been done. This attitude helps explain why Mexicans migrated at the turn of the century. When they moved north, they intended not so much to stay as to continue their lives in their Mexican village, the center of their world. Thus it was usually an able-bodied young man who came north to make money to supplement his family's meager wages so that they and their *ranchito*, or tenant farm, could survive. Roughly two-thirds of the migrants were single men, and most assumed that they would go back to Mexico some day, as did one of Romo's interviewees, who "left Mexico with the dream of eventually returning to his homeland." Virtually no Mexican immigrants initiated and completed naturalization procedures in the United States; it is unlikely that it even occurred to them to do so. Their social and political aspirations and consciousness remained oriented toward Mexico even after the journey north. Although many stayed and sent for their families, many others, if not most, intended to return to the old ways in the familiar place. Remaining north of the border was an unintended consequence of their effort to survive in Mexico.[31]

California Pastoral

The penetration of the market into a culture liquidates previous effective forms of social organization. Kinship and neighborhood networks and rootedness to ancestral lands fall prey to the commodification of production and producers. This process affected the Mexican peasantry during the Porfiriato. The market also brought such changes to those cultures that created and controlled it. Such cultures, including Anglo-American commercial culture, equated market relationships with freedom. But to other cultures, the unfolding of the market and its ways only translated into destruction. Mexicans perceived that the old bonds that defined the individual were destroyed along with traditional systems of land tenure. Instead, the labor market bound people to it for their subsistence; either they worked on land to which they once had access or joined the migrant pool. In capitalist cultures, however, the same allegiances to kin, social relationships, and the land restrained an individual's liberty and freedom to make a profit from people and the land. Capitalism hardly initiated exploitation, but its form—the market—surely was new. "To separate labor from other activities of life and to subject it to the laws of the market," Karl Polanyi notes, "was to annihilate all organic forms of existence and to replace them by a different type of organization, an atomistic and individualistic one."[32] This dissolution proved the difference. Economics, or the distribution system, had always created the rich and the poor, but the unfolding of production now tended to isolate them from the various ties that had provided some solace. These historical patterns also meant that Anglo-American attitudes changed toward Mexicans and their culture. I shall now proceed to analyze first how the Americans created a fantasy heritage of the old Californios and then how they justified further capitalizing on Mexican labor.

Individuals, if on the free side rather than the bound side of the market, can have the material wherewithal to encourage domestic happiness and can pursue private fancies. But they do so in an atomized fashion. Disengaged from such ties as those to kin and land, a person loses certain restraints. These have been important consequences, usually unacknowledged, of the individual freedom that accrued when the market came to mediate between human beings. "The effect," says Norman O. Brown, "is to substitute an abstraction, *Homo economicus*, for the concrete totality of human nature, and thus to dehumanize human nature." People, things, and land then become useful and desirable only insofar as they have a market value. In other words, something was lost when all this freedom was gained because "in this dehumanized human nature man loses contact with his own body, more specifically with his senses, with sensuality and with the pleasure-principle." These gaps in the "totality of human nature" needed to be filled.[33]

Material success in the rugged marketplace means people have given up something of themselves and certain vital ties to humanity by seeing others as competitors, as people off of whom money can be made. The new materialists of southern California, consumed with production, recalled nonmarket mission and rancho California. They gave birth to the story of California Pastoral to fulfill something of what was lost to them in the inhuman marketplace. This myth captured the popular imagination of Californians—it was even taught in the schools—for many decades. The society pages of southern California newspapers reported how Anglo-Americans re-created such California rituals as the *rancheros visitadores*, or the visits caballeros would make with one another. "Ostensibly a gay affair," Carey McWilliams noted with respect to the *rancheros visitadores*, "the annual ride represents a rather grim and desperate effort to escape from the bonds of a culture that neither satisfies nor pleases." Its images consisted of Indians learning civilization from kindly padres, of hospitable and genteel dons and happy-go-lucky peons, and of Anglo traders bringing liberty and the marketplace to all of these charmingly backward people. This caricature of the reality of California history blossomed in California Days fiestas (without Mexicans), the rehabilitation of the missions (without Indians), and the rewriting of history (with the connivance of nostalgic Californios). "And so they lived," wrote Hubert Howe Bancroft in his fanciful *California Pastoral*, "opening their eyes in the morning when they saw the sun; they breathed the fresh air, and listened to the song of the birds; mounting their steeds they rode forth in the enjoyment of healthful exercise; they tended their flocks, held intercourse with each other,

and ran up a fair credit in heaven." California Pastoral con-
veyed a nice life, especially for market-oriented consumers of
such reveries. "How many," asks Bancroft, "among the states-
men, among the professional and business men and artisans
of our present high civilizations, can say this much?"[34]

The myth has several origins. Many Anglo-Americans who
arrived before 1846 did not condemn the California life-style
they encountered but adopted aspects of it. Said one visitor
in 1843, "Such was life in California in those early days, a
simple Arcadian sort of life with happy contented people who
were rich in lands and cattle [and] cared nothing for wealth."
Old Californios added to the image. The Los Angeles *Star* of
November 6, 1852, reported about Doña Vallejo, who "tells
many a fine yarn of the merry gay times of the old padres,
when all was dancing, *pasearing* in the then simple and primitive land." Now déclassé, Californios conjured up images of
happier times past before the cholos and the Yankee army
annihilated their Arcadia. "The old lady says the ancient times
were the happiest—plenty to eat, no hard work—all California living as one family," the *Star* reported to its English-
speaking readership, many of whom were new arrivals. But
then it continued, "The Mexicans, the revolution, the Yankees and the gold mines, have put off all the happiness for
the next world, and spoiled the young people. It is nothing
but work and getting old now. . . . Ah! for the good old times
of the 'dolce far niente,' never to return."[35]

This seductive image drew in many emotionally hungry
Anglo-Americans. Ironically, only a few decades earlier the
very same culture had railed at Californio indolence and ir-
religion. Now, as California Pastoral grew in their imaginations, many Americans immortalized the fiestas and the missions. The celebration of the centennial of Los Angeles included
"old, creaking *carretas* that had seen service in pioneer days;
there were richly-decorated saddles, on which rode gay and
expert horsemen." Everything was hauled out for the occasion. "Two Mexican Indian women, . . . one named Benja-
mina—alternately scowling and smiling, and declared to be,
respectively, one hundred and three and one hundred and
fourteen years old, formed a feature of the procession." There

23. Caballeros at a plaza fiesta, 1901. (Courtesy of the Huntington Library.)

was even some genuine realism, as "the celebration concluded with a Spanish *baile,* at which dancing was continued until the following morning."

The height of the Spanish fiestas came after the boom of the 1880s. These thoroughly gringo affairs took place at the Americans' most acquisitive moment of popular culture in Los Angeles. For the fiesta of 1894 the Los Angeles *Times* reported that "genuine Indians will be part of the parade." History was literally recalled: "They will be brought in from the reservations." Lending its columns to the support of the Fiesta Fund, the *Times* referred to Los Angeles as "the Chicago of the West—the ambitious, prosperous city of the Western Hemisphere." The city was a far cry from the *suertes, solares,* and *ejidos* of its origins. Nevertheless, according to Harris Newmark, "it is considered by all who have seen Los Angeles grow, that this first fiesta and the resulting strengthening of the [Merchants] Association have been among the earliest, and in some respects, the most important elements contributing to the growth and development of our city." For this fiesta,

Chinese merchants rented all the horses in town for three dollars a day and then rented them to the paraders for five dollars.[36] This plainly mercenary celebration appropriated the Californios' hospitable and disaccumulationist rituals. By doing so, the Anglo-Americans could feel genteel as they avidly pursued their business.

The rancheros, formerly deemed the wasteful monopolizers of the land, entered the pastoral scene as well. "There is one old tough customer left, old Manuel Domínguez, who owns leagues and leagues of land on the sea, extending back nearly to Los Angeles," wrote a traveling correspondent back to the San Francisco *Alta Californian* in May 1869, "and he won't sell an acre." As we saw in the previous chapter, Domínguez (the mestizo prohibited from testifying in court, who collected a gold piece in his pouch as each of his cattle boarded the train to the slaughterhouse) and his ilk had been previously thought of as indolent and unenterprising. Now, however, "he sits in lonely grandeur, defying alike taxes, Yankees, and compound interest; nothing can induce him to sell." (After his death in 1882, his six daughters partitioned the rancho.) "It is probably true," wrote Charles Nordhoff, "that the old Californios were . . . perhaps the happiest people who ever lived on the face of the earth." In contrast to the non-seigneurial ways of Anglo culture, Nordhoff believed that "poverty was unknown, for he who was poor lived on his rich relations; their houses were always open to everyone." He still needed to point out that "they had none of the energy and ingenuity of civilized life," but rather mournfully now, not disapprovingly.[37]

At least one Anglo, herself mythologized, genuinely understood that the white-supremacist market culture had quashed all that the Californios held dear. Helen Hunt Jackson acknowledged this sentiment when she spoke through Señora Moreno in the novel *Ramona:* for the señora, "the idea of having to wage a war with peddlers was to her too monstrous to be believed." Her house was built with its back to the new road, so she could say, " 'Let their travel be where it belongs, behind our kitchens; and no one have sight of the front doors of our houses, except friends who have come to visit us.' Her enjoyment of this never flagged. Whenever she saw, passing the place, wagons or carriages belonging to the hated Americans, it gave her a distinct thrill of pleasure to think that the house turned its back on them." Yet Jackson, the Gilded Age's most sincere and earnest critic of United States policies toward Indians, enshrined the missions in California Pastoral.[38]

Published in 1884 to bring attention to the plight of the Indians of southern California, *Ramona* called forth a storm of protest on the part of those who had grabbed up the Indians' remaining lands. It is both a love story and a bitter tale about the Anglo treatment of the Indians. Ramona, born of an Irish father and an Indian mother, is raised by the severe Señora Moreno, who dislikes cholos as much as she detests Yankee riffraff and peddlers. Ramona and Alessandro, the Temecula Indian who comes with his people from the hills to shear sheep, fall passionately in love. Alessandro's end parallels that of his people generally: an Indian-cursing Anglo murders him after Alessandro has been falsely accused of stealing a horse. The gentle and pious Father Salvierderra represents the remnants of the mission period in *Ramona*. Through his character it appears that the humble and innocent Indians were treated with heavenly and blessed kindness as they received civilization. But Jackson's fantastically popular book ignored the complexities of the mission and rancho periods. Thus was born the inviolable venerability of the missions.[39]

Helen Hunt Jackson held up a mirror to the business practices of the Americans with respect to Indian lands, and many took offense at what they saw. But the mythology coming to surround the missions served an important purpose for the entrepreneurs of southern California. The nostalgia market provided something else to sell the tourists—the missions. Everything from postcards of Ramona's life to pageants depicting her wedding at the mission became a part of southern California Anglo Protestant culture. Curiously enough, the Catholic church did not join the movement, and, needless to say, neither did Mexicans. In 1888 John Fletcher Lummis founded the Association for the Preservation of the Missions, later known as the Landmarks Club, which undertook the

24. Alessandro's people were not always as forebearing as Helen Hunt Jackson's *Ramona*, or this photo, would have us believe. The caption in the archives reads: "Pechanga (Temecula) Indian school about 1890. Mrs. Platt, teacher, . . . was killed by the Indians and the school burned." (Courtesy of the Huntington Library.)

restoration of the crumbling mission buildings. "A thoughtful man," Nordhoff had already written, "cannot visit these and other old missions . . . without feeling a deep respect for the good men who erected these now ruined churches." The padres became as saints: they "gathered around them communities of savages, and patiently taught them not only to worship in a Christian church, but also the habit of labor, the arts of argriculture, and some useful trades." "What a picture that would have made for the artist!" exclaimed E. B. Webb in *Indian Life at the Old Missions,* published in 1952. "It was a sight never again to be seen in California," she (and, presumably, her readers) lamented. Her otherwise-remarkable book is infused with the spirit of *Ramona* and California Pastoral: "It is said that the Indians eagerly looked forward to taking part in this performance in which the Nativity was represented." "The good old padres" and the missions received new life: "The bells rang merrily calling the neophytes. . . .

25 and 26. The missions, which Anglo-Americans once vilified as
coercive toward the neophytes and as monopolizers of land, eventually came to be seen as the saviors of the primitive and unfortunate Indians. In the top photo (c. 1887) an Indian woman is on
display as a basket maker at a Pastoralist celebration, though she
appears to be grinding. In the bottom photo some ancient Indian
women have been brought out for the rededication of Mission San
Luis Rey. (Courtesy of the Huntington Library.)

From the choir loft came the clear, melodious voices of the Indians, their singing mingling with sweet, haunting music of flutes, violins, bass-viols, and trumpets rendering the old hymns and chants taught them by the padres."[40]

The late nineteenth century in California was the era of the white man's burden, and it lasted at least through most of the twentieth century with regard to the California missions. This romanticization also served to blur the jagged edges of cultural genocide in the mission period and of racial hostility and more genocide in the years after the American conquest. Moreover, the embroidering of the missions and ranchos softened both the nature and the implications of the continuing routine of using colored labor. All of these notions combined nicely with the need to create a past for the uprooted Anglo immigrants to southern California and the need for nonmarket social relations to give them some humanity. In this way the missions returned to the southern California landscape.

"No state has a more romantic nor heroic history than California," reads a form letter from Lummis to urge support for "Candle Day" at Mission San Fernando in 1916. The lighting of the candles, "sold at $1 each," was "the romantic and unique feature . . . for this event," which celebrated "the 147th anniversary . . . of the first discovery of this enchanted valley by white men." The story of Andrés Pico, victor at San Pascual and later indigent resident of Mission San Fernando, was further embellished. "I can hear him call yet," declared the daughter of the Methodist developer of Ex-Mission San Fernando, " 'Viene aqui mi chiquito, quiere V. sandilla [*sic*] ' " (" 'Come here my little one, would you like some watermellon?' "). Josephine Maclay Walker recalled of Mission San Fernando that there were "two of the old mission Indians still alive, . . . [One] claimed to be 104 years old. Every day he came to the mission for food. General Pico told us never to give it to him to take home for he had two young wives who would take it away and trade it for whiskey. They were like children and had to be treated as such."[41]

History is our relationship with the past. How a particular history is written or told can reveal as much about those producing it (and this one is probably no exception) as it does about the particular subject. The Americans in the decades at the turn of the century identified personal fulfillment with success in the marketplace. "Running up and down everywhere seeking money, like dogs with their noses to the ground," in Señora Moreno's harsh words, they sought to gain some nobility and *cariño* for themselves in the past they facilely appropriated. "Actually," Carey McWilliams said, "there is something rather pathetic about the spectacle of these frustrated business men cantering forth in search of *ersatz* weekend romance, evoking a past that never existed to cast some glamour on an equally unreal today."[42]

The creation of California Pastoral did not mark the first time that any of the players in that historical drama made up some history. Peoples' relationships to the land, to the productive apparatus, and to those considered alien give strangely varied perceptions of reality. The lonely economic men exaggerated the country's importance, as if Anglo culture had improved on all those before it, and adhered to such abstractions as those embodied in the concept of manifest destiny. The nation prided itself on uniqueness and superiority, and its writers of history were self-congratulatory as well as disparaging of those cultures and colors the United States had conquered. Overvaluing themselves and their commercial mission, but never questioning or reflecting on the loss of their organic ties to people and land, Americans could not comprehend their yearnings, which surfaced in the form of pastoralist fantasies and the crushing of those who maintained those ties, which both repulsed and attracted them. Such disordered thinking and confusion emerging in the guise of self-importance and sense of entitlement can only be interpreted as profound cultural narcissism. An editorial in the *Pacific Rural Press* of 1909 stated:

We desire American prominence and leadership in the commercial, intellectual and social advancement of all Pacific border nations. This means recognition of American mastery if Americans are broad enough to attain it. It also means the wonderful building up of the Pacific Coast States of this nation. It is not reasonable to obscure this clear line of progress by throwing a lot of political or diplomatic litter over it.

America took this grandiose sense of its unique and progressive mission into the twentieth century.[43]

"Feelings of entitlement, interpersonal exploitativeness, relationships that alternate between the extremes of overidealization and devaluation, and lack of empathy" characterize narcissists' "responses to threats to self-esteem" and "disturbances in interpersonal relationships," according to the clinical literature.[44] This description fits many American views regarding the consistent devaluation of other peoples' notions of land and lifeways; it explains Americans' exploitation of others through real-estate schemes and certain labor practices; their alternation between pastoral and derogatory views of Hispanics; and their remarkable lack of compassion for people who suffer the destructive consequences of manifest destiny and the penetration of their market into traditional social relations. The mission padres thought themselves culturally superior to Indians and caused them tremendous pain, but they initially approached the heathens with compassion. A narcissistic culture, by contrast, cannot reflect the reality of another culture because it has severed its ties with "other." Such others are only important or meaningful insofar as they contribute to the idealization of the narcissist. The self, then, is actually the object of the gaze. In such a looking glass American culture appeared as grandiose, an image Americans greatly admired.

There is much more to understanding the relationships of Anglo-Americans to people of color besides their lack of empathy and their sociopathy, of course. The expansiveness resulting from the internal dynamics of the capitalist economic system may be the primary explanation of Anglo-American actions. Certainly, the application of contemporary psychological labels to past cultures is problematic. Nevertheless, the concept of narcissism uncannily characterizes the "personality" of Anglo-American culture, both as it looked backward to the nineteenth century and appropriated a pastoralized Californio history and as it looked forward to Mexico to provide a solution to its labor problems.

With this feeling of entitlement Americans continued throwing the few Indians remaining in southern California off their lands, even in the twentieth century. At the Warner ranch in 1902, 301 Indians, in "their ancient homes, to which they are so pathetically attached," were "under judgment of eviction by the Supreme Court of the United States." According to the Indian Advisory Commission, the land was "worthless except as a stock ranch, for which purpose it is now used by the successful claimants in the litigation by which the Indians are dispossessed." The "Captain of the Indians," Cecilio Blacktooth, said to the commission:

You see that graveyard over there? There are our fathers and grandfathers. You see that Eagle Nest Mountain and that Rabbit-Hole Mountain? When God made them he gave us this place. We have always been here. We would rather die here. Our fathers did. We cannot leave them. . . . If Harvey Downey says he owns this place, that is wrong. The Indians always here.

If you [the commission] do not buy this place [to make it a protected reservation], we will go into the mountains like quail and die there, the old people and the women and children. Let the government be glad and proud. It can kill us. We do not fight. We do what it says. If we cannot live here, we want to go into those mountains and die.[45]

This same sense that conferred to the Americans rights to the land also permitted them to treat similarly those who would come to produce on that land.

The emerging economic elites of Los Angeles (as well as its small employers) and everyone in agriculture felt both compelled and and entitled to use Mexicans as cheap labor. The competitive market and the need to maintain low wages provided the motivation for his compulsion. Mexicans saved the women and children of landowning families from having to do peasant labor. Thus, family virtue justified and called forth more cheap laborers. American self-importance included the sense that Mexicans existed for Americans to use. The Americans objectified them so they could more appropriately serve labor needs, just as they objectified Californio history to serve emotional needs. Moreover, their actual and genuine success in the marketplace, freeing family members from backbreaking toil, further validated the Anglo-Americn worldview. This success gave them even more optimism about a controllable future of which they could take charge.

La Gente Mexicana after 1848

Mexicans, of course, were real people. Most of them in California neither owned a large rancho nor were employed as cholos. Nevertheless the chaos and meanness that Mexicans generally experienced after the conquest profoundly influenced them. Richard Griswold del Castillo admirably portrays how the mass of Hispanic Californians fared in the half-century after 1848. Economic misfortunes plagued the small landholder who lived in Los Angeles sooner than they did the rancheros. Only about 3 percent of the ten thousand Mexican Californios in 1850 owned a large rancho. Yet Griswold del Castillo shows that "in 1850, 61 percent of Mexican-American heads of families owned small parcels of land worth more than 100 dollars." Only ten years later that figure had dropped to 29 percent and by 1870 to 21 percent. If we include those who did not head households, only 5 or 10 percent held on to land in the decades after the conquest. Not all those lands, which included many small shops, were alienated to whites, however. Newly arrived Mexican immigrants acquired some of those properties, especially in the economically turbulent 1860s, though they usually lost them fairly quickly.[46]

Nearly 75 percent of those Mexicans employed in 1844 worked in lowly occupations, and that figure would not change through the 1870s. Actually, according to Griswold del Castillo, the era brought a slight increase in opportunities for skilled workers. But many, if not most, landless Mexicans in southern California worked with the cattle, where stable seigneurial relations between owner and worker prevailed. Albert Camarillo's study of Santa Barbara shows that "either out of pride, or preference, or job discrimination, most remained tied to the ever diminishing pastoral economy." The decline of cattle thrust these people into the unskilled labor market, where itinerant work became the norm. As the productive landscape changed, so did work for Mexicans in southern California. During the 1870s Santa Barbara adobe construction

gave way to brick and lumber as the city became American-
ized in its population and tastes, and the demand for skilled
Mexican adobe masons disappeared. By the 1890s, after the
Chinese had departed from Santa Barbara, Mexicans typically
worked the unskilled day labor jobs in building and street
construction. They continued in unskilled work as the economy changed, though the quality and quantity of those jobs
changed with it. Once the land base had been transferred to
the Americans, Mexicans could find neither independence as
small producers nor a sympathetic *patrón* to attach themselves to. Dependence on a seasonal and illiberal labor market proved the only opportunity for unskilled Mexicans in the
late nineteenth century.[47]

As with the imposition of new forms of work discipline on
missionized Indians, the structure of labor imposed new demands on Mexicans as economic activity commercialized in
the decades following the war. Family structure felt the consequences of the labor market. Ideally, men headed Mexican
families, providing food and protection, whereas women
maintained the home, taking care of the men and children.
Children learned respect for their elders, expressed as formality and deference. Girls received *consejos* (advice) from all
manner of sources—newspapers, popular plays, folk songs—
about remaining faithful to the proper female roles of wife
and mother and disciplining the extravagant sexual urges that
nineteenth-century culture anxiously attributed to women. The
upper classes could best afford adherence to such cultural expectations regarding roles, whereas the demands of lower-class
life meant that poorer women often had to do jobs intended
for men. The claims of work on the male elders, though, meant
that working-class families had an even more difficult time
maintaining family norms. Dangerous seasonal labor produced
widowhood and both temporary and permanent abandonment
of husbands among southern California Mexicans. Griswold
del Castillo finds that "more than 31 percent of Mexican-
American families were headed by women" by the 1880s. Yet
surprisingly, rates of female employment were low. Women,
usually house servants, comprised only 13 percent of Mexican
wage laborers in Los Angeles during that time. As *vendadores*

27. A Mexican ranch hand and his family in front of their adobe at Rose Ranch, largely vineyards, near Pasadena in the late 1870s. (Courtesy of the Huntington Library.)

in the marketplaces, however, they provided picturesque images for Anglo newcomers and tourists and subsistence for their families. The demands of work pressed laboring Mexicans into conflict with their cultural norms regarding the proper roles of women and men.[48]

No better sign of the Mexicans' situation can be found than their geographic instability. The structure of the labor market and the presumptions about who should fill it remained the same. Now, however, people moved in and out of it because of its itinerant, rather than seigneurial, nature. Griswold del Castillo calculates that only about a quarter of the heads of household before 1848 remained in Los Angeles during the 1850s. A remarkably low one-tenth of the Mexican inhabitants maintained residence in Los Angeles in the following two decades. (In other cities of the United States usually 40 to 50 percent persisted over those decades.) According to Griswold del Castillo, "by 1880, more than 90 percent of the total population [of Los Angeles] had migrated there after the Mexican War of 1848." Only 12 percent of those who lived in Los An-

28. One of the original adobes of Los Angeles that Señora Magdalena Cacia (?) built in 1837. (It was destroyed in 1925.) In this photo from the 1890s the building is inhabited by recent Mexican migrants. (Courtesy of the Huntington Library.)

geles in 1844 still did so in 1880. Yet the overall number of Spanish-speaking residents of Los Angeles remained rather stable. In 1844 there were 1,469, in 1850, 1,215, and in 1860, 2,069. Griswold del Castillo finds no significant increase in the 1860s and 1870s. Similarly, in Santa Barbara "a veritable exodus of Mexicans of the post-1848 migration had occurred," states Camarillo. Of the 117 Mexican-born households enumerated in 1860, the census listed only 8 of these remaining in 1880, though the total population remained about the same. Discontinuity now came to characterize the Mexican population of southern California. The ravages of violence, the market, and discrimination had clearly taken their toll.[49]

Yet no doubt those very beseiged families sheltered Mexicans from the dilapidating influences of the market. *Compadrazco*, the extended family, and an ideology that put the family above the self both connected individual Mexicans to something larger than the impersonal world of work and provided them shelter during times of unemployment or sickness. So too did the *mutualista*, or mutual-aid society. These self-help organizations, which local middle-class Mexicans or elites usually organized, sought to maintain the culture in the midst of Anglo presumptuousness, outright hostility, and overwhelming numbers. They celebrated Mexican holidays and functioned as fraternal societies. They gave loans to Mexican-American business people and, most important, offered life insurance to working-class Mexicans, which provided for the care of the beneficiary's family and a proper Catholic burial. Present throughout Mexico and the United States, these societies furnished an organizational structure to Mexican communities, which Chicano scholars are beginning to discover and analyze. Mexicans created and participated in, or at least had available to them, a rich institutional life that facilitated their everyday needs for physical aid and comradeship. La Sociedad Hispano-Americano de Beneficia Mutua, one such organization formed in Los Angeles in 1875, stated that "unity constitutes strength" for "*nuestra raza*," the term the mutualistas most commonly used to refer to themselves. Mexicans formed mutualistas—social, cultural, and prepolitical organizations—to sustain themselves when they were "thrown among those who were strangers," and these societies further rooted Mexicans in the north.[50]

In the context of the Americans' effective monopolization of political power and violence, Mexicans could only adapt to their marginalization. They did not participate significantly in the developing southern California economy or its culture of production. The market and the exclusionary nature of Anglo-American economics either debarred or eliminated Mexican property owners large and small. The new labor market proved oppressive to traditional Mexican life-styles or unattractive to many others who preferred the old ways and occasional work to the menial tasks available. The economic and cultural place of Mexicans on the changing southern California landscape translated into their geographic isolation as well. As the Americans brought the peculiarities of their labor relations, architectural aesthetics, and language, that landscape became more and more unfamiliar to Mexicans. Thus the barrio, So-

29. Mexican workers at the Sansevain Winery about 1900. They replaced the Indians whom such wine killed. (Courtesy of the Seaver
Center for Western History Research, Los Angeles County Museum.)

nora Town in Los Angeles, became more and more attractive
to them because of its unconfused Mexican temper and appearance. Geographically unsteady, Mexicans in the Southwest moved in and out of the various barrios, where they
found cultural stability and identity.

California would have been, and would be today, a different place indeed if people had done more of their own work.
Perhaps Indian women would not have left for the foreigners'
missions, or the Indians would not have been perceived as
only good for work and drink, or Californios would not have
assumed that work is for peons and Indians and not for hidalgos. The greater efficiency and leisure that the division of
labor has brought some people has come at a high cost for
many others. Pain, turmoil, dislocation, and death, in the case
of the Indians, emerged from these processes and notions.

The interaction of cultures need not be such a negative ordeal. It can be an enriching experience if carried out in an
atmosphere of openness and tolerance. But when two cultures

act on one another within the context of power relations, as usually happened in California, the resulting tensions are neither enlightening nor creative but destructive and spiritually alienating. Work and notions of other were of central importance to the unfolding of these tensions in California. Questions of race and labor based the cultural interactions analyzed in this book firmly within the context of power relations. Throughout California history, technology has not saved elites and the middle class from labor—Mexicans and Indians did. Having people darker than themselves do their work for them was one factor that united Californio and interloping American elites. This notion has proved crucial to understanding why so many would be thrown among strangers so often and why their lives would be ones of often perplexing or agonizing acculturation to the production demands that those strangers made on them.

Epilogue

The chief difference between the man of the archaic and traditional societies and the man of the modern societies with their strong imprint of Judeo-Christianity lies in the fact that the former feels himself indissolubly connected with the Cosmos and the cosmic rhythms, whereas the latter insists that he is connected only with History.

Mircea Eliade, *Cosmos and History: The Myth of the Eternal Return*

*Returning it back, returning
it back, you will go on, life will go on.
That's what the People say.
That's what the land says.*

*If we don't do that,
life will continue to be exploited,
the land will be used up
and the People will remain colonized and powerless,
and the city jail
will still be full of Indians.*

Simon Ortez, *Fight Back: For the Sake of the People, For the Sake of the Land*

In agricultural societies, men believed that time consisted simply of cycles, of seasons. Each winter solstice contained the same moment. An individual grew old of course, but that was simply because he wore himself out: a man was the fuel which made the machine of the seasons go. Capitalism will supply the idea of time-as-highway. Highway of the sun, the highway of progress. The idea of progress was that the conquerors hadn't simply won a battle, but that they had been chosen and designated because they were superior beings. Their superiority would inevitably span the cycles and the seasons. It transformed them into cork-screws of which they, the conquerors, were the tip. And with that tip they opened the bottles of the lesser cultures, one after another. They drank until their thirst was quenched and tossed aside the bottles, assuring themselves that they would break. This was a new kind of violence. The arrow or the sword had previously killed, but what killed now was the verdict of history. The history of the conquerors of course. With this new violence arose a new fear among the conquerors: the fear of the past, fear of the lesser beings in their broken bottles.

Alain Tanner and John Berger, *Jonah Who Will Be Twenty-Five in the Year 2000*

People and History

An End and a New Beginning

This narrative about Indian, Spanish, and Mexican California came to a close at the turn of the century because time had changed so thoroughly by then. For the Mexicans and the Anglos, time was a highway. Progress, with strikingly different outcomes for each group, brought them to new ways of being on the landscape of southern California and to new conflicts, usually with strange others. For the Indians, though, time ended.

Eliade, Ortiz, and Tanner and Berger—the Romanian-American scholar of religion, the Ácoma poet, and the Swiss filmmaker and the contemporary British writer quoted in the epigraph—all acknowledge that history has not been a positive record for all people. Even for those who succeeded, progress has meant the sacrifice of certain aspects of their humanity. In this book I have related the remarkable productive attainments of the mission priests and the American entrepreneurs and the compelling graciousness of the rancheros. I also chronicled the enormous human destruction that accompanied these achievements. We saw in chapter 1 how Indian peoples always had to renew the cosmos, "returning it back" to nature so that "life will go on," as Ortiz writes. "That's what the land says" for humans to do to maintain the proper relationships. The Indians ritualized return in the dual sense of giving back to nature in propitiation for having taken from her, and of repeating the ways of the ancestors. Such activity maintained the people, in the words of Eliade, "indissolubly connected with the Cosmos and the cosmic rhythms." The Spanish and the Americans, for different reasons, separated the Indian peoples from their sacred histories, rituals, and spirits (through missionization and alcohol) and from their lands (through reduction, secularization, and commodification). Thus they became "colonized and powerless"; the city jails of California filled with Indians, and they died out. The Indians were not simply "thrown among strangers" but were thrown onto the highway of history. When that happened, time could not regenerate itself; it was now moving forward, and the Indians' relationship to the archaic cycles dissolved. When the natives no longer affirmed these ancient and revivifying rhythms, they ceased to be as a people. For them to have an existence, they had to be joined to the cycles. Previously they seemed to be able to maintain the cycles through rituals and adherence to the sacred ways. The movement flew out of their control now; the conquerors made time linear with such notions as ten years' neophyte training, secularization, and wage labor. The "idea of time-as-highway" made it a terrible journey, one from which they did not return. On it they encountered diseases against which they proved helpless; new ways of work and body discipline that separated them from the spirits that animated their old worlds; and addictions that chained them to linear history, which careened down the highway. Entrance into history killed them, not simply the microbes, guns, alcohol, and labor systems. For a long time the conquerors held that the Indians' passing was either a virtue, because they were disgusting savages, or pitiable, because they remained in the way of progress. It was inevitable either way. In these pages, though, the story has been told— too late for them to continue—of "the lesser beings in their broken bottles."

The others carried on, but progress took them to different places. For Anglo-Americans in southern California, history proceeded along a highway the curves of which their commercial mission deemed unimportant, their self-importance allowed them to ignore, or their armed manpower simply straightened out. Southern California grew phenomenally in the early twentieth century because so much money flowed there to fuel the bonanzas in real estate, agriculture, and industry; because so many people moved there to consume its yield; because transportation further developed to take the rest of the output to market; and because so many more Mexicans, and other peoples, came there to do the actual labor needed to produce the fortunes.

The history of Mexicans, and of work and acculturation to its demands, would proceed in twentieth-century California from the history of Indians that I have here analyzed. I wonder if there is not something unflattering about this situation in which work is central to the history of Mexicans in the United States. America admires the entrepreneurial and frontier spirits. Thus, it celebrates migratory Puritans, forty-niners, and homesteaders, not Mexicans who came to labor or Africans who came in chains. The English and the Spanish both spoke of a civilizing mission to the savages of the New World. Disease and guns, however, twisted this endeavor into one of destruction. Nevertheless, Europeans and Anglo-Americans persist in believing in the virtue of their migrations because they spread civilization—understood as Christianity, body discipline, language, and European ways of organizing politics. But actually, no one's migrations are all that exalted. The Puritans' fabled errand into the wilderness was an escape from the perceived chaos and sinfulness of England, which they feared God would punish; the Spaniards moved to conquer (spiritually and economically) and to secure a life of leisure based on Indio labor; and westering Americans sought wealth in the goldfields or real estate schemes or sought free land, which often as not enslaved them to toil and misery. People moved for a variety of reasons, usually to fill their bellies or their coffers or because the old place was perceived as intolerable. None of them willfully and freely moved: something pushed them out. Thus, I do not think that anyone's story of migration to a new place is more praiseworthy than anyone else's. The issue, more likely, has to do with the tossing aside of the bottles they found there.

When the conquerers drank of the labor of the savages, they usually disparaged them to justify doing so and to maintain the natives as dependents or captives. Americans depreciate, or do not find interesting, the despised and dependent beings that their economic system has brought forth. Thus, they have rarely found in Mexicans a worthwhile story, or perhaps they secretly have feared it. But this has been a good story, one that will continue along the difficult highway of twentieth-century history.

Labor and production persistently defined the history of Mexicans in the United States, at least through World War II. Itinerant gang labor in agriculture and on the railroads of the Southwest was always essential. Mexicans worked in urban service industries as well, though not in great numbers. What some have called a secondary labor market of dead-end, low-paying jobs defined the work lives of Mexicans north of the border. Mexicans responded with a variety of adjustments, resignation, and resistance. In the twentieth century Mexican workers acted to improve or even fundamentally change the productive relations they inherited in southern California. The activity and ferment around the Mexican revolution stimulated nationalist union organization in the first decades of the century, not only on the old mission grounds but also in the agricultural fields of California. Usually Mexican radicals, or Anglo communists, led such efforts, which promised comprehensive changes in the distribution of wealth. Later, in the late 1930s, Mexicans joined and led racially mixed unions within the Congress of Industrial Organizations, helping integrate them structurally into the American pluralist system. Such union organization, whether radical or reformist, exclusively Mexican or racially mixed, meant that they were setting down roots in the new land and investing energy in creating a better life there. Often with the help of their CIO unions Mexicans pushed into better jobs in the 1930s and especially during the expansive war years. Many men served in the United States Army in World War II and returned with a sense of themselves as Americans.

Thus, Mexicans acted to change the trajectory on which Indian history had set them. The adaptation of aspects of American popular culture, particularly among American-born youth, and the desire for political inclusion in the years after

World War II, produced a new *mestizaje*. A diversity of responses to their often-oppressive situation and aspirations for a better life characterized Mexicans' efforts to live in the north. Out of these various endeavors to resist, adapt to, assimilate, integrate into, and change American work and politics would come a new journey, a new story.

Notes

Chapter 1: If Its Inhabitants Are Addicted to Independence

1. Interrogatorio of 1813, quoted in Zephyrin Engelhardt, *San Fernando Rey, the Mission of the Valley* (Chicago, 1927), 30; Hugo Reid, letters of 1851 nos. 16 and 17 to the Los Angeles *Star*, reprinted in Susanna Bryant Dakin, *A Scotch Paisano: Hugo Reid's Life in California, 1832–1852* (Berkeley, 1939), 262; Bernice Eastman Johnston, *California's Gabrielino Indians* (Los Angeles, 1962), 129; George Harwood Phillips, *Chiefs and Challengers: Indian Resistance and Cooperation in Southern California* (Berkeley and Los Angeles, 1975), 6–7; A. L. Kroeber, *Handbook of the California Indians* (Washington, D.C., 1925), 631.

2. Zephyrin Engelhardt, *San Gabriel Mission and the Beginnings of Los Angeles* (San Gabriel, Calif., 1927), 4; Fray Pedro Cambón to Fray Rafael Verger, February 28, 1772, in Francis J. Weber, ed., *The Pride of the Missions: A Documentary History of the San Gabriel Mission* (Los Angeles, 1978); Fray Junípero Serra to Fray Don Antonio María Bucareli, May 21, 1773, in *Writings of Junípero Serra*, ed., Antoine Tibesar (Washington, D.C., 1966), 1:359.

3. Prevailing wisdom has it that the word *indios*, or Indians in English, derives from Columbus's mistaken belief that he had reached the East Indies. It is just as likely that he referred to the people he encountered in the Carribean variously as *sindioses* (Godless ones) or *en Diós* (in God), which by corruption became *indios*. That is

the opinion of some Pueblo elders. See also Russell Means, "Fighting Words on the Future of the Earth," *Mother Jones* 5 (December 1980), 25. Christopher Columbus, "The Letter of Christopher Columbus to Rafael Sanchez, Written on Board the Caravel While Returning from His First Voyage" (1493), facsimile ed. (Murfreesboro, N.C., 1970) contains the usual version, though one wonders how well the Genoan's Spanish made it into the Latin in which the letter was published as a popular broadside.

4. For the various adjectives preceeding *gentiles,* see, for example, José de Gálvez, "Patentes e Instruciones a los Empleados de la Expedición Marítima de Monterrey, 29 de Deciembre—12 de Febrero"; his letters to de Croix, December 16, 1768, and August 29, 1769, Archivo General de Indias, Seville (henceforth AGI), Wright Collection, Huntington Library; de Anza to Bucareli, Tubac, March 7, 1773, in Herbert Eugene Bolton, *Anza's California Expeditions,* 5:603; E. B. Webb, *Indian Life at the Old Missions* (Los Angeles, 1952), 52.

5. Means, "Fighting Words," 25.

6. Kroeber, *Handbook,* 620–22, 831–32; Sherburne F. Cook, *The Conflict between the California Indian and White Civilization* (Berkeley and Los Angeles, 1976), 193; Johnston, *California's Gabrielino Indians,* 10–15.

7. Kroeber, *Handbook,* 930, 633, 839; Alfonso Ortiz, *The Tewa World: Space, Time, Being, and Becoming in Pueblo Society* (Chicago, 1969), 45–51; Frank Waters, *Book of the Hopi* (New York, 1977), 7, in regard to the importance of femaleness in Pueblo culture, notes: "With the pristine wisdom granted them, they understood that the earth was a living entity like themselves. She was their mother; they were made from her flesh; they suckled at her breast. For her milk was the grass upon which all animals grazed and the corn which had been created specially to supply food for mankind. But the corn plant was also a living entity with a body similar to man's in many respects, and the people built its flesh into their own. Hence corn was also their mother. Thus they knew their mother in two respects which were often synonymous—as Mother Earth and the Corn Mother." According to Preston Holder, *The Hoe and the Horse on the Plains: A Study of Cultural Development among North American Indians* (Lincoln, Nebr., 1974), 57–59, among the agricultural Caddoans the Grandmother Leaders were central figures in the tribes, and the peoples' most sacred object, the bundle, had names like Mother Born Again or Lucky Woman Leader. For a modern feminist discussion of these notions, see Ad-

rienne Rich, *Of Woman Born: Motherhood as Experience and Institution* (New York, 1977), 70–105.

8. Kroeber, *Handbook*, 930, 633, 839; Ortiz, *The Tewa World*, 45-51; Fermín Lasuén, "Refutation of Charges" (1801), in *Writings of Fermín Lasuén*, ed. and trans. Finbar Kenneally (Washington, D.C., 1965), 2:204; Hugo Reid, "Letter no. 3 to the Los Angeles *Star*" (1852), reprinted in Dakin, *Scotch Paisano*, 226.

9. Christopher Vecsey, "American Indian Environmental Religions," in Christopher Vecsey and Robert W. Venables, eds., *American Indian Environments: Ecological Issues in Native American History* (Syracuse, N.Y., 1980), 19–24; Calvin Martin, *Keepers of the Game: Indian-Animal Relationships and the Fur Trade* (Berkeley and Los Angeles, 1978), 33–36; Frank Hamilton Cushing, "Zuñi Fetiches" (1883), in *Zuñi: Selected Writings of Frank Hamilton Cushing*, ed. Jesse Green (Lincoln, Nebr., 1979), 195–203; my fortunate experience of team-teaching a course at Colorado College on the cultures of the Southwest, in spring 1983, with José Rey Toledo, an elder of Jémez pueblo, has significantly influenced this discussion. It may be of some consequence that I gained this knowledge through oral, not written, communication with Mr. Toledo. The choice of verb tenses in this section on Indian ways may seem a bit awkward. Indeed, most California Indians "were," but many Indians still "are." Simon Ortiz, in his short story "What Indians Do," wonders at the audacity of white academics who refer to the "recovery" of Indian village sites and the need for Indian languages to be "preserved." Indians actually exist, and they need not preservation but feeding through ritual. Indians continue; hence the use of the present perfect in this text, because "Returning it back, returning / it back, you will go on, life will go on. / That's what the People say. / That's what the land says." Those who have kept the rituals have continued. Simon J. Ortiz, "What Indians Do," in his *Fightin'* (New York, 1983), 104–11, and Simon J. Ortiz, "Returning It Back, You Will Go On," in *Fight Back: For the Sake of the People, For the Sake of the Land* (Albuquerque, 1980), 41-44. The author has benefited from several readings by, and discussions with, Simon Ortiz as part of the Colorado College Southwest Studies Program.

10. "Diary by Serra of the Expedition from Loreto to San Diego, March 28 to July 1, 1769," in *Serra Writings*, 1:109; Sir George Simpson, *Narrative of a Journey round the World, during the Years 1841 and 1842* (London, 1847), 1:345; J. F. G. de la Pérouse, *A Voyage round the World, Performed in the Years 1785, 1786, 1787,*

and 1788, 3d ed. (London, 1807), 2:193. For more on *"las pulgas,"* see "The Flea in California History and Literature," *California Historical Society Quarterly* 15 (December 1936), 329-37; K. T. Khlebnikov, *Memoirs of California* (1829), translated from the Russian with a biographical sketch of the author by Anatole G. Mazour, *Pacific Historical Review* 9, no. 2 (September 1940), 324; Alfred Robinson, *Life in California before the Conquest* (1846; San Francisco, 1925), 141–42.

11. La Pérouse, *Voyage round the World*, 2:193; *The Portolá Expedition of 1769–1770, Diary of Miguel Costansó*, Publications of the Academy of Pacific Coast History, 2:29, 33, quoted in E. B. Webb, *Indian Life at the Old Missions* (Los Angeles, 1952), 14–15; "Font's Complete Diary of the Second Anza Expedition," in Herbert Eugene Bolton, ed. and trans., *Anza's California Expeditions* (Berkeley, 1930), 4:251; Kroeber, *Handbook*, 628, 624; Johnston, *California's Gabrielino Indians*, 1, 60.

12. Kroeber, *Handbook*, 633, 646, 832–33; Marvin Harris, *Cows, Pigs, Wars, and Witches: The Riddles of Culture* (New York, 1975), 111–24; Marshall Sahlins, "The Spirit of the Gift," in his *Stone Age Economics* (Chicago, 1974), 168–71; Douglas Monroy, "The Sun Chief and the Accumulationist Personality," *Southwest Economy and Society* 11, no. 2 (Fall 1983), 46–55.

13. Cook, *Conflict*, 139; Kroeber, *Handbook*, 647; Sahlins, *Stone Age Economics*, 171–79; la Pérouse, *Voyage round the World*, 2:202.

14. Kroeber, *Handbook*, 647; Harris, *Cows, Pigs*, 83–87; a good example of a violent culture devaluing women is that of the Yanomamo of Brazil and Venezuela. Perhaps the most fierce people known, their "society is decidedly masculine. . . . There is a definite preference to have male children." Females have no recourse against the constant violence the men inflict on them and "are largely pawns to be disposed of by their kinsmen, and their wishes are given very little consideration." Napoleon A. Chagnon, *Yanomamo: The Fierce People* (New York, 1968), 81–84.

15. Kroeber, *Handbook*, 647.

16. Kroeber, *Handbook*, 626, 640–41, 668–73.

17. Kroeber, *Handbook*, 627, 650, 851–54.

18. Martin, *Keepers of the Game*, 113-18; Vecsey, "American Indian Environmental Religions," 22–23; Barry Holstun Lopez, *Of Wolves and Men* (New York, 1978), 90–97; Cushing, "Zuñi Fetishes," 194–97, and "On the Trail," in Cushing, *Zuñi*, 310; Kroeber, *Handbook*, 624.

19. Cook, *Conflict*, 99; Harris, *Cows, Pigs*, 126–30; Kroeber,

Handbook, 652; Sahlins, "The Original Affluent Society," in *Stone Age Economics,* 1–32.

20. Mircea Eliade, *Cosmos and History: The Myth of the Eternal Return* (New York, 1959), 88–89; Calvin Martin, "Time and the American Indian," and Richard Drinnon, "The Metaphysics of Dancing Tribes," both in *The American Indian and the Problem of History,* ed. Calvin Martin (New York, 1987), 192–220 and 109–11.

21. E. Bradford Burns, *Latin America: A Concise Interpretive History* (Englewood Cliffs, N.J., 1972), 11–14; Charles C. Cumberland, *Mexico: The Struggle for Modernity* (New York, 1968), 41–43; Charles Gibson, *Spain in America* (New York, 1966), 3–16; James D. Cockcroft, *Mexico: Class Formation, Capital Accumulation, and the State* (New York, 1983), 23–24; *The Poem of the Cid,* trans. Rita Hamilton and Janet Perry (New York, 1984), especially 47–53 and 63–65, which tells "what a great day it was for Christendom when the Moors fled from the place. . . . There was great rejoicing in the Christian host when they found that they had lost only fifteen of their number. They brought in endless quantities of gold and silver and all the Christians were enriched with the booty they had won" (63, 65).

22. Cockcroft, *Mexico,* 31, 46–47; Hubert Howe Bancroft, *History of California* (1884; San Francisco, 1963), 1:110–13; John Francis Bannon, *The Spanish Borderlands Frontier, 1513–1821* (New York, 1970), 49–54.

23. Carlos Francisco de Croix to Julian de Arriaga, May 28, 1778 (Ciudad Mexico), Arriaga to Croix, October 18, 1768, and Bucareli to Arriaga, May 27, 1774, Chapman documents nos. 1014 and 2625, AGI (Julian de Arriaga was "Teniente General de Estado y del Despacho de la Marina é Indias"); C. Alan Hutchinson, *Frontier Settlement in Mexican California: The Híjar-Padrés Colony, and Its Origins, 1769–1835* (New Haven, Conn., 1969), 2–10.

24. *Gazeta de Madrid,* March 19 and May 14, 1776, quoted in Hutchinson, *Frontier Settlement,* 12. For an example of the inability to see the unity of the Spanish efforts, see John Francis Bannon, *The Spanish Borderlands,* 155, who describes the military preparations for California and then adds, "And since no Spanish frontier was complete without the mission . . . ," as if establishing a mission were an afterthought.

25. Gálvez to Rivera y Moncada, August 20, 1768 (Ciudad Mexico), Chapman document no. 1050, AGI; Gálvez, "Instrucción . . . [para] Don Gaspar de Portolá, February 20, Chapman document no. 1206, AGI; "Diaz's Diary from Tubac to San Gabriel, 1774," in

Bolton, *Anza's California Expeditions*, 2:288–89; Bucareli to Arriaga, November 26, 1774 (Mexico City), in Bolton, *Anza's California Expeditions*, 5:195; Charles III to Croix, April 8, 1770, Chapman document no. 1460, AGI; Gálvez to Croix, December 16, 1768, Chapman document no. 1128; Serra to Neve (reminding the latter what he had said before) January 7, 1780, in *Writings of Serra*, 3:410–11.

26. Statement "de un particular," Prov. Int. Tom. 23, Wright Collection, Archivo General de México (henceforth AGM).

27. Gibson, *Spain in America*, 82–83; Nancy M. Farriss, *Crown and Clergy in Colonial Mexico, 1759–1821: The Crisis of Ecclesiastical Privilege* (London, 1968), 88–89, 91–92, 99–100, 136–37; Hutchinson, *Frontier Settlements*, 43–44; Robert Archibald, *The Economic Aspects of the California Missions* (Washington, D.C., 1978), 2–3.

28. Serra to the Superiors of San Fernando College, October 17, 1767, and Serra, "Diary of the Expedition from Loreto to San Diego, March 28 to July 1, 1769," both in Serra, *Writings*, 1:33, 67; Farriss, *Crown and Clergy*, 43–44.

29. Eulalia Pérez, "Una Vieja y Sus Recuerdos" (1877), Bancroft Library, 6, 20; Diary of José María Zalvidea, July 19 to August 14, 1806, Santa Barbara Mission Archives; Julio César, "Recollections of My Youth at San Luis Rey Mission," trans. Nellie Van de Grift Sanchez, *Touring Topics* 22 (November 1930), 43.

30. Hubert Howe Bancroft, *California Pastoral, 1769–1848* (San Francisco, 1888), 618; José María Amador, "Memorias sobre la Historia de California" (1877), Bancroft Library, 99, 108; Bancroft, *History of California*, 3:642n; José Eusebio Galindo, "Apuntes para la Historia de California" (1877) Bancroft Library, 6; Maynard Geiger, "Biographical Data on the Missionaries of San Fernando College Serving the California Missions in 1817 and 1820," *California Historical Society Quarterly* 48 (June 1969), 129–36 (reprints Fray Sarría's report).

31. Neve to Bucareli y Urzua, Monte Rey, June 3, 1777, Prov. Int. Tom. 121, AGM, 43; Gálvez, "Decreto," November 23, 1768, Chapman document no. 1114, AGI; Serra to Bucareli y Ursua, August 17, 1775, in Serra, *Writings*, 2:306; "Font's Complete Diary," 179–80; Bancroft, *History of California*, 1:589.

32. These laws of the Indies are quoted in Francis F. Guest, "An Examination of the Thesis of S. F. Cook on the Forced Conversion of Indians in the California Missions," *Southern California Quarterly* 61 (Spring 1979), 2, and Dora P. Crouch and Daniel J. Garr,

Spanish City Planning in North America (Cambridge, Mass., 1982), 13, 16, 19; Pope Paul III's bull "Sublimis Deus," June 9, 1537, is quoted in Lewis Hanke, *The Spanish Struggle for Justice in the Conquest of America* (Philadelphia, 1949), 73; Bancroft, *History of California*, 1:607–8; Herbert E. Bolton, "The Mission as a Frontier Institution in the Spanish-American Colonies," *American Historical Review*, 23, no. 1 (October 1917), 46–47.

33. Gálvez, "Decreto"; Zumárraga is quoted in Daniel Garra, "Planning, Politics, and Plunder: The Missions and Indian Pueblos of Hispanic California," *Southern California Quarterly* 54 (Winter 1972): 291–92; Croix to Fages, Mexico, November 12, 1770, In Maynard Geiger, ed. and trans., "The First Expansion of the Mission Field of California, 1770–1771," *Southern California Quarterly* 48 (June 1966), 190; Gordon R. Miller, "Shaping California Water Law, 1781 to 1928," *Southern California Quarterly* 55 (Spring 1973), 11.

34. Padre Font is quoted in Bolton, *Anza's California Expedition*, 1:241; Palóu to the Guardian of the College of San Fernando, April 22, 1774, and Lasuén to Fray Pangua, April 23, 1774, are both reprinted in Bolton, *Anza's California Expedition*, 4:135, 141.

35. Serra to Bucareli, May 21, 1773, in Serra, *Writings*, 1:359–63; Francisco Palóu, *Historical Memoirs of New California* (1926), ed. and trans. Herbert Eugene Bolton (New York, 1966), 2:325–26; Bancroft, *History of California*, 1:180–82; Engelhardt, *San Gabriel Mission*, 13; Serra on San Luis Obispo is quoted in Bancroft, *History of California*, 1:189n.

36. Serra to Bucareli, in Serra, *Writings*, 1:363; Bancroft, *History of California*, 1:181.

37. Bolton, *Anza's California Expeditions*, 1:360–61; Hugo Reid, letter no. 16, in Dakin, *Scotch Paisano*, 262; Engelhardt, *San Gabriel Mission*, 90.

38. Hugo Reid, letter no. 22 in Dakin, *Scotch Paisano*, 284; Webb, *Indian Life*, 284–85; Cook, *Conflict*, 150–51.

39. Stanley Diamond, *In Search of the Primitive: A Critique of Civilization* (New Brunswick, N.J., 1981), 4; N. Scott Momaday, *House Made of Dawn* (New York, 1977), 86–91; Claude Lévi-Strauss, *Tristes Tropiques*, trans. John Weightman and Doreen Weightman (New York, 1984), 298–300; the Venetian Bible is on display at Mission San Gabriel.

40. Pangua is quoted in Webb, *Indian Life*, 24–25; "Anza's Return Diary," in Bolton, *Anza's California Expeditions*, 2:224, 110; Rafael Verger to Bucareli, December 25, 1772, Chapman document

no. 1939, AGI; Bucareli to Arriaga, May 27, 1774, Chapman document no. 2625, AGI; Serra to Bucareli, August 15, 1775, in Serra, *Writings*, 2:306–7; Guest, "Thesis of S. F. Cook," 64.

41. Serra to Bucareli, May 21, 1773, in Serra, *Writings*, 1:363; Palóu, *Historical Memoirs*, 2:326; Lasuén, *Writings*, 2:204, 206.

42. Carlos N. Híjar, "California in 1834: Recollections" (1877), Bancroft Library, 11; F. W. Beechey, *Narrative of a Voyage to the Pacific and Beerings Straight* [*sic*] (London, 1831), 2:16; Webb, *Indian Life*, 260; Phillips, *Chiefs and Challengers*, 24; the padres' original vestments are on display at Mission San Gabriel.

43. Padre Cambón is quoted in Thomas Workman Temple II, "Founding of Misión San Gabriel Archángel," Part 2, "Padre Cambón's Contemporary Report of the Founding," *The Masterkey* 33 (October–December 1959), 159–60; Jorge Juan y Antonio de Ulloa, *Noticias Secretas de América, 1749* (Madrid, 1918), 2:31; Bancroft, *History of California*, 1:387; Beechey, *Narrative*, 2:19; Cook, *Conflict*, 74–76.

44. A. Duhaut-Cilly, *Voyage autour du Monde, principalment à la Californie et aux Isles Sandwich, pendant les années 1826, 1827, 1828 et 1829* (Paris, 1834–35), in "Duhaut-Cilly's Account of California in the Years 1827," ed. and trans. Charles Franklin Carter, *California Historical Society Quarterly* 7 (1929), 215; Lasuén, *Writings*, 2:205; Cook, *Conflict*, 76–80.

45. Anastasio Carrillo to de la Guerra, February 21, 1822, de la Guerra Papers; Nellie Van de Grift Sanchez, *The Spanish Period* (Chicago, 1926); Cook, *Conflict*, 76–79. José María Amador, "Memorias sobre la Historia de California" (1877), Bancroft Library, 14–15, 36. Francis F. Guest, a defender of the missions, contends that "there is no valid or reliable documentation which proves that a governor, presidio commander, or missionary sent an armed party of soldiers or missionized Indians into the wilderness to force non-Christian Indians to be reduced in a mission in violation of this law." His evidence, though, is the testimony of the padres. Guest does allow, however, that the authorities could punish "rebellion" or "harboring fugitives" with "capture." Guest, "Thesis of S. F. Cook," 2–10.

46. Juana Machado, "Los Tiempos Pasados de la Alta California" (1878), Bancroft Library, 2–4; Beechey, *Narrative*, 24. Defenders of the missionaries' methods include Webb, *Indian Life at the Old Missions*, Zephyrin Engelhardt, *The Franciscans in California* (Harbor Springs, Mich., 1897) and *The Missionaries of California* (San Francisco, 1912), and Guest, "Thesis of S. F. Cook." See Bancroft,

History of California, and Cook, *Conflict,* for critical views of these conversion methods.

47. Archibald, *Economic Aspects of the California Missions,* 153–55.

48. Padre Cambón is quoted in Temple, "Founding of Misión San Gabriel," 159; Toypurina and Nicolás José are quoted in Thomas Workman Temple II, "Toypurina the Witch and the Indian Uprising at San Gabriel," *The Masterkey* 32 (September–October 1958), 146–49; Phillips, *Chiefs and Challengers,* 25–26.

49. Bancroft, *History of California,* 1:249–55; Cook, *Conflict,* 65–66; Serra to Pangua, April 13, 1776, in Serra, *Writings,* 1:417; "Anza's Diary of the Second Anza Expedition, 1775–1776," in Bolton, *Anza's California Expeditions,* 3:87; "Garcés Diary from Tubac to San Gabriel, 1774," in Bolton, *Anza's California Expeditions,* 3:339–40; Palóu, *Historical Memoirs of New California,* 4:61. Only Palóu believed that the neophyte Indians were largely faithful. Anza, Lasuén, Bancroft, and Cook are all convinced that renegade Christians participated in the San Diego revolt.

50. Pedro Fages, "Report on the Californias, 30 November, 1775," Chapman document no. 3042, AGI, 16–17; Serra to Croix, August 22, 1778, in Serra, *Writings,* 3:255. Serra continued in the same lengthy letter to Croix that in regard to "pueblos composed of Spaniards, or of people of mixed blood," he could "not see or recognize any advantage in it [a secular settlement] whatever, either on the temporal or spiritual side."

51. Fages, "Report on the Californias," 25; Serra to Bucareli, Mexico City, March 13, 1773, Serra to Pangua, April 17, 1776, Serra to Pangua and the Discretorium, Monterrey, December 8, 1782, in Serra, *Writings,* 1:299, 301, 3:2, 4:169; Bancroft, *History of California* 1:191, 383; Bannon, *Spanish Borderlands Frontier,* 160, 164.

52. Bancroft, *History of California* 1:200, 634, 2:189; Fray Francisco González de Ibarra to de la Guerra, July 11, 1822 (San Fernando Rey), de la Guerra Papers; Serra to Bucareli, Mexico City, April 22 and June 11, 1773; Serra to Pangua and Discretorium, July 18 and July 19, 1774, and June 6, 1777; Serra to Bucareli, January 8, 1775; Serra to Neve, January 7, 1780; Serra to Lasuén, July 10, 1778, in Serra, *Writings,* 1:341, 357, 2:107, 109, 121, 198, 203, 3:205, 415.

53. Serra to Croix, August 22, 1778, in Serra, *Writings,* 3:252–53; Pérez, "Una Vieja," 6; Padre Calzada is quoted in C. Alan Hutchinson, "The Mexican Government and the Mission Indians of Upper California, 1821–1835," *The Americas* 21 (April 1965), 340–41.

54. José del Carmen Lugo, "Life of a Rancher," *Historical Society of Southern California Quarterly* 32 (September 1950), 227; Pablo Tac, "Conversion of the San Luiseños of Alta California," ed. Ninna Hewes and Gordon Hewes, *The Americas* 9 (July 1952); Lasuén, *Writings*, 202; Webb, *Indian Life*, 149.

55. Juan Bojorges, "Recuerdo sobre la Historia de California" (1877), Bancroft Library, 9; Bucareli to Arriaga, Mexico City, January 27, 1773, in *Anza's California Expeditions*, 5:53; Serra to Bucareli, August 17, 1775, in Serra *Writings*, 2:306; the San Gabriel padres are quoted in Webb, *Indian Life*, 43.

56. Gil y Taboada and Zalvidea are quoted in Webb, *Indian Life*, 47; Pérez, "Una Vieja," 20; the responses to the "Contestación" are in Cook, *Conflict*, 143–44; Lorenzo Asisara's narrative is in Amador, "Memorias."

57. Bancroft, *History of California* 1:590; Durán is quoted in Irving Berdine Richman, *California under Spain and Mexico, 1535–1847* (Boston, 1911), 254; Lasuén, *Writings*, 204; W. S. W. Ruschenberger, *Sketches in California in 1836* (Los Angeles, 1953), 8; Cook, *Conflict*, 145–57.

58. Pérez, "Una Vieja," 15; Webb, *Indian Life*, 248–51; José del Carmen Lugo, "Vida de un Ranchero" (1877), Bancroft Library, 105; José Arnaz, "Recuerdos" (1878), Bancroft Library, 31; Intelligent Bostonian, *Northwest Coast of America and California: 1832, Letters from Fort Ross, Monterey, San Pedro, and Santa Barbara* (Los Angeles, 1952), 18–19; Encarnación Piñedo, "Early Days at Santa Clara," *The Owl* (April 1934), quoted in Webb, *Indian Life*, 252; Duhaut-Cilly, *Voyage*, 164.

59. Santa Barbara Presidio Comandancia Militar, "Diligencia practicada en esta referida Misión para la veriguación de indicios de echiseria, de cuyo crimen es acusado el Neofito y carpintero de esta muy referida Misión nombrado Tomás," Juez Cabo Antonio Solorzano, July 30, 1826, Mission Santa Inez, Miscellaneous legal documents dealing with military, civil, and criminal cases, chiefly in Los Angeles and Santa Barbara, in de la Guerra Papers; Cook, *Conflict*, 144–57, at 149.

60. Juan Bandini to Eustace Barron, December 8, 1828, Stearns Papers, box 4; Hugo Reid, letter no. 22, in *Scotch Paisano*.

Chapter 2: Brutal Appetites

1. Christopher Caudwell, *Further Studies in a Dying Culture* (1938; New York, 1971), 94–98, 124–27; Michael Paul Rogin, *Fa-*

thers and Children: Andrew Jackson and the Subjugation of the American Indian (New York, 1975), 12.

2. Webb, *Indian Life*, 32-38 (the padres from San Luis Rey are quoted on page 36); Lasuén, *Writings*, 2:202, 207.

3. This discussion derives from John Berger, "Why Look at Animals," in his *About Looking* (New York, 1980), 1–13; Lopez, *Of Wolves and Men*, 98–113; Diamond, *In Search of the Primitive*, 8–9; and Carolyn Merchant, *The Death of Nature: Women, Ecology, and the Scientific Revolution* (San Francisco, 1982), 99–215; *The Little Flowers of St. Francis*, ed. and trans. Raphael Brown (Garden City, N.J., 1958), 88–91, 321–22.

4. Lewis Mumford, *Technics and Civilization* (New York, 1934), 31–33, 107–12; Michel Foucault, *Discipline and Punish: The Birth of the Prison* (New York, 1979), 135–56; Fray Antonio Peyri to Juan Bandini, December 25, 1828, Stearns Papers.

5. Mumford, *Technics and Civilization*, 33–36; Lasuén, *Writings*, 2:202.

6. Padre Venegas is quoted in Alexander Forbes, *California: A History of Upper and Lower* (London, 1839), 184.

7. Lasuén to Fray Antonio Nogueyra, January 21, 1797, in Lasuén, *Writings*, 2:6; Serra to Lasuén, January 12, 1780, in Serra, *Writings*, 3:418.

8. Pérez, "Una Vieja," 16; Apolinaria Lorenzana, "Memorias de La Beata" (1878), Bancroft Library, 7–8; "Font's Complete Diary of the Second Anza Expedition," in Bolton, *Anza's California Expeditions*, 4:181–82; Lugo, "Vida," 100; Carlos N. Híjar, "California in 1834: Recollections" (1877), Bancroft Library, 33; Amador, "Memorias," 90; Bancroft, *California Pastoral*, 232; Webb, *Indian Life*, 27–28; Sanchez, *Spanish Period*, 306; Antonia Castañeda, "Comparative Frontiers: The Migration of Women to Alta California and New Zealand," in *Western Women: Their Land, Their Lives*, ed. Lillian Schlissel, Vicki Ruiz, and Janice J. Monk (Albuquerque, 1988), 290.

9. Lasuén, *Writings*, 2:206–7; la Pérouse, *Voyage round the World*, 2:200; Engelhardt, *San Gabriel Mission*, 91 (the San Gabriel fathers are quoted on page 82); Lugo, "Vida," 22; Michel Foucault, *The History of Sexuality*, vol. 1, *Introduction* (New York, 1980), 24–27.

10. "Font's Complete Diary," in *Anza's California Expeditions*, 4:270; Douglas Monroy, "They Didn't Call Them Padre for Nothing: Patriarchy in Hispanic California," in *Between Borders: Essays on Mexicana/Chicana History*, ed. Adelaida R. Del Castillo (Encino, Calif., 1990).

11. La Pérouse, *Voyage round the World*, 2:201; Cook, *Conflict*, 86, 89–90. Oddly, no one mentions flea infestation as a factor in the Indians' new lives in the missions.

12. "Diary of Juan Bautista de Anza," in Bolton, *Anza's California Expeditions*, 2:205; "Garcés' Diary from Tubac to San Gabriel," in *Anza's California Expeditions*, 2:347; "Font's Complete Diary," in *Anza's California Expedition*, 4:178; Archibald, *Economic Aspects*, 11; Webb, *Indian Life*, 40–41, 168–71; Cook, *Conflict*, 142.

13. Bancroft, *History of California*, 1:613–16; Lugo, "Life of a Rancher," 225–26; Archibald, *Economic Aspects*, 145; Webb, *Indian Life*, 100, 130–31; Lasuén to Don José Arguello, November 20, 1792, to Don Diego de Borica, January 26, 1796, and January 29, 1796, Lasuén, *Writings*, 1:258–59, 369–71; Amador, "Memorias," 194.

14. Bancroft, *History of California*, 1:591–92; Lasuén, *Writings*, 207; Sanchez, *Spanish Period*, 305; Cook, *Conflict*, 91–94; la Pérouse, *Voyage round the World*, 2:197.

15. Archibald, *Economic Aspects*, 11, 159; Engelhardt, *Mission San Gabriel*, 58, 71–74; Lugo, "Vida de un Ranchero," 98–99, 113; Bancroft, *History of California*, 1:617–18; J. M. Guinn, *Historical and Biographical Record of Southern California* (Chicago, 1902), 41.

16. Bancroft, *History of California*, 1:387–88, 577; Archibald, *Economic Aspects*, 179; Guinn, *Historical and Biographical Record*, 50.

17. The following table, compiled from data in Archibald, *Economic Aspects*, 154–79, compares the number of cattle and the number of Indians living in the California missions.

Year	Number of Neophytes	Number of Cattle	Neophytes:Cattle
1785	5,123	6,813	1:1.33
1791	8,425	25,180	1:2.99
1795	11,025	31,167	1:2.83
1800	13,688	54,321	1:3.97
1805	20,372	95,035	1:4.67
1810	18,770	116,306	1:6.20
1815	19,467	139,596	1:7.17
1820	20,473	149,489	1:7.30

18. The San Gabriel padres are quoted in Webb, *Indian Life*, 41; Pérez, "Una Vieja," 18; Lugo, "Vida," 100; Amador, "Memo-

rias," 188; Híjar, "California in 1834," 34; la Pérouse, *Voyage round the World*, 2:197; Cook, *Conflict*, 40–48; Richard Sutch, "The Care and Feeding of Slaves," in Paul A. David, Herbert G. Gutman, Richard Sutch, Peter Temin, and Gavin Wright, *Reckoning with Slavery: A Critical Study on the Quantitative History of American Negro Slavery* (New York, 1976), 261–67; Neal Salisbury, *Manitou and Providence: Indians, Europeans, and the Making of New England, 1500–1643* (New York, 1984), 31–32.

19. Archibald, *Economic Aspects*, 11, 109–14 (Governor Solá is quoted on page 110); Engelhardt, *San Gabriel Mission*, 59; Hutchinson, "Mexican Government," 336–37; Engelhardt, *San Fernando Rey*, 36–37; Fray Antonio Peyri to Juan Bandini, October 6, 1828, Stearns Papers, Box 49.

20. Governor Solá to Father Payeras, San Juan Bautista, June 27, 1918, Santa Barbara Mission Archives, quoted in Archibald, *Economic Aspects*, 110; Fray Pascual Nuez to Prefect Mariano Payeras, San Gabriel, June 5, 1820, de la Guerra Papers.

21. Sanford A. Mosk, "Price-Fixing in Spanish California," *California Historical Society Quarterly* 17 (June 1938), 118–21; Archibald, *Economic Aspects of the California Missions*, 14–16, 22–26; Fray Francisco González de Ibarra to de la Guerra, San Fernando Rey, May 2, 1825, de la Guerra Papers; Nuez to Payeras, June 5, 1820.

22. Rafael Verger to Bucareli, December 25, 1772, AGI, Chapman Document no. 1939; Lasuén to Don Jacobo Ugarte y Loyola, October 20, 1787, Lasuén, *Writings*, 1:168.

23. Archibald, *Economic Aspects*, 103–4; Engelhardt, *San Gabriel Mission*, 94–95; Fray José María de Zalvidea to de la Guerra y Noriega, San Gabriel Mission, October 18, 1815, de la Guerra Papers; Bancroft, *History of California*, 1:614.

24. Archibald, *Economic Aspects*, 130–32; Hutchinson, "Mexican Government," 335; Tomás Almaguer, "Interpreting Chicano History: The World-System Approach to Nineteenth-Century California," *Review* 4 (Winter 1981), 473–77 (Shaler is quoted on page 475).

25. Archibald, *Economic Aspects*, 130, 185; Bancroft, *History of California*, 2:195, 3:89–90; Juan Bandini to Eustace Barron, December 8, 1828, Stearns Papers, Box 4; Lugo, "Life," 229–30.

26. Archibald, *Economic Aspects of the California Missions*, 63–65; Lugo, "Vida," 78.

27. Tac, "Conversion of the San Luiseños," 100.

28. Father Narciso Durán to Governor Figueroa, June 17, 1833, quoted in Webb, *Indian Life*, 222–23; a sign at the Mission San

Gabriel winery tells how the Indians made the wine under the supervision of the padres. The first vines planted in California were at Mission San Juan Capistrano and Mission San Diego in 1779. They first bore fruit in 1781 or 1782, according to Webb. The present author remembers driving on the San Bernardino Freeway in the 1950s and seeing the vineyards on land that once belonged to Mission San Gabriel. By the mid-1960s the smog had killed those remaining vines.

29. César, "Recollections of My Youth," 42; Lugo, "Life," 27; Antonio Olivera, "List of Those Who Ride Horses at the Mission," March 4, 1818, de la Guerra Papers; Francisco González de Ibarra to de la Guerra, Mission San Fernando, July 11, 1821, de la Guerra Papers.

30. Archibald, *Economic Aspects*, 153–55; Guinn, *Historical and Biographical Record*, 69; Phillips, *Chiefs and Challengers*, 34; Cook, *Conflict*, 3–5, 16.

31. Cook, *Conflict*, 9–11, 80.

32. Engelhardt, *San Gabriel Mission*, 82, 90; Cook, *Conflict*, 23; Serra to Bucareli, May 21, 1773, in Serra, *Writings*, 1:363; Zalvidea is quoted in Guest, "Thesis of S. F. Cook," 27; Serra to Bucareli, August 24, 1774, September 9, 1774, and to Don Melchor de Peramas, January 27, 1774, in Serra, *Writings*, 2:145, 177, 31; Fages edict is quoted in Cook, *Conflict*, 106; Bancroft, *History of California*, 1:640.

33. Engelhardt, *San Gabriel Mission*, 90; Bannon, *Spanish Borderlands Frontier*, 157; Bancroft, *History of California*, 1:132; Mumford, *Technics and Civilization*, 97.

34. Diamond, *In Search of the Primitive*, 1; David Carrasco, *Quetzalcoatl and the Irony of Empire: Myths and Prophecies in the Aztec Tradition* (Chicago, 1982), 150–59; Monroy, "They Didn't Call Them Padre for Nothing"; Susan Brownmiller, *Against Our Will: Men, Women and Rape* (New York, 1975), 23–34.

35. Bolton, *Anza's California Expeditions*, 1:360–61; Reid, letter no. 16, in Dakin, *Scotch Paisano*, 262; Engelhardt, *San Gabriel Mission*, 90; Durán is quoted in Cook, *Conflict*, 106; Serra to Neve, Monterey, January 7, 1780, in Serra, *Writings*, 3:415.

36. Reid, letter no. 16, in Dakin, *Scotch Paisano*, 262; Serra to Bucareli, October 4, 1778, in Serra, *Writings*, 3:265; Cook, *Conflict*, 24; Bolton, *Anza's California Expeditions*, 1:453.

37. Amador, "Memorias," 217; Cook, *Conflict*, 30–32; the San Fernando padre is quoted in Engelhardt, *San Fernando Rey*, 30; the San Gabriel padre is quoted in Engelhardt, *San Gabriel Mis-*

sion, 104, and Cook, *Conflict,* 26; Lorenzana, "Memorias," 7; Simpson, *Narrative,* 1:317.

38. Zalvidea to Governor [?], San Juan Capistrano, December 3, 1832, Santa Barbara Mission Archives; Payeras' first statement is quoted in Engelhardt, *Mission San Gabriel,* 109, and his second is quoted in Archibald, *Economic Aspects,* 157; Cook, *Conflict,* 28.

39. Lasuén, "Refutation of Charges," and Memorandum of July 8, 1789, in Lasuén, *Writings,* 2:220, 1:193–94; A. R. Boscana, "Chinigchinich: A Historical Account of the Origin, Customs, and Traditions of the Indians at the Missionary Establishment of San Juan Capistrano, Alta California," in Alfred Robinson, *Life in California before the Conquest* (1846; San Francisco, 1925), 335.

40. Sanchez, *Spanish Period,* 301–2; Serra to Neve, January 7, 1780, in Serra, *Writings,* 3:412; Bojorges, "Recuerdos," 9; Híjar, "California in 1834," 32, 57, 196; Reid is quoted in Guinn, *Historical and Biographical Record of Southern California,* 41; la Pérouse, *Voyage,* 2:194, 199; Webb, *Indian Life,* 50–51; Foucault, *Discipline and Punish,* 43–50.

41. Serra to Neve, January 7, 1780, in Serra, *Writings,* 3:413–15; César, "Recollections of My Youth at San Luis Rey Mission," 42; Amador, "Memorias," 77, 93–94, 98–99; Angustias de la Guerra Ord, *Occurrences in Hispanic California,* ed. and trans. Francis Price and William H. Ellison (Washington, D.C., 1956), 9; Fray Francisco González de Ibarra to de la Guerra, Mission San Fernando Rey, February 23, 1823, de la Guerra Papers; Pérez, "Una Vieja," 20.

42. Florian F. Guest, "The Indian Policy under Fermín Francisco de Lasuén, California's Second Father President," *California Historical Society Quarterly* 45 (September 1966), 210; Fray Tapis is quoted in Webb, *Indian Life,* 49.

43. Fray Tapis is quoted in Webb, *Indian Life,* 49 (see page 27 for Webb's discussion of the necessity of punishment); Cook, *Conflict,* 62–63.

44. Robinson, *Life in California,* 44–45; Duhaut-Cilly, *Voyage,* 215; la Pérouse, *Voyage round the World,* 2:194–95, 199; Bancroft, *History of California,* 2:345; Amador, "Memorias," 67; Lugo, "Life," 227; Lorenzana, "Memorias," 13–14.

45. Monroy, "They Didn't Call Them Padre for Nothing"; Marcia Westkott, *The Feminist Legacy of Karen Horney* (New Haven, Conn., 1986), 101, 109; Foucault, *History of Sexuality,* 25–35.

46. Cook, *Conflict,* 58–61, 70.

47. William Mason, "Indian-Mexican Cultural Exchange in the

Los Angeles Area, 1781–1834," *Aztlán* 15, no. 1 (Spring 1984), 136–37; Bancroft, *History of California*, 2:323–24, 345; Richman, *California under Spain and Mexico*, 219–20.

48. The story of Quintana and his neophytes relies largely on the recollection of Amador, "Memorias," 67–77, which includes the narrative of the neophyte Lorenzo Asisara; Bancroft, *California Pastoral*, 596; José María Estudillo to Fray Marcelino Marquinez, October 15, 1812, California Historical Documents Collection, Huntington Library; Engelhardt, *Franciscans in California*, 376; Bancroft, *History of California*, 2:387–89; Foucault, *Discipline and Punish*, 60–65.

49. Amador, "Memorias," 74.

50. Amador, "Memorias," 74; Ripoll to Father President Vicente Francisco Sarría, Santa Barbara, May 5, 1824, in "Fray Antonio Ripoll's Description of the Chumash Revolt at Santa Barbara in 1824," ed. and trans. Maynard Geiger, *Southern California Quarterly* 52 (December 1970), 354; "Testimony, June 1, 1824," de la Guerra Documents, quoted in Cook, *Conflict*, 108; Bancroft, *History of California*, 2:527–37; Webb, *Indian Life*, 51; Ord, *Occurrences*, 7–9.

51. Bancroft, *History of California*, 2:527.

Chapter 3: To Join as Neighbors

1. Harry Kelsey, "A New Look at the Founding of Old Los Angeles," *California Historical Quarterly* 55, no. 4 (Winter 1976), 327–37; Antonio Ríos-Bustamante and Pedro Castillo, *An Illustrated History of Mexican Los Angeles, 1781–1985* (Los Angeles, 1986), 25–33; Bancroft, *History of California*, 1:340–46; Guinn, *Historical and Biographical Record*, 57–60; Edwin A. Beilharz, *Felipe de Neve: First Governor of California* (San Francisco, 1971), 107–9; Workers of the Writers' Program of the Work Projects Administration in Southern California, *Los Angeles: A Guide to the City and Its Environs* (New York, 1941), 27–28. The planting fields were called suertes because the grantees drew *suertes*, or lots, to see who got the fields closest to the pueblo. Indeed, one depended on *suerte*, which also means luck, to get a prime location for the family field.

2. Eugene Genovese, *The World the Slaveholders Made: Two Essays in Interpretation* (New York, 1971), 3–113; Almaguer, "Interpreting Chicano History," 486–90, 498–501.

3. Bancroft, *History of California*, 1:633n and 2:634n; Don Meadows, descendant of Yorba, is quoted in Robert Glass Cleland,

The Cattle on a Thousand Hills: Southern California, 1850–1880 (San Marino, Calif., 1975), 52–53; Carey McWilliams, *Southern California: An Island on the Land* (1946; Santa Barbara, 1979), 52.

4. Foucault, *History of Sexuality*, 1:92–95.

5. Neve to Bucareli, Monterey, June 7, 1777, Mexico, Prov. Int. 121, AGM, reprinted in *Los Angeles: Biography of a City*, ed. John Caughey and LaRee Caughey (Berkeley and Los Angeles, 1977), 63–66; Fages, "Report on the Californias," 16; Croix's instructions for the recruitment of settlers for the new pueblo are also reprinted in *Los Angeles*, 66–68.

6. Bancroft, *History of California*, vol. 1, reprints these *bandos, instrucciones,* and *reglamentos,* 343–47nn, and 608–9; Kelsey, "New Look," 328–32; Guinn, *Historical and Biographical Record,* 58–61, 92; Hutchinson, *Frontier Settlement,* 43–46; Crouch and Garr, *Spanish City Planning,* 159.

7. Ríos-Bustamante and Castillo, *Illustrated History,* 30–33; Kelsey, "New Look," 333–336.

8. Theodore Grivas, "Alcalde Rule: The Nature of Local Government in Spanish and Mexican California," *California Historical Society Quarterly* 40, no. 1 (March 1961), 11–19; Guinn, *Historical and Biographical Record,* 84–89; Dakin, *Scotch Paisano,* 63.

9. Mason, "Indian-Mexican Cultural Exchange in the Los Angeles Area, 133–35; Guinn, *Historical and Biographical Record,* 62.

10. Bancroft, *History of California,* 1:361–63; Ríos-Bustamante and Castillo, *Illustrated History,* 42–43.

11. Bancroft, *History of California,* 1:319–28, and Neve's letter to Croix is on page 324n.

12. George Vancouver is quoted in John Caughey, "The Country Town of the Angels," in *Los Angeles,* 74–75; Bancroft, *History of California,* 1:558–61; Fray Isidro Antonio Salazar to Viceroy Branciforte, Mexico, May 11, 1796, Santa Barbara Mission Archives, quoted in Archibald, *Economic Aspects,* 94–95; Mason, "Indian-Mexican Cultural Exchange," 126.

13. Cockcroft, *Mexico,* 48–49; Bancroft, *History of California,* 1:460–61, 605–6, 659; Ríos-Bustamante and Castillo, *Illustrated History,* 42–46; Castañeda, "Comparative Frontiers," 287–90; Guinn, *Historical and Biographical Record,* 59–62, 89–90; Sanchez, *Spanish Period,* 468–69; Archibald, *Economic Aspects,* 94–95.

14. Guinn, *Historical and Biographical Record,* 89; Mason, "Indian-Mexican Cultural Exchange," 125–27, states that "in all probability, the letter, if not the spirit, of [Fages's] regulations were observed"; Bancroft, *History of California,* 2:415; William Marvin

Mason, "Fages' Code of Conduct toward Indians, 1787," *Journal of California Anthropology* 2, no. 1 (Summer 1975), 94–98 (Ortega is quoted on page 94); George Harwood Phillips, "Indians in Los Angeles, 1781–1875: Economic Integration, Social Disintegration," *Pacific Historical Review* 49 (August 1980), 431–32, states that Fages's "instructions were often ignored"; Duhaut-Cilly, *Voyage*, 158, 163; Durán is quoted in Hutchinson, "Mexican Government," 339, and in Mason, "Indian-Mexican Cultural Exchange," 129; Richard Henry Dana, *Two Years before the Mast* (New York, 1963), 63.

15. Señan is quoted in Engelhardt, *San Gabriel Mission*, 63; Zalvidea to Governor Sola is quoted in Mason, "Indian-Mexican Cultural Exchange," 131; Archibald, *Economic Aspects*, 94–95; J. Gregg Layne, "Annals of Los Angeles," Part 1, "From the Founding of the Pueblo to the American Occupation," *California Historical Society Quarterly* 13 (September 1934), 204; Serra to Croix, Monterey, August 22, 1778, in Serra, *Writings*, 3:263; Simpson, *Narrative*, 1:402.

16. Cleland, *Cattle on a Thousand Hills*, 7–17 (Fages's request is quoted on page 7); Bancroft, *History of California*, 1:609–11, 659–65; W. W. Robinson, "The Dominguez Rancho," *Historical Society of Southern California Quarterly* 35 (December 1953), 343; George Shochat, "The Casa Adobe de San Rafael in Glendale, California," *Historical Society of Southern California Quarterly* 32, no. 4 (December 1950), 270–77 (Fages is quoted on page 272).

17. Cleland, *Cattle*, 25–29; Bancroft, *History of California*, 4:533.

18. Cleland, *Cattle*, 19; Lugo "Vida," 79–80.

19. Fray Santa María is quoted in Caughey, "Country Town of the Angels," 76; José Bandini, *A Description of California in 1828* (Berkeley, 1951), 9; Duhaut-Cilly, *Voyage*, 311; Dana, *Two Years before the Mast*, 137.

20. Caughey, "Country Town of the Angels," 76; Mason, "Indian-Mexican Cultural Exchange," 130.

21. Duhaut-Cilly, *Voyage*, 311; K. T. Khlebnikov, *Memoirs of California, 1829*, translated from the Russian with a biographical sketch of the author by Anatole G. Mazour, *Pacific Historical Review* 9, no. 2 (September 1940), 325.

22. Durán is quoted in Richman, *California under Spain and Mexico*, 254; Borica is quoted in Guinn, *Historical and Biographical Record*, 66; Juan Bandini to Eustace Barron, December 8, 1828, Stearns Papers, Box 4.

23. Cook, *Conflict*, 218–31; Bancroft, *History of California*, 2:332–34 and 3:358–59; Phillips, *Chiefs and Challengers*, 42.

24. David J. Weber, *The Mexican Frontier, 1821–1846: The American Southwest under Mexico* (Albuquerque, 1982), 60–63; Hutchinson, *Frontier Settlements*, 22, 27–28, 141; Vallejo is quoted in Daniel Garr, "Planning, Politics, and Plunder," 297–98; Bandini to Barron, December 8, 1828.

25. La Pérouse, *Voyage* 2:195; Bandini to Barron, December 8, 1828; de la Guerra Ord, *Occurrences*, 25; Bancroft, *History of California*, 2:527; Weber, *Mexican Frontier*, 63.

26. Hutchinson, *Frontier Settlement*, 96, 141 (Zúñiga is quoted on page 402); Manuel Servín, "The Secularization of the California Missions: A Reappraisal," *Southern California Quarterly* 47 (June 1965), 135–39; Guinn, *Historical and Biographical Record*, 66.

27. Alamán is quoted in Bancroft, *History of California*, 2:488n.

28. Ord, *Occurrences*, 25; Cleland, *Cattle*, 19–20; Hutchinson, "Mexican Government," 335; Weber, *Mexican Frontier*, 63–64; Bancroft, *History of California*, 3:301–2 and 4:42–43, 181–85.

29. Ríos-Bustamante and Castillo, *Illustrated History*, 76–79; Bancroft, *History of California*, 3:186–211; Cleland, *Cattle on a Thousand Hills*, 33, 187; Lillian Charlotte Lederer, "A Study of Anglo-American Settlers in Los Angeles County previous to the Admission of California to the Union" (M. A. thesis, University of Southern California, 1927), 38–46.

30. Ord, *Occurrences*, 25; Cleland, *Cattle*, 19–20; Hutchinson, "Mexican Government," 335; Weber, *Mexican Frontier*, 63–64 (Figueroa is quoted on page 64); the secularization order is quoted in Guinn, *Historical and Biographical Record*, 66–67; Bancroft, *History of California*, 4:42–43, 181–185.

31. Durán to José Figueroa, San Gabriel, August 6, 1833, Santa Barbara Mission Archives; Bancroft, *History of California*, 3:308.

32. W. W. Robinson, "The Indians of Los Angeles as Revealed by the Los Angeles City Archives," *Quarterly of the Historical Society of Southern California* 20 (December 1938), 33–34; Amador, "Memorias," 113.

33. Durán, "Notas y Comentarios al Bando de Echandía sobre las Misiones, 1831," December 31, 1831, in Bancroft, *History of California*, 3:310n, see also 348–49; Ord, *Occurrences*, 31–32; Pérez, "Una Vieja," 14–15.

34. Bancroft, *History of California*, 3:445–57; Ord, *Occurrences*, 42.

35. Webb, *Indian Life*, 304–306 (Duflot de Mofras is quoted on page 296); Ord, *Occurrences*, 49; Bancroft, *History of California*, 3:645; Weber, *Mexican Frontier*, 65–67; Pío Pico, "Regulations for

Sale of the Missions," October 28, 1845, California Historical Documents, Huntington Library.

36. Durán is quoted in Hutchinson, "Mexican Government," 350–351; Cook, *Conflict*, 5; Bancroft, *History of California*, 3:619, 643–48, 656; Cave J. Couts to Benjamin Wilson, Guajomito Rancho, August 15, 1853, Benjamin Wilson Papers; Hugo Reid, letter no. 21, in Dakin, *Scotch Paisano*, 282; Robinson, "Indians of Los Angeles," 16–17; Phillips, "Indians in Los Angeles," 436–37.

37. Bancroft, *History of California*, 2:323–24; Cook, *Conflict*, 218–31; Anastasio Carrillo to de la Guerra, Los Angeles, August 5, 1821, de la Guerra Papers; Juana Machado, "Los Tiempos Pasados de la Alta California" (1978), Bancroft Library, 17.

38. Machado, "Los Tiempos Pasados," 11–15; Bancroft, *History of California*, 3:614–15 and 4:67–77; Arguello is quoted in Robert F. Heizer and Alan F. Almquist, *The Other Californians: Prejudice and Discrimination under Spain, Mexico, and the United States to 1920* (Berkeley and Los Angeles, 1971), 17–18; Engelhardt, *San Fernando Rey*, 51–52; Simpson, *Narrative*, 1:353.

39. Robert Glass Cleland, *This Reckless Breed of Men: The Trappers and Fur Traders of the Southwest* (Albuquerque, 1976), 270, 308–10; Phillips, *Chiefs and Challengers*, 42–43.

40. Heizer and Almquist, *Other Californians*, 18; Simpson, *Narrative*, 1:353; Phillips, *Chiefs and Challengers*, 43; Bancroft, *History of California*, 4:67–77.

41. Phillips, "Indians in Los Angeles," 436–37; Hutchinson, "Mexican Government," 350–51; Bancroft, *History of California*, 4:52–53; Vicente Guerrero is quoted in Guinn, *Historical and Biographical Record*, 67; the ayuntamiento proceedings for February 1846 are quoted in Robinson, "Indians of Los Angeles," 167; de la Portilla is quoted in Phillips, *Chiefs and Challengers*, 37; George O. Schanzer, "A Russian Visit to the Spanish Franciscans in California, 1836," *The Americas* 9, no. 4 (April 1953), 456.

42. Max Horkheimer, "The End of Reason," in *The Essential Frankfort School Reader*, ed. Andrew Arato and Eike Gebhardt (New York, 1978), 30.

43. Horkheimer, "End of Reason," 32; Bancroft, *History of California*, 3:633–44n, lists those who received grants between 1831 and 1840; Cleland, *Cattle*, 23–24; J. W. Wood, *Pasadena, California: Historical and Personal* (n.p., 1917), 29–30, 34–35.

44. Helen Tyler, "The Family of Pico," *Historical Society of Southern California Quarterly* 35, no. 3 (September 1953), 229–36; Weber, *Mexican Frontier*, 214; Cleland, *Cattle*, 67.

45. Machado, "Los Tiempos Pasados," 16; Lugo, "Vida," 86–97; Amador, "Memorias," 216; Dana, *Two Years before the Mast*, 191–92; Robinson, *Life in California*, 67; Bancroft, *California Pastoral*, 373–74.

46. Mumford, *Technics and Civilization*, 128–31.

47. Khlebnikov, *Memoirs of California*, 324–25; William Henry Brewer, *Up and Down California in 1860–1864: The Journal of William H. Brewer* (Berkeley and Los Angeles, 1966), 13; Simpson, *Narrative*, 1:383; Duflot de Mofras is quoted in Nellie Van de Grift Sanchez, *Spanish Arcadia* (Los Angeles, 1929), 309; Gloria E. Miranda, "Hispano-Mexican Childrearing Practices in Pre-American Santa Barbara," *Southern California Quarterly* 65, no. 3 (Winter 1983), 313.

48. Sanchez, *Spanish Arcadia*, 264, 374; José Antonio Rocha and Juan Antonio Carrillo, "Report as to the Value of the Mission Warehouse at San Pedro," April 7, 1834, Stearns Papers, Box 81.

49. Lugo, "Vida," 75–76, 84–85, 98.

50. José del Carmen Lugo, "The Days of a Rancher in Spanish-California," translated by Nellie Van de Grift Sanchez, *Touring Topics* 22, no. 4 (April 1930), 22; Amador, "Memorias," 228; Híjar, "Recollections," 22; Sanchez, *Spanish Arcadia*, 355.

51. Simpson, *Narrative*, 1:383; Duhaut-Cilly, *Voyage*, 311; Ord, *Occurrences*, 25; Arnaz, "Recuerdos," 24–25; Miranda, "Hispano-Mexican Childrearing Practices," 308–13; Sanchez, *Spanish Arcadia*, 266–77; Sepúlveda is quoted in Bancroft, *California Pastoral*, 329; in Latin *famulus* means slave, and *familia* for the Romans denoted the household—slaves as well as kin of the patriarch.

52. Bancroft, *California Pastoral*, 329; Sanchez, *Spanish Arcadia*, 264.

53. Bancroft, *California Pastoral*, 333–34; Bancroft, *History of California*, 2:575; Amador, "Memorias," 207–8.

54. Lugo, "Life of a Rancher," 223–24; William Henry Thomes, *Recollections of Old Times in California, or California Life in 1843*, edited with an introduction by George R. Stewart (Berkeley, 1974), 14; Salvador Vallejo and J. B. Dye are quoted in Sanchez, *Spanish Arcadia*, 41–42 and 444, resp.; Híjar, "Recollections," 21; Simpson, *Narrative*, 1:381, 387; Joseph B. Chiles, *A Visit to California in 1831, as Recorded for Hubert Howe Bancroft* (Berkeley, 1970), 16.

55. Karl Polanyi, *The Great Transformation: The Political and Economic Origins of Our Time* (Boston, 1957), 46.

56. Híjar, "Recollections," 21.

57. Dana, *Two Years before the Mast*, 190–93; Robinson, *Life in*

California, 101, 171; Arnaz, "Recuerdos," 14; Híjar, "Recollections," 16–18; Amador, "Memorias," 226–27; the gowns worn at the wedding fiesta Dana describes are on display at the Santa Barbara Historical Museum.

58. Gloria B. Miranda, "Gente de Razón Marriage Patterns in Spanish and Mexican California: A Case Study of Santa Barbara and Los Angeles," *Southern California Quarterly* 63, no. 1 (Spring 1981), 8.

59. Robinson, *Life in California*, 73–75, 171; Híjar, "Recollections," 9–12, 17, 23; Vicente Gómez, "Lo que sabe sobre cosas de California" (1876), Bancroft Library, 8, 72; Amador, "Memorias," 229; Lugo, "Vida," 116–28; Sanchez, *Spanish Arcadia*, 287–89, 300, 307–8, 446.

60. S. M. Lee, *Glimpses of Mexico and California* (Boston, 1887), 71; Arnaz, "Recuerdos," 23–24; Amador, "Memorias," 206–11; Bancroft, *California Pastoral*, 362–63; Eliza W. Farnham, *California, Indoors and Out; or, How We Farm, Mine, and Live Generally in the Golden State* (New York, 1856), 186–87; Sanchez, *Spanish Arcadia*, 50.

61. Lugo, "Vida," 82–83; Arnaz, "Recuerdos," 17–18; Amador, "Memorias," 116, 206–11; Bancroft, *California Pastoral*, 364–65; Sanchez, *Spanish Arcadia*, 443, 446, 451–52.

62. Robinson, "The Indians of Los Angeles," 162–71; Sanchez, *Spanish Period*, 472; Phillips, "Indians in Los Angeles," 436–37.

63. Híjar, "Recollections," 16–17; Cleland, *Cattle*, 30–31; Sanchez, *The Spanish Period*, 445; Edwin Bryant, *What I Saw in California; Being the Journal of a Tour in the Years 1846–1847* (New York, 1848), 448; Lugo, "Life," 216; Robert Cameron Gillingham, *The Rancho San Pedro: The Story of a Famous Rancho in Los Angeles County and of Its Owners the Dominguez Family* (Los Angeles, 1961), 227; Dr. Marsh is quoted in Sanchez, *Spanish Arcadia*, 109; Bandini to Barron, December 8, 1828.

64. Bryant, *What I Saw in California*, 448; Bandini, *Description of California in 1828*, 10; Lugo, "Vida," 76–77; Híjar, "Recollections," 9, 207; Bancroft, *California Pastoral*, 312, 333, 508.

65. Guest, "Thesis of S. F. Cook," 8; Señora Vallejo is quoted in Sanchez, *Spanish Period*, 434; Albert Ferdinand Morris, *The Journal of a "Crazy Man": Travels and Scenes in California from the Year 1834 to the American Conquest*, ed. Charles L. Camp, *California Historical Society Quarterly* 15, nos. 2, 3 (June, September 1936), 237.

66. "Prayers, religious verses . . . of José Antonio de la Guerra y Noriega," in Personal Papers File, de la Guerra Papers.

67. Ruschenberger, *Sketches in California in 1836*, 4; T. J. Farn-

ham, *The Early Days of California: Embracing What I Saw There, with Scenes in the Pacific* (Philadelphia, 1860), 117; Almaguer, "Interpreting Chicano History," 478; Lederer, *Study of Anglo-American Settlers*, 24–25; Max Weber, *The Protestant Ethic and the Spirit of Capitalism* (New York, 1958), 51.

68. José Antonio Pico to Abel Stearns, February 28, 1836, Stearns Papers, Box 49; Sanchez, *Spanish Arcadia*, 39.

69. Antonio José Rocha and José Antonio Ezequiel Carrillo, "Purchase of Old Warehouse by Don Abel Stearns from the Fathers . . .," April 7, 1834, Papers Relating to San Pedro, Stearns Papers, Box 81; Dakin, *Scotch Paisano*, 88; Lederer, *Study of Anglo-American Settlers*, 24–26; Cleland, *Cattle*, 187–89; John A. Hawgood, "The Pattern of Yankee Infiltration in Mexican Alta California, 1821–1846, *Pacific Historical Review* 27 (1958), 28.

70. Lederer, *Study of Anglo-American Settlers*, 2–4, 12, 28; Sanchez, *Spanish Arcadia*, 132–36; J. M. Guinn, Review of *Sixty Years in Southern California, Historical Society of Southern California Quarterly* 10 (1915–1916), 128; James M. Jensen, "John Forster–A California Ranchero," *California Historical Society Quarterly* 48, no. 1 (March 1969), 37–38; Dana, *Two Years before the Mast*, 63; Ruschenberger, *Sketches in California in 1836*, 4.

71. Ord, *Occurrences*, 54–55; Leonard Pitt, *The Decline of the Californios: A Social History of the Spanish-Speaking Californians, 1846–1900* (Berkeley and Los Angeles, 1966), 6–7; Sanchez, *Spanish Arcadia*, 132; Miranda, "Gente de Razón Marriage Patterns," 8, 20n, 24; Weber, *Mexican Frontier*, 214–15.

72. Híjar, "California in 1834," 22; Sanchez, *Spanish Arcadia*,133–35, 273; Gayle Rubin, "The Traffic in Women: Notes on the 'Political Economy' of Sex," in *Toward an Anthropology of Women*, ed. Rayna Reiter (New York, 1975), 170–84.

73. Stearns Papers, Boxes 4, 5, 7; Lederer, *Study of Anglo-American Settlers*, 60; Jensen, "John Forster," 39; Cleland, *Cattle*, 64–65, 189, 332 n. 13; McWilliams, *Southern California*, 53.

74. Cleland, *Cattle*, 190–93, 311 n. 28, 113; Jensen, "John Forster," 39–40; Security Trust and Savings Bank, *El Pueblo: Los Angeles before the Railroads* (Los Angeles, 1928), 21; Dakin, *Scotch Paisano*, 51–52.

75. Bancroft, *California Pastoral*, 289; Ruschenberger, *Sketches in California in 1836*, 4; Robinson, *Life in California before the Conquest*, 53, 55, 102; Dana, *Two Years before the Mast*, 136–37.

76. Cleland, *Cattle*, 190; Amador, "Memorias," 226–27; Arnaz, "Recuerdos," 15.

77. Arnaz, "Recuerdos," 15.

310 Notes to Pages 164–72

Chapter 4: Heaven, or Some Other Place

1. Pío Pico is quoted in Security Trust and Savings Bank, *El Pueblo*, 81; Alvarado is quoted in Sanchez, *Spanish Arcadia*, 132; Guerrero to Castro, January 24, 1846, Castro Documents 6, no. 309, Bancroft Library, is quoted in Robert Glass Cleland, "Early Sentiment for the Annexation of California," *The Southwestern Historical Quarterly* 18, no. 2 (October 1914), 151; Manuel Mier y Terán, "I am warning you," in *Foreigners in Their Native Land: Historical Roots of the Mexican Americans*, ed. David J. Weber (Albuquerque, 1973), 104; Castro is quoted in Juan B. Alvarado, *Historia de California* 2, 133–34, and Alvarado is quoted in Cleland, "Early Sentiment," no. 2, 151.

2. Cleland, "Early Sentiment," no. 1, 26.

3. Dana, *Two Years before the Mast*, 135; Robinson, *Life in California*, 101; Simpson, *Narrative*, 1:410; Khlebnikov, *Memoirs of California*, 323.

4. Bryant, *What I Saw in California*, 447; Simpson, *Narrative*, 1:410; Philip L. Edwards, *California in 1837* (Sacramento, 1890), 17.

5. Dana, *Two Years before the Mast*, 135–36; David J. Weber quotes Francis Parkman in the editor's introduction to section 2 in *Foreigners in Their Native Land*, 60; Robinson, *Life in California*, 101; John Berger, *Ways of Seeing* (London, 1977), 45–47.

6. Norman O. Brown, *Life against Death: The Psychoanalytic Meaning of History* (Middletown, Conn., 1970), 238; J. B. Dye is quoted in Sanchez, *Spanish Arcadia*, 186.

7. Farnham, *Early Days of California*, 61; Farnham, *California, Indoors and Out*, 295.

8. Edwards, *California in 1837*, 17.

9. "Sirvientes los alamitos," Stearns Papers, Box 84; Dakin, *A Scotch Paisano*, 52–55; Webb, *Indian Life*, 300; Jensen, "John Forster," 39–40; N. Pryor to Stearns, May 24, 1839, and Nov. 12, 1838, Stearns Papers, Box 50.

10. Cleland, 198–202; J. M. Guinn, "The Passing of the Rancho," *Annual Publications of the Historical Society of Southern California* 10, part 1 (1915–16), 46–47.

11. Ezequiel Williams of the Missouri Fur Company is quoted in Cleland, *This Reckless Breed of Men*, 123; Robinson, *Life in California*, 19–23, 31; Farnham, *Early Days of California*, 83–84.

12. Duhaut-Cilly, *Voyage*, 162; Layne, "Annals of Los Angeles," 2:208; Bancroft, *History of California*, 3:642; Weber, *Mexican Frontier*, 149–51.

13. Bancroft, *History of California*, 4:81, 375.

14. Lederer, Anglo-American Settlers, 17; Bancroft, *History of California*, 3:393, 4:380; Weber, *Mexican Frontier*, 179–206 (Almonte is quoted on page 202).

15. Bancroft, *History of California*, 4:304–13; Amador, "Memorias," 162; Bryant, *What I Saw in California*, 327; Simpson, *Narrative*, 1:409–10.

16. Bryant, *What I Saw in California*, 427; Alex Forbes to Stearns, Tepic, April 18, 1831, Stearns Papers, Box 27; Farnham, *Early Days of California*, 117; Dana, *Two Years before the Mast*, 136; Simpson, *Narrative*, 1:409; Smith to Calhoun, December 30, 1845, is quoted in Cleland, "Early Sentiment," 2:144; Thomas Oliver Larkin to Abel Stearns, Monterey, May 27, 1846, Stearns Papers, Box 40.

17. Bancroft, *History of California*, 4:480–525.

18. Cleland, "Early Sentiment," 2:135–36, 152–59; Robinson, *Life in California*, 213–14; Manuel Micheltorena to Reverend Father Superior of Mission San José, Mission San Juan Bautista, June 29, 1844, de la Guerra Papers; Weber, *Mexican Frontier*, 206, 269–70; Amador, "Memorias," 116.

19. Gene M. Brack, *Mexico Views Manifest Destiny: An Essay on the Origins of the Mexican War* (Albuquerque, 1975), 88–166; Polk is quoted in Glenn W. Price, *Origins of the War with Mexico: The Polk-Stockton Intrigue* (Austin, Tex., 1976), 36; Bancroft, *History of California*, vol. 5, is the most complete account of the Mexican War in California, and Bandini is discussed on pages 282–283.

20. Bancroft, *History of California*, 5:265–83; Helen V. Shubert, "The Men Who Met the Yankees in 1846," *California Historical Society Quarterly* 13, no. 1 (March 1934), describes the efforts of the "pastoral dragoons."

21. Pío Pico to Francisco Figueroa, Abel Stearns, et al., Santa Barbara, June 27, 1846, Stearns Papers, Box 49; "Pronunciamiento de Varela y otros Californios contra los Americanos, 24 de Set. 1846," is reprinted in Bancroft, *History of California*, 5:310n.

22. Bancroft, *History of California*, 5:305–20; Steven Clark Foster, "Angeles from '47 to '49" (1877), Bancroft Library, 42–44.

23. Bancroft, *History of California*, 5:314–47, 389–407.

24. Pitt, *Decline of the Californios*, 83–103; Richard Griswold del Castillo, *The Los Angeles Barrio, 1850–1890: A Social History* (Berkeley and Los Angeles, 1979), 42; Guinn, "Passing of the Rancho," 46; Cleland, *Cattle*, 35, 102, 106, 146.

25. Horace Bell, *Reminiscences of a Ranger, or Early Times in Southern California* (Los Angeles, 1881), 83; Bancroft, *History of California*, 5:312–13.

26. Bell, *Reminiscences of a Ranger*, 83; Lederer, *Anglo-Amer-*

ican Settlers in Los Angeles, 23.

27. Cleland, *Cattle*, 206, quoting Alfred Robinson; John Forster to C. J. Couts, San Juan Capistrano, August 2, 1868, and February 25, 1869, Couts Papers; Jensen, "John Forster," 42; Simpson, *Narrative*, 1:409; Brewer, *Up and Down California*, 121; postcard of the Griffith Park Planetarium to Miss M. McKelvie, May 4, 1939, found in a Chicago bric-a-brac store; "Ordinances and Regulations of Los Angeles (1832–1888)," compiled by Marco R. Newmark, *Historical Society of Southern California Quarterly* 30, no. 1 (March 1948), 34; Harris Newmark, *Sixty Years in Southern California, 1853–1913* (New York, 1916), 81.

28. Charles Nordhoff, *California: For Health, Pleasure, and Residence* (New York, 1873), 153; Cleland, *Cattle*, 106.

29. Stearns's account books are in Stearns Papers, Box 84; Gillingham, *Rancho San Pedro*, 80; Nordhoff, *California*, 155; "Daily Occurrences at Azusa," vols. 2 and 3, Henry Dalton Papers; Sheldon G. Jackson, *A British Ranchero in Old California: The Life and Times of Henry Dalton and the Rancho Azusa* (Glendale and Azusa, Calif., 1977), 194–95.

30. Gillingham, *Rancho San Pedro*, 225; Stearns's account books, Stearns Papers, Box 84; account book of Rancho Santa Ana del Chino, 1840–59, California Historical Documents, Huntington Library; "Day Book, Servants, 1853," Couts Papers.

31. The "Act for the Government and Protection of the Indians" is reprinted in Edward O. C. Ord, *The City of the Angels and the City of the Saints, or a Trip to Los Angeles and San Bernardino in 1856* (Los Angeles, 1978), 37–39; Hizer and Almquist, *Other Californians*, 36–40; Cook, *Conflict*, 308–9; the Los Angeles ordinance is quoted in Phillips, *Chiefs and Challengers*, 58.

32. Cook, *Conflict*, 305–7; Phillips, *Chiefs and Challengers*, 65.

33. Farnham, *California, Indoors and Out*, 97; Los Angeles *Star*, March 13, 1852; Heizer and Almquist, *Other Californians*, 23–40; Robinson, *Indians of Los Angeles*, 26–27.

34. D. A. Shaw, *Eldorado, or California as Seen by a Pioneer, 1850–1900* (Los Angeles, 1900), preface, 187.

35. D. L. Phillips, *Letters from California: Its Mountains, Valleys, Plains, Lakes, Rivers, Climate and Productions* (Springfield, Ill., 1877), 98; T. Butler King, *Report on California* (Washington, D.C., 1850), 17; Governor Peter H. Burnet in California, *Senate Journal*, 3d session, 1852, 714, is quoted in Heizer and Almquist, *Other Californians*, 26.

36. Governor John Bigler to General E. Hitchcock, Sacramento,

April 8, 1852, quoted in Heizer and Almquist, *Other Californians*, 207; Phillips, *Letters from California*, 98.

37. C. T. Hopkins, *Common Sense Applied to the Immigrant Question: Showing Why the "California Immigrant Union" Was Founded and What It Expects to Do* (San Francisco, 1869), 22.

38. Bell, *Reminiscences of a Ranger*, 35–36; Robinson, *Life in California*, 1–3; Los Angeles *Star*, December 3, 1853, and March 31, 1855; Cleland, *Cattle*, 58–60, which also quotes Horace Bell; Rockwell D. Hunt, *The American Period* (Chicago, 1926), 347–48; Phillips, *Chiefs and Challengers*, 57–59; Helen Hunt Jackson, *A Century of Dishonor: A Sketch of the United States Government's Dealings with Some of the Indian Tribes*, new ed. (Boston, 1893), 462–63.

39. Los Angeles *Star*, March 31, 1855 and December 3, 1853.

40. Los Angeles *Star*, January 4, 1855, September 17, 1853, June 18, 1853, and January 18, 1855.

41. Cave Johnson Couts to Don A. Hollister (petition for binding out several Indian servants), Rancho Guajome, January 10, 1861; "Indenture wherein Jesús Delgado & Paula Delgado bind an Indian child Sasaria to Isidora Bandini de Couts," San Luis Rey, January 25, 1854; "Indenture wherein Indian woman Jacinta binds over her son to Isidora Bandini Couts," San Diego County Justice of the Peace, San Luis Rey, August 13, 1866; "Judgment rendered by William Caswell Ferrell, Justice of the Peace, in case of Cave Johnson Couts vs. Francisco, an Indian Boy," San Diego County, May 6, 1858—all in Couts Papers; Couts to Benjamin Wilson, Guajomito, May 7, 1854, Wilson Papers.

42. Cook, *Conflict*, 301, 323–24, Bryant, *What I Saw in California*, 266; King, *Report on California*, 16.

43. Nordhoff, *California*, 155; King, *Report on California*, 17; Los Angeles *Semi-Weekly News*, February 11, 1869, quoted in Cleland, *Cattle*, 59.

44. John Forster to Couts, Santa Margarita, February 23, 1870, Couts Papers.

45. Cook, *Conflict*, 295–98; Phillips, *Chiefs and Challengers*, 119, 124; Pablo de la Guerra to David C. Broderick, Santa Barbara, 1857, de la Guerra Papers.

46. Cook, *Conflict*, 280–92, 470; Hunt, *Spanish Period*, 345–46.

47. Phillips, *Chiefs and Challengers*, 44–46.

48. Phillips, *Chiefs and Challengers*, 47–70.

49. Phillips, *Chiefs and Challengers*, 71–110; Robinson, *Indians of Los Angeles*, 30–31.

50. Los Angeles *Star* of December 6, 1851, quoted in Cleland, *Cattle*, 67.

51. Cook, *Conflict*, 294.

52. Phillips, *Chiefs and Challengers*, 130–76; Cleland, *Cattle*, 64–68, 301n; Los Angeles *Star*, June 26, 1852; Lorenzana, "Memorias," 43; Foster, "Angeles from '47 to '49," 47–57.

53. Newmark, *Sixty Years in Southern California*, 650; Los Angeles *Semi-Weekly News*, September 8, 1868, and March 16, 1869, quoted in Cleland, *Cattle*, 175.

54. Eric Foner, *Free Soil, Free Labor, Free Men: The Ideology of the Republican Party before the Civil War* (New York, 1971), 11–29; Fred A. Shannon, *The Farmer's Last Frontier: Agriculture, 1860–1897* (New York, 1968), 51–52; Alex Forbes to Stearns, Tepic, April 18, 1831, Stearns Papers, Box 27.

55. Bancroft, *History of California*, 6:539–40.

56. Pitt, *Decline of the Californios*, 60–67; Hizer and Almquist, *Other Californians*, 143–48; Rudolfo Acuña, *Occupied America: A History of Chicanos* (New York, 1981), 100–101; Bancroft, *History of California*, 6:404–8; Antonio Franco Coronel, "Cosas de California" (1877), Bancroft Library, 1877, 176–84, is reprinted in *Foreigners in Their Native Land*, 169–73; King, *Report on California*, 68.

57. Pitt, *Decline of the Californios*, 68; Coronel, "Cosas de California," 170–71.

58. Cleland, *Cattle*, 36–46; Bancroft, *History of California*, 6:575–78.

59. The treaty and James Buchanan are quoted in *Foreigners in Their Native Land*, 164, 167; Pitt, *Decline of the Californios*, 83–103.

60. Bancroft, *History of California*, 6:576.

61. McWilliams, *Southern California*, 58–61; Pitt, *Decline of the Californios*, 148–55; Acuña, *Occupied America*, 11–17; Mario T. García, "The Californios of San Diego and the Politics of Accommodation," *Aztlán* 6, no. 1 (Spring 1975), 76–79.

62. Cary McWilliams, *North from Mexico: The Spanish-Speaking People of the United States* (New York, 1968), 36–44.

63. Los Angeles *Star*, February 28, 1853, December 10, 1853.

64. Newmark, *Sixty Years in Southern California*, 91.

65. *El Clamor Público*, February 14, 1857.

66. Los Angeles *Star*, January 31, 1857; *El Clamor Público*, May 9, 1857, March 21, 1857.

67. Los Angeles *Star*, December 10, 1853, July 21, 1855, July 8, 1854, May 6, 1854, July 16, 1853, January 11, 1855; *El Clamor Público*, January 31, 1857; Pitt, *Decline of the Californios*, 154.

68. Pablo Neruda, *Splendor and Death of Joaquín Murieta*, trans. Ben Belitt (New York, 1973), 143–45; Richard G. Mitchell, "Joaquín Murieta: A Study of Social Conditions in Early California" (Master's thesis, University of California, Berkeley, 1927), excerpted in *Furia y Muerte: Los Bandidos Chicanos*, ed. Pedro Castillo and Albert Camarillo (Los Angeles, 1973), 37–51; Pitt, *Decline of the Californios*, 69–82; Murieta's alleged words are in Ireneo Paz, *Life and Adventures of the Celebrated Bandit Joaquín Murieta: His Exploits in the State of California* (Chicago, 1937), 167; Bancroft, *History of California*, 6:203; Bancroft, *California Pastoral*, 645.

69. Los Angeles *Star*, October 22, 1853; *La Estrella*, January 18, 1855; Newmark, *Sixty Years in Southern California*, 205.

70. J. Gregg Layne, "Annals of Los Angeles," part 2, "From the American Conquest to the Civil War," *California Historical Society Quarterly* 13, (December 1934), 328; Cleland, *Cattle*, 91.

71. Pitt, *Decline of the Californios*, 167–71; Griswold del Castillo, *Los Angeles Barrio*, 109–13; Bancroft, *California Pastoral*, 643; Newmark, *Sixty Years in Southern California*, 207–9; Cleland, *Cattle*, 250–63, reprints many of the Los Angeles *Star* articles on the exploits of the Flores gang.

72. Los Angeles *Star*, May 16, 1874, is conveniently reprinted in Cleland, *Cattle*, 274–79; Ernest May, "Tiburcio Vasquez," *Historical Society of Southern California Quarterly* 29 (1947), 122–35, reprinted in *Furia y Muerte*, 17–31; Will H. Thrall, "The Haunts and Hide-outs of Tiburcio Vasquez," *Historical Society of Southern California Quarterly* 30, no. 2 (June 1948), 93–94; Acuña, *Occupied America*, 113–14.

73. Vallejo is quoted in Sanchez, *Spanish Arcadia*, 41–42; Cleland states, "The lawless conditions revealed by the foregoing illustrations were the inevitable result of a backwash from the mines; the bitter resentment of a wild, resentful element among the Spanish-Californian population, made landless by the passing of the ranchos into other hands; and the coming of large numbers of frontier 'bad men' and outlaws to the wild hinterland of southern California" (*Cattle*, 101).

74. *El Clamor Público*, July 24, 1855, December 22, 1855, April 25, 1857; Pitt, *Decline of the Californios*, 181–94.

75. *El Clamor Público*, January 12, 1856, August 9, 1856, January 31, 1857, December 1, 1855, March 7, 1857; Michael Weiss, "Education, Literacy, and the Community of Los Angeles in 1850," *Southern California Quarterly* 60, no. 1 (Summer 1978), 125–28.

76. *El Clamor Público*, July 24, 1855.

77. Edmund S. Morgan, *American Slavery, American Freedom: The Ordeal of Colonial Virginia* (New York, 1975), 363–87.

78. King, *Report on California*, 4; Shaw, *Eldorado*, 183.

79. Los Angeles *Star*, February 26, 1853; Cleland, *Cattle*, 94–95; Pitt, *Decline of the Californios*, 125–26. Pitt asserts that Andrés Pico fired the shots that killed Elias Cook and Dr. J. T. Overstreet, but the *Star* attributes them to Colonel Watson.

80. Pitt, *Decline of the Californios*, 149–53, 202; Acuña, *Occupied America*, 107–9; García, "Californios of San Diego," 71–76.

81. Cleland, *Cattle*, 110–11; Guinn, "Passing of the Rancho," 46.

82. Gillingham, *Rancho San Pedro*, 141–42; Wood, *Pasadena*, 38–43; Los Angeles *Star*, September 18, 1852, October 23, 1852; Cleland, *Cattle*, 112–13; Shochat, "Casa Adobe de San Rafael," 277–88; Lugo, "Vida," 129.

83. Josephine Maclay Walker, "Life and Personal Reminiscences of General Andrés Pico" (c. 1920), Charles Maclay Papers, Huntington Library; Lugo, "Vida," 129–30; Newmark, *Sixty Years in Southern California*, 99–100; Ygnacio Sepúlveda to Antonio Coronel, Sacramento, February 17, 1864, Antonio Coronel Papers, Los Angeles County Museum.

84. Cleland, *Cattle*, 113, 198–206; Guinn, "Passing of the Rancho," 46–47; Henry Preston to Stearns, Los Angeles, August 4, 1862, Stearns Papers, Box 50; John Forster to Cave Couts, San Juan Capistrano, August 2, 1868, and February 25, 1869, Couts Papers.

85. *Southern Vineyard*, March 22, 1859, quoted in Cleland, *Cattle*, 116; Harris Newmark, *Sixty Years in Southern California*, 252.

86. Antonio Coronel, "Miscellaneous Writings," no. 262, Coronel Papers; Sepulveda to Coronel, Sacramento, February 17, 1864.

87. "Petition of the California Landowners to the Honorable Senate and House of Representatives of the United States of America," Stearns Papers, and reprinted in Cleland, *Cattle*, 238–43, cf. 43.

88. Guinn, "Passing of the Rancho," 46; Cleland, *Cattle*, 130–35; Juan Forster to Cave Couts, Rancho Santa Margarita, May 17, 1862, and Los Angeles, January 8, 1863, and Forster to Willie Blount Couts, San Francisco, May 9, 1862, Couts Papers; Juan Bautista Bandini to Cave Couts, Rancho los Coyotes, February 18, 1863, Couts Papers.

89. Ida May Shrode, "The Sequent Occupation of the Rancho Azusa de Duarte, a Segment of the Upper San Gabriel Valley of California" (Ph.D. diss., University of Chicago, 1948), 72; Gillingham, *Rancho San Pedro*, 225–26; Cleland, *Cattle*, 139–43, 183; Lederer, "Anglo-American Settlers," 23.

Chapter 5: At Considerable Less Wages

1. Alexander Saxton, *The Indispensable Enemy: Labor and the Anti-Chinese Movement in California* (Berkeley and Los Angeles, 1971), 92–100; Cleland, *Cattle*, 160–67.

2. Cleland, *Cattle*, 172–83; Newmark, *Sixty Years in Southern California*, 31.

3. McWilliams, *Southern California*, 91–92, 113–18; Cleland, *Cattle*, 208–27; Shrode, "Sequent Occupation of the Rancho Azusa," 84–86; Richard Gird, journal, 1881–1907, Huntington Library, 2.

4. Glenn S. Dumke, "The Real Estate Boom of 1887 in Southern California," *Pacific Historical Review* 11 (December 1942), 427–38; McWilliams, *Southern California*, 118.

5. McWilliams, *Southern California*, 121–24; Fogelson, *Fragmented Metropolis*, 66–68.

6. Cook, *Conflict*, 256–59.

7. Phillips, *Chiefs and Challengers*, 140–49; Bancroft, *History of California* 7: 485–94; Jackson, *Century of Dishonor*, 459–60, 495.

8. Nordhoff, *California*, 149; Shrode, "Sequent Occupation of the Rancho Azusa," 70; Michael Forbes to Stearns, Laguna, July 29, 1873, Stearns Papers, Box 27; Jackson, *Century of Dishonor*, 459; Juan Bautista Bandini, diary, vol. 1, in Spanish with English translation by Margaret Gaffey Mel, Huntington Library.

9. Max Weber, "Religious Rejections of the World and Their Directions," in *From Max Weber: Essays in Sociology*, ed. H. H. Gerth and C. Wright Mills (New York, 1958), 331; Gird, journal, 4, 6, 42, 44; Forster to Couts, San Juan Capistrano, December 27, 1863, Couts Papers.

10. Gird, journal, 31–48.

11. Nordhoff, *California*, 155–56.

12. Henry Dalton, "Daily Occurrences (at Azusa)," vols. 3, 5, 7, Huntington Library.

13. Henry Dalton, "Indian Books—Wages and Accounts for Indian Employees on Azusa Ranch, 1857–1862," vols. 1–2, Dalton Papers; Miscellaneous Papers, Lake Vineyard Wine Company, 1869, Benjamin Wilson Papers. I could not help but feel the death contained in the "Indian Books" as I perused them in the Huntington Library.

14. Los Angeles *Star*, January 15 and December 3, 1853, January 4 and 18, 1855; *La Estrella*, March 17, 1855; *El Clamor Público*, October 16 and December 1, 1855.

15. Newmark, "Ordinances and Regulations of Los Angeles," 38;

Cook, *Conflict*, 273, 277; Robinson, "Indians of Los Angeles," 24–25; Cleland, *Cattle*, 80.

16. Cook, *Conflict*, 262–63.

17. Cook, *Conflict*, 3–5, 350–57, 379–82; Hunt, *Spanish Period*, 345–46; Los Angeles *Daily News*, February 13, 1872.

18. Henry Nash Smith, *Virgin Land: The American West as Symbol and Myth* (New York, 1957), 123–44, 165–73; Foner, *Free Soil*, 11–29.

19. George B. Ironside to Benjamin Wilson, Lake Vineyard Ranch, April 11, 1869, Wilson Papers; Dalton, "Daily Occurrences," vol. 7; Bandini, diary, vol. 1, June 3 and 21, July 5, October 7, September 30, November 11, 1881.

20. William Marsh to Benjamin Wilson, Lake Vineyard (San Marino), July 13, 1854, Wilson Papers; Bandini to Couts, Tijuana, April 28, 1864, Couts Papers; James Debarth Shorb to Wilson, Lake Vineyard, March 20, 1874, Wilson Papers.

21. Los Angeles *Star*, December 12, 1868; "Hagar, a Many Sided Question," *Pacific Rural Press*, February 7, 1874.

22. Los Angeles *Star*, December 12, 1868; Bandini, diary, vol. 1, November 12, 1879, March 5, April 25, 1880, May 5 and 6, 1881; vol. 2, June 13, October 7 and 13, November 21, 1883, April 3, July 27, 28, and 30, August 3, September 2 and 8, 1885, February 3, 1889; vol. 4, August 23, 1889, March 26, 1891. Arcadia's boozing and slumbering second husband had a black personal servant—"el Negrito George"—in February 1889.

23. Shrode, "Sequent Occupation of the Rancho Azusa," 81; "Hagar"; *Pacific Rural Press*, July 30, 1881, January 15, 1881.

24. *Pacific Rural Press*, June 30, 1877, April 19, 1879, March 5, 1881, March 17, 1883.

25. Pacific Rural Press, December 10, 1881; "Hagar."

26. McWilliams, *Southern California*, 122–23; Fogelson, *Fragmented Metropolis*, 67–68; Griswold del Castillo, *Los Angeles Barrio*, 35; Cleland, *Cattle*, 233.

27. Carlton Beals, *Porfirio Díaz, Dictator of Mexico* (1932; Westport, Conn., 1971), 332–46; John Kenneth Turner, *Barbarous Mexico* (1910; Austin, Tex., 1969), 220–23; Cockcroft, *Mexico*, 89–93.

28. Ricardo Romo, *East Los Angeles: History of a Barrio* (Austin, Tex., 1983), 34–40; Beals, *Porfirio Díaz*, 336, 342; Cockcroft, *Mexico*, 88.

29. Romo, *East Los Angeles*, 31–59.

30. Romo, *East Los Angeles*, 34–39; Cockcroft, *Mexico*, 86–99; "California—Labor and Social Conditions of Mexicans," *Monthly Labor Review* 32, no. 1 (January 1931), 84.

31. John Berger, *Pig Earth* (New York, 1979), 11, 202–9; Ricardo Romo, "Mexican Workers in the City: Los Angeles, 1915–1930" (Ph.D. diss., University of California, Los Angeles, 1975), 9; Los Angeles City Survey, The Interchurch World Movement, *The Mexican in Los Angeles* (Los Angeles, 1920), 22; Governor C. C. Young's Mexican Fact-Finding Committee, *Mexicans in California* (San Francisco, 1930), 73; Robin Fitzgerald Scott, "The Mexican-American in the Los Angeles Area, 1920–1950: From Acquiescence to Activity" (Ph.D. diss., University of Southern California, 1971), 9; Romo, *East Los Angeles*, 56; Blanche A. Sommerville, "Naturalization from the Mexican Viewpoint," *Community Exchange Bulletin* 6, no. 4 (May 1928), 11; William Wilson McEuen, "A Survey of the Mexicans in Los Angeles" (M.A. thesis, University of Southern California, 1914), 12.

32. Polanyi, *Great Transformation*, 163.

33. Brown, *Life against Death*, 238.

34. McWilliams, *Southern California*, 82; Bancroft, *California Pastoral*, 360.

35. Los Angeles *Star*, November 6, 1852; Thomes, *Recollections of Old Times in California*, 24.

36. Christina Wiebus Mead, "La Fiestas de Los Angeles: A Survey of the Yearly Celebrations, 1894–1898," *Historical Society of Southern California Quarterly* 31, nos. 1 and 2 (March and June 1949), 68–72, who quotes the Los Angeles *Times* of March 28 and April 8, 1894, on page 69; Newmark, *Sixty Years in Southern California*, 528, 608.

37. San Francisco *Alta Californian*, May 7, 1869, is quoted in Gillingham, *Rancho San Pedro*, 253; Nordhoff, *California*, 160.

38. Helen Hunt Jackson, *Ramona* (New York, 1970), 17, 25; Monroy, "They Didn't Call Them Padre for Nothing."

39. McWilliams, *Southern California*, 70–83.

40. McWilliams, *Southern California*, 77–78; Nordhoff, *California*, 158; Webb, *Indian Life at the Old Missions*, 262; postcards in my possession.

41. Charles Lummis, "Form Letter for Special Committee on San Fernando Mission 'Candle Day.'" Los Angeles, July 10, 1916, Maclay Papers; Walker, "Personal Reminiscences of General Andrés Pico."

42. Jackson, *Ramona*, 14; McWilliams, *Southern California*, 82.

43. American Psychiatric Association, *Diagnostic and Statistical Manual of Mental Disorders*, 3d ed. (Washington, D.C., 1980), 315–17, which adds that narcissists have "a grandiose sense of self-importance or uniqueness [and] preoccupation with fantasies of un-

limited success"; *Pacific Rural Press*, February, 13, 1909.

44. American Psychiatric Association, *Diagnostic and Statistical Manual of Mental Disorders*, 3d ed., 315–17.

45. Charles F. Lummis, *Preliminary Report of the Warner's Ranch Indian Advisory Commission* (Los Angeles, 1902), 23, 26, 29, 31.

46. Griswold del Castillo, *Los Angeles Barrio*, 31, 46–51.

47. Griswold del Castillo, *Los Angeles Barrio*, 53–54; Albert Camarillo, *Chicanos in a Changing Society: From Mexican Pueblos to American Barrios in Santa Barbara and Southern California, 1848–1930* (Cambridge, Mass., 1979), 18–19.

48. Richard Griswold del Castillo, *La Familia: Chicano Families in the Urban Southwest, 1848 to the Present* (Notre Dame, Ind., 1984), 27–39, 78–81; Griswold del Castillo, *Los Angeles Barrio*, 65, 73.

49. Griswold del Castillo, *Los Angeles Barrio*, 33–41; Camarillo, *Chicanos in a Changing Society*, 65.

50. *La Crónica*, June 13, 1877; "Invitation to Join Sociedad Española de Beneficia Mutua," San Francisco, October 25, 1877, del Valle Papers; Griswold del Castillo, *La Familia*, 40–55. In the twentieth century these institutions often transformed themselves into other organizations, particularly labor unions. See Jose Amara Hernandez, *Mutual Aid for Survival: The Case of the Mexican American* (Malabar, Fla., 1983); Griswold del Castillo, *Los Angeles Barrio*, 134–38; Romo, *East Los Angeles*, 148–55; Francisco E. Balderrama, *In Defense of La Raza: The Los Angeles Mexican Consulate and the Mexican Community, 1929 to 1936* (Tucson, 1982), 37–50.

Bibliography

Archival Sources

Many of the important documents of early California history have been gathered together at the Huntington Library in San Marino, California, and at the Bancroft Library at the University of California, Berkeley. The Chapman Collection and the Wright Collection in the Huntington Library contain a small but remarkable assemblage of photographed copies and typescripts of crucial documents from the Archivo General de las Indias (AGI) in Seville and the Archivo General de México (AGM), which A. G. Chapman and H. R. Wright, respectively, collected in the 1920s. The Huntington's California Historical Documents collection also provided important original sources on Spanish and Mexican California. Many of the letters and reports on which I rely in the first two chapters were found in these collections and are cited in the notes. The Huntington Library also has a number of collections of the papers of important personages of southern California history, and I have listed the ones used herein below. The Bancroft Library has the singular series of interviews, called *recuerdos* (remembrances), of Californios, which Thomas Savage collected for Hubert Howe Bancroft in 1877 and 1878. Although they must be read with a particularly critical eye, these first-hand accounts provide crucial information and insights about frontier California. A few of the documents cited I found during a brief trip to the Santa Barbara Mission Archives.

Huntington Library Papers

Couts, Cave Johnson
Dalton, Henry
de la Guerra y Noriega, José

Maclay, Charles
Stearns, Abel
Wilson, Benjamin Davis

Bancroft Library Recuerdos

Amador, José María
Arnaz, José
Bojorges, Juan
Foster, Steven Clark
Galindo, José Eusebio
Gómez, Vicente

Híjar, Carlos N.
Lorenzana, Apolinaria
Lugo, José del Carmen
Machado, Juana
Pérez, Eulalia

Los Angeles County Museum Papers

Coronel, Antonio
del Valle, Ignacio

Periodicals

El Clamor Público
Los Angeles *Daily News*
Los Angeles *Estrella*
Pacific Rural Press
Los Angeles *Star*

Works

Acuña, Rudolfo. *Occupied America: A History of Chicanos.* New York, 1981.

Almaguer, Tomás, "Interpreting Chicano History: The World-System Approach to Nineteenth-Century California." *Review* 4 (Winter 1981).

American Psychiatric Association. *Diagnostic and Statistical Manual of Mental Disorders.* 3d ed. Washington, D.C., 1980.

Archibald, Robert. *The Economic Aspects of the California Missions.* Washington, D.C., 1978.

Balderrama, Francisco E. *In Defense of La Raza: The Los Angeles Mexican Consulate and the Mexican Community, 1929 to 1936.* Tucson, 1982.

Bancroft, Hubert Howe. *California Pastoral, 1769–1848.* San Francisco, 1888.

―――. *History of California.* 6 vols. Facsimile of 1884 edition. San Francisco, 1963.

Bandini, José. *A Description of California in 1828.* Berkeley, 1951.

Bandini, Juan Bautista. Diary. In Spanish, with English translation by Margaret Gaffey Mel. Huntington Library, San Marino, Calif.

Bannon, John Francis. *The Spanish Borderlands Frontier, 1513–1821.* New York, 1970.

Barrera, Mario. *Race and Class in the Southwest: A Theory of Racial Inequality.* Notre Dame, Ind., 1984.

Beals, Carlton. *Porfirio Díaz, Dictator of Mexico.* 1932. Westport, Conn., 1971.

Beechey, F. W., *Narrative of a Voyage to the Pacific and Beerings Straight* [*sic*]. Vol. 2. London, 1831.

Beilharz, Edwin A. *Felipe de Neve: First Governor of California.* San Francisco, 1971.

Bell, Horace. *Reminiscences of a Ranger, or Early Times in Southern California.* Los Angeles, 1881.

Berger, John. *About Looking.* New York, 1980.

―――. *Pig Earth.* New York, 1979.

―――. *Ways of Seeing.* London, 1977.

Bolton, Herbert Eugene. *Anza's California Expeditions.* Vol. 1, *An Outpost of Empire.* Berkeley, 1930.

―――, ed. and trans. *Anza's California Expeditions.* Vol. 2, *Opening of a Land Route to California: Diaries of Anza, Díaz, Garcés, and Palóu;* vol. 3, *The San Francisco Colony: Diaries of Anza, Font, and Eixarch, and Narratives by Palóu and Moraga;* vol. 4, *Font's Complete Diary of the Second Anza Expedition;* vol. 5, *Correspondence.* Berkeley, 1930.

―――. "The Mission as a Frontier Institution in the Spanish-American Colonies." *American Historical Review* 23, no. 1 (October 1917).

Boscana, A. R. "Chinigchinich: A Historical Account of the Origin, Customs, and Traditions of the Indians at the Missionary Establishment of San Juan Capistrano, Alta California." In Alfred Robinson, *Life in California before the Conquest.* 1846. San Francisco, 1925.

Brack, Gene M. *Mexico Views Manifest Destiny: An Essay on the Origins of the Mexican War.* Albuquerque, 1975.

Brewer, William Henry. *Up and Down California in 1860–1864: The Journal of William H. Brewer.* Berkeley and Los Angeles, 1966.

Brown, Norman O. *Life against Death: The Psychoanalytic Meaning of History*. Middletown, Conn., 1970.

Brownmiller, Susan. *Against Our Will: Men, Women and Rape*. New York, 1975.

Bryant, Edwin. *What I Saw in California; Being the Journal of a Tour in the Years 1846–1847*. New York, 1848.

Burns, E. Bradford. *Latin America: A Concise Interpretive History*. Englewood Cliffs, N.J., 1972.

"California—Labor and Social Conditions of Mexicans." *Monthly Labor Review* 32, no. 1 (January 1931).

Camarillo, Albert. *Chicanos in a Changing Society: From Mexican Pueblos to American Barrios in Santa Barbara and Southern California, 1848–1930*. Cambridge, Mass., 1979.

Carrasco, David. *Quetzalcoatl and the Irony of Empire: Myths and Prophecies in the Aztec Tradition*. Chicago, 1982.

Castañeda, Antonia. "Comparative Frontiers: The Migration of Women to Alta California and New Zealand." In *Western Women: Their Land, Their Lives*, edited by Lillian Schlissel, Vicki Ruiz, and Janice J. Monk. Albuquerque, 1988.

Caudwell, Christopher. *Further Studies in a Dying Culture*. 1938. New York, 1971.

Caughey, John. "The Country Town of the Angels." In *Los Angeles: Biography of a City*, edited by John Caughey and LaRee Caughey. Berkeley and Los Angeles, 1977.

César, Julio. "Recollections of My Youth at San Luis Rey Mission." Translated by Nellie Van de Grift Sanchez. *Touring Topics* 22 (November 1930).

Chagnon, Napoleon A. *Yanomamo: The Fierce People*. New York, 1968.

Chiles, Joseph B. *A Visit to California in 1831, as Recorded for Hubert Howe Bancroft*. Berkeley, 1970.

Cleland, Robert Glass. *The Cattle on a Thousand Hills: Southern California, 1850–1880*. San Marino, Calif., 1975.

———. "Early Sentiment for the Annexation of California." *Southwestern Historical Quarterly* 18, nos. 1 and 2 (July 1914 and October 1914).

———. *This Reckless Breed of Men: The Trappers and Fur Traders of the Southwest*. Albuquerque, 1976.

Cockcroft, James D. *Mexico: Class Formation, Capital Accumulation, and the State*. New York, 1983.

Columbus, Christopher. "The Letter of Christopher Columbus to Rafael Sanchez, Written on Board the Caravel While Returning from His First Voyage." 1493. Facsimile ed. Murfreesboro, N.C., 1970.

Cook, Sherburne F. *The Conflict between the California Indian and White Civilization*. Berkeley and Los Angeles, 1976.

Crouch, Dora P., and Daniel J. Garr. *Spanish City Planning in North America*. Cambridge, Mass., 1982.

Cumberland, Charles C. *Mexico: The Struggle for Modernity*. New York, 1968.

Cushing, Frank Hamilton. "Zuñi Fetiches." 1883. In *Zuñi: Selected Writings of Frank Hamilton Cush*, edited by Jesse Green, 195–203. Lincoln, Nebr., 1979.

Dakin, Susanna Bryant. *A Scotch Paisano: Hugo Reid's Life in California, 1832–1852*. Berkeley, 1939.

Dalton, Henry. "Daily Occurrences (at Azusa)." Henry Dalton Papers. Huntington Library, San Marino, Calif.

———. "Indian Books—Wages and Accounts for Indian Employees on Azusa Ranch, 1857–1862." Henry Dalton Papers. Huntington Library, San Marino, Calif.

Dana, Richard Henry. *Two Years before the Mast*. 1845. New York, 1963.

Diamond, Stanley. *In Search of the Primitive: A Critique of Civilization*. New Brunswick, N.J., 1981.

Drinnon, Richard. "The Metaphysics of Dancing Tribes." In *The American Indian and the Problem of History*, edited by Calvin Martin. New York, 1987.

Duhaut-Cilly, A. *Voyage autour du Monde, principalment à la Californie et aux Isles Sandwich, pendant les années 1826, 1827, 1828 et 1829*. Paris, 1834–35. In "Duhaut-Cilly's Account of California in the Years 1827," edited and translated by Charles Franklin Carter, *California Historical Society Quarterly* 7 (1929).

Dumke, Glenn S. "The Real Estate Boom of 1887 in Southern California." *Pacific Historical Review* 11 (December 1942).

Edwards, Philip L. *California in 1837*. Sacramento, Calif., 1890.

Eliade, Mircea. *The Myth of the Eternal Return, or Cosmos and History*. Princeton, N.J., 1971.

Engelhardt, Zephyrin. *The Franciscans in California*. Harbor Springs, Mich., 1897.

———. *The Missionaries of California*. San Francisco, 1912.

———. *San Fernando Rey, the Mission of the Valley*. Chicago, 1927.

———. *San Gabriel Mission and the Beginnings of Los Angeles*. San Gabriel, Calif., 1927.

Fages, Pedro. "Report on the Californias, 30 November 1775," Archivo General de las Indias. Chapman Documents. Huntington Library, San Marino, Calif.

Farnham, Eliza W. *California, Indoors and Out; or, How We Farm, Mine, and Live Generally in the Golden State.* New York, 1856.

Farnham, T. J. *The Early Days of California: Embracing What I Saw There, with Scenes in the Pacific.* Philadelphia, 1860.

Farriss, Nancy M. *Crown and Clergy in Colonial Mexico, 1759–1821: The Crisis of Ecclesiastical Privilege.* London, 1968.

"The First Expansion of the Mission Field of California, 1770–1771." Edited and translated by Maynard Geiger. *Southern California Quarterly* 48 (June 1966).

"The Flea in California History and Literature." *California Historical Society Quarterly* 15 (December 1936).

Fogelson, Robert M. *The Fragmented Metropolis: Los Angeles, 1850–1930.* Cambridge, Mass., 1967.

Foner, Eric. *Free Soil, Free Labor, Free Men: The Ideology of the Republican Party before the Civil War.* New York, 1971.

Forbes, Alexander, *California: A History of Upper and Lower.* London, 1839.

Foucault, Michel. *Discipline and Punish: The Birth of the Prison.* New York, 1979.

———. *The History of Sexuality.* Vol. 1, *An Introduction.* New York, 1980.

"Fray Antonio Ripoll's Description of the Chumash Revolt at Santa Barbara in 1824." Edited and translated by Maynard Geiger. *Southern California Quarterly* 52 (December 1970).

García, Mario T. "The Californios of San Diego and the Politics of Accommodation." *Aztlán* 6 (Spring 1975).

Garr, Daniel. "Planning, Politics, and Plunder: The Missions and Indian Pueblos of Hispanic California." *Southern California Quarterly* 54 (Winter 1972).

Geiger, Maynard. "Biographical Data on the Missionaries of San Fernando College Serving the California Missions in 1817 and 1820." *California Historical Society Quarterly* 48 (June 1969).

Genovese, Eugene. *The World the Slaveholders Made: Two Essays in Interpretation.* New York, 1971.

Gibson, Charles. *Spain in America.* New York, 1966.

Gillingham, Robert Cameron. *The Rancho San Pedro: The Story of a Famous Rancho in Los Angeles County and of Its Owners, the Dominguez Family.* Los Angeles, 1961.

Gird, Richard. Journal, 1881–1907. Huntington Library, San Marino, Calif.

Governor C. C. Young's Mexican Fact-Finding Committee. *Mexicans in California.* San Francisco, 1930.

Griswold del Castillo, Richard. *La Familia: Chicano Families in the Urban Southwest, 1848 to the Present.* Notre Dame, Ind., 1984.

――――. *The Los Angeles Barrio, 1850–1890: A Social History.* Berkeley and Los Angeles, 1979.

Grivas, Theodore. "Alcalde Rule: The Nature of Local Government in Spanish and Mexican California." *California Historical Society Quarterly* 40 (March 1961).

Guest, Florian. "The Indian Policy under Fermín Francisco Lasuén, California's Second Father President." *California Historical Society Quarterly* 45 (September 1966).

Guest, Francis F. "An Examination of the Thesis of S. F. Cook on the Forced Conversion of the Indians in the California Missions." *Southern California Quarterly* 61 (Spring 1979).

Guinn, J. M. *Historical and Biographical Record of Southern California.* Chicago, 1902.

――――. "The Passing of the Rancho." *Annual Publications of the Historical Society of Southern California* 10, part 1 (1915–16).

――――. Review of *Sixty Years in Southern California. Annual Publications of the Historical Society of Southern California* 10, part 1 (1915–16).

"Hagar, a Many Sided Question." *Pacific Rural Press,* February 7, 1874.

Hanke, Lewis. *The Spanish Struggle for Justice in the Conquest of America.* Philadelphia, 1949.

Harris, Marvin. *Cows, Pigs, Wars, and Witches: The Riddles of Culture.* New York, 1975.

Hawgood, John A. "The Pattern of Yankee Infiltration in Mexican Alta California, 1821–1846." *Pacific Historical Review* 27 (1958).

Heizer, Robert F., and Alan F. Almquist. *The Other Californians: Prejudice and Discrimination under Spain, Mexico, and the United States to 1920.* Berkeley and Los Angeles, 1971.

Hernández, José Amara. *Mutual Aid for Survival: The Case of the Mexican American.* Malabar, Fla., 1983.

Holder, Preston. *The Hoe and the Horse on the Plains: A Study of the Cultural Development among North American Indians.* Lincoln, Nebr., 1974.

Hopkins, C. T. *Common Sense Applied to the Immigrant Question: Showing Why the "California Immigrant Union" Was Founded and What It Expects to Do.* San Francisco, 1869.

Horkheimer, Max. "The End of Reason." In *The Essential Frank-*

. *fort School Reader*, edited by Andrew Arato and Eike Gebhardt. New York, 1978.

Hunt, Rockwell D. *The American Period*. Chicago, 1926.

Hutchinson, C. Alan. *Frontier Settlement in Mexican California: The Híjar-Padrés Colony and Its Origins, 1769–1835*. New Haven, Conn., 1969.

————. "The Mexican Government and the Mission Indians of Upper California, 1821–1835." *The Americas* 21 (April 1965).

Intelligent Bostonian. *Northwest Coast of America and California: 1832, Letters from Fort Ross, Monterey, San Pedro, and Santa Barbara*. Los Angeles, 1952.

Jackson, Helen Hunt. *A Century of Dishonor: A Sketch of the United States Government's Dealings with Some of the Indian Tribes*. New ed. Boston, 1893.

————. *Ramona*. New York, 1979.

Jackson, Sheldon G. *A British Ranchero in Old California: The Life and Times of Henry Dalton and the Rancho Azusa*. Glendale and Azusa, Calif., 1977.

Jensen, James M. "John Forster—A California Ranchero." *California Historical Society Quarterly* 48 (March 1969).

Johnston, Bernice Eastman. *California's Gabrielino Indians*. Los Angeles, 1962.

Kelsey, Harry. "A New Look at the Founding of Old Los Angeles." *California Historical Society Quarterly* 55 (Winter 1976).

King, T. Butler. *Report on California*. Washington, D.C., 1850.

Klebnikov, K. T. *Memoirs of California*. 1829. Translated from the Russian with a biographical sketch of the author by Anatole G. Mazour. *Pacific Historical Review* 9, no. 2 (September 1940).

Kroeber, A. L. *Handbook of California Indians*. Washington, D.C., 1925.

Kushing, Frank Hamilton. "Zuñi Fetiches" (1883). In *Zuñi: Selected Writings of Frank Hamilton Cushing*, edited by Jesse Green. Lincoln, Nebr., 1979.

la Pérouse, J. F. G. de. *A Voyage round the World, Performed in the Years 1785, 1787, and 1788*. 2 vols. 3d ed. London, 1807.

Lasuén, Fermín. Writings of Fermín Lasuén. 2 vols. Edited and translated by Finbar Kenneally. Washington, D.C., 1965.

Layne, J. Gregg. "Annals of Los Angeles." Part 1, "From the Founding of the Pueblo to the American Occupation." Part 2, "From the American Conquest to the Civil War." *California Historical Society Quarterly* 13 (September, December 1934).

Lederer, Lillian Charlotte. "A Study of Anglo-American Settlers in

Los Angeles County previous to the Admission of California to the Union." Master's thesis, University of Southern California, 1927.

Lee, S. M. *Glimpses of Mexico and California.* Boston, 1887.

Lévi-Strauss, Claude. *Tristes Tropiques.* Translated by John Weightman and Doreen Weightman. New York, 1984.

The Little Flowers of St. Francis. Edited and translated by Rafael Brown. Garden City, N.J., 1958.

Lopez, Barry Holstun. *Of Wolves and Men.* New York, 1978.

Los Angeles: Biography of a City. Edited by John Caughey and LaRee Caughey. Berkeley and Los Angeles, 1977.

Los Angeles City Survey. The Interchurch World Movement. *The Mexican in Los Angeles.* Los Angeles, 1920.

Lugo, José del Carmen. "The Days of a Rancher in Spanish-California." Translated by Nellie Van de Grift Sanchez. *Touring Topics* 22 (April 1930).

————. "Life of a Rancher." *Historical Society of Southern California Quarterly* 32 (September 1950).

————. "Vida de un Ranchero" (1877). Bancroft Library, Berkeley, Calif.

Lummis, Charles F. *Preliminary Report of the Warner's Ranch Indian Advisory Commission.* Los Angeles, 1902.

Martin, Calvin. *Keepers of the Game: Indian-Animal Relationships and the Fur Trade.* Berkeley and Los Angeles, 1978.

————. "Time and the American Indian." In *The American Indian and the Problem of History,* edited by Calvin Martin. New York, 1987.

Mason, William Marvin. "Fages' Code of Conduct toward Indians, 1787." *Journal of California Anthropology* 2 (Summer 1975).

————. "Indian-Mexican Cultural Exchange in the Los Angeles Area, 1781–1834." *Aztlán* 15, no. 1 (Spring 1984).

May, Ernest. "Tiburcio Vásquez," *Historical Society of Southern California Quarterly* 29 (1947). Reprinted in *Furia y Muerte: Los Bandidos Chicanos,* edited by Pedro Castillo and Albert Camarillo. Los Angeles, 1973.

McEuen, William Wilson. "A Survey of the Mexicans in Los Angeles." Master's thesis, University of Southern California, 1914.

McWilliams, Carey. *Southern California: An Island on the Land.* 1946. Santa Barbara, 1979.

Mead, Christina Wiebus, "Las Fiestas de Los Angeles: A Survey of the Yearly Celebrations, 1894–1898." *Historical Society of Southern California Quarterly* 31 (March 1949 and June 1949).

Means, Russell. "Fighting Words on the Future of the Earth." *Mother Jones* 5 (December 1980).

Merchant, Carolyn. *The Death of Nature: Women, Ecology, and the Scientific Revolution.* San Francisco, 1982.

Miller, Gordon R. "Shaping California Water Law, 1781 to 1928." *Southern California Quarterly* 55 (Spring 1973).

Miranda, Gloria E. "Gente de Razón Marriage Patterns in Spanish and Mexican California: A Case Study of Santa Barbara and Los Angeles." *Southern California Quarterly* 63 (Spring 1981).

————. "Hispano-Mexican Childrearing Practices in Pre-American Santa Barbara." *Southern California Quarterly* 65 (Winter 1983).

Mitchell, Richard G. "Joaquín Murieta: A Study of Social Conditions in Early California." Master's thesis, University of California, Berkeley, 1927. Excerpted in *Furia y Muerte: Los Bandidos Chicanos*, edited by Pedro Castillo and Albert Camarillo. Los Angeles, 1973.

Momaday, N. Scott. *House Made of Dawn.* New York, 1977.

Monroy, Douglas. "The *Sun Chief* and the Accumulationist Personality." *Southwest Economy and Society* II, no. 2 (Fall 1983).

————. "They Didn't Call Them Padre for Nothing: Patriarchy in Hispanic California." In *Between Borders: Essays on Mexicana/Chicana History*, edited by Adelaida R. Del Castillo. Encino, Calif., 1990.

Morgan, Edmund S. *American Slavery, American Freedom: The Ordeal of Colonial Virginia.* New York, 1975.

Morris, Albert Ferdinand. "The Journal of a 'Crazy Man': Travels and Scenes in California from the Year 1834 to the American Conquest." Edited by Charles L. Camp. *California Historical Society Quarterly* 15, nos. 2, 3 (June, September 1936).

Mosk, Sanford A. "Price-Fixing in Spanish California," *California Historical Society Quarterly* 17 (June 1938).

Mumford, Lewis. *Technics and Civilization.* New York, 1934.

Neruda, Pablo. *Splendor and Death of Joaquín Murieta.* Translated by Ben Belitt. New York, 1973.

Newmark, Harris. *Sixty Years in Southern California, 1853–1913.* New York, 1916.

Nordhoff, Charles. *California: For Health, Pleasure, and Residence.* New York, 1873.

Ord, Angustias de la Guerra. *Occurrences in Hispanic California.* Edited and translated by Francis Price and William H. Ellison. Washington, D.C., 1956.

Ord, Edward O. C. *The City of the Angels and the City of the*

Saints, or A Trip to Los Angeles and San Bernardino in 1856. Los Angeles, 1978.

"Ordinances and Regulations of Los Angeles (1832–1888)." Compiled by Marco R. Newmark. *Historical Society of Southern California Quarterly* 30 (March 1948).

Ortiz, Alfonso. *The Tewa World: Space, Time, Being, and Becoming in Pueblo Society*. Chicago, 1969.

Ortiz, Simon J. *Fight Back: For the Sake of the People, for the Sake of the Land*. Albuquerque, 1980.

———. *Fightin'*. New York, 1983.

Palóu, Francisco. *Historical Memoirs of New California*. 1926. 4 vols. Edited and translated by Herbert Eugene Bolton. New York, 1966.

Paz, Ireneo. *Life and Adventures of the Celebrated Bandit Joaquín Murieta: His Exploits in the State of California*. Chicago, 1937.

Phillips, George Harwood. *Chiefs and Challengers: Indian Resistance and Cooperation in Southern California*. Berkeley and Los Angeles, 1975.

———. "Indians in Los Angeles, 1781–1875: Economic Integration, Social Disintegration." *Pacific Historical Review* 49 (August 1980).

Phillips, D. L. *Letters from California: Its Mountains, Valleys, Plains, Lakes, Rivers, Climate and Productions*. Springfield, Ill., 1877.

Piñedo, Encarnación. "Early Days at Santa Clara." *The Owl* (April 1934).

Pitt, Leonard. *The Decline of the Californios: A Social History of the Spanish-Speaking Californians, 1846–1900*. Berkeley and Los Angeles, 1966.

The Poem of the Cid. Translated by Rita Hamilton and Janet Perry. New York, 1984.

Polanyi, Karl. *The Great Transformation: The Political and Economic Origins of Our Time*. Boston, 1957.

Price, Glenn W. *Origins of the War with Mexico: The Polk-Stockton Intrigue*. Austin, Tex., 1976.

The Pride of the Missions: A Documentary History of the San Gabriel Mission. Edited by Francis J. Weber. Los Angeles, 1978.

Rich, Adrienne. *Of Woman Born: Motherhood as Experience and Institution*. New York, 1977.

Richman, Irving Berdine. *California under Spain and Mexico, 1535–1847*. Boston, 1911.

Ríos-Bustamante, Antonio, and Pedro Castillo. *An Illustrated History of Mexican Los Angeles, 1781–1985*. Los Angeles, 1986.

Robinson, Alfred. *Life in California before the Conquest*. 1846. San Francisco, 1925.

Robinson, W. W. "The Indians of Los Angeles as Revealed by the Los Angeles City Archives." *Historical Society of Southern California Quarterly* 20 (December 1938).

Robinson, W. W. "The Dominguez Rancho." *Historical Society of Southern California Quarterly* 35 (December 1953).

Rogin, Michael Paul. *Fathers and Children: Andrew Jackson and the Subjugation of the American Indian.* New York, 1975.

Romo, Ricardo. *East Los Angeles: History of a Barrio.* Austin, Tex., 1983.

————. *Mexican Workers in the City: Los Angeles, 1915–1930.* Ph.D. diss., University of California, Los Angeles, 1975.

Rubin, Gayle. "The Traffic in Women: Notes on the 'Political Economy' of Sex." In *Toward an Anthropology of Women,* edited by Rayna Reiter. New York, 1975.

Ruschenberger, W. S. W. *Sketches in California in 1836.* Los Angeles, 1953.

Sahlins, Marshall. *Stone Age Economics.* Chicago, 1974.

Salisbury, Neal. *Manitou and Providence: Indians, Europeans, and the Making of New England, 1500–1643.* New York, 1984.

Sanchez, Nellie Van de Grift. *Spanish Arcadia.* Los Angeles, 1929.

————. *The Spanish Period.* Chicago, 1926.

Saxton, Alexander. *The Indispensable Enemy: Labor and the Anti-Chinese Movement in California.* Berkeley and Los Angeles, 1971.

Schanzer, George O. "A Russian Visit to the Spanish Franciscans in California, 1836." *The Americas* 9 (April 1953).

Scott, Robin Fitzgerald. "The Mexican-American in the Los Angeles Area, 1920–1950: From Acquiescence to Activity." Ph.D. diss., University of Southern California, 1971.

Security Trust and Savings Bank. *El Pueblo: Los Angeles before the Railroads.* Los Angeles, 1928.

Serra, Junípero. *Writings of Junípero Serra.* 3 vols. Edited by Antoine Tibesar. Washington, D.C., 1966.

Servín, Manuel. "The Secularization of the California Missions: A Reappraisal." *Southern California Quarterly* 47 (June 1965).

Shannon, Fred A. *The Farmer's Last Frontier: Agriculture, 1860–1897.* New York, 1968.

Shaw, D. A. *Eldorado, or California as Seen by a Pioneer, 1850–1900.* Los Angeles, 1900.

Shochat, George. "The Case Adobe de San Rafael in Glendale California." *Historical Society of Southern California Quarterly* 32 (December 1950).

Shrode, Ida May. "The Sequent Occupation of the Rancho Azusa de Duarte, a Segment of the Upper San Gabriel Valley of California." Ph.D. diss., University of Chicago, 1948.

Shubert, Helen V. "The Men Who Met the Yankees in 1846." *California Historical Society Quarterly* 13 (March 1934).

Simpson, Sir George. *Narrative of a Journey round the World, during Years 1841 and 1842.* 2 vols. London, 1847.

Smith, Henry Nash. *Virgin Land: The American West as Symbol and Myth.* New York, 1957.

Sommerville, Blanche A. "Naturalization from the Mexican Viewpoint." *Community Exchange Bulletin* 6, no. 4 (May 1928).

Sutch, Richard. "The Care and Feeding of Slaves." In *Reckoning with Slavery: A Critical Study on the Quantitative History of American Negro Slavery,* ed. Paul A. David, Herbert G. Gutman, Richard Sutch, Peter Temin, and Gavin Wright. New York, 1976.

Tac, Pablo. "Conversion of the San Luiseños of Alta California." Edited by Ninna Hewes and Gordon Hewes. *The Americas* 9 (July 1952).

Temple, Thomas Workman, II. "Founding of Misión San Gabriel Arcángel." Part 2, "Padre Cambón's Contemporary Report of the Founding." *The Masterkey* 33 (October–December 1959).

————. "Toypurina the Witch and the Indian Uprising at San Gabriel." *The Masterkey* 32 (September–October 1958).

Thomes, William Henry. *Recollections of Old Times in California, or California Life in 1843.* Edited with an introduction by George R. Stewart. Berkeley, 1974.

Thrall, Will H. "The Haunts and Hide-outs of Tiburcio Vásquez." *Historical Society of Southern California Quarterly* 30, no. 2 (June 1948).

Turner, John Kenneth. *Barbarous Mexico.* 1910. Austin, Tex., 1969.

Tyler, Helen. "The Family of Pico." *Historical Society of Southern California Quarterly* 35 (September 1953).

Ulloa, Jorge Juan y Antonio de. *Noticias Secretas de América, 1749.* Vol. 2, Madrid, 1918.

Vecsey, Christopher. "American Indian Environmental Religions." In *American Indian Environments: Ecological Issues in Native American History,* edited by Christopher Vecsey and Robert Venables. Syracuse, N.Y., 1980.

Walker, Josephine Maclay. "Life and Personal Reminiscences of General Andrés Pico" (c. 1920). Charles Maclay Papers. Huntington Library, San Marino, Calif.

Waters, Frank. *Book of the Hopi.* New York, 1977.

Webb, E. B. *Indian Life at the Old Missions.* Los Angeles, 1952.

Weber, David J. *Foreigners in Their Native Land: Historical Roots of the Mexican Americans.* Albuquerque, 1973.

———. *The Mexican Frontier, 1821–1846: The American Southwest under Mexico.* Albuquerque, 1982.

Weber, Max. *The Protestant Ethic and the Spirit of Capitalism.* New York, 1958.

———. "Religious Rejections of the World and Their Directions." In *From Max Weber: Essays in Sociology,* edited by H. H. Gerth and C. Wright Mills. New York, 1958.

Weiss, Michael. "Education, Literacy, and the Community of Los Angeles in 1850." *Southern California Quarterly* 60, no. 1 (Summer 1978).

Westkott, Marcia. *The Feminist Legacy of Karen Horney.* New Haven, Conn., 1986.

Wood, J. W. *Pasadena, California: Historical and Personal.* N.p., 1917.

Workers of the Writers' Program of the Work Projects Administration in Southern California. *Los Angeles: A Guide to the City and Its Environs.* New York, 1941.

Index

Compositor: Edwards Brothers, Inc.
Text: 11/13 Galliard
Display: Galliard
Printer: Edwards Brothers, Inc.
Binder: Edwards Brothers, Inc.